THE VIKING-AGE RUNE-STONES

THE VIKING-AGE RUNE-STONES

Custom and Commemoration in Early Medieval Scandinavia

Birgit Sawyer

OXFORD
UNIVERSITY PRESS

OXFORD
UNIVERSITY PRESS

Great Clarendon Street, Oxford OX2 6DP
Oxford University Press is a department of the University of Oxford.
It furthers the University's objective of excellence in research, scholarship,
and education by publishing worldwide in

Oxford New York

Auckland Bangkok Buenos Aires Cape Town Chennai
Dar es Salaam Delhi Hong Kong Istanbul Karachi Kolkata
Kuala Lumpur Madrid Melbourne Mexico City Mumbai Nairobi
São Paulo Shanghai Taipei Tokyo Toronto

Oxford is a registered trade mark of Oxford University Press
in the UK and certain other countries

Published in the United States
by Oxford University Press Inc., New York

First published 2000

First published in paperback 2003

British Library Cataloguing in Publication Data
Data available

Library of Congress Cataloging in Publication Data
Sawyer, Birgit.
The Viking-age rune-stones : custom and commemoration in early medieval
Scandinavia / Birgit Sawyer.
Includes bibliographical references.
1. Inscriptions, Runic. 2. Vikings—History. 3. Vikings—Social life and customs.
4. Scandinavia—History. I. Title.
PD2013 .S27 2000 948′.022—dc21 00-037501

ISBN 0-19-820643-7 (Hbk)
ISBN 0-19-926221-7 (Pbk)

1 3 5 7 9 10 8 6 4 2

Typeset by SNP Best-set Typesetter Ltd., Hong Kong
Printed in Great Britain
on acid-free paper by
Biddles Ltd,
Guildford and King's Lynn

To Peter

PREFACE

In 1988 I published a preliminary report about my research on the runic inscriptions in late Viking-Age Scandinavia. It was then—and still is—my conviction that this material is a very important source, which has hitherto been largely untapped by historians.

The first stages of my research (and the publishing of the preliminary report) were financed by the Swedish Research Council for Humanities (HSFR), to which my first thanks are due. Thanks are also due to the Norwegian Research Council for a grant towards the cost of illustrating this book. Without the help of many colleagues in different disciplines, however, I would not have been able to pursue the project, and heartfelt thanks are due to all of them, above all to Börje Westlund and Rune Palm, who have also read and commented on this manuscript. Börje has encouraged me from the very start and has since then always been ready to guide and advise me; during the final months of writing the telephone line between Trondheim and Linköping was busy for hours on end! Rune, whose own work (on regional differences in the runic material) has been a source of inspiration, has likewise been prepared to help whenever needed. I am also indebted to Torgunn Snædal and Helmer Gustavson (Swedish 'Runverket', Riksantikvarieämbetet, Stockholm), James Knirk (Norwegian 'Oldsaksamlingen'), and Marie Stoklund (Danish National Museum), who have generously and patiently helped me over the years.

For help with linguistic questions I would especially like to thank Lena Peterson (Uppsala University), and I also owe a great debt to Jan Owe (Hässelby), who has gone through the Catalogue with a fine-tooth comb. Indeed, *all* of us who work on runic material are indebted to Jan, who is untiring in collecting and systematizing every runic inscription he comes across!

For large parts of the contents in this book I have benefited from discussions in different seminars, at Scandinavian, English, Austrian, American, and Canadian universities. For having arranged these rune seminars and for valuable contributions to the discussions special thanks are due to Else Mundal (University of Bergen), Gro Steinsland (University of Oslo), Janet Nelson (King's College, London), Patrick Wormald (Christ Church, Oxford), Simon Keynes (Trinity College, Cambridge), Heide Dienst, Otto Gschwantler, Herwig Wolfram (University of Vienna), Kaaren Grimstad (University of Minnesota), Jesse Byock (UCLA), and Roberta Frank (University of Toronto). Other scholars who have been very helpful and to whom thanks are due are Klaus Düwel (Universität Göttingen), Anne-Sofie Gräslund (Uppsala University), and—for help with maps—Ingemar Jansson (Stockholm University) and Sigurd Rahmqvist (Riksantikvarieämbetet, Stockholm).

Finally I must thank my husband, Peter Sawyer, who has not only prepared all the maps and revised my English, but was the first to put the idea of investigating these inscriptions into my head. He has ever since been my inspiration, as well as my worst/best critic, and, most important of all has been his enthusiastic support and preparedness to have 'runatic' discussions at any time of the day—or night. His contribution to my discussion about the 'good people' of Scandinavia has been particularly important.

Despite all the help I have been given, some errors will undoubtedly remain; they are all my responsibility.

This book should have been ready at least two years ago, but because of my move from Sweden to Norway there was an inevitable delay. I cannot, however, say that I regard the work as 'finished' yet, but somewhere one has to draw the line and leave it to others to pick up threads, ideas, and suggestions, to develop them or to question them, to take account of new discoveries, and offer new and exciting solutions.

I have gradually changed my mind on the question of how to explain the different sponsorship patterns found in Scandinavia (as some readers who have followed my publications since the mid-80s have noticed!), and I am willing to change it again, if my critics can convince me that my main hypothesis, as presented here, is not supported by other contemporary evidence.

B.S.

Trondheim
April 1999

CONTENTS

CATALOGUE

LIST OF PLATES

(For an explanation of the codes DR, NIyR, U, etc. see the Abbreviations List below, pp. xvii–xx)

Photographic credits

Denmark and Bornholm: Copenhagen, Nationalmuseet, Pls. 1, 17, 18, 21, 38 A–C. Norway: Oslo, Oldsaksamlingen, Pl. 12 (Photo: James Knirk); Trondheim, Pl. 2 (photo: Per E. Fredriksen). Sweden: Antikvarisk-topografiska arkivet (ATA), Pls. 3, 4, 8, 9, 11, 19, 29, 31, 32, 33, 34; Riksantikvarieämbetet (photos: Bengt A. Lundberg), Pls. 5–7, 10, 13–16, 20, 22–28, 30, 35–37.

LIST OF FIGURES

LIST OF MAPS

LIST OF TABLES

SOURCES, ABBREVIATIONS, AND CONVENTIONS

For further abbreviations, symbols, etc. used in the Catalogue, see the Explanatory Notes on pp. 191–8

Sources

The standard editions

DR *Danmarks runeindskrifter*, ed. L. Jacobsen and E. Moltke, 2 vols. (Copenhagen, 1941–2)

NIyR *Norges innskrifter med de yngre runer*, ed. M. Olsen and A. Liestøl, 5 vols. (Oslo, 1941–60)

SRI *Sveriges runinskrifter*, pub. by Kungliga Vitterhets Historie och Antikvitetsakademien (Stockholm, 1900–)

Other editions

Since the edition of *Ölands runinskrifter* (*SRI* i) is now out of date, references here are to the numbers given them by Nilsson (see abbr. 'Öl' below). *SRI* has not yet published the inscriptions of Hälsingland and Medelpad, and for these provinces I have used Åhlén (see abbr. Hs below) and Hellbom (see abbr. M below). For the only stone in Jämtland, see *Jämtlands kristnande* (1996).

Identification numbers, new finds, and new interpretations

All inscriptions are identified by means of a number preceded by a code indicating the country or province of origin. The identification numbers of inscriptions from Denmark are prefixed with 'DR', and those from Norway with 'NIyR'. The provincial prefixes for inscriptions from Sweden are given in the Abbreviations List below. I have given new finds my own numbers, combined with the appropriate country/province abbreviation, e.g. Dk N[ew] 1.

Many new Danish finds were published by Moltke (1985), and for help with the unpublished finds I am indebted to Marie Stoklund of the Nationalmuseum in Copenhagen. For new finds in Norway I am indebted to Professor James Knirk of Oldsaksamlingen in Oslo. New Swedish finds and new interpretations are published annually in the periodical *Fornvännen*.

Abbreviations

ATA Antikvarisk-topografiska arkivet, Riksantikvarieämbetet, Stockholm

Born — Bornholm; for inscriptions see DR below

DGL — *Danmarks gamle landskabslove med kirkelovene*, ed. J. Brøndum-Nielsen, 8 vols. (Copenhagen, 1933–61)

Dk — Denmark (for new finds)

DR — code for inscriptions of Denmark, published together with inscriptions of Bornholm in *Danmarks runeindskrifter*, ed. L. Jacobsen and E. Moltke, 2 vols. (Copenhagen, 1941–2)

F — Otto von Friesen's handwritten register of Gotland's runic inscriptions; two notebooks in Uppsala University Library

FV — *Fornvännen* (Tidskrift för svensk antikvarisk forskning, 1906–)

G — Gotland; for inscriptions see *Gotlands runinskrifter*, ed. S. B. F. Jansson, E. Wessén, and E. Svärdström, 2 vols. (= *SRI* xi–xii; Stockholm, 1962–77)

GF — Gotlands Fornsal

Gs — Gästsrikland; for inscriptions see *Gästriklands runinskrifter*, ed. S. B. F. Jansson (= *SRI* xv.1; Stockholm, 1981)

Hov — S. B. F. Jansson, *Stenfynden i Hovs kyrka* (Filologiskt arkiv, 9; Stockholm, 1962)

HR — S. B. F. Jansson, 'Ett par hälsingska runstenar', *Hälsingerunor—en hembygdsbok* (Norrala, 1951), 15–23

Hs — Hälsingland; for inscriptions see M. Åhlén, 'Runinskrifter i Hälsingland', *Bebyggelsehistorisk tidskrift*, 27 (1994), 33–50

KHL — *Kulturhistorisk leksikon for nordisk middelalder*, 22 vols. København) (Malmö, 1956–78)

L — J. G. Liljegren, *Runurkunder* (Stockholm, 1833)

M — Medelpad; for inscriptions see A. Hellbom, *Medelpads runstenar* (Sundsvall, 1979)

MÖLM 1960 — S. B. F. Jansson, 'Törnevalla kyrkas runstenar', *Meddelanden från Östergötlands och Linköpings stads museum* (1960–1), 219–37

Nä — Närke; for inscriptions see *Närkes runinskrifter*, ed. S. B. F. Jansson (= *SRI* xiv.1; Stockholm, 1975)

NGL — *Norges gamle love indtil 1387*, ed. R. Keyser, P. A. Munch, G. Storm, and E. Hertzberg, 5 vols. (Christiania, 1846–95)

NIyR — code for inscriptions of Norway; see *Norges innskrifter med de yngre runer*, ed. M. Olsen and A. Liestøl, 5 vols. (Oslo, 1941–60)

No — Norway (for new finds)

NOR — *Nytt om runer: Meldingsblad om runeforskning*, 1– (1986–)

NTS — *Norsk tidsskrift for sprogvidenskap*, 1–31 (1928–77)

Ög — Östergötland; for inscriptions see *Östergötlands runinskrifter*, ed. E. Brate (= *SRI* ii; Stockholm, 1911–18)

Öl	Öland; for inscriptions see B. E. Nilsson, *The Runic Inscriptions of Öland* (Ann Arbor 1973 (University Microfilms International))
RAÄ	Riksantikvarieämbetet, Stockholm
RR	*Runor och runinskrifter: Föredrag vid Riksantikvarieämbetets och Vitterhetsakademiens symposium 8–11 september 1985* (Konferenser 15; Stockholm, 1987)
RS	Otto von Friesen, *Runorna i Sverige: En kortfattad översikt* (Föreningen Urds skrifter, 4.3 uppl.; Uppsala, 1928)
S	C. Säve, *Gutniska urkunder* (Stockholm, 1859)
SB	S. B. F. Jansson, 'Några nyfunna sörmländska runristningar', *Sörmlandsbygden*, 34, 9–22
SHM	Statens Historiska Museum
SKL	S. Curman and E. Lundberg, *Vreta klosters kyrka* (Sveriges kyrkor, 43: Östergötland, 2; Stockholm, 1935)
SLL	*Svenska landskapslagar tolkade och förklarade för nutidens svenskar*, ed. A. Holmbäck and E. Wessén, 5 vols. (Stockholm, 1933–46)
Sm	Småland; for inscriptions see *Smålands runinskrifter*, ed. R. Kinander (= *SRI* iv; Stockholm, 1935–61)
Sö	Södermanland; for inscriptions see *Södermanlands runinskrifter*, ed. E. Brate and E. Wessén (= *SRI* iii; Stockholm, 1924–36)
SRI	*Sveriges runinskrifter*, pub. by Kungliga Vitterhets Historie och Antikvitetsakademien (Stockholm, 1900–)
SVS	S. B. F. Jansson, 'Mellby kyrkas runsten', in *Svenska studier från runtid till nutid tillägnade Carl Ivar Ståhle på 60-årsdagen den 27 juni 1973* (Skrifter utgivna av Nämnden för svensk språkvård, 48; Stockholm, 1973)
THS	*Runristningar i Täby: En vägledning. Sammanställd och kommenterad av S. E. Vingedal, ny utvidgad och rev. uppl.* (Täby hembygdsförenings skriftserie, 10; Täby, 1971)
U	Uppland; for inscriptions see *Upplands runinskrifter*, ed. E. Wessén and S. B. F. Jansson (= *SRI* vi–ix; Stockholm, 1940–)
VA	Rimbert, *Vita Anskarii*, ed. W. Trillmich, in W. Trillmich and R. Buchner, *Quellen des 9. und 11. Jahrhunderts zur Geschichte der hamburgischen Kirche und des Reiches* (Berlin, 1961), 16–133
Vg	Västergötland; for inscriptions see *Västergötlands runinskrifter*, ed. H. Jungner and E. Svärdström (= *SRI* v; Stockholm, 1940–70)
Vr	Värmland; for inscriptions see *Värmlands runinskrifter*, ed. S. B. F. Jansson (= *SRI* xiv.2; Stockholm, 1978)
Vs	Västmanland; for inscriptions see *Västmanlands runinskrifter*, ed. S. B. F. Jansson (= *SRI* xiii; Stockholm, 1964)

The following signs and conventions are also employed:

~	means 'commemorating'
——	missing or illegible element in personal names (e.g. ——björn)
. . .	missing or illegible word(s) in inscriptions
/	marks half strophe in verse inscriptions
m	men
w	women
bold type	indicates transliterated (in some cases, uninterpreted) text

The pomp of funerals has more regard to the vanity of the living than to the honour of the dead.

La Rochefoucauld, *Maximes*

INTRODUCTION

COMPARED with western Europe, Scandinavia is poorly provided with written evidence for its early medieval history; there are no charters before 1085, and the earliest law codes and histories were compiled in the twelfth century (in Sweden not until the thirteenth century). The only texts preserved from earlier periods (apart from some coin legends) are runic inscriptions, some of which are scratched on pieces of wood or on metal objects such as spear-heads or brooches, but most are on stones erected as memorials or grave-markers. There are also similar memorials inscribed on exposed rock surfaces. For convenience all these memorial inscriptions will here be called rune-stones. In Scandinavia about 3,000 are known, most of them made in the tenth and eleventh centuries. In so far as they have been used as a historical source, most attention has been paid to the monuments that commemorate men who died abroad, which may give the impression that such inscriptions are typical; in fact, they amount to less than 10 per cent of the whole corpus. Most monuments were for people who lived and died at home and constitute a body of contemporary evidence for the period that has been largely untapped by historians. It is true that the inscriptions seldom provide information about events or identifiable persons, and that not much historical knowledge can be gained if only single stones are considered. The main purpose of this book is to show that studied as a *whole*, the corpus of rune-stones is a most rewarding source for the social, economic, religious, and political history of Scandinavia in the tenth and eleventh centuries.

THE AIM OF THIS STUDY—AND HOW IT BEGAN

Sometime in the middle of the eleventh century the widow Inga commemorated her husband Ragnfast with no less than four rune-stones, all in the parish of Markim, *c.* twenty kilometres east of Sigtuna in Uppland. In one of the inscriptions she states that she had also had a bridge built 'for his soul'. To sponsor a rune-stone was a costly business, to sponsor four and *also* build a bridge required significant resources. How had Inga acquired her wealth? She gives part of the answer herself, stating that she had inherited after her son, Ragnfast's heir, and, having survived him too, she was now the owner of her dead husband's property. The rest of the answer is given in a long inscription in Hillersjö parish, on an island in Lake Mälaren about twenty kilometres south of Sigtuna, which tells us that Inga was also the sole heiress after her father, Germund. When Inga died, all that she owned went to her mother, Gerlög (see pp. 49–50 and Fig. 3.1 below).

On first meeting Inga and Gerlög many years ago I was very curious to know if there were many women like them in eleventh-century Scandinavia and decided to have a closer look at other runic inscriptions, beginning with those in Uppland. It was a disappointment to discover that such explicit statements about inheritance are very rare indeed, but, by then, I was fascinated by the material itself, above all by the fact that it was so often women who acted as sponsors, commemorating their husbands, sons, fathers, or even brothers. Since most of the rune-stones were sponsored by men, I began to wonder in what situations it was accepted—or even expected—that women should undertake this responsibility on their own. It seemed clear that these women, left as widows or brotherless daughters, were all independent property-owners, and the suspicion grew that in commemorating their deceased relatives *all* sponsors, male and female, were at the same time stating their claims to what had been owned and controlled by the dead.

This idea encouraged me to go through all the rune-stone material systematically, an investigation that led to the hypothesis that the runic inscriptions reflected customs of inheritance understood in a wide sense, involving not only land and/or goods, but also status in society, rights, and duties. This was suggested by the fact that the rune-stones are not simply memorials to the dead; unlike most medieval (and modern) grave monuments that only name the dead, the runic inscriptions name the sponsors and do so first of all. The prominence given to sponsors shows that Viking-Age rune-stones are monuments to the *living* as much as to the *dead*. Another characteristic, in virtually all inscriptions, is the care taken to define the *relationship* of sponsors to the dead. That relationship was obviously significant throughout Scandinavia.

One important result of this preliminary investigation was the recognition of different sponsorship patterns in different parts of Scandinavia; while in western Scandinavia most stones were sponsored by single individuals, in eastern Sweden most stones were sponsored by two or more persons acting together.[1] Other significant regional differences are discussed in Chapters 3 and 4. If the explanations for these regional differences offered here are not accepted, the different patterns remain and other explanations will have to be sought. The investigation revealed many other interesting features in the inscriptions that cast light on religious, social,

[1] B. Sawyer (1988).

and political conditions in general. Some of these are presented below, in Chapters 5 and 6 and in the Excursus, and in Chapter 7 an attempt will be made to explain the rune-stone fashion itself.

The tenth- and eleventh-century rune-stones are an invaluable source of knowledge about the late Viking Age; they throw light on such varied matters as the development of language and poetry, kinship and habits of name-giving, settlement, place-names and communications, Viking as well as trading expeditions, and, not least, the spread of Christianity. Many of these topics have been investigated or are currently being studied (see Chs. 1 and 2), but much remains to be done. Whatever one chooses to focus on, it is essential to consider the whole body of material; only then do different features and patterns emerge. Most of the systematic investigations published hitherto, however, have concentrated on particular regions or provinces. Uppland in particular has been the subject of many valuable studies in different disciplines. An exception to this regional or provincial approach is that used by the linguist Rune Palm, who has studied all Scandinavian (including Icelandic) rune-stones, from the Migration period to the end of the Middle Ages, and analysed their types, as well as the content and language of the inscriptions.[2]

The present study is an attempt to collect as much *historical* information as possible from all tenth- and eleventh-century rune-stones in Scandinavia, including new discoveries made before 1995. I am aware that I must have missed some important details and that my figures of proportions may not always be 100 per cent correct. In uncertain cases—where different interpretations of inscriptions are possible—the ones I have chosen to accept may be questioned. It is, however, my hope that this work will stimulate discussion and encourage further investigations, all the more so since my work in these 'runatic' years has perhaps raised more questions than it has yielded answers.

My data-base, described in Chapter 2.1, makes many different kinds of analyses possible; some are presented in this book, others will be used in future publications. Above all, it is my hope that other scholars will find it helpful in their own work. The final section of the book (pp. 189–262) consists of a Catalogue of the main corpus, and the complete data-base will be made available through 'Runverket' (the Department of Runes, Central Board of National Antiquities) in Sweden, within six months of the publication of this book.

In the text of the book (as well as in the data-base) I follow the convention of using bold type for transliterated text (most often to indicate

[2] Palm (1992).

uninterpreted words), and italic type for the normalized, i.e. transcribed/translated forms.[3]

Since my first chapters below are necessarily technical, readers who are unfamiliar with this material may find it helpful to begin with the Conclusion (Ch. 7).

[3] However, ordinary roman type is employed for a few frequently used terms (such as 'thegn', 'dreng', 'härad', explained below).

SURVEY

1

RUNE-STONES, THEIR DISTRIBUTION AND HISTORICAL BACKGROUND

More than 3,000 rune-stones are known in Scandinavia, and the majority of them were made in the tenth and eleventh centuries. Most of these 'late Viking-Age rune-stones' were upright, but some are horizontal slabs that covered graves and are here called 'recumbent stones', and some inscriptions are carved on natural rock faces. They differ in size, shape, and design, but the content of the inscriptions is very uniform, and everywhere the language is Old Scandinavian.

The examples in Plates 1–4 illustrate both regional and chronological variations; the Danish and Norwegian stones (Pls. 1 and 2), mostly unornamented, with the inscription in straight rows or bands, are earlier than the ones in eastern Sweden (Pl. 3), where inscriptions are often placed in the body of serpents, and decoration of various kinds is common. The recumbent stone from Västergötland (Pl. 4), with the inscription along its edge, represents a late stage but is nevertheless contemporary with many of the upright stones.

The chronology and regional distribution of these rune-stones is discussed below and in Chapter 2; suffice it to say here that the fashion for commemorating the dead with rune-stones was most common in eastern Sweden; Uppland alone has more than 1,300 examples. The uniformity of these 'late Viking-Age inscriptions' throughout Scandinavia, despite their uneven distribution, raises many questions—above all, where and why the fashion started, why it spread as it did, and why it ceased.

1.1. THE RUNE-STONES AND THEIR DISTRIBUTION

In Scandinavia rune-stones were already being erected in the fourth century AD.[1] These 'older' Norse inscriptions, from the fourth century to *c.*800, are cut with runes belonging to the 24-character rune series (*fuþark*), the script once employed all over the Germanic area. There are relatively few inscriptions from this period; their language is sometimes hard to understand and their contents are often obscure. The absence of

[1] This survey is based on Palm (1992), 18–19, 245–7, and Jansson (1987), 11–12, 25–7.

PLATE 1. DR 41, Jelling. Example of inscription in straight rows or bands: 'King Gorm made this monument in memory of Thorvi (Thyre), his wife, Denmark's adornment.'
PLATE 2. NIyR 449, Kuli. Example of inscription in straight rows or bands: 'Tore and Hallvard raised this stone in memory of X. Twelve winters had Christianity improved (things) in Norway.'

'old' Norse rune-stones in Denmark has been explained by assuming that the 'custom' spread from the north and reached what is now southern Sweden by the seventh century. A group of inscriptions in Blekinge in the south of Sweden shows significant changes in the language as well as some change in the form of the runes, and is therefore considered to belong to a time of transition. These transitional rune-stones are thought to have stimulated the development of the oldest Danish runic monuments.

Before 800 the writing system had been adapted to solve the problems raised by the changes that the language was undergoing; the 24-rune *fuþark* was simplified and reduced to the 16-rune series. From the start we

PLATE 3. U 279, Skälby. Example of inscription placed in the body of a serpent: 'Björn and Igulfast and Jon had this bridge built in memory of Torsten, their brother. Öpir cut the runes.'

PLATE 4. Vg 165, Södra Ving. A late stage of development, with the inscription written along the edge of a recumbent stone: 'Bothild had this tomb made in memory of Sven Dyrmod's son. Harald "stone-master" made it.'

meet this new *fuþark* in two forms; long-twig ('normal') runes and short-twig runes (mainly cut in wood with shorter side-strokes, and probably used for recording more personal matters).

Although the custom of erecting rune-stones was apparently a northern innovation, it was in Denmark, more precisely in Jutland, that it was first widespread among the higher classes. Here the forms of the runes and the formula of inscriptions was conventionalized and this new type of monument quickly spread to southern and middle Sweden, certain parts of Norway, and the British Isles. The high period of rune-stone erection started *c.*950; in Denmark, Norway, and southern Sweden it lasted for about eighty years, while in Uppland and Bornholm it continued until the early twelfth century. It is the uniformity of the inscriptions on these late Viking-Age monuments that permits us to speak of a fashion. They are remarkably similar in language and with few exceptions they have the same basic formula: 'X raised this stone in memory of Y'; most specify the relationship between sponsor and deceased, and many have additional details giving the title (e.g. 'thegn', 'dreng') of the deceased or more information about his or her family.

There were, however, regional and chronological differences.[2] One is in the way the inscription is arranged on the face of the stone; while most of the older inscriptions are arranged in vertical rows, the younger are placed either in a single band running around the edge/outline of the stone or in several bands, sometimes most elegantly shaped, that fill the whole face. The band is commonly in the form of a serpent ('rune animal') with head and tail, often drawn round a Christian cross.

Runic inscriptions commemorating the dead are also found on sarcophagi or grave covers in churches and churchyards, above all in Iceland and Sweden. It has been supposed that these 'medieval' types of monument are younger than the 'Viking-Age' types, but Rune Palm has shown that this is wrong; some of the so-called 'medieval' inscriptions are so similar to those of the Viking Age in content and formulation that they must be treated together. He has redefined the types so that Viking-Age inscriptions include all that contain the commemorating formula (X raised/laid this stone in memory of Y) in contrast to later inscriptions that name only the deceased. This distinction, based on the *content* of the inscriptions whatever the type of monument, is, to some extent, confirmed by runographic, linguistic, and ornamental differences.[3]

Palm is clearly right to argue that the content of the inscriptions ought to be decisive; the chronological distinction between upright and recumbent stones is based on the unproved assumption that these types could not have existed at the same time. Following Palm, it will here be accepted that erect and recumbent stones with inscriptions naming both sponsor

[2] For linguistic differences see Palm (1992). [3] Palm (1992), 245–7.

and deceased can be contemporary. What is more, in some areas these two types of monument have different, exclusive distributions, which suggests that they were complementary, possibly being used by different groups in society. Thomas Neill and Stig Lundberg have suggested that the richly decorated grave monuments were one way in which the magnates manifested their power.[4]

The material on which this study is based thus comprises *all rune-stones with the commemorating formula* (together with a few that lack it but are undoubtedly from the Viking Age) amounting to a total of 2,307 stones. Their distribution is as follows: Denmark 199 (8.6%), Norway 51 (2.2%), Sweden 2,057 (89.2%). The Danish total includes 31 on Bornholm. As these are much later than those from other parts of Denmark they will here be treated separately and the total of 'Danish' inscriptions is thus 168 for the purpose of this book. The names above do not denote the modern countries but, by and large, the medieval kingdoms. This means that the modern Swedish provinces of Blekinge, Halland, and Skåne are treated as Danish and that Gotland—and Jämtland—are treated as Swedish.[5] The medieval kingdoms have served as the basis for the standard editions of the inscriptions, and consequently provide the main geographical framework in this study.

The distribution of rune-stones within these kingdoms is also very uneven (for details see App. 1 and Map 1 A–B). Uppland has almost half of the Swedish rune-stones, and most of the others are found in the densely populated provinces of Södermanland, Östergötland, Västergötland, and Småland. In Denmark the majority of stones are situated in northern Jutland and Skåne, and in Norway the main concentration is in Rogaland. Even if the number of Norwegian rune-stones seems small, it should be pointed out that, in relation to the population, the custom of erecting them was almost as common (or uncommon) there as in Denmark (which had at least three times more inhabitants than Norway).[6]

The fact that new discoveries of rune-stones are nearly always made in areas that already have some suggests that the original distribution of these monuments was much the same as it is today. The introduction of the Roman alphabet did not mean that the art of writing and reading runes was forgotten; runes continued to be used throughout the middle ages and in some parts of Scandinavia until the nineteenth century. An active interest in early runic inscriptions was evidenced as early as the twelfth century by the Danish historian Saxo Grammaticus' report that King Valdemar I was curious about a rock in Blekinge, 'chequered with strange symbols'.

[4] Neill and Lundberg 1994; see also Lundberg (1997), 5, 80–1.

[5] From the end of the 12th cent. Jämtland belonged politically to Norway but ecclesiastically to Sweden.

[6] Sawyer and Sawyer (1993), 42.

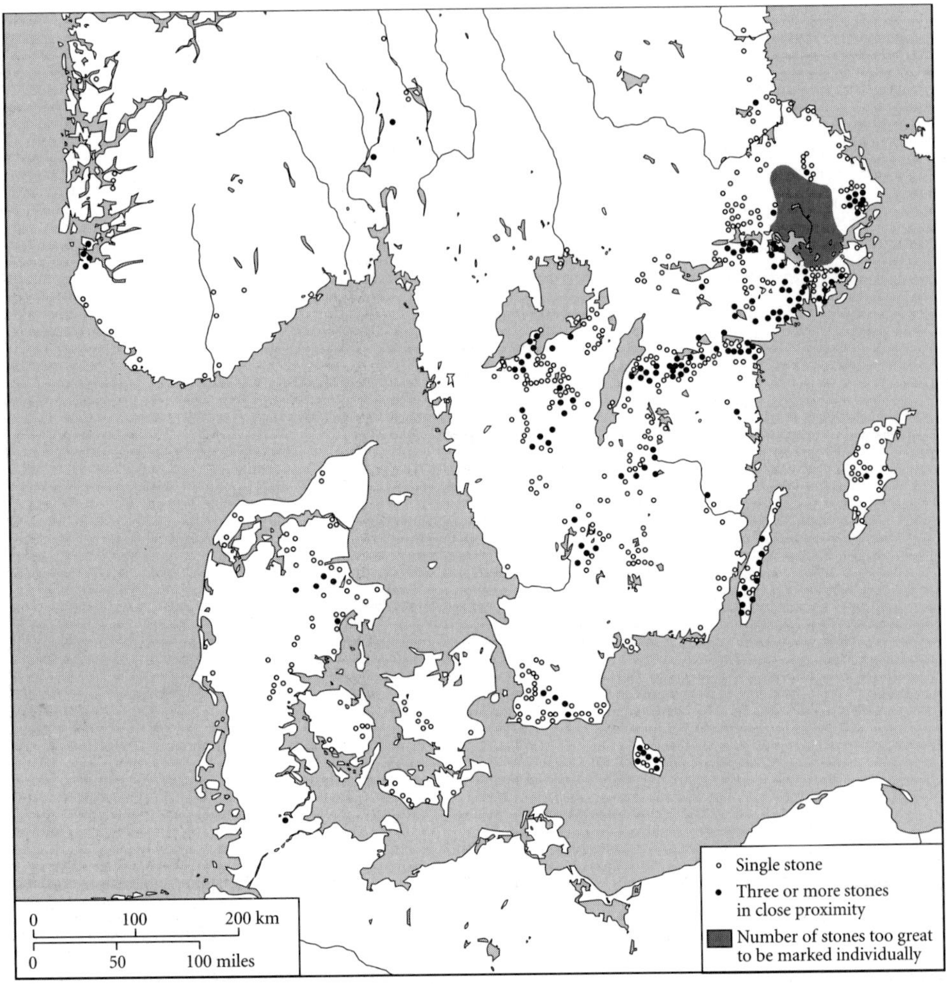

Map 1a. Distribution of inscriptions in the corpus: South Scandinavia

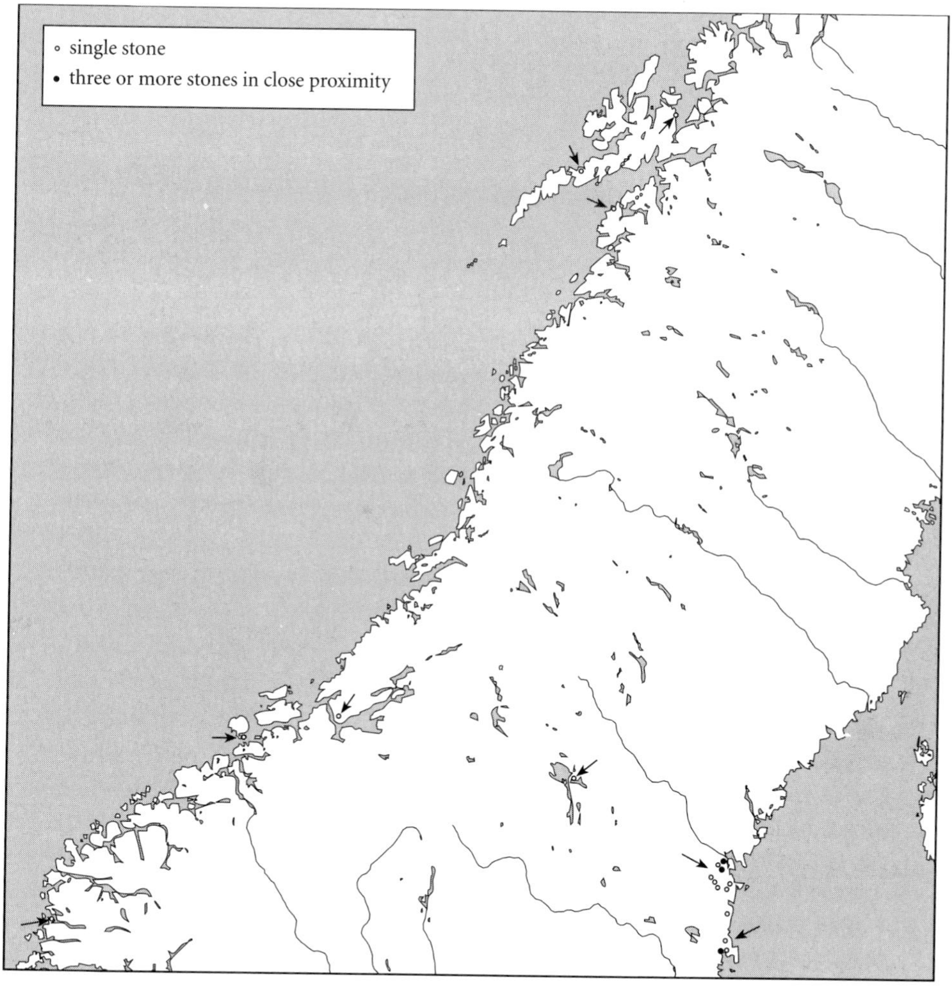

Map 1b. Distribution of inscriptions in the corpus: North Scandinavia

He sent men there 'to pace the rock, make a closer investigation of the rows of characters there and copy the twiggy outlines of the letters'.[7] This early runologic expedition could not, however, find any significance in these 'symbols', probably because they were not runes but natural cracks in the rock.

Some, perhaps many, rune-stones have been lost, but there is no reason to suppose that this has seriously distorted the overall distribution. There is no evidence that many have been deliberately destroyed; indeed, all the signs are that they have normally been treated with respect. A large number of stones are now in the fabric of churches or in churchyard walls, but that was not due to the shortage of building material (see next paragraph). Many of the churches in which they are found are in areas with abundant suitable building stone. Some stones were transported several kilometres to a church. For example, two monuments commemorating Jarlabanke (the self-commemorator, see Ch. 6.3.3a) that probably stood originally in Täby north of Stockholm have been found, intact, in Fresta and Danderyd churches, respectively six kilometres west and eleven kilometres south of Täby (U 197, 261). Another example is the rune-stone found in 1978 on what was formerly the bed of Klejtrup lake, near Viborg in north Jutland (DR N2). It was apparently being taken across the frozen lake on a wooden sledge together with smaller building stones when the ice broke and the whole load was lost. The most plausible explanation is that its destination was Klejtrup church on the far side of the lake, 1.5 kilometres away.[8]

There is now a wide measure of agreement that rune-stones were put in churches for symbolic reasons, although opinions differ about what those reasons were. Lars Wilson has argued for 'place-continuity', claiming that such rune-stones originally stood on the sites of the churches in which they were put, which he suggests were in many cases places where *things*, or local assemblies, met.[9] This may sometimes have been so, but a more likely explanation is that it was a way of honouring early converts who had supported missionaries and played an important role in the early stages of Christianization.[10] A systematic study of the placing of rune-stones in church buildings throughout Scandinavia is badly needed. It is, however, clear that in many instances they were placed in significant parts of churches, as threshold stones, as foundations—notably in Uppsala cathedral where several very large stones support major columns—or even as altars.[11] It is true that many have been broken but this must often have happened when churches were rebuilt. It is more significant that many are intact, or almost so, and are placed so that the inscription can be read.

7 Saxo Grammaticus (1979 edn.), p. 7.
8 See Iversen (1985), 56–65.
9 Wilson (1994), 125–31.
10 Cf. Zachrisson (1998), 161–2.
11 U 760=796 see *FV* 1995, 45–7, U 799 (recumbent stone), U 978; DR 365. G 218 was found under the altar in Follingbo church.

There are, therefore, good reasons for thinking that the present distribution of rune-stones in Scandinavia as a whole, as well as within its different regions, is a reliable guide to their distribution in the tenth and eleventh centuries, and shows where the fashion for such monuments was, or was not, adopted. If the inscriptions are to be used as historical evidence it is first necessary to consider the reasons for this pattern.

1.2. PREVIOUS WORK

The modern study of runic inscriptions was begun in the seventeenth century by Johannes Bureus in Sweden and Ole Worm in Denmark (which then included Norway).[12] Various attempts were subsequently made to catalogue the inscriptions in each kingdom, but it was not until the end of the nineteenth century that the Dane Ludwig Wimmer, the Norwegian Sophus Bugge, the Swede Otto von Friesen, and other scholars well versed in philology began to put runic studies on a sound basis and laid firm foundations for the standard national editions: *Danmarks runeindskrifter* (*DR*), 1941–2; *Norges innskrifter med de yngre runer* (*NIyR*), 1941– ; *Sveriges runinskrifter* (*SRI*), 1900– .

These works, especially *DR*, include some general surveys of the material in which reference is also made to inscriptions in other parts of Scandinavia, but the topics discussed by the various editors naturally tend to reflect their own special interests, making direct comparisons very difficult, and, on some topics, impossible. Apart from textbooks, notably those by Lucien Musset and Klaus Düwel,[13] there are no comprehensive surveys of the whole body of material. Rune Palm is as far as I know the only scholar who has used *all* Scandinavian (including the Icelandic) rune-stones in his study of regional variations.[14]

In modern scholarship the runic inscriptions are studied by, among others, archaeologists, cultural geographers, historians of both art and religion, and above all by linguists.[15] Publications between 1880 and 1993 have been listed by Jan Owe,[16] and since 1986 an annual bibliography has been edited by James E. Knirk.[17] Many scholars have expressed views on topics discussed in this book, such as the purposes served by rune-stones, the social group(s) to which the sponsors belonged, or the relation between the rune-stones and other monuments or archaeological discoveries. These various opinions will be referred to where they are relevant.

[12] Svärdström (1936) and (1971); Moltke (1958).

[13] Musset (1965); Düwel (1983).

[14] Palm (1992).

[15] Among recent linguistic work the Swedish project, 'The Chronology of Viking-Age Runic Inscriptions', should be mentioned; in the series 'Runrön' (Department of Nordic Languages, Uppsala University) several studies have been published, to which references will be made in this book.

[16] Owe (1995).

[17] Published in *NOR* (Runearkivet IAKN, Oldsaksamlingen, Oslo University).

1.3. WHY WERE THE RUNE-STONES ERECTED?

In order to use the rune-stones as a historical source it is necessary to understand *why* they were erected. There is general agreement that this fashion answered certain needs, but there is little agreement about what these were. Two explanations for the sudden proliferation of rune-stones, Viking activity or religious change, have been widely accepted.

1.3.1. Viking raids

Viking raids are a possible explanation for the stones erected in honour of men who died abroad (see Pl. 5), but since these would account for only a small minority of the commemorations they cannot explain the fashion. It is, however, hardly surprising that the erection of rune-stones is commonly connected with Viking voyages or trading expeditions, since inscriptions concerned with such activities have tended to attract most attention in both specialist studies and general works on the period,[18] thus obscuring the fact that the overwhelming majority of stones were erected in memory of people who lived, worked, and died at home. The view of such eminent experts as Erik Moltke and Sven B. F. Jansson that Viking raids were the key to the phenomenon has contributed to the relative neglect of the many monuments commemorating the less spectacular stay-at-homes. It appears that these scholars—and many others besides—regarded the 'voyage-stones' as the *proper* rune-stones, setting the style that other sponsors followed. That is the clear implication of Sven B. F. Jansson's assertion:

> When the great expeditions were over, the old trade routes closed, and the Viking ships no longer made ready each spring for voyages to east and west, then that meant the end of the carving and setting up of rune stones in the proper sense of the term. They may be called the monuments of the Viking voyages, and the sensitive reader may catch in many of their inscriptions the Viking's love of adventure and exploits of boisterous daring. (Jansson (1987), 38).

Even if the so-called 'voyage-stones' were the model for other inscriptions this would not explain why so suddenly towards the *end* of the Viking Age sea-going relatives were honoured in this special way, and in so many different parts of Scandinavia. Memorials of different kinds and voyages abroad had been made for several centuries without leading to the erection of rune-stones like those of the tenth and eleventh centuries. It follows that other factors must be sought to explain the fashion and its spread.

[18] Moltke (1985); Jansson (1987).

Plate 5. Sö 338, Turinge. Stone commemorating Torsten, who 'fell in battle, east in Gårdarike' (for full text of inscription, see p. 132).

1.3.2. Christianization

The process of Christianization was certainly one factor, for these monuments reflect the transition from pagan to Christian burial customs.[19] Some scholars argue that the erection of rune-stones answered emotional needs among the newly converted who, having buried their relatives in

[19] Both Otto von Friesen (1933) and Sune Lindkvist (1915) regard the custom as closely connected with the Christian mission, at least in Uppland. See also Helge Ljungberg (1938: 272) and Torun Zachrisson (1998: 123–64).

new ways and new places, that is in churchyards, wanted to honour them in traditional places—at home, beside a road, or in a place of assembly.[20] It is, of course, possible that this was sometimes the case, but many rune-stones were moved at an early date from their original sites to stand in churchyards or to be built into the fabric of churches. This suggests that it was rather the lack of churches and churchyards that created the need to erect Christian rune-stones. In Uppland, churches began to be built and churchyards consecrated later than in many parts of southern and western Scandinavia, and in this province many rune-stones seem to have functioned as Christian gravestones in pagan cemeteries.[21]

The rituals associated with burial are not only for the sake of the dead, they are also a means of demonstrating the wealth and status of the survivors. Missionaries objected to the furnishing of graves with weapons, tools, and other goods and urged that gifts should be made to them instead, as payment for their prayers on behalf of the dead.[22] In a transitional period, when the new Christian—and simple—burial customs must have been perceived as an enormous breach with the old rituals, and before churches and churchyards became the natural places for memorials, ostentatious rune-stones in public places were one way of displaying status and wealth. In Denmark rune-stones certainly marked status, but it is difficult to decide whether they also indicated that the deceased had been given a Christian burial; few are overtly Christian. Nevertheless it seems likely that these 'neutral' stones were erected by people who had accepted the new customs; in Denmark, where conversion was by royal command, there was only a need to declare one's faith if it differed from what was publicly accepted. There are about twenty Danish inscriptions with apparently pagan characteristics that can be interpreted as declarations of nonconformity,[23] about the same number as are explicitly Christian. Conversely, the fact that most rune-stones in Uppland are ostentatiously Christian suggests that *there* it was the Christian faith that was deviant.

The distribution and regional characteristics of the runic inscriptions may therefore reflect the process of conversion. The relatively few Danish rune-stones were erected during a short period, most of them in the decades immediately before and after the year 1000, and there are roughly equal numbers of pagan and Christian inscriptions. This is consistent with the fact that here Christianity was imposed by a king with effective authority, which ensured a relatively short period of transition. The pagan inscriptions may indeed have been as much political as religious protests.

[20] von Friesen (1933), 169; Palme (1959), 93, 144.

[21] Gräslund (1987*a*), (1987*b*).

[22] Cf. Hyenstrand (1973).

[23] The pagan character of some inscriptions is uncertain. The Danish inscriptions that are undoubtedly pagan include three with the formula *Tor vige*, 'May Thor hallow', four with magical invocations, and five decorated with Thor's hammer; see further Ch. 6.1.

Moreover, churches were being built and Christian cemeteries consecrated much earlier in Denmark than in eastern Sweden. The inscriptions in Götaland are very much like those in Denmark; they are relatively few and only a small number are explicitly Christian. What is more, Västergötland has three of Sweden's six overtly pagan inscriptions.[24] This is consistent with the fact that here too conversion was effected by royal authority; it was in Västergötland that the Swedish king Olof Skötkonung, who died *c.*1022, founded the first Swedish bishopric.

In the rest of Sweden the weakness or, in some areas, absence of effective royal authority meant that conversion was a more prolonged process. In Uppland missionaries had to contend with the continuation of pagan rituals at Uppsala, a cult centre that was famous throughout Scandinavia, until about 1080. Pagan burials continued in parts of Uppland throughout the eleventh century and very few, if any, churches were built there before the twelfth century. The fact that many of the rune-stones in Uppland contain declarations of Christian faith suggests that the decision to convert was taken by individuals, or families, and that new conversions were taking place throughout the eleventh century. It is, therefore, not surprising that a very large number of rune-stones were erected there, and over such a long period, from *c.*1020 to the early twelfth century. In Öland and Bornholm the situation appears to have been much like that in Uppland, while Södermanland shares some features with Götaland.

Even if the erection of rune-stones answered religious and social needs in a period of transition, the change of faith and the abandonment of traditional burial customs, however, cannot alone explain the origin, distribution, and uniformity of the fashion. As Map 1 A–B (and App. 1) shows there are large areas with few or no rune-stones of the tenth and eleventh centuries. Moreover, in regions that are otherwise richly endowed with runic monuments of that period, there are districts in which they are scarce or entirely absent, for instance southern Jutland, eastern Småland, Kinnekulle in Västergötland, and the area near Alvastra in Östergötland. The distribution suggests that rune-stones were not needed everywhere, either because circumstances were different or because in those areas the functions of the inscriptions were effected in some other way.

Any attempt to discover what these functions were must, in the first place, take account of the fact that they were memorials not only to the dead but also to the people who raised them; the sponsors are always named first. These inscriptions thus differ markedly from medieval (and most modern) tombstones, which normally only name the deceased.

[24] One with *Tor vige* (Vg 150), one with a hammer (Vg 113), and one with a magical invocation (Vg 67, the same type as in Denmark). In Södermanland there is one with *Tor vige* (Sö 140) and two with hammers (Sö 86, 111). See discussion, Ch. 6.1.

Another significant difference is that, while tombstones are laid over women as well as men, the Viking-Age rune-stones were erected mainly in memory of *men*. Thus the transition to Christian burial customs cannot be the only reason; that would explain neither the uneven distribution, nor why so few women were commemorated by rune-stones (only 7%; half of them together with men). Since the proportion of richly furnished women's graves in the Iron Age was much higher than that, the relatively few rune-stones erected in memory of women shows that the fashion can only *partly* reflect changes in religion and burial customs. The wider context is suggested by the fact that only certain individuals, mostly men, are honoured, and that the emphasis is put on the sponsors (i.e. those responsible for the monuments) and their *relationship to the deceased*. Only eight of the (more or less complete) inscriptions lack a commemoration formula,[25] but four of them are parts of double monuments and the formula is found on the other stone.[26] Two others (U29 and 73) will be discussed in Chapter 5.6.

It is obvious that the relationships between sponsors and the dead were significant in determining who commemorated whom. A systematic study of all relationships has revealed patterns with distinct differences between regions that cannot be explained as due to chance; there must have been rules, principles, or customs determining who should commemorate the dead in this monumental way, and they were not the same throughout Scandinavia.[27]

1.4. HISTORICAL BACKGROUND

In order to explain the fashion for runic monuments in late Viking-Age Scandinavia it is necessary to consider the political as well as the religious changes that transformed Scandinavia between the ninth century and the twelfth.[28]

In the tenth century *Denmark* was the only well-established territorial kingdom in Scandinavia. By the early eighth century there are both literary and archaeological indications that powerful Danish rulers were based in South Jutland. During the first two-thirds of the ninth century two different dynasties competed for the royal power, and even if the Danish kingdom was sometimes ruled by more than one king, it was not divided. This relative stability broke down during the last decades of the

[25] J 1; Sö 138; U 29, 73, 315, 344, 348, and 541.

[26] Thus Sö 138 is likely to have the same sponsor as Sö 137. U 315 refers to U 316; U 344 refers to U 343; and U 348 refers to U 347.

[27] B. Sawyer (1988), (1989).

[28] The historical background given here is based on new research—presented in Sawyer and Sawyer (1993)—which differs somewhat from the traditional view.

century; English, Frankish, and Irish sources refer to several Viking leaders as 'kings of the Danes', and it is likely that the old royal dynasties had died out shortly before the year 900. At the beginning of the tenth century, however, Gorm, thought to be a descendant of a certain Sven *a Nortmannia* (from Norway or Normandy?), established himself in Jutland, and by marrying Thyre, the daughter of a powerful chieftain in Sjælland or Skåne, he sought to extend Danish royal power to the areas east of the Store Bælt ('Great Belt'), an object that was pursued by his son Harald and at last achieved by his grandson Sven ('Forkbeard'). Gorm's and Harald's monuments at Jelling tell us about their success; the opposition they met with can only be deduced (see Excursus).

1.4.1. The formation of the Norwegian and the Swedish kingdoms

The first known attempt to create a Norwegian kingdom (mainly in western Norway) was by Harald Fairhair (*c.*900—when Denmark was weakened), but it soon fell apart under his successors. From the middle of the tenth century Norway remained under Danish overlordship for almost a century, with short periods of independence during the reigns of Olav Tryggvason (*c.*995–1000) and Olav Haraldsson (1015–28). It was under these kings that Christianity, already well on its way, became finally established in Norway.

The first king known to have been acknowledged by the two main groups in Sweden, the *Götar* and the *Svear*, was Olof Eriksson (*c.*995–*c.*1020), whose father Erik ('the Victorious') was probably the founder of Sigtuna (*c.*975) in the Mälar valley. Sigtuna was a royal centre and a base from which a new Christian form of kingship was gradually extended over the region. There is much to indicate that Olof Eriksson was under Danish overlordship, from which he freed himself after the death of the Danish king Sven Forkbeard (in 1014). Whatever success Olof and his sons had, their authority was much less than that of their Danish contemporaries, which is clearly shown by the process of conversion in the two kingdoms. In Denmark Sven Forkbeard's father, King Harald Bluetooth, had been converted and baptized *c.*965, and by the end of the century pagan rituals and burials had been abandoned. In eastern Sweden, however, pagan rituals continued until *c.*1080, although most of the eleventh-century kings and many Svear were Christian. By 1060, when the diocesan organization of Denmark was complete, there was only one Swedish bishopric, in Västergötland. In Norway dioceses were organized later than in Denmark but earlier than in Sweden (*c.*1070–90).

The process of territorial consolidation in Sweden was delayed by the tensions and differences between the Götar and the Svear; the former occupying the plains of central southern Sweden, divided by Lake Vättern into east and west Götar (after whom the medieval provinces Östergötland and Västergötland were named). A wide belt of forest lay between the

Götar and the Svear, who lived in the region around Lake Mälaren and along the east coast of Sweden.

The formation of both the Norwegian and the Swedish kingdoms should be seen against the background of Danish hegemony in Scandinavia and the fact that Viking raids, having for more than two hundred years enabled chieftains and their retainers to enrich themselves, were now coming to an end.

1.4.2. Danish hegemony

Danish domination can be traced as far back as to the late eighth century. The reason for their supremacy was that the Danes had many advantages: a relatively numerous population, easy access to all parts of their territory, and, above all, their control of the entrance to the Baltic. This enabled the Danish kings to regulate and benefit from the trade between western Europe and the Baltic region, a trade of growing importance. By extending their authority to Norway the Danes also profited from the trade along the Norwegian coast (that is to say, the 'North way', after which the kingdom was named). We do not know how much (if any) of Sweden was dominated by the Danish kings; it is clear, though, that many Swedes accepted Danish kings as their overlords, and that was obviously what the Danes wanted, rather than territorial control.

As already mentioned, the Swedish king Olof Eriksson also apparently accepted Danish overlordship; he was the stepson of the Danish king Sven Forkbeard (who had married his mother), and Olof's base in Västergötland, where he established a bishop's see, brought him into closer contact with the Danes, who had probably played some part in the conversion of this province. The prestige of Danish overlordship was enormously enhanced by Sven's conquest of England in 1013, and it was as a king of England that his son Knut later became king of the Danes as well. While Knut devoted most of his attention to the English part of his empire, both Norwegians and Swedes repudiated Danish overlordship. The Norwegian king Olav Haraldsson and the Swedish king Anund (Olof Eriksson's son) joined forces against Knut but without success; Knut overthrew Olav Haraldsson, conquered Norway, and claimed to have authority in Sweden too: in a letter (1027) he calls himself king of the English and of Denmark, king of the Norwegians and 'some of the Swedes'. A number of runic inscriptions in Sweden commemorate men who had served in England, and some of them had obviously fought under Knut there. Other inscriptions tell us about 'thegns' and 'drengs' who are likely to have been Knut's or his father's retainers both at home and abroad (see further Ch. 5.4).

After Knut's death (1035) the Danish hegemony in Scandinavia came to an end. The Norwegian kingdom had already become stronger during the latter half of the eleventh century, while in Sweden the kingdom was not consolidated until almost a hundred years later.

1.4.3. The end of the Viking Age

In western Scandinavia the rune-stone period coincides with the reigns of Harald Bluetooth, Sven Forkbeard, and Knut; in eastern Sweden the oldest stones were sponsored during Knut's reign, but the majority coincide with the turbulent remainder of the eleventh century, when rival kings were trying to establish themselves and promote Christianity. In the whole of Scandinavia, however, the rune-stone period also coincides with the last phase of Viking activity, the causes of which have been much debated. It is clear that a key factor in the outburst of piracy was the commercial expansion in north-western Europe, beginning towards the end of the seventh century. Soon, however, Viking activity involved not only plundering but colonization. While, during the ninth and tenth centuries, there had been room for many free enterprises, things changed when the defences in western Europe grew stronger and Sven Forkbeard monopolized the riches of England by conquering it. But in the east there still remained the sort of possibilities referred to in many runic inscriptions; apart from raiding, many Swedes also took part in trading expeditions as well as serving Byzantine emperors as their guards.

Viking activity caused many changes in Scandinavia, the most fundamental being the conversion to Christianity. Missionaries and bishops opened new channels of communication with other parts of Europe, bringing knowledge of more developed forms of government, administration, and law. Links were also forged by traders, and the expanding commerce resulted in the development of towns, functioning not only as centres of secular authority but also as places in which royal churches symbolized the new, Christian kingship, early examples being Lund in Denmark, Sigtuna in Sweden, and Trondheim in Norway.

2

PRESENTATION OF THE CORPUS AND ITS SUBGROUP; BASES OF ANALYSES

I. The Corpus

The corpus comprises all inscriptions that yield a minimum of textual information. These are all listed below in the Catalogue. As described at page xvii above, most of the inscriptions are identified by the numbers assigned to them in the standard editions (*DR*, *NIyR*, *SRI*), but since the edition of *Öland's* inscriptions is out of date, these are referred to by the numbers given in Nilsson (1973). For inscriptions not included in these editions (new finds and lost ones that have now been recovered) it is customary to refer to their archival number or to the publications in which they have been reported. However, I have found it more practical to adopt another system for these finds, using the abbreviations 'Dk' for Denmark, 'No' for Norway, and the standard abbreviations for Swedish provinces (listed in the Abbreviations, above, and in App. 1), with my own numbers preceded by 'N' (=new).

2.1. VARIABLES

In the data-base there are thirty-three variables, the most important of which are fully described in the Explanatory Notes at the beginning of the Catalogue (pp. 191–8), thus making it possible to search the material for many different purposes. These variables may be grouped under the following headings.

Identification: reference number; provenance (region, district,[1] parish, place); type of find-spot (e.g. beside a road, in a church).

Outer features: type of stone (upright, on a rock-face, recumbent); material (granite/sedimentary); state (fragments, parts); height, width/breadth; form of inscription (in bands, serpents); ornament (e.g. cross, animal, figures).

[1] The districts have different names in different regions, e.g. 'härad', 'hundare', 'ting', so for the sake of simiplicity I have chosen to refer to 'districts'.

Contents: inscription (in modern Scandinavian languages, sometimes with the original language in bold type); relationship between sponsor(s) and deceased; prayer; signature (of rune-carver); personal names; place-names; other characteristics (e.g. titles; 'thegns', 'drengs'); references to travel abroad or bridge-building; additional information (see below Ch. 3.1.2); miscellaneous comments and comparisons, cross-references, etc.

2.2. GENERAL FEATURES

2.2.1. Type

Ninety per cent of the inscriptions are on *upright* stones; in Norway, Denmark, and Bornholm almost all are of this type, but in Uppland and Södermanland inscriptions on *rock faces* are relatively common.[2] In the rest of Sweden there are a number of *recumbent* (grave)stones: in Västergötland the proportion is as high as 19% and in Östergötland 12%.

The heights of upright stones differ; the tallest stones are found in Norway where 60% are taller than 2 metres, and as many as 20% even exceed 3 metres; in Västergötland too the stones are generally taller than in other regions.[3]

2.2.2. Lost stones

Less than 17% of the known stones have disappeared; the proportion of lost stones is highest in Öland and Östergötland[4] and lowest in Bornholm and Denmark.[5]

2.2.3. Material

Granite (or gneiss) is the most common material, but sedimentary rock was also used in all parts of Scandinavia, especially in eastern Sweden, and most frequently in Öland and Gotland (limestone). According to Stefan E. Hagenfeldt and Rune Palm sandstone was more often used at a later stage; rune-stones of this material have to a large extent (80%) been found in or near churches, and it is suggested that they functioned in the same way as the medieval types of monument, with which they may be contemporary. The reason why sandstone was chosen could be the relative ease with which this material could be cut and carved, making it possible to satisfy a growing demand, and—in areas where sandstone was not locally available—the sponsors' wish to mark their status.[6]

[2] Respectively, 8% and 11%.

[3] Stones taller than 2 m.: in Vg, 36%; in Ög, 28%; in U, 26%; in Sm and Sö, 20%; in Dk 17%.

[4] Respectively, 24% and 23%.

[5] Respectively, 3% and 11%.

[6] Hagenfeldt and Palm (1996), 9, 48, 56.

2.2.4. Find-spots

We know where 95% of the stones were found but this was apparently the original location of less than half of them. Almost 40% have been found in churches, or in or near churchyards; this may have been where many of them were initially placed, but some have certainly been moved there from their original sites. The highest proportion of rune-stones in or near churches are in Öland (98%) and the lowest in Småland (37%). In Uppland and Södermanland, however, a larger proportion have been found beside roads (*c.*30%) than in or close to churches (*c.*27%). Many stones have also been found beside roads in Småland (25%), Västergötland (15%) and Östergötland (13%).

In regions with the most rune-stones, many have been found close to waterways,[7] and 7% are close to bridges or causeways. About 13% are situated close to prehistoric graves or gravefields, most frequently in Småland (22%), least frequently in Östergötland and Bornholm, with only one (Öl 1) in Öland. In Norway almost a third are close to farms, which is proportionately a less common location in the rest of Scandinavia.

2.2.5. Design

The design—that is to say, the layout—of 90% of the inscriptions is known: rows or bands are typical in Norway, Denmark, and southern Sweden (Vg, Ög, Sm), while serpents dominate in Uppland and Södermanland (see Ch. 1, Pls. 1–3). In Sweden (most frequently in Östergötland, 25%) there is also a 'transitional' design, between band and serpent, in which the band is curved and sometimes has ornamented ends, often shaped as serpents' heads. Gotland is exceptional; the rune-stones there have the same mushroom-shape as the earlier picture stones, with the inscription round the edge, and there are often one or more horizontal bands across the stone under a cross (Pl. 6). There is also a special, 'Ölandic' style, also with the inscription round the edge but with interlaced band ornaments in the middle (Pl. 7). For further illustrations, see Figure 1 in the Explanatory Notes to the Catalogue.

2.2.6. Crosses and other kinds of ornament

Christian crosses are found on 47% of the stones, most commonly in Uppland (59%) and Södermanland (54%), less frequently in Norway (21%) and Denmark (11%). Overall, 10% of the stones (but none in Bornholm) have other types of pictorial ornament, e.g. ships, masks, and beasts (for beasts, see Ch. 4.8 and Pl. 16; for masks, see Ch. 6.1.3 and Pl. 29); and sometimes these are combined with a cross.[8] For illustrations of crosses, see Figure 2 in the Explanatory Notes to the Catalogue.

[7] Between 7% and 9%.

[8] Thus 'pictorial ornaments' do not include serpent or ribbon patterns.

PLATE 6. G 134, Sjonhem. Example of Gotlandic design. *Inscription*: 'Rodvisl and Rodälv, they had these stones raised in memory of (their) three sons. This one in memory of Rodfos. Valachians (?) betrayed him on a voyage. May God fail those who failed him.'
PLATE 7. Öl 55, Sandby. Example of Ölandic design. *Inscription*: 'Gudfast and Helgun and Nenne, mother and sons, had this stone raised in memory of the father Sven.'

2.2.7. Signature

A rune-master's signature is found in 13% of the inscriptions, most frequently in Uppland (18%) and in Södermanland (11%) but relatively rarely in the rest of Scandinavia. Professional rune-carvers were apparently more common towards the end of the period.[9] One function of the rune-masters' signature is suggested in Ch. 4.2.

2.3. REGIONAL GROUPINGS

The above presentation has revealed significant differences within Scandinavia in types of rune-stone, the places where they have been found, their design and ornament, and the occurrence upon them of crosses and sig-

[9] Zachrisson (1998), 126.

TABLE 2.1. *Characteristic regional features of rune-stones*

	South/West	Intermediate	East
Type (other than upright):	few	recumbent: Vg 19%; Ög 12%	on rocks: Sö 11%; U 8%
Main types of:			
Find-spot	church; farm	church; roadside	roadside; church
Design	rows; bands	bands; 'transitional'; serpents	serpents
Stones incorporating:			
Ornament (%)	11	4 in Sm+Ög; 17 in Vg	10
Cross (%)	Dk 11 (No 21.5)	42[a]	57[b]
Signature (%)	Dk 5 (No 8)	4[c]	14.5[d]

[a] Percentages by district: Sm 41.5; Vg 38; Ög 47.
[b] Percentages by district: Sö 54.5; U 59.
[c] Percentages by district: Sm 2; Vg 7; Ög 3.
[d] Percentages by district: Sö 11; U 18.

natures. These variations make it possible to distinguish three 'regions' each with common features: a South/West-Scandinavian region (Dk and No), an East-Swedish one (Sö and U), and an intermediate one (Sm, Vg, Ög); see Table 2.1.

2.4. CHRONOLOGY AND DATING PROBLEMS

Very few inscriptions (less than 2%) can be dated historically, and then only approximately; examples are: Harald Bluetooth's stone at Jelling (DR 42), dating from before his death *c.*987; a stone (NIyR 184) commemorating a man who took part in Knut's conquest of England after 1015; the stones commemorating men who took Knut's *geld* or 'payment' (U 344 and U 194) in England (?1018); and the stones commemorating men who followed their leader Ingvar on an eastern expedition (*c.*25 stones) after *c.*1040.

This does not seem very encouraging, but the historically dated inscriptions sometimes contain information that link them with others so that a *relative* chronology is possible for many more. In some cases the name of the rune-master can serve as a link,[10] in other cases a link is provided by

[10] Most of the signed inscriptions are in Uppland and Södermanland, where, according to *KHL* xiv, cols. 496–505, the 'rune-master' chronology was: early 11th cent.: Fasttegn, Gunnar; *c.*1020–50: Åsmund Kåresson; *c.*1030–50: Livsten; *c.*1040–?: Balle; *c.*1050–?: Fot, Visäte, Öpir. (See modifications in Gräslund (1992).)

PLATE 8. U 335, Orkesta. Inscription in serpent placed in the middle: 'Holme had this stone raised and this bridge (built) in memory of Hära, his father, Sigröd's housecarl.'

reference to events or persons that are common to two or more stones. It is occasionally possible, especially in eastern Sweden, to reconstruct genealogies.

Nevertheless, for the overwhelming number of inscriptions the dating is based on typology. For this the crucial features are the content (of text and ornament), the language, and the design of the inscription—in rows, bands, or serpents. It appears that the editors of the standard works have generally put greater weight on the design than on the other variables, and on this basis the following relative chronology has been established:[11]

Design	*Ornament*
Inscription in rows or bands:	
without framing lines (Pl. 2, Ch. 1) }	none
with framing lines (Pl. 1, Ch. 1) }	
Inscription in serpents:	
placed in the middle (Pl. 8)	simple
placed round the edges (Pl. 9) }	developed: (*a*) serpents
placed randomly (Pl. 10) }	(*b*) beasts (Pl. 11)

Typological dating does not correspond to real dating.[12] In some cases archaism may have been deliberate, and in others the features are due not to chronological but to regional differences. As far as content is concerned,

[11] After Palm (1992), 31 f. [12] Palm (1992), 33.

PLATE 9. U 330, Snottsta. Inscription in serpent placed round edges: 'Inga had these stones raised and this bridge built in memory of Ragnfast, her husband. Assur was his housecarl.'

it is not possible to date rune-stones by Christian or pagan features; many monuments lack both, and the presence or absence of Christian prayers seems to have more to do with local custom than anything else. In Uppland there is a slight tendency for prayers to be more frequent in the older inscriptions.[13] The formula 'May Thor hallow' may be younger than some of the Christian prayers, in reaction to the Conversion.[14] Even the significance of a Christian cross has been questioned; we do not know what its function was, nor if it was sometimes a later addition.

[13] Cf. also Zachrisson (1998), 126, with references given there.
[14] Cf. Palm (1992), 31, and B. Sawyer (1989), 188.

PLATE 10. U 29, Hillersjö. Inscription in serpents placed randomly (for full inscription, see pp. 49–50).

Harald Bluetooth's stone at Jelling is a good illustration of the complexities involved in typology; as far as ornament is concerned, it represents a far more developed stage than his father's monument, while linguistically it represents an older stage.[15]

Neither language nor orthography has served as a reliable guide to chronology; in modern runology more attention has been paid to *regional* variations.[16] There is no doubt that linguistically there were two main areas, a southern one and a northern one.[17] Two stylistic areas can also be discerned; on the basis of form and ornament Hans Christiansson has distinguished a southern and a northern style, with the forests south of Lake Mälaren as the boundary between them.[18]

A new attempt to establish a chronology has been made by the Swedish archaeologist Anne-Sofie Gräslund, who has concentrated on the zoomorphic runic carving of the Mälar region with the heads seen in profile. Her stylistic analysis of the serpents (the design of the animals' heads, feet, coils, and tails, the arrangement of the patterns, and the overall impression) has led her to distinguish five Profiles, the main features of which can be seen in the characteristic examples illustrated in Figure 2.1. While

[15] Palm (1992), 33.
[16] Lagman (1990); Williams (1990); Palm (1992).
[17] Palm (1992), 34, 253.
[18] Christiansson (1959).

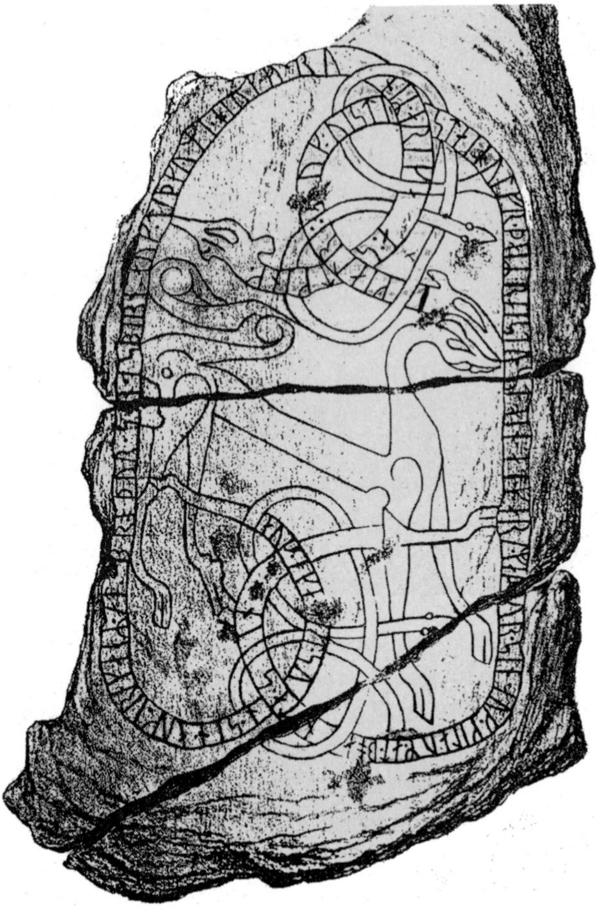

Plate 11. Sö 205, Överselö. Inscription in serpents, with beast: 'Ingjald and Visäte and Stenulv, they raised this stone in memory of Karl, their father, and Gillög in memory of her husband, and Inga in memory of her son, and Ärnger after his brother. Äsbjörn and Tidkume cut the runes, Orökja painted.'

Profiles 1 and 2 are closely connected with the Ringerike style, Profiles 3, 4, and, to a certain extent, 5 are closely connected with the Urnes style.[19] Gräslund has concluded that the stones without serpents ('straight' stones) belong to the decades around the year 1000, and that stones with serpents' heads seen from above ('bird's-eye view' stones) were contemporary with Profile 2.

[19] Gräslund (1992) and (1998); for the complete analysis—heads, feet, coils, and tails, see Gräslund (1998).

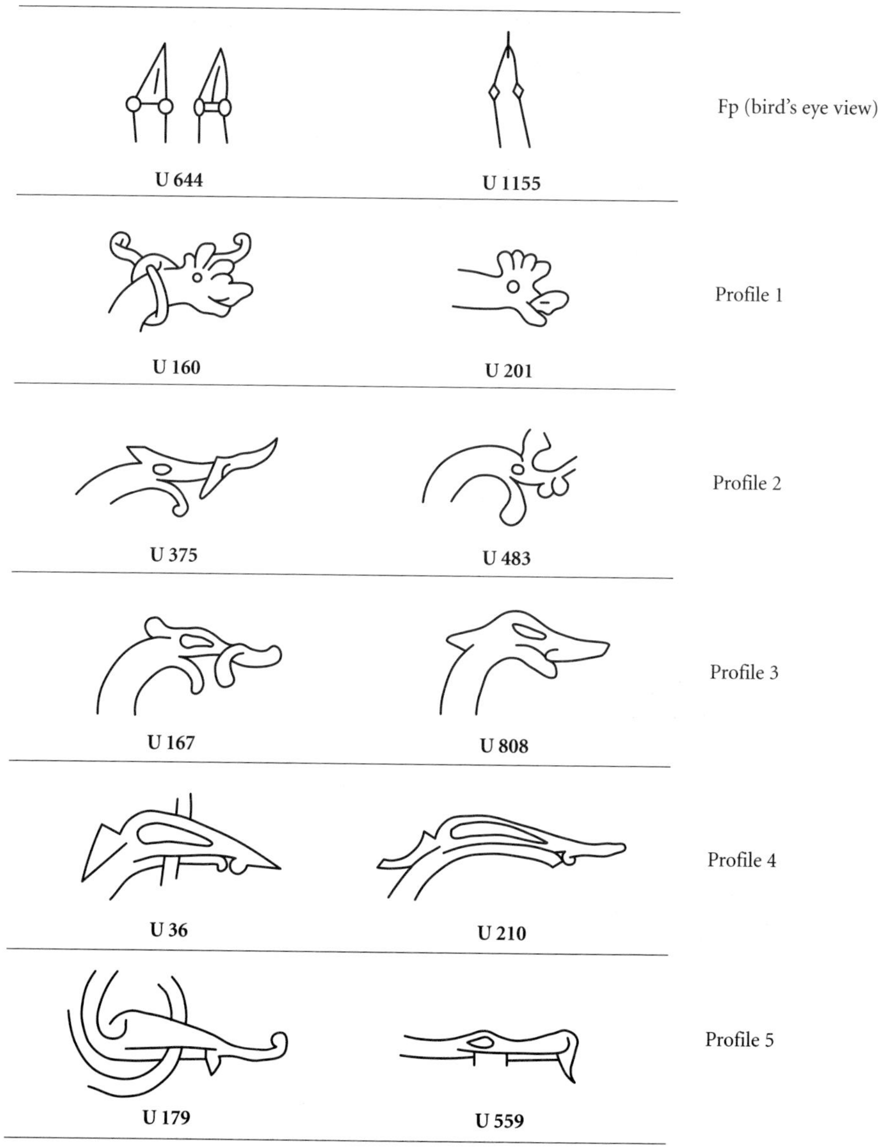

FIGURE 2.1. Gräslund's Serpent Profiles

The dating of inscriptions adopted in this volume, and summarized below, inevitably has a large margin of uncertainty. It is an attempt to combine Gräslund's stylistic chronology for the East with chronologies that have been proposed for other regions on different grounds.

Periodization in this volume	*Gräslund's chronology*
1. *c*.750/800–960	
2. 960–1050	
2a. 960–1020	straight[20] + Profile 1
2b. 1020–1050	bird's-eye view + Profile 2
3. 1050–1100	
3a. 1050–1070	Profile 3
3b. 1070–1100	Profile 4
4. after 1100	Profile 5

My periodization differs partly from the one used in *DR*, where period 1 refers to early inscriptions (before 750/800) that are not dealt with in this study. Thus, my period 1 (before *c*.960) corresponds to *DR*'s period 2.1 (750/800–900) and partly to its period 2.2 (900–1050). The overlap of sixty years will not, however, create problems, since it is likely that few stones of *DR*'s period 2.2 were sponsored before the mid-tenth century.

Admittedly *DR*'s period 2.2 includes stones that the editors dated to the beginning of the tenth century, including the following that are relevant here: DR 26, 29, 34, 209, and 230. Their arguments for such an early dating are, however, not convincing, and here these stones will be treated as belonging to my period 2. Runographically and linguistically they correspond to the Jelling group, but their contents were judged to be closer to the earlier so-called Helnæs–Gørlev group. The argument is that they belong to a pagan milieu and must therefore be older than the Jelling group; DR 26 has a hammer sign (DR 29 and 34 are sponsored by the same man as DR 26); DR 209 and 230 (see Ch. 5, Pls. 18 and 17) contain pagan spells, the former also the 'May Thor hallow' formula. It has, however, been pointed out above that these features do not exclude the possibility that they were more or less contemporary with the Jelling group of stones.

With this exception I have followed the dates given by the standard works. As far as Norway is concerned it is difficult to generalize, since the date of many inscriptions is most uncertain, but it seems that the majority belong to the period before *c*.1050. In Denmark too most of the stones were erected before *c*.1050, while in Bornholm the majority are more recent than that. Most of the stones in Östergötland, Västergötland, and Småland

[20] i.e. without a serpent.

TABLE 2.2. *Incidence of characteristic features in Uppland before and after* c.*1050 (%)*

	Before *c.*1050	After *c.*1050
Signature	9.5	27
Pictorial ornament	7	15
Cross	76.5	62
Prayer	46.5	16.5
Cross and prayer	38	12

seem to be more or less contemporary with the Danish ones, while many stones in other parts of Sweden are later.

In my data-base 65% of the Uppland and 63% of the Södermanland stones can be dated, thanks to Gräslund's chronology. In Södermanland most of these stones were erected before *c.*1050; only 22.5% are later. In Uppland, however, as many as 71% belong to the period *after c.*1050, and 45% are later than *c.*1070.

Following Gräslund's chronology the following generalizations can be made about the stones in Uppland: here signed and ornamented stones were more common towards the end of the period, while prayers, and stones with both prayer and cross, were more common in the early period. Stones with crosses are slightly less common in the latter part of the period (see Table 2.2).

II. The Relationship Subgroup and Categories of Relationship

Many inscriptions in the corpus are incomplete, so in order to assess the proportion of men and women in the material, as well their different relationships, I have distinguished a subgroup containing only inscriptions that specify both sponsors and deceased (the Relationship Subgroup). This subgroup includes 1,776 of the 2,307 inscriptions in the main corpus.[21]

Thus in 77% of all inscriptions the sex of the sponsors and deceased is known. These inscriptions can be classified in nine *main categories* (namely A, B, AB, C, D, CD, E, F, EF) according to the sex of the sponsors and deceased: see Table 2.3 below.

Table 2.3 shows that the overwhelming majority of stones were raised in memory of men exclusively; that women were seldom commemorated

[21] Bornholm: main corpus, 31 inscrs. / subgroup, 26 inscrs.; Denmark: 168 / 149; Norway: 51 / 40; Sweden: 2,057 / 1,561.

TABLE 2.3. *Categorization of 1,776 stones according to sex of sponsors and deceased (%)*

Sponsors									Deceased	
Men			Women			Men + Women				
A	m~m	66.6	C	w~m	11.1	E	m+w~m	14.6	92.3	men
B	m~w	3.6	D	w~w	0.4	F	m+w~w	0.2	4.2	women
AB	m~m+w	2.7	CD	w~w+m	0.2	EF	m+w~m+w	0.5	3.4	men+women
TOTAL		72.9			11.7			15.3	99.9	

Note: m = men; w = women; swung dash (~) = 'commemorating'; plus sign = 'together with'. For a survey of the categories in the main regions, see Appendix 2.

exclusively, and that memorials commemorating both men and women are even less common.

It is thus mainly as sponsors that we encounter women. Their proportion is especially high in Uppland, Södermanland, and Öland, where they often act together with men. In the rest of Scandinavia it is relatively unusual for women and men to act as co-sponsors, and in Norway it seems never to have happened. The main regional variations can be summarized as follows.

The deceased. As a rule the stones were raised in memory of a single person, but in over 13% of the inscriptions two or more people, mostly men, are commemorated together, for example, father and son, several brothers, or son and brother. Inscriptions commemorating both men and women are not frequent, though there are occurrences everywhere except in Norway and Gotland. Inscriptions commemorating women only also occur in most regions (except Närke, Hälsingland, Medelpad, and Jämtland), although there are few in Uppland and Södermanland, and they are even scarcer in Småland. Women, whether alone or together with men, are very rarely commemorated by other women; there are only six (? seven) examples: one each in Norway and Denmark, one (possibly two) in Södermanland, and three in Uppland.[22]

The sponsors. In Scandinavia as a whole it was as common for sponsors to act on their own as together with others, but there are considerable differences between areas and categories. In Norway only 12.5% of the stones are sponsored by two or more persons, in Denmark and Västergötland about 18%, in Småland about 22%, while the corresponding proportion lies between about 58% and 64% in Södermanland and Uppland (see further Ch. 4.2).

22 NIyR 68 (mother~daughter); DR 55 (daughter~mother); Sö 73 (woman~woman), and perhaps Sö 15 (daughter~mother?); U 314 and 489 (both mother~daughter). In U 605 a woman commemorates herself.

2.5. THE NATURE OF RELATIONSHIPS BETWEEN SPONSORS AND DECEASED

The proportion of specified relationships is lower in Denmark and Norway than in Sweden. In order to analyse the different kinds of relationships the following subcategories are used (for a complete account of the system of analysis (A 1, C 1, etc.), see the Catalogue: Explanatory Notes, pp. 195–6).

Subcategory	*Examples*
1. child~parent	A 1=son~father; C 1=daughter~father; E 1=son+daughter~father
2. sibling~sibling	B 2=brother~sister
3. parent~child	C 3=mother~son; F 3=parents~daughter
4. kin~kin[23]	A 4=(sometimes) nephew~uncle
5. partner~partner (=co-owners)	in category A=trading partners or comrades-in-arms; in other categories=spouses. In these cases the sponsor and deceased were not blood relations but may have had property in common.
6. unspecified relationships	i.e. when names only are mentioned and only the sexes can be determined
7a. superior~inferior	A 7a=king~'hirdman' (i.e. 'retainer')
7b. inferior~superior	A 7b=man~leader
8. person~him/herself	i.e. the 'self-commemorative' inscriptions

2.5.1. Identical commemorations

Some sponsors commemorated the same person(s) on two (or more) monuments. Since I have found only 38 cases (of which 28 are in Uppland) it is not likely to have much effect on the analysis; these identical commemorations are spread over the main categories A, B, AB, C, and E, as well as over the most common subcategories within each.[24]

[23] This category contains both consanguinity and affinity and many different terms of kinship, e.g. nephew (brother's or sister's son), grandson (son's or daughter's son), uncle (father's or mother's brother), unspecified consanguinity (*frændi*), and affinity (*magʀ*), i.e. son/brother/father-in-law.

[24] This total includes only the cases with *exactly* the same relationship; in four more cases people have been commemorated both by the same and by other sponsors; see Catalogue, under respective Further Particulars sections. Individuals who have commemorated themselves twice or more are dealt with separately (see Ch. 6.3).

2.5.2. The subcategories; simple and complex relationships

Most inscriptions concern simple relationships, as shown in the list above, but everywhere, and especially in Uppland and Södermanland, various combinations of relationships occur. A very common combination is a son and a widow commemorating a man together, for example:

> Stenulv had this stone raised in memory of Sigfast, his father, and Holmgärd in memory of her husband. (U 30, Kvarsta)

The ways these complex relationships are dealt with will be explained below (pp. 41–2).

2.6. SPONSORSHIP PATTERNS

In most cases (88%) the sponsors were closely related to, or married to, or were partners of, the deceased, but in Denmark and Norway the proportion of such relationships is lower. In the few inscriptions that do not specify the relationship between sponsors and the deceased, the people named may nevertheless have been related, if only by marriage, but that cannot be taken for granted (see Ch. 3.5).

In discussing this topic, attention will be concentrated first on the commemorations of only men (categories A, C, and E), next on the commemorations of only women (categories B, D, and F), and finally on the commemorations of both men and women (categories AB, CD, and EF). The discussion will refer mainly to the regions with the most inscriptions: Uppland, Södermanland, Östergötland, Västergötland, Småland, Denmark, and Norway—the latter for the sake of comparison, despite the small number of inscriptions.

It has been suggested that sponsorship by women increased in the period, and that this could explain their relatively high proportion in Uppland.[25] This, however, does not seem to be the case; both as single sponsors (category C) and together with men (category E) women are as well represented in the period before *c.*1050 as after.[26] Women commemorated on their own (categories B, D, and F), however, seem to be more frequent towards the end of the period, but the number of those that can be dated is so small in Uppland (fourteen in all) that no certain conclusions can be drawn. Women commemorated together with men (categories AB and CD) seem to be as frequent—or rare—both before and after *c.*1050.[27]

[25] Zachrisson (1998), 159.

[26] Of the dated stones category C accounts for *c.*11% and category E for 22% both before and after *c.*1050.

[27] The six cases where men and women together commemorate men and women (category EF), however, all belong to the latter half of the 11th cent.

A: *men~men*

Erlend carved these runes in memory of Olve, (his) father. (NIyR 271, Gjerde)

Most stones commemorating men were raised by men (66.6%), generally by their sons, brothers, or fathers; Norway and Denmark, however, have a considerably lower proportion of sons than the rest of Scandinavia. In Denmark brothers are in the majority, and in Norway, Västergötland, and Småland there are proportionately more fathers as sponsors than in other areas. Other male relatives are fairly common in Norway, Västergötland, and Östergötland, but not in Uppland and Södermanland, and partners are exceptional outside Denmark.

C: *women~men*

Åse set up this stone in memory of her husband Ømunde, who was Finnulv's 'hirdman' (retainer). (DR 155, Sjørind)

The proportion of women commemorating men on their own is roughly the same in the main areas, between *c.*10.5% and 15.5%. Since this percentage (11.1% as an average) cannot be supposed to reflect demographic reality, it was probably the result of rules or customs that determined when it was appropriate or necessary for women to act on their own. If so, those rules seem to have been much the same in most areas of Scandinavia, with the exception of Norway (three cases) and Småland (four cases), and possibly also of Gotland and Öland (two cases each).[28]

In order to discover what these rules may have been, I have investigated how often wives, mothers, daughters, and sisters acted as sponsors on their own, in comparison with sons, fathers, brothers, and other male relatives acting on their own. This has cast light on the rules regulating when women could, or were expected to, act on their own. The result suggests that in Scandinavia as a whole it was not normally the custom for women to raise stones on their own as long as sons, brothers, and fathers of the deceased were alive. In western Scandinavia male relatives other than sons, brothers, or fathers are more common as sponsors commemorating men than daughters and sisters together; in Denmark and Norway there are no daughters or sisters commemorating men at all. This suggests that in western Scandinavia women did not put up stones so long as even more remote male kinsmen or partners were alive. Among women who commemorate men on their own we most often meet the wife (4%) or mother (3.5%) of the deceased, only half as often his daughter (2%), and very seldom his sister (not even 1%). Most of these women who acted independently were widows; the others were probably unmarried women without male relatives.

[28] NIyR 61, 66, 213; Sm 46, 64, 76, 105; G 138, N6; Öl 31, 51.

E: *men and women~men*

Torbjörn and Frölög had this stone raised in memory of Önd, their son. (Sö 50, Jogersta)

In Scandinavia as a whole women acted together with men more frequently than on their own (14.6%), but it should be emphasized that this mixed category is very unusual outside Uppland, Södermanland, and Öland, and totally absent in Norway. Most of the inscriptions in this category were sponsored by the son and wife or the father and mother of the deceased. With few exceptions it is only in Uppland and Södermanland that sons and daughters act together.

B: *men~women*

Frösten made this memorial to Tora, his wife . . . (Vg 67, Saleby)

This is a very small group—on average only 3.6% of all inscriptions—but there are great regional variations: less than 2% in Uppland and Södermanland, but as high as *c.*7% in Denmark and 8.5% in Västergötland. Most men commemorating women did so in their capacity as husbands or sons, and more seldom (only in Uppland, Östergötland, and Småland) as fathers.

D: *women~women*

Gunnvor, Trydrik's daughter, built a bridge in memory of Astrid, her daughter. She was the most accomplished maiden in Hadeland. (NIyR 68, Nordre Dynna)

This is an even smaller group (0.4%), represented only in Norway, Denmark, Uppland, and Södermanland. They are all daughters commemorating their mothers or vice versa.[29]

F: *men and women~women*

Gunnar and Kättilö had the stones raised and the bridge built in memory of Olog, their daughter . . . (U 377, Velamby)

The four cases where this occurs are unique to Uppland and Södermanland.[30]

AB: *men~men and women*

Unnulv and Fjolvar (?) raised this stone in memory of Djure, their father, Redulv's son, and in memory of **harlau**, their mother . . . (Hs 6, Järvsö)

This category amounts to 2.7% of the inscriptions but is unrepresented in Norway. In most cases we find sons commemorating both parents; other relationships occur only in Uppland and Södermanland.

[29] NIyR 68; DR 55; U 314, 489, 605; Sö 15, 73.

[30] U 311, 313, 377; Sö 128.

CD: *women~men and women*

Estrid (?) had this stone raised in memory of Hedenfast, her father, and Öda in memory of her husband and of Ödgärd, her daughter. (U 821, Mysinge)

There are only four cases—all in Uppland.[31]

EF: *men and women~men and women*

Hagbard and Ingegärd had these stones raised in memory of their father, Runfast, and their mother, Runa. Ingulv carved the runes. Hagbard built the bridge. (U 1041, Golvasta)

This is also a very small category, occurring in Uppland, Södermanland, Medelpad, and Östergötland.[32]

In several respects it is possible to distinguish two main patterns of sponsorship, one in the south and west of Scandinavia, the other in the east. The terms 'South/West' and 'East' can therefore serve as a convenient shorthand description of the two main zones. The East comprises Södermanland, Uppland, and Öland, but not Östergötland, which, although geographically in the east, has much the same sponsorship pattern as the South/West zone.

In the South/West, i.e. mainly Denmark and Norway, but also to a certain extent Västergötland, Östergötland, and Småland, most rune stones were sponsored by a single person; in the East by two or more people, often by men and women together. Further, the proportion of women (as sponsors and deceased) is generally lower in the South/West than in the East, and is particularly low in Norway—and Småland.

Norway, Denmark, and Västergötland have proportionately more unspecified relationships than the other Swedish provinces. Moreover, in Scandinavia as a whole about 86.5% of the sponsors were close kin of the deceased, while in Norway and Denmark such close kinship was less common, the proportion being only *c.*70%.

In general it can be said that the main contrast is between Denmark together with Norway in the South/West, and Uppland together with Öland in the East. The areas in between share characteristics with both, but in varying degrees.

2.7. COMPLEX RELATIONSHIPS

As pointed out above, most inscriptions concern simple relationships but there are many cases where various combinations of relationships occur, for example:

[31] U 133, 652 (both by women in memory of their sons and themselves), 821, N9.

[32] U 11, 100, 867, 914, 1041, 1093; Sö 331; M 3; Ög 84.

Visäte and Halvdan had this stone carved in memory of Holme, their father, and of Holmfast, their brother. (Vs 29, Sala)

In this case the sponsors have commemorated both their father and their brother (a combination indicated in the Catalogue by a solidus between the relationship digits listed on pp. 36–7 above: A 1/2).

Anund and Svarald and Finnvid had this stone raised in memory of Ögisl, their father, and Björn in memory of his brother. (Sö 190, Ytterenhörna)

Here the sponsors have different relationships to the deceased; three sons commemorate their father, and are joined by their uncle, who commemorates his brother (an association indicated in the Catalogue by an intervening full point between the relationship digits: A 1.2).

In the following examples the deceased or the sponsors are of both sexes:

Håkan had this stone raised in memory of Skygne, his brother, and of Altrud, his mother . . . (M 5, Attmar)

Stenulv had this stone raised in memory of Sigfast, his father, and Holmgärd in memory of her husband . . . (U 30, Kvarsta)

In such cases the sex of the sponsor and/or deceased is shown in the Catalogue by combining the relationship digit with a zero (0), placed *before* for a woman and *after* for a man; for instance AB (=men commemorating both men and women) 20/01: a man has commemorated both his brother and his mother (e.g. M 5, above). E (=both men and women commemorating men) 10.05: a man has been commemorated both by his son(s) and by his wife (e.g. U 30, above). For a fuller descriptions of the principles used, see the Catalogue: Explanatory Notes (pp. 195–6).

III. Bases of Analyses

In discussing the categories of relationships I have used two different ways of dealing with the complex ones:

2.8. INSCRIPTIONS

Inscriptions containing complex relationships can be counted several times as examples of different kinds of relationships: for example, son commemorating father, *and* brother commemorating brother, *and* wife commemorating husband, etc. Thus the numbers of relationships cannot be added up to correspond to the total of the inscriptions (see Ch. 3). (So, for example, there are 772 inscriptions containing the relationship son~father, but many of them *also* contain other relationships, e.g. brother~brother, the total of which is 355 inscriptions.)

2.9. RELATIONSHIPS

In order to make a comprehensive survey of all kinds of relationships and a complete assessment of their proportions possible, it has been necessary to break down all complex relationships into simple ones. An inscription in which, for example, a man commemorates his father and his brother at the same time is thus counted as evidence of two relationships, both son~father (A 1) and brother~brother (A 2). Another example is when a man is commemorated by several persons, for instance by his sons, wife, mother, and brothers, which is counted as four different relationships (E 10.05.03.20).[33] In the Relationship Subgroup of 1,776 inscriptions 2,280 relationships occur. The analysis of all these relationships is presented below in a 'Relationship Survey' (Table 2.4 below), and is also used in Chapter 3.1–2).

2.9.1. Three different zones

As already pointed out above (section 2.6, end), we can discern two main sponsorship patterns in Scandinavia; with the help of this comprehensive Relationship Survey we can see that there is also an Intermediate zone, between South/West and East.

2.9.1a. South/West (Denmark and Norway)

Admittedly Denmark has a somewhat higher proportion of female sponsors than Norway, but common to both areas is the almost total absence of daughters and sisters among the sponsors; this is also true of Västergötland. In contrast to Norway, however, Denmark has mothers sponsoring stones in memory of their sons, though proportionately fewer than in the East zone. Most women sponsors in Norway and Denmark were wives commemorating their husbands.

A striking feature of both Norway and Denmark is the high proportion of stones commemorating brothers and, by contrast, the low proportion of sons commemorating their fathers. Norway has a very high proportion of fathers commemorating their sons, while in Denmark few fathers put up stones; partners were responsible for more. In Norway the categories of male relatives (A 4) and unspecified relationships (A 6) together amount to almost 36% of the relationships in inscriptions commemorating men, in Denmark 25.5%.

2.9.1b. East (Södermanland, Uppland, Öland)

Even if Södermanland, Uppland, and Öland have a higher proportion of women sponsoring stones than Denmark and Norway, this does not apply to the category of *sole* female sponsors. The main differences are (*a*) that

[33] See Catalogue: Explanatory Notes, p. 195.

TABLE 2.4. *Percentage of all relationships in the Relationship Subgroup with their codes*

Relationship	%	Code
son~father	31.5	A 1, AB 10, E 10
brother~brother	14.8	A 2, AB 20, E 20
father~son	10.4	A 3, AB 30, E 30
wife~husband	8.0	C 5, CD 50, E 05
man~man	7.6	A 6, AB 60, E 60
mother~son	7.2	C 3, CD 30, E 03
daughter~father	3.8	C 1, CD 10, E 01
kinsman~kinsman	3.4	A 4, AB 40, E 40
woman~man	2.1	C 6, CD 60, E 06
son~mother	2.1	B 1, AB 01, F 10
person~him/herself	1.7	subcategories 8, 80, 08
husband~wife	1.6	B 5, AB 05, F 50
sister~brother	1.2	C 2, CD 20, E 20
male partner~male partner	1.1	A 5, AB 50, E 50
brother~sister	0.6	B 2, AB 02, F 20
father~daughter	0.6	B 3, AB 03, F 30
mother~daughter	0.4	D 3, CD 03, F 03
kinswoman~kinsman	0.4	C 4, CD 40, E 04
man~woman	0.4	B 6, AB 06, E 06
superior~inferior inferior~superior	0.4	A 7a, AB 70a, E 70a A 7b, AB 70b, E 70b
kinsman~kinswoman	0.3	B 4, AB 04, F 40
daughter~mother	0.2	D 1, CD 01, F 01
kinswoman~kinswoman	0.04	D 4, CD 04, F 04
woman~woman	0.04	D 6, CD 06, F 06
TOTAL	99.9	

Notes: Category EF is not included; its relationships are always explained in terms of categories A, B, C, and D: see Catalogue, Explanatory Notes (p. 195–6).

For each main region, see Appendix 3, which presents ten frequent relationships indicating inheritance and/or joint property.

in the East zone women often acted together with men, (*b*) that we meet not only wives and mothers but also daughters and sisters among the sponsors. The proportion of sons commemorating their fathers is as high as 36.5%, and in these provinces we seldom meet male relatives other than sons, brothers, and fathers, and the proportion of partners and unspecified sponsors is relatively low.

It is also mainly in Södermanland and Uppland that we have examples of sons and daughters acting together. It should, however, be emphasized that there is a certain difference between the two provinces: in Södermanland female sponsors are not so frequent as in Uppland, and this applies, above all, to the wives, the proportion of whom is actually lower in Södermanland than in Denmark, Västergötland, and Östergötland.

In most respects the pattern in Öland agrees with that of Uppland, but not with regard to daughters, who are totally absent.

2.9.1c. Between South/West and East—the Intermediate zone

In terms of this analysis, if not geographically, Östergötland, Västergötland, Småland, Gotland, Västmanland, Gästrikland, and Närke lay between the two well-defined zones described above. The four latter are very difficult to place, since their material is so meagre, but it can at least be said about Gotland that the high proportion of 'group-sponsored' stones echoes the pattern of the East zone, while the proportion of women sponsors is low, as in the South/West.

Västergötland and Östergötland show similar patterns, with more features of the South/West zone than of the East: relatively low proportions of both 'group-sponsored' stones and stones sponsored by men and women together (and a total lack of stones raised by women in memory of other women), but a higher proportion of female sponsors than Norway and Denmark. What separates these two provinces is the relatively large number of fathers commemorating sons in Västergötland and the very occurrence of stone-raising daughters and sisters in Östergötland.

Småland, finally, has some extraordinary contrasts, with points of similarity with both the main zones: the proportion of women sponsors is the lowest in the whole of Scandinavia, while the proportion of explicitly

Table 2.5. *Sponsorship patterns of the three zones in percentage of relationships*

Sponsors	South/West	Intermediate	East
(i) *% of all relationships*			(*Öland included*)
single	83	73	33
male+female	No 0; Dk 6	11	27.5
(ii) *% of relationships in commemorations of men*			(*Öland excluded*)
son~father	14.5[a]	28	34[b]
brother~brother	24	16.5	14[c]
father~son	No 15; Dk 7	15.5	10.5[d]
male relative~male relative	5.5	6.5	2.5[e]
daughter~father	0	2.5	5[e]
sister~brother	0	1	1.8[e]
mother~son	No 0; Dk 2.5	4.5	9[f]
wife~husband	6.5	6	8[g]

[a] Dk 19%; No 10%.
[b] As high as over 41% in Öland.
[c] Uppland only 12%.
[d] Södermanland as high as 12%; cf. Östergötland, 11.5%.
[e] Does not occur in Öland.
[f] Only 4% in Öland.
[g] As high as 11% in Öland.

family-stones is the highest. Here there is only one single example of a wife commemorating a husband; but, on the other hand, there are some sisters, so rare in the South/West, and there is one daughter. Table 2.5 summarizes the main features of the three main zones defined above, giving average percentages for the South/West, viz. Norway and Denmark; for the East, viz. Södermanland and Uppland (Öland being excluded under (ii) and, instead, commented on in the footnotes); and for the 'Intermediate' zone, viz. Småland, Västergötland, and Östergötland. It should be pointed out that in two cases (brother~brother, and father~son) Södermanland differs from Uppland and has the same proportions as Östergötland. The main contrasts are between Denmark and Uppland.

On the basis of the frequency of relationships, the two main zones (South/West and East) correspond to the results from other types of investigations—runological, art historical, and dialectological.[34] The fact that the ethnologist Sigurd Erixon (on the evidence of different kinds of farm buildings) and the linguist Manne Eriksson (on the evidence of different names of farming tools) have also distinguished between a south-western and an eastern zone, suggests that the cultural border between these two main zones, however blurred in detail, has had a very long history.[35]

The pattern, or rather patterns, of relationships between sponsors and deceased presented here reinforces the assumption that it was not simple chance that decided who commemorated whom, but that there were certain established principles, some prevailing all over Scandinavia, others only in certain regions. What were these principles?

[34] Palm (1992), 34–40.

[35] For references, see Palm (1992), 37–8.

3

PROPERTY AND INHERITANCE

I. The Inscriptions as Declarations of Inheritance

Throughout Scandinavia the sponsors were normally closely related to the deceased. With few, if any, exceptions they, as survivors, can be assumed to have had an interest in property that had been owned by the deceased, whether by inheritance or because it had been jointly owned, for example by man and wife or by trading partners. There are, indeed, various indications that it was the new owner of the property that had belonged to the person being commemorated who commissioned the inscription and determined how it was formulated. The heirs' natural interest in marking their status and in proclaiming the inheritance could explain the care taken to state the nature of the relationship in the inscriptions.

The thought that *some* rune-stones may have functioned as declarations of inheritance is not new.[1] What is claimed here, however, is that almost *all* inscriptions reflect inheritance and property rights. I would, though, not go so far as Knut Carlqvist, who has argued that inheritance issues played the decisive role in the erection of rune-stones;[2] the purposes must have been manifold and have varied in different regions.

It is, however, not only the careful definition of relationships that supports the hypothesis that the inscriptions reflect claims to property by inheritance. It is a reasonable assumption that everything in an inscription is significant—the order in which the sponsors are named, the formulas used, and the additional information that is sometimes given. The facts that the stone was not easily worked and that the space at the disposal of the rune-master was limited suggest that inscriptions would not include superfluous or unimportant details. This can be illustrated by a very common type of inscription:

Otrygg and Bonde and Alvrik raised this stone in memory of Kåre, their father, and Gunned in memory of her husband. God help his spirit. Torbjörn carved the runes. (U 37, Säby)

[1] Ruprecht (1958), 81; Jansson (1963), 97; Hyenstrand (1973), 187; Page (1987), 46–7, 50.
[2] Carlqvist (1977).

Despite the fact that the different relationships lengthen and complicate the inscription, it was obviously considered important in the circumstances to spell them out. The most satisfactory explanation is that the sponsors, because of their different relationships to Kåre, had different claims upon his property. Kåre's sons were his heirs, and his widow had a right to dispose of her own property, whether inherited or given as dowry and dower. She may also have had a right to a share of what she and Kåre had owned jointly. As a widow she is not likely to have had any claims to direct inheritance—in no early Germanic law do spouses inherit from each other—but she might well have had a future claim through reverse inheritance, if she survived her sons. Other inscriptions, notably that at Hillersjö, discussed below (U 29), show that in Uppland property was transferred by reverse inheritance at that time.

The hypothesis that most inscriptions reflect claims to property by inheritance is greatly strengthened by those that name women among the sponsors; it is difficult to see in what context other than the ownership of property women were often omitted from the close family circles described in the inscriptions but were sometimes included, occasionally to the exclusion of all others. In order to avoid misunderstanding it must be emphasized that this hypothesis does not involve the assumption that all sponsors were heirs of the deceased. In some cases the sponsor may have been a guardian acting on behalf of a son who was too young to dispose of his inheritance, or perhaps one acting on behalf of a daughter;[3] other sponsors may have had no claim to inherit but were entitled to a share of the property that they had owned jointly with the deceased, for example in a trading partnership or a marriage.

Since most property changed hands by inheritance, an obvious question is whether the sponsorship pattern can provide any clues to the inheritance customs of Viking-Age Scandinavia. This will be discussed in greater detail below, but it may be helpful first to give some account of the assumptions that underlie this interpretation of the inscriptions.

The point of departure has been that women in Scandinavia, as elsewhere in Europe, had some right to inherit and dispose of property; no Germanic law excludes them. As there are no Scandinavian law codes, even fragmentary ones, from the period of the rune-stones, the Continental Germanic laws that were compiled during the sixth, seventh, and eighth centuries have provided the framework within which my interpretation has been developed. This is not the place to discuss the different Germanic

[3] e.g. Sö 302: 'Östen had this stone raised in memory of Torgärd, his sister, Hallbjörn in memory of his mother'. Probably Hallbjörn was too young to sponsor a stone commemorating his mother on his own, so his maternal uncle did it as his guardian (and potential heir?).

inheritance rules in any detail; but some salient features need to be outlined.[4]

In these Germanic laws a woman's claim to a share of her paternal inheritance was as a rule postponed, particularly when land was involved, as long as there were male descendants. A woman who married had a share of the property of her own family; at her wedding she was given a dowry (most often movable wealth) that might have been very valuable. A woman did not, however, have a legal right to this; it was her guardian, commonly her father or brother, or another close male relative, who decided about her marriage and negotiated the dowry with the suitor's family. After the wedding the woman's property was administered by her husband, her new guardian; it was only as a widow that she could dispose of it herself. Spouses did not inherit from each other, but property could pass from one spouse to the other via their children, so-called reverse inheritance.

All Germanic law codes were influenced by Roman law, some more so than others. This influence is evident in the different rules regulating inheritance from a man. According to Roman law, sons and daughters had equal rights, but of the Germanic law codes only the Visigothic and Burgundian gave a daughter the right to share with her brother, and then with the important limitation that sons preceded daughters in the inheritance of land. In the other Germanic law codes sons always, and grandsons sometimes, precede daughters, and in Thuringian law male offspring to the fifth degree excluded females.

In Roman law if a man died after his father and had no living children, his brothers and sisters had equal inheritance rights, but if there were no brothers, the sisters shared the inheritance with his mother. If there were no brothers or sisters, the mother shared (equally) with the paternal kin of her son, and she had full rights of ownership over her share even if she remarried. The Germanic law codes have different rules in such cases; while the Burgundian rules are the same as the Roman, the Visigothic and Salic laws let the mother precede her son's brothers and sisters, but she only had the usufruct, and that only as long as she did not marry again.

These rules governing inheritance help to elucidate the inscriptions.

The Hillersjö inscription (U 29, see Ch. 2, Pl. 10), which has frequently been discussed, illustrates the acquisition of paternal inheritances successively by a daughter and her mother. The full text is:

Read! Germund got Gerlög, a maiden, as wife. Then they had a son before he (Germund) was drowned and then the son died. Thereafter she got Gudrik as her husband. He . . . this . . . [damaged part; the reference is probably to Gudrik as the owner of Hillersjö]. Then they had children but only one girl survived, her name

[4] Murray (1983), *passim*.

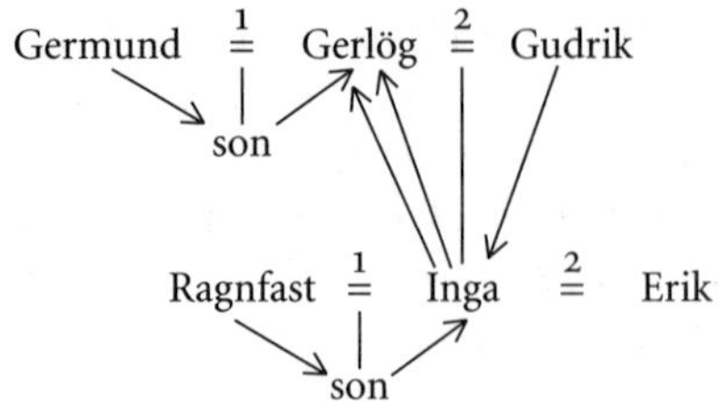

Figure 3.1. Gerlög's inheritances

Note. The arrows show the transmission and reversion of inheritances

was Inga. Ragnfast of Snottsta got her as wife. Thereafter he died and then the son. And the mother (Inga) inherited from her son. Then she had Erik as her husband. Then she died. Then Gerlög inherited from Inga, her daughter. Torbjörn the skald carved the runes.

In giving such detail the Hillersjö inscription is unique, and the inheritance it describes must have been remarkable; it shows how, on several occasions, paternal land passed from one family to another by means of reverse inheritance, and how, in the end, the widow Gerlög inherited from no less than three different families (see Fig. 3.1). Her daughter Inga also commissioned several inscriptions that supplement the information in the inscription at Hillersjö; she commemorated her husband Ragnfast with four inscriptions in Markim parish, some thirty kilometres north of Hillersjö. Three of these inscriptions are at Snottsta: U 330 (for which see Ch. 2, Pl. 9); U 331, which states that Ragnfast had inherited Snottsta farm from his father, Sigfast; and U 329, which mentions that he had two sisters, Gyrid and Estrid. The fourth of Inga's inscriptions (U 332, at Vreta) explains that she inherited from her child.

With her stones Inga asserted her independence as a widow, and proclaimed not only her husband's status as the owner of Snottsta, but also her own status as the mother of Ragnfast's heir, implying that she had the right to inherit from her son after the death of his father. But why are Ragnfast's sisters named? In the light of the rules regulating a mother's right in the different Germanic law codes, it may be suggested that Inga was proclaiming the right of her sisters-in-law to share the inheritance with her. The rule that applied in the Snottsta case was obviously one that gave the mother property rights even if she remarried, which makes it likely that (as, for example, in Burgundian law) she first had to share the inheritance with the paternal kin of her dead husband, that is, his sisters.

This interpretation differs from that given by Elias Wessén and Sven B. F. Jansson, who simply assert that Ragnfast's sisters were left without a share (*SRI*, U 330–2). The fact that they are not only mentioned but also *named*, casts doubt on this interpretation. We do not know what share the sisters had; one of Inga's stones (U 331), says explicitly that 'he (Ragnfast) alone was the owner of this village (*by*) after his father, Sigfast', which clearly implies that he did not share the inheritance of Snottsta with anyone. We can assume that it also passed undivided to his son; but when, in the absence of close male kinsmen, the inheritance passed to women, division was a natural consequence.

3.1. THE IMPORTANCE OF INDIVIDUAL DETAILS IN INTERPRETING RUNIC INSCRIPTIONS

The assumption that every detail in a runic inscription is significant deserves to be emphasized. The hypothesis advanced here provides a natural explanation for many formulations and additional references in the inscriptions. Some examples will serve to illustrate this.

3.1.1. Formulation

Torbjörn and Frölög had the stone raised in memory of Önd, *their* son. (Sö 50, Jogersta)

This very simple and common type of inscription conveys important information: the possessive *their* marks that Önd was the son of both of them. This had legal consequences, it meant that after they were dead both their families were entitled to inherit. This formulation may be compared with the following:

Holmsten and Vigunn, they had the stone raised in memory of *her* son, and Vihjälm in memory of Ingefast. (Sö 37, Vappersta)

Here the possessive *her* marks that Holmsten was not the father of Ingefast and was therefore not entitled to inherit from him. We are not told who Vihjälm was, but perhaps he was Ingefast's brother, mentioned because of his inheritance right.

The way the inscription was formulated was particularly important when family circumstances were as in the following case:

-björn and Underlög, mother and son, had this stone hewn in memory of Ulvrik and . . . [X], father and son, and in memory of . . . [Y], *Underlög's son.* (Sö 280, Strängnäs)

This inscription probably means that -björn was the heir of his father Ulvrik and of his brother (X), while his mother Underlög was the sole heiress of *her* son (Y), who was not the son of Ulvrik and consequently only -björn's half-brother. If Underlög were to survive -björn, she could also inherit from him.

The three examples above may be compared with the following four dealing with step-relations:

Toke raised these stones and made this memorial to his stepfather? (*magR*), Ebbe, a good 'thegn', and to his mother, Tove. They are both lying in this mound. Ebbe gave Toke all his property. (DR 143, Gunderup)

Ospak had the memorial raised to Fader, his stepson (*stiupsunn*). (Sm 113, Tångerda)

(The following two inscriptions are sponsored by the same man:)

Gunnald had this stone raised in memory of Orm, his stepson (*stiupsunn*), a good 'dreng', and he had gone east with Ingvar. God help his soul. (Vs 19, Berga)

Gunnald had this stone raised in memory of Gerfast, his son, a good 'dreng', and he had gone to England. God help his soul. (Vs 18, Berga)

That stepsons and stepfathers normally did not inherit from each other is confirmed by the Gunderup inscription (DR 143), which emphasized that Ebbe had made Toke his heir, presumably in a public assembly, or by some other legal procedure. In both Sm 113 and Vs 19 a stepfather commemorated his stepson. We do not know if there was any agreement between them concerning property. There must have been remarriages and, as is shown by Vs 18 and 19 together, people were careful to mark the difference between their own children and those of their spouses. This is further illustrated by a group of five rune-stones put up in Harg (Skånela parish in Uppland).[5] The inscriptions inform us that Gunnar and Holmdis had a son, Tord, together, and that Holmdis also had a daughter, Juvurfast, from an earlier marriage. In commemorating Juvurfast the couple took great care to mark the difference; she is commemorated on three stones: on one by the couple together; on one by her stepfather; and on one by her mother:

(U 313) Gunnar had this stone hewn in memory of Juvurfast, *his stepdaughter*, and Holmdis in memory of *her daughter*.

(U 312) Gunnar, Farulv's son, had this monument made for Juvurfast's soul, *his stepdaughter, Holmdis' daughter*.

(U 314) Holmdis had this monument made in memory of Juvurfast, *her daughter*.

3.1.2. Additional references

Additional references can help trace where the inheritance came from:

Bläsa had this beautiful stone memorial raised to his son Svarthövde. *Fridälv was his mother.* (Gs 19, Ockelbo church)

We are here probably witnessing a case of reverse inheritance, from son to father, and the reference to Fridälv suggests that the son had inherited from his mother.

[5] U 312–16; on U 315 and 316 the same couple commemorate their son Tord.

Gylla and Ragntrud, they raised the stone in memory of Vred, their father, *husband of Olof, brother of Björn.* God help his soul. (Sö 8, Nybble)

Olof and Björn were probably dead; otherwise they would have been expected to act as sponsors themselves. It is my suggestion that they are mentioned in order to declare (1) that the daughters, Gylla and Ragntrud, had inherited from their mother, Olof, and could now, after their father's death, dispose of this inheritance themselves; and (2) that their inheritance from their father also included what he had inherited from his brother Björn.

Sven raised these stones in memory of Åslak and of Göte, his son, *and Åslak was Sven's brother.* (Sm 122, Uppgränna)

This formulation, somewhat clumsy in modern language, was presumably necessary to make clear whose son Göte was. As the brother of Göte's father Åslak, Sven claimed the property of both.

Gåse's sons raised this stone in memory of Gunnar *(their) brother's son.* (NIyR 84, Vang)

Here we can see how an inheritance goes to the paternal uncles of the deceased; the stone is richly decorated, see Plate 12.

3.1.3. One or more sponsors

Several questions are raised by the following, very common, types of inscription:

(a) Tore raised this stone in memory of Gunnar, *his father.* (DR 122, Glenstrup)

(b) Torbjörn and Ingefast had this stone raised in memory of Sigtorn, *their father.* He died on a journey/voyage . . . (Vs 27, Gällsta)

In western Scandinavia individual sponsors (type (a)) are more frequent than in the east, where stones with two or more sponsors (type (b)) are in the majority. When a single son commemorated his father, he may of course have been the only son, but this explanation can hardly cover all cases. First, it is not very likely that in Scandinavia as a whole almost 40% of the sons commemorating fathers had no brothers.[6] Secondly, the regional differences suggest that we are probably dealing with different principles regulating the rights to property and inheritance. In the East (Uppland, Södermanland, and Öland) only *c.*28% of the sons commemorating their fathers are single sponsors, while in the South/West the proportion of sons as single sponsors is as high as *c.*70% . All the single sponsors in these parts of Scandinavia cannot have lacked brothers, especially as here, above all in Norway and Denmark, the proportion of

[6] See App. 4(d).

PLATE 12. NIyR 84, Vang. Note the 'great beast': cf. Ch. 4.8 (for the inscription, see text above).

'brother-stones' is higher than anywhere else;[7] here brothers acted as single sponsors in nearly nine cases out of ten (85%), which strongly suggests that undivided inheritances were the rule in these parts, while divided inheritances (with individual shares) were more common in the East (where less than 40% of the brothers are single sponsors).

The fact that Torbjörn and Ingefast (Vs 27) commemorated their father together could mean that they shared the inheritance, without necessarily splitting it up and forming separate households. The information that 'he died on a journey/voyage' presumably served the purpose of publicly announcing his death; not until then was it possible to claim his property. During the Viking Age, when many men went abroad, there must have been a great need for such public declarations of death. For the people who remained at home and were for a long time ignorant of the fate of their relatives, it was necessary to have some form of legal procedure, probably in a public assembly, before property could be transferred and a rune-stone raised.[8]

The close connection between the raising of a stone and the transfer of property by inheritance is illustrated by the Norwegian Skadberg stone:

Members of the ale-guild raised this stone in memory of Skarde when they drank his 'inheritance ale'. (NIyR 247)

3.1.4. The order in which sponsors are mentioned

When two or more sponsors acted together, the order in which they are named is significant: those who are most important in the context are mentioned first, men before women, older children probably before younger. How is the order in the following example to be explained?

Östen had this stone raised in memory of Torgärd, his sister, Hallbjörn in memory of his mother. (Sö 302, Bergaholm)

Since it is not likely that the brother inherited before the son, the explanation seems to be that Hallbjörn was under age and therefore under his uncle's tutelage. With the inscription Östen also signalled that he was closest to the inheritance, if something should happen to Hallbjörn.

3.1.5. Two or more inscriptions interpreted together

The following examples from Ardre in Gotland illustrate how the significance of the additional details given in some inscriptions is revealed by the content of other inscriptions:

Sibba raised the stone in memory of Rodiaud, his wife, *daughter of Rodgair in Anga.* She died young, leaving infant children. (G 111)

Sibba had this stone made in memory of *his and Rodiaud's daughter.* (G 112)

[7] See Ch. 4.4.1. [8] See further Ch. 5.7.

In discussing G 111 the editors quote, with approval, a comment to the effect that, touching in its simplicity, it is the oldest example in Swedish literature of 'a widower's worries about his motherless children'. With all due respect for Sibba's sad situation, I suggest that the reference to the small children was not so much emotionally motivated as it was important in the context of inheritance; Sibba thus emphasized that he and Rodiaud, who had apparently inherited from her father ('daughter of Rodgair in Anga'), had had children to whom her property would pass. In Gotland as in Uppland and, indeed, the rest of Europe, in childless marriages property normally went back to the family it originally came from (cf. the reversion of the inheritance after the death of Inga of Snottsta, where her second husband Erik was excluded (Fig. 3.1 above)). Sibba mentioned his children to demonstrate his claim to their maternal inheritance. We do not know how many children the couple had, but when Sibba raised the stone in memory of his and Rodiaud's daughter (G 112), the property had presumably passed to him via the daughter mentioned, but not named, in G 112. Taken together these inscriptions show how a paternal inheritance (from Rodgair's family) became a maternal inheritance (via Rodiaud) that finally reverted (via Rodiaud and Sibba's daughter) to Sibba and thereby passed into the hands of a different family.

The following examples, also from Gotland (see Ch. 2, Pl. 6), together constitute what can be called the Sjonhem monument. It consists of three stones raised by two parents in memory of each of their three sons:

Rodvisl and Rodälv, they had these stones raised in memory of (their) three sons. This one in memory of Rodfos. Valachians (?) betrayed him on a voyage. May God fail those who failed him. (G 134)

This one in memory of Ai——. He died in Vindau. Two sisters . . . [von Friesen supplies 'outlived'] three brothers. Rodald (?) and Rodgut, Rodar and Torstain, they are father's brothers. (G 135)

This one in memory of Hailfos (?) He died at home and had a daughter. She is called Hailvi. Valdinga-Udd (?) made the stones, and . . . Dan and Botbjärn carved. (G 136)

The inscription G 135 shows that the dead brothers had two sisters, whom it was obviously considered important to mention, and that there were, moreover, four uncles, who are named immediately after the sisters. This makes von Friesen's guess about the missing words highly probable; since the father Rodvisl no longer had any male offspring, the two daughters and his brothers were closest in line to inherit after him—but not on their own. The inscription G 136 tells us that one of the deceased sons, Hailfos, had a daughter, mentioned by name because of her importance in the context: as Hailfos' child she presumably took over his right to inherit from Rodvisl, but according to the rules in the later law of Gotland she is likely to have had to share the inheritance from her grandfather with his daughters and four brothers. From her own father, Hailfos, she should have been able to inherit without competition.

3.2. THE SPONSORSHIP PATTERN AS REFLECTING PROPERTY RIGHTS

If the hypothesis that most runic inscriptions reflect rights to property by inheritance is accepted, a whole body of new material becomes available for the study of property rights in tenth- and eleventh-century Scandinavia. Above I have tried to show that this hypothesis provides an explanation for the general emphasis on the nature of relationships, the specific formulations, many of the additional details given in the inscriptions, and the order in which sponsors are named in individual inscriptions. In what follows I will consider what patterns emerge if the whole body of material in the Relationship Subgroup is interpreted as reflecting rights to property by inheritance.

The sponsorship pattern as a whole shows important regional differences that can be interpreted as reflecting a preference for undivided inheritances in some areas, but for divisions with individual shares in others. It is therefore worth considering whether these patterns can contribute more to our understanding of inheritance and ownership. It is, for example, possible that the patterns can provide clues to the order of precedence in claiming inheritance. To test this possibility reference may be made to the analysis of all inscriptions in terms of relationships (Table 2.4 above). The following list repeats the eight most common types of relationship found in the inscriptions (see Ch. 2.9). For a detailed survey of frequencies in each of the main regions, see Appendix 4(b–d).

Percentage frequency of the eight most common relationships out of a total of 2,280

son~father	31.5
brother~brother	14.8
father~son	10.4
wife~husband	8.0
man~man	7.6
mother~son	7.2
daughter~father	3.8
kinsman~kinsman	3.4

The list above does not, of course, reflect the Scandinavian inheritance pattern directly; if it did, Scandinavia would be unique in Western Europe in setting aside inheritance by daughters not only in favour of sons but also in favour of the brothers and parents of the deceased! Similarly, the high proportion of mothers as sponsors cannot be interpreted as reflecting a rule that gave mothers the right to inherit before daughters; nowhere would a female ascendant be preferred to a descendant. What the list does reflect, is the frequency with which different members of a family—e.g. sons, daughters, and brothers—acted as independent property owners. The assumption that their relationship to the deceased can reveal how they had acquired at least part of their property, is a useful starting-point for discussion. If any conclusions can be drawn directly from the above list, they are that, among the stone-raisers, (1) daughters were generally passed over in favour of sons in cases of paternal inheritance, (2) the right of a brother was very strong, generally stronger than that of the mother, and (3) reverse inheritance was a common phenomenon.

With some regional exceptions, reverse inheritance is very frequent among the stone-raisers, amounting to *c.*18.5% of all relationships. Fathers and mothers commemorating sons constitute 17.6% of the relationships, while parents commemorating daughters account for not even 1%.[9] There are, however, differences inside Scandinavia: in Denmark the proportion of reverse inheritance is very low (less than 7%), while in Småland it is relatively high (*c.*25%). How should these regional differences be explained? Surely it cannot have been that much more dangerous to be a young man in some parts of Scandinavia than in others; rather, it seems to be due to different preferences in inheritance customs.

In reality reverse inheritances might well have been even more common than is explicitly indicated; 8% of all relationships are widows commemorating husbands, sometimes on their own, sometimes together with their sons or (more seldom) other male relatives.[10] If these widows were subsequently to survive their sons/relatives, they would be entitled to reverse inheritance; indeed, the main reason for a woman to sponsor a rune-stone together with sons/relatives might have been to mark the right to a future inheritance. On the other hand, reverse inheritance might not always have been the expectation, even though it appears to have been so; in some cases the father (and perhaps the mother) may have taken responsibility for the raising of a memorial on behalf of heirs who were under age, as is suggested by Sö 302 and G 136 quoted above.[11]

[9] Only in Uppland does the proportion of *mothers* commemorating sons equal the proportion of *fathers* (both *c.*11%). In Denmark the proportion of mothers is more than half of the proportion of fathers, while in other areas their proportion is significantly lower.

[10] In Uppland and Södermanland it is slightly less common for widows to act on their own, while it is the other way around in the rest of Scandinavia; in Norway and Bornholm there are no cases of widows acting together with other male relatives.

[11] Cf. also U 203: 'Alle had this stone raised in memory of Ulv, his son, father of Frögärd in Väsby . . .'

In any case, the figures as they stand indicate that many parents in Viking-Age Scandinavia survived their off-spring.

II. The Sponsors as Holders of Joint or Inherited Property

A disadvantage with *relationships* as a basis for analysis is that it does not show how often several persons, men or women—or men *and* women—acted together. In the rest of this chapter the analyses will therefore be based on the *inscriptions* (of the Relationship Subgroup specifying both sponsors and deceased). Since many inscriptions contain different types of inheritance, the number of inheritances is more than the number of inscriptions. For percentages for each main region, see Appendix 4.

3.3. JOINT OWNERSHIP

Before discussing inheritance customs, those cases will be considered where agreements of joint ownership are likely to have been made, agreements that needed to be fulfilled after the death of one partner. This subcategory (see Ch. 2.5) includes stones raised in memory of (*a*) spouses and (*b*) trading partners or comrades-in-arms.

3.3.1. Spouses

As has been pointed out above, spouses do not inherit from each other under any of the early Germanic law codes, and the examples of spouses commemorating each other should therefore be interpreted as implying that the surviving spouse claimed, among other things, his or her share of what had been jointly owned. Such joint ownership in marriage (Dan. *fællig*; Norw. *félag*) is supposed to have been introduced into Scandinavia during the Viking Age and was regulated in all the later provincial law codes. By commemorating her husband a widow might have declared her right to dispose of the property she had brought with her to the marriage (dowry and perhaps inherited wealth) as well as the property she had acquired through the marriage itself (dower and share of the joint property).

Husbands commemorate their wives in only *c.*2% of the inscriptions, in contrast to the *c.*11% in which wives commemorate their husbands.[12] The proportion of wives as sponsors may be so much higher because they survived their husbands more often than vice versa; even if the rate of

[12] Percentages of the Relationship Subgroup. Husbands commemorating wives: 35 cases out of 1,776 inscriptions=1.97%; wives commemorating husbands: 190 cases out of 1,776 inscriptions=10.7%.

mortality was very high among women of childbearing age, archaeological investigations indicate that during the Viking Age women—having survived their fertile period—lived longer than men. There was, moreover, all the more reason for a widow to make her claims known by raising a rune-stone; nobody would, presumably, have questioned the economic independence of a man, while a woman's acquisition of independent status—an exception to the rule—needed to be clearly marked.

Another consideration in the inscriptions commemorating a spouse might have been the possibility of a future claim to reverse inheritance. So, for example, at Snottsta Inga marked her status as Ragnfast's widow in no less than four inscriptions, and the Hillersjö inscription shows that in the end she inherited his property from the son they had in common. In certain inscriptions the possibility of a future claim (via the children) probably explains the care the surviving spouse took to specify who was the deceased spouse's closest relative, that is, the person, whose heir he or she had been. This might very well have been the case in the following examples of wives commemorated by their husbands:

Tore Hordsson raised this stone in memory of Åsgerd, his wife, *daughter of Gunnar, (who was) the brother of Helge at Klepp.* (NIyR 225, Klepp)

Ketil raised this stone in memory of Jorun, his wife, *daughter of Utyrme.* (NIyR 251, Stavanger)

Frösten made these monuments in memory of Tora, his wife, *she was the daughter of* . . . , the best of people . . . (Vg 67, from Saleby, now at Dagsnäs)

Sibba raised this stone in memory of Rodiaud, his wife, *daughter of Rodgair in Anga* . . . (G 111, Ardre)

Vibjörn had this stone hewn in memory of *Gunne's daughter*, his wife. (U 280, Smedby)

The good 'bonde' (landowner) Holmgöt had (this stone) raised in memory of Odendis, his wife. To Hassmyra a better housewife, administering the farm, will never come. Rödballe cut these runes. *Odendis was a good sister of Sigmund.* (Vs 24, Hassmyra; see Pl. 13)

In the following example the widower/father had probably acquired property through reverse inheritance, as in the case of Sibba in Gotland (G 111–12) discussed above:

Gunnar laid this stone in memory of Gudlög, his good wife, and of Asa, his good daughter. God help both their souls. (Ög 239, Skänninge)

Some of the widows who commissioned inscriptions may also have wanted to demonstrate their former status as wives of famous and important men in the hope of retaining that status after the husband's death. Where the husbands had been 'thegns', i.e. landowners of substance who were probably royal agents (see below, Ch. 5.2), the widows may even have claimed the privilege of taking over at least some of their husbands' rights and duties

PLATE 13. Vs 24, Hassmyra. A husband commemorates his wife (for the inscription, see text above).

themselves. (See, for example, DR 98, 99, 277, and 293; Vg 115, 150, and 152. A husband is mentioned as a 'dreng' (young warrior, member of a retinue) in Vg 154. These titles will be discussed more fully in Chapter 5.4.)

Some regional differences in the distribution of 'spouse-stones' should be noted; in all there are only thirty-six inscriptions where a husband commemorates his wife. Outside the main rune-stone areas there are only 4;[13] in the East zone (U, Sö, Öl) there are 13,[14] while in the South/West there are 19.[15]

Examples of wives commemorating their husbands occur everywhere, but Småland has only two cases, in one of which (Sm 64) the woman commemorated her sons at the same time, and was thus also acting in her capacity as a mother.[16]

Eastern Sweden (the East) is divided between on the one hand Uppland and Öland, with *c.*14.5% commemorations by widows, and on the other hand Södermanland, with only *c.*7.5%. Southern and western Scandinavia (the South/West)—with the exception of Småland—has an average proportion of *c.*8.5%, somewhat higher than that of Södermanland but significantly lower than those of Uppland and Öland. Another difference is that in the East it was most common for widows to act together with other male relatives (most often sons), while in the South/West widows normally acted on their own.[17]

If, however, we compare only the cases where widows acted on their own the proportion is almost the same everywhere—on average *c.*5.5%: higher in Östergötland, Västergötland, and Uppland, lower in Södermanland.[18] A cautious conclusion is that the rules regulating when a widow took responsibility were roughly the same in the whole of Scandinavia—with some exceptions, above all Småland.

3.3.2. Trading partners and comrades-in-arms

Stones of this kind are infrequent in Sweden; there are only nine: three each in Uppland (all in Sigtuna) and Västergötland,[19] two in Östergötland,[20] and one in Södermanland.[21] In Norway there are no cases, but in

[13] Two are in Västmanland (Vs 17 and 24), one in Gotland (G 111), and one in Bornholm (DR 378).

[14] Out of a total of 1,100: 9 in Uppland; 1 in Södermanland; 3 in Öland.

[15] Out of a total of 594: 4 in Östergötland; 5 in Västergötland; 1 in Småland; 6 in Denmark; 2 in Norway; 1 in Bornholm. Four of the Danish examples have been regarded as erected by someone other than the husband; see further, Excursus (pp. 158–66).

[16] The same is true of Gotland, also with two cases, in one of which the woman is also acting as a mother (G 138).

[17] Widows acting together with sons: in the East, 46.5%; in South/West Scandinavia, 20%.

[18] Ög 7.8%; Vg 6.8%; U 6.3%; Sö 3.3%, (Öl 2.7%, Bo 3.8%, and Sm 1.2%); Dk 6%; No 5%.

[19] U 379, 385, and 391; Vg 112, 122, and 182.

[20] Ög 64 and Ög N19.

[21] Sö 292.

Denmark there are sixteen, of which some were raised by trading partners, some apparently by comrades-in-arms.[22] As regards the former, the death of one partner might have led to the surviving partner either taking over the dead man's share of what they had owned jointly (for example a ship or a stock of goods), or simply claiming his own share from the heirs. As far as the comrades-in-arms are concerned, it is conceivable that agreements were sometimes made under which the survivor was entitled to his comrade's equipment; in any case we can certainly expect mutual promises to ensure that an appropriate memorial would be erected when the time came.

3.4. INHERITANCE CUSTOMS

Under this heading I shall refer to the four classes in the Relationship Subgroup, as listed in Appendix 4(b–d), namely:

1. paternal inheritances (772 inscriptions)
2. fraternal inheritances (355)
3. reverse inheritances (339)
4. maternal inheritances (55)

3.4.1. Sons and daughters

In *c.*38% of the inscriptions in the total Relationship Subgroup sons commemorated their fathers on their own or together with their mothers or other female relatives apart from their sisters; in 2.7% daughters did so, mostly on their own; and in 2.7% sons and daughters acted together. This means that, of the 772 paternal inheritances (class 1) 87.6% went to sons only, 6.2% to daughters only, and 6.2% to sons and daughters jointly. The very large difference in the percentages of inheritances going to sons and those going to daughters appears to be due to the 'postponement' of female beneficiaries; that is to say (according to the gradual principle, see Ch. 4.3), women had a right to inherit but they always had to wait until no male relative of the same degree remained alive: i.e. son inherited before daughter; brother before sister, etc. But even if the postponement of daughters seems to have been common in Scandinavia, there are indications that sometimes they were not postponed: in the East, particularly in Uppland, there are several cases of sons and daughters commemorating their fathers jointly[23] and even a few cases of brothers and sisters commemorating their brothers (see Ch. 4.2).

This is one of the many differences that are revealed by comparing the

[22] DR 1 (Sønderjylland); 62, 66, 68, 125, and 127 (Nørrejylland); 262, 270, 279, 316, 318, 321, 329, 330, 335, and 339 (Skåne).

[23] The 38 cases out of 398 paternal inheritances in Uppland = 9.5%.

sponsorship patterns in different regions. Another difference is that it is mainly in the East, again particularly Uppland, that the widows and sons of the deceased sponsor rune-stones jointly. This could be evidence of joint ownership in the family, a principle that in the later laws goes together with the inclusion of daughters in paternal inheritances. In the East almost half the widows acted together with their son(s) when commemorating husbands; in the South/West only a fifth did so.[24]

3.4.2. Daughters and sisters

Postponed or included, the individual inscriptions show that in some areas daughters and sisters inherited from their fathers and brothers much more often than is suggested by the sponsorship pattern, according to which daughters took or shared in only *c.*12.5% of all paternal inheritances, sisters in only *c.*7.5% of all fraternal ones.[25] Again these average figures are misleading, since women do not figure as sponsors commemorating their fathers or brothers in Denmark, Norway, Bornholm, or Öland, while this happened quite often in Uppland, Södermanland, and Östergötland.[26]

These percentages, however, do not show how common it was for daughters and sisters to inherit; many heiresses are hidden behind their husbands, sons, or other close male relatives, who raised the stones on their behalf. For example:

Gulle raised this stone in memory of *his wife's brothers* Äsbjörn and Jule, very good 'drengs'. But they died in the east. (Vg 184, Smula)

Öbjörn and Torgils raised this stone in memory of Åslek, his **siuhr** (father-in-law or brother-in-law?).[27] (U 774, Hjulsta)

Ögöt raised this stone in memory of Sigfus, his *magʀ* (father-in-law or brother-in-law?). (Ög 219, Lundby)

In these cases it is likely that the husbands acted on behalf of their wives; in Vg 184 Gulle's wife may have inherited after her brothers, and in Ög 219 the sponsor is related with the deceased Sigfus via marriage and may be claiming his daughter's or sister's inheritance.

In the following cases the mothers were probably heiresses who are 'hidden' by their sons, who acted as sponsors:

Kjell raised this memorial to Lek (?), *his mother's brother.* (Sm 121, Rogberga churchyard)

Redulv and Gere raised this stone in memory of Ofag, *their mother's brother*, a good 'bonde' [see Ch. 5.5.1]. (Ög 207, Viby)

[24] In Uppland, Södermanland, and Öland widows and sons act together in 65 out of 140 'widow-inscriptions' (46.5%), while in the rest of Scandinavia this happens in only 10 out of 50 such cases (20%). In Norway and Bornholm it never occurs.

[25] The percentages are based on classes 1 (772 paternal inheritances) and 2 (355 fraternal inheritances).

[26] See App. 4.

[27] For **siuhr**, see *SRI*, U 774.

Even if the sisters were dead at the time of the commemorations and thus did not inherit themselves, it was through them that the inheritances were traced.

The proportion of men commemorating their kinsmen is low in the East (in Uppland and Södermanland *c.*3–4%), but high in Norway, Västergötland, and Östergötland (7.5–8.5%). Since the latter three regions have a much lower proportion of female sponsors, it can be deduced that, as sponsors, further removed male kin were preferred to more closely related women. In some cases kinsmen may have acted on behalf of an heiress, in others they might themselves have been the preferred—or only—heirs. It is of course impossible to know the background of all cases.

Another way of tracing daughters and sisters who inherited from their fathers or brothers is through the additional details given in many inscriptions, for example:

[father commemorating his son, who was the] father of Frögärd in Väsby. (U 203, Angarn church)

[man commemorating a man, who was] Ingrid's father. He was Vide's heir. (U 60, Ängby)

[three men commemorating a man, who was] Åsgerd's father. (U 1177, Hässelby)

[parents commemorating their son] he . . . had a daughter. She is called Hailvi (G 136, Sjonhem)

In U 203 the deceased's father may have taken care of his granddaughter's paternal inheritance; in U 60 and U 1177 relatives may have tried to ensure that the inheritance left by the deceased men would go to their daughters Ingrid and Åsgerd. G 136 has been commented on above (section 3.1.5).

3.4.3. Mothers

There are only fifty-five cases of maternal inheritance in the Relationship Subgroup (*c.*3% compared with 43.5% cases of paternal inheritance), but it is clear that many more mothers left property that they had inherited from, for example, fathers, brothers, or children of an earlier marriage. Even though women could inherit property, here, as elsewhere in Europe, it was probably administered by their husbands. In some cases a son commemorating his father also refers to his father's wife, who was almost certainly already dead.[28] In this way they could show that there was a maternal as well as a paternal inheritance. For example:

[two sons commemorating their father, who was] Aldriv's husband (Sö 31, Nora)

[two sons commemorating their father, who was] Vigerd's husband, Torgerd's good son (U 79, Skesta)

[28] Nä 28, 32; Sö 31, 306; U 35, 38, 43, 79, 88 (?), 121 (?), 819, 829, 873; Ög 194.

Since many inscriptions indicate that women must have inherited much more often than is shown by the sponsorship pattern, it is clear that, among the sponsors, we meet only economically independent men and women. The regional differences suggest that, while in the South/West women rarely achieved this status, in the East, particularly Uppland, women seem to have had a better chance of doing so. There, as well as in Öland and Södermanland, married women who inherited were not always represented by their husbands, but could appear together with them in the inscriptions. Moreover, it seems that in these provinces daughters were not always postponed by sons but could inherit together with them.

In Scandinavia as a whole, however, it is clear that women were normally kept under male guardianship as long as possible, and that almost the only way for them to achieve independence was to be left as widows. It is likely that unmarried women could only rarely obtain a similar status—that is, only when they were of age and had no known living male relatives.

Thus, even if postponement of daughters and sisters was the general rule—in Uppland as elsewhere—many women became sole heiresses as a result of their superior longevity and the high mortality of children. A good example is provided by Gerlög from Hillersjö and her daughter Inga discussed above (pp. 49–51 and Fig. 3.1). Gerlög may have been unusual in inheriting from three different families, but there were many other widows who inherited from their children, and via them from their husband's family; in the Relationship Subgroup there are 339 cases of reverse inheritance (class 3), in almost half of which women were the sole or joint heiresses, more often as widows than as wives sharing with their husbands.[29] In addition there were potential heiresses, i.e. the many widows who commemorated their husbands and were likely to survive their children; women commemorated their husbands in *c.*11% of the inscriptions of the subgroup, half of them on their own.

While the proportion of 'widows' is much the same everywhere, the proportion of 'mothers' varies; it is high in the East, lower in Götaland and Denmark, and, with one exception (a mother commemorating her daughter), non-existent in Norway.

3.5. UNSPECIFIED RELATIONSHIPS

In 199 of the 1,776 inscriptions of the Relationship Subgroup (=*c.*11%) we know only the names (and sex) of the people involved—as sponsors or deceased—not their relationship.[30] This subcategory (see Appendix 5), especially large in Norway, Denmark, and Västergötland, needs to be

[29] Reverse inheritance to women in 168 out of 343 cases=49%: to widows in 101 cases and to wives together with husbands in 67 cases. See App. 4(c).

[30] Subcategory 6 in the list given at Ch. 2.5 above.

discussed at some length. In the first place, it should be emphasized that this is a very heterogeneous category and can be divided into the three following groups:

I. 47 incomplete inscriptions (lost, damaged, fragmentary, partly illegible or uninterpreted) that are likely to have included specified relationships.[31]

II. 29 complete inscriptions specifying some relationships but not all. Since some of the relationships are carefully stated, it can be assumed that it was taken for granted who the unspecified people were.[32]

III. 123 complete inscriptions that do not specify any relationships.[33]

Strictly, it is only the third of these groups that should be treated as inscriptions in which relationships are not specified. Even so, this still means that a significant proportion (7%) of the Relationship Subgroup appears to be inconsistent with my hypothesis that rune-stones reflect claims to property by inheritance. Considering the emphasis normally put on kinship, the omission of any reference to relationship may indicate that no kinship could be claimed. It is impossible to say what claims—if any—the sponsors of these stones had, but at least thirty-five of them show in various ways that the identity of the individuals in question was an important issue by describing them (*a*) as the son/daughter, father, or other relative of a named person;[34] or (*b*) as having lived in or owned a named place;[35] or (*c*) as having gone to or died in a named place.[36] These additional references indicate that the property of the deceased was at stake. The commemorations of men 'who went to or died in such-and-such a place' imply that the time had come to deal with the property of the deceased.[37]

Unspecified or not, the content of some of these inscriptions suggests that the relationships were kin-based and thus reflect claims to inherit: for example, where *a woman commemorates a man* (considering the frequency of all known relationships it is not very likely that a woman would act as a sponsor in any capacity other than that of wife, mother, or—though less

[31] e.g. U 115: '. . . Finnvid, Ragnfrid's son, had . . . who had Ingegärd as wife and Kvick's and Finnvid's(?) . . .'

[32] e.g. Ög 23: 'Torlak had this stone raised in memory of Röde, his father, and in memory of Gunne.'

[33] e.g. DR 109: 'Thore raised this stone in memory of Fastulv Myge.'

[34] e.g. DR 81: 'Sægerd, Finulv's daughter, raised this stone in memory of Odinkar, Osbjørn's(?) son (. . .).'

[35] Ög 94: 'Asgöta and Gudmund raised this monument in memory of Oddlög(?), who lived in Haddestad. He was a good "bonde", died in Greece(?).'

[36] e.g. Sö 165: 'Gudrun raised the stone in memory of Hidin, he was nephew of Sven. He was in Greece and shared gold . . .'

[37] For examples, see nn. 35 and 36 above.

likely—daughter or sister).[38] Claims to inherit may also be reflected where *similar names* indicate that the persons involved belonged to the same family.

It was common for the same type of names to run in a particular family; so, for example, in U 1172 (Holm), '*Björn* and his brothers raised this stone in memory of *Sigbjörn* in Holm', we can be fairly certain that the sponsors were Sigbjörn's sons. Another case is Sö 254 (Vansta):[39] 'Sven and *Sten* raised this stone in memory of *Toste*, their father, who died in Ingvar's *lið* [retinue], and in memory of *Torsten* and of *Östen*, Alvhild's son.' Presumably Torsten and Östen were also Toste's sons (Toste being an abbreviated form of Torsten), Sven's and Sten's brothers. The fact that Östen is referred to as 'Alvhild's son' must indicate that he had a different mother from his brothers.[40]

On the grounds adduced in the above two paragraphs it can be argued that at least 56 (18 in Uppland) of the 123 'strictly unspecified' relationships (group III) nevertheless reflect claims to property and inheritance.[41] The other 67 in group III are proportionately most common in Norway, Denmark, Västergötland, and Småland.

Finally it is significant that inscriptions without specified relationships are more common in western Scandinavia and thus belong to the earlier stages of the 'rune-stone period'.[42] In Uppland, where most stones (71%) were erected during the second half of the eleventh century, almost half of the unspecified relationships are in inscriptions made before 1050. It is plausible that in areas where—and at a time when—this way of commemorating the dead was still fairly exclusive and confined to a narrow—and well-known—élite, there was no need to specify relationships, but when the fashion spread to other areas and—as in the East—to broader sections of society, a careful specification of all persons involved became necessary.

3.6. CONCLUSION

While a full analysis of every inscription is necessary for a better knowledge of Scandinavian inheritance customs, the sponsorship pattern shows who controlled property, whether inherited or acquired in some other way.

[38] e.g. Vg 9: 'Gunnur erected this stone in memory of Olov *nacke* [the neck], Torkel's father.' Gunnur was probably Olov's widow, securing their son Torkel's paternal inheritance.

[39] Other examples are DR 354; NIyR 259; G 207; Gs 14; Hs 2; Sö 124; U 319, 659, 757, 775, 827, 951, 1053, 1177; Vg 32, 66, 107, 151; Öl 92.

[40] Cf. Brate and Wessén's discussion of Sö 254 in *SRI*, p. 222.

[41] See App. 5, group III(a+b).

[42] In Norway almost every fourth inscription is without a specified relationship (i.e. 9 out of 40, or 22.5%); in Denmark, Västergötland, and Småland the average figure is 11.5%, while in Östergötland it is less than 7%. In the East (Uppland, Södermanland, and Öland) the average proportion lies between 5% and 5.5%.

Both the sponsors, whether they were heirs themselves or guardians of heirs, and the people commemorated were all economically independent property owners.

We have seen that 92.3% of all stones were erected exclusively in memory of men, 4.2% exclusively in memory of women, and almost 3.5% in memory of both men and women. Even if claims to property underlay the inscriptions on stones commemorating only those individuals who had full disposal rights, the proportion of women commemorated seems extremely low. Since a minimum figure for women enjoying control of property is 11.7% (i.e. the proportion of women acting as sponsors on their own), the question arises as to why more women were not commemorated. One answer is, of course, that some women gained independent status because they had no surviving male relatives and consequently nobody to commemorate them and claim their property, but this can hardly be the whole explanation. Where there *were* male relatives alive, they may have preferred to trace their title back to the man from whom the woman had inherited. There may also have been other reasons for the difference in the proportions of commemorated and sponsoring women: perhaps it reflects a change in women's rights of disposal. Such a change would first be evidenced among the sponsors, and only later among the deceased.

Commemorations of women, either on their own or together with men, account for 7.7% of all inscriptions in the Relationship Subgroup. There are, however, regional differences; the proportion is lower in Uppland and Södermanland (6.8% and 5.1% respectively), higher in Denmark and the rest of Sweden (9.4% in both cases). It is interesting that in both Uppland and Södermanland commemorations of women tend to be later than commemorations of men; in Uppland, where 71% of all datable rune-stones were erected after 1050, 82.1% of those commemorating women belong to this period. In Södermanland the tendency is even clearer, here only 22.5% of all datable stones were erected after 1050, while as many as 38.5% of those commemorating women belong to this period. The fact that the rune-stones in the South/West are much earlier than those in the East shows, however, that in general the commemoration of women was not a late development.

It is possible that a woman had to be unusually rich or of extraordinary social status in order to be commemorated in her own right. Manifestly, these prestigious memorials normally belonged to the world of men, where masculine qualities and warlike achievements were highly valued, and where the honour and reputation of the deceased was an important element in the inheritance he passed on. Men of only moderate means may well have been commemorated because of their reputation. Stones commemorating women members of ruling families (most of them in Denmark) constitute a special group in which political considerations probably played an important role.

Women sponsored inscriptions on their own in almost 12% of all cases, and it is perhaps significant that this average figure correlates with the proportion in the main regions, where the average lies between 11% (Södermanland) and 13% (Denmark), and is somewhat higher only in Östergötland (15.5%).[43]

This similarity contrasts with the proportion of inscriptions sponsored by women and men together. These consitute over 15% of the Relationship Subgroup, but this figure is most misleading since there are great differences between the regions: in Norway and Bornholm there are no occurrences at all, in Denmark, Västergötland, and Östergötland they are fairly rare (3.5–5%), in Småland and Öland they are somewhat more common (8.5–11%), while Södermanland has more than the average for Scandinavia as a whole (16%) and in Uppland the proportion is over 24%! How are these differences to be explained?

Since most of the runic inscriptions in the South/West zone are earlier than those in the East, these regional differences may in part be due to changes that occurred during the rune-stone period. The most revolutionary novelty was the introduction of Christianity, and it is worth considering whether men and women raised stones (or were commemorated) together because of Christian influence. This influence deeply affected economic conditions; to make it possible for each individual, female as well as male, to give to the Church 'for the sake of their souls', the Church encouraged individual shares and rights of disposal for women as well as men (see Ch. 6). It was also under Christian influence that the institution of joint ownership (Dan. *fællig*) developed, enabling both spouses to own a share in the family property. Since this idea is likely to have taken some time to be accepted, this could explain why mixed sponsorship, with husbands acting together with wives, or widows together with their children, occurs more frequently in areas where most of the rune-stones are relatively late.

Another striking difference is between multiple and single sponsorship. This, as well as the other differences presented here, will be discussed in the following chapter.

[43] In Småland, Öland, and Bornholm it is significantly lower, only 4–5%.

4

INHERITANCE: CUSTOMS AND LAWS

A widely held interpretation of early Scandinavian society has been that it was based on clans (Sw. *ätter*), in the sense of descent groups that were responsible for many of the functions that were later taken over by kings and the Church.[1] Belief in their existence largely depends on interpreting the medieval laws as reflecting such a clan society in the last stages of dissolution, and some provisions of these laws have been taken to be relics of a time when the clan was supposed to have owned land collectively. For such a society to function each clan would have to be a well-defined, distinct group, which in turn requires that descent was traced from fathers only—or from mothers only. It has been supposed that Scandinavian clans were patrilineal and that upon marriage a woman left her own clan to join that of her husband. As a consequence, women are supposed to have had no right to inherit land; otherwise clans could not have had permanent rights over their own land.

There is, however, no evidence for such well-defined descent groups in Scandinavia—or in other Germanic societies.[2] The laws that have been taken to show the transformation of such a society do nothing of the sort. On the contrary, they show that for purposes of inheritance kinship was traced through both sexes, and they all recognize that women have a right, even if postponed or limited, to inherit. What is more, the laws provide for reverse inheritance, when a surviving parent inherits from a child. In that way a widow could acquire her husband's inherited land, which after her death would pass to her heirs, and thus to a different family.[3]

If a patrilinear clan society ever existed in Scandinavia, which is extremely doubtful, it had disappeared long before the laws began to be compiled in the twelfth century. The runic inscriptions of the tenth and eleventh centuries confirm this, for they show that the kinship system was bilateral; many inscriptions refer to relatives by marriage (e.g. brothers-in-law and mothers-in-law), and often record the name of the wife, mother,

[1] This view is repeated in modern textbooks and has been widely disseminated by Anderson (1978: 107–8, 176–7).

[2] See Murray (1983).

[3] Winberg (1985), 24–7; B. Sawyer (1991*a*) and (1991*b*).

or daughter of a dead man. The fundamentally bilateral character of kinship is further underlined by the terminology used in inscriptions for certain relatives; an uncle, for example, is described either as a 'mother-brother' or a 'father-brother'.

The inscriptions that explicitly deal with property and inheritance clearly show that property rights were individual and that women were entitled to inherit. If, as suggested here, the sponsorship pattern reflects inheritance customs, it shows that in Scandinavia as a whole women (on their own or together with men) were beneficiaries of at least 50% of all reverse, 12.5% of all paternal, and 7.5% of all fraternal inheritances. As we have seen, customs were apparently not the same in all regions; in Denmark, Norway, Småland, and Gotland women generally seem to be postponed by men in the order of inheritance, while in Uppland and Södermanland there are indications that they could inherit together with men.

Further, the inscriptions show that in eleventh-century Scandinavia a woman did not sever all links with her own family when she married. In the new family, created with her husband, they both, together with their children, had property rights or expectations. It cannot be proved that wives owned a share of the household property at that time, as they did later, but it does seem likely that they often did. That many inscriptions were sponsored by widows, either on their own or together with other members of the family, suggests that as wives they had a leading role in their families, most probably as co-owners. With some regional exceptions it seems to have been the widow's task to sponsor her husband's memorial if his sons, brothers, or father did not survive him, or if his sons were too young. In such a situation the widow apparently took over the headship of the household, the guardianship of minors, and control of the property, suggesting that she also had well-defined rights as co-owner when her husband was alive. Thus the many memorials sponsored jointly by a widow and her sons confirm not only the nuclear character of families but also indicate the existence of what in Danish is called *fællig*, the joint ownership by spouses.

4.1. INHERITANCE—AND OTHER DEVOLUTIONS OF PROPERTY

Even where women were postponed by men as heirs, they were not denied a portion of the family property; women who married (in the landowning class, most probably did) normally received a dowry, in effect a prepaid inheritance, which could sometimes have been greater than the portions that were left for their unmarried brothers. Therefore, in discussing inheritance rules we need to consider the role of heirs in rural societies. An heir, especially of a major landowner, inherited not only property but also the rights and duties that went with the land; he or she in effect stepped into the shoes of the former owner, taking over his social and political responsibilities. In most pre-modern societies this role was normally played by men; it is, therefore, interesting that often—for demographic reasons—it had to be played by women.

According to both literary evidence and the oldest laws, property-owners could give away large parts of the family property to children who married. The size of dowries and dowers was the subject of negotiation and could vary greatly. In order to achieve advantageous matches a father could, for example, give away such large marriage portions in his lifetime that there was relatively little left for the unmarried children to inherit. This freedom of action was later limited, however, as a result of ecclesiastical and royal demands.

The Church pressed the claim that Christ should be coheir in all inheritances, but as long as heads of families could freely dispose of property in their lifetimes, large amounts of land could be transferred to heirs without the Church having a chance to claim its share. The Church also urged everyone to make gifts in alms for the sake of their souls. It was, therefore, important that women as well as men should have a fair share of the family property, but the shares could not be finally decided until the head of the family died. When that happened any children who had been given some portion of the family estate when they married could either be excluded from a further share, or return what they had been given so that a new and just division could be made. For such a redistribution to be fair it was desirable that the amount each heir was entitled to should be fixed legally. It was also in the interest of both the Church and secular government that all heirs should have a right to a predetermined share of the family property so that they would be better able to pay any legal penalties that might be imposed (and so that the shares of their coheirs would be protected). The principle eventually accepted was that family property should be divided equally into what the laws called 'head-shares', with men counting as whole and women as half heads. The justification for this was, perhaps, that a man had to give his wife dower from his portion.

The transition from a free devolution of family property to systems in which the individual shares in inheritances were fixed for both men and women is reflected in the medieval Scandinavian laws. The change was completed in Denmark by the beginning of the thirteenth century, in Norway in 1274 (with the national law), but in Sweden as a whole not until the acceptance of the national law, which was issued in about 1350. Earlier there had been great variations in the way family members were treated.

4.2. THE RUNIC EVIDENCE

Thanks to the runic evidence we can trace different ways of dealing with inheritances and property rights back to the late tenth and the eleventh centuries; my suggestion is that multiple sponsorship was necessary when individual shares—both of joint properties held by spouses and of divided inheritances—were claimed, while single sponsorships reflect claims to an inheritance (or an important part of an inheritance) that could—or should—not be divided, be it land, a title, or specific rights.[4] We do not know whether, or to what extent, primogeniture was customary in Scandinavia, but in Icelandic saga-literature there are occasions when one son was preferred to the others.[5] Another way of avoiding division for which there is evidence in the laws was for sons to take the inheritance jointly, under the headship of one (usually the eldest) among them (see Pl. 14).

4.2.1. Single and multiple sponsorship

In eastern Sweden, especially Uppland, multiple sponsorships dominate, while in south/west Scandinavia single sponsorships are most common. In Uppland, Södermanland, and Öland 691 out of 1,100 inscriptions (63%) have multiple sponsors, while in Denmark, Norway, Östergötland, Västergötland, and Småland the figure is 120 out of 568 inscriptions (21%).[6] In those provinces that have too few inscriptions to make percentages meaningful, it is possible only to indicate the main *tendencies.* Gotland generally follows the pattern of the East, Närke and Västmanland have more similarity with that of the South/West. Medelpad, Hälsingland, Gästrikland, and Bornholm have a slight majority of single sponsorships.

The averages obscure the fact that there are significant differences within the regions; for example, although Uppland as a whole has a clear majority of multiple sponsors,[7] in four of its districts they form only a minority.[8] Leaving such local variations aside for the moment, the question is how the contrast between the East and the South/West should be explained. If multiple sponsorship reflects the division of an inheritance into individual shares, why were individual shares more common in eastern Sweden than in the rest of Scandinavia?

The insistence of churchmen that all children should have a share in an

[4] See also B. Sawyer (1991*b*). [5] Jochens (1985), 95–112.

[6] In Norway there are only five cases of multiple sponsorship.

[7] Esp. in: Sjuhundra (6 out of 7), Hagunda (27/30), Ulleråker (18/24), Örbyhus (6/7), Fröśåker (4/5), Värmdö (1/1), and Väddö and Häverö (1/1)=on average 84% multiple sponsorships.

[8] Sigtuna (4 out of 10), Trögd (17/41), Åsunda and Enköping (14/29), and Bro and Vätö (1/4)=on average only *c.*43% multiple sponsorships.

PLATE 14. U 130, Nora. The inscription may be an example of sons inheriting jointly: 'Björn, Finnvid's son, had this rock carved in memory of Olev, his brother. He was deceived [killed] at Finnheden. May God help his soul. This farm is their property (*oðal*) and family inheritance, belonging to Finnved's sons at Älgesta.'

inheritance cannot explain this contrast between east and west Scandinavia, for the process of Christianization advanced far more rapidly in Denmark and Norway than in east Sweden. The relative abundance of new or unsettled land in the East, together with alternative resources, notably iron, could well have been a factor that encouraged the division of inheritances, but this in itself is not a satisfactory explanation for the contrast revealed by the eleventh-century rune-stones. The most probable explanation is that in the East, especially in Uppland and Södermanland, one of the main functions of rune-stones was to proclaim the acceptance of Christianity (see Ch. 1.3.2). In that region royal authority was too weak to provide the support that missionaries needed, and indeed obtained in the west. In Uppland and other parts of the East they depended for their protection and maintenance on converts. This would suggest that sponsors of manifestly Christian rune-stones in that region had not only declared their faith but had also publicly acknowledged responsibility for protecting and supporting the clergy. It was, therefore, in the interest of all that claims to inheritances and property should be clearly stated. This would help to explain the custom of multiple sponsorship; if a convert donated land or movable wealth to the Church, the assent of potential heirs was needed to ensure that they would not revoke the gift. Such assent was later registered by having them witness diplomas; in the eleventh century the same result was achieved by multiple sponsorship of the monuments commemorating converts. One form of donation, explicitly mentioned in about 145 inscriptions, is the building of a bridge.[9] It is possible that many inscriptions were 'authorized' by the clergy, and it is worth considering the possibility that the signatures of the 'rune-masters' had the function of declaring such authorization, and were not only a confirmation that alms had been given, but offered some promise of support, spiritual and secular, for all those named as sponsors.

If the high degree of multiple sponsorship in Uppland can be at least partly explained by the religious situation there, the high degree of single sponsorhip in western and southern Scandinavia may be explained by political circumstances. In the light of developments in other parts of Europe, it may be suggested that undivided claims were a consequence of increasing royal authority. This suggestion seems consistent with the evidence of the development of royal power inside Scandinavia. It developed first in Denmark and Norway, but in Sweden it took a long time for the kings to extend their authority throughout what was to become the Swedish kingdom. Where royal power was expanding, it was important for magnates to defend old family rights, and at the same time it was important for the new men, endowed with land and prerogatives by the king, to defend *their* rights. In order to defend privileges, old or new, it was desirable to ensure that only one man at a time was responsible for the inheritance, either by adopting primogeniture, or by joint inheritance under the leadership of one heir. A strategy where a single heir was preferred is consistent with the literary evidence mentioned earlier; it is also worth considering the possibility that, as in some other parts of Europe, only one son was allowed to marry.

This interpretation was part of the hypothesis I put forward some years

[9] See Ch. 6.3.2.

ago that the rune-stones were a crisis symptom, a response to the social and economic changes caused by religious and political developments during the tenth and eleventh centuries.[10] The inscriptions made public and permanent claims to old or new rights to land, title, and power. The distribution of rune-stones may therefore reflect the degree of political and religious change in different areas; the main concentrations of inscriptions occurring where change was greatest.

4.3. GRADUAL AND PARENTELA PRINCIPLES

It will be argued here that the different systems of inheritance reflected in the inscriptions, whatever their causes, can be classified as the *parentela* system in the East and the *gradual* elsewhere in Scandinavia. The former system is that found in the Justinian code, the latter in most Germanic codes, most clearly in the Lombard laws. Both systems are found later in the medieval Scandinavian law codes (see below).

According to the gradual principle those who are nearest in grade of kinship inherit first, so that collaterals and ascendants exclude more distant descendants (such as grandchildren): see Figure 4.1(a). In the parentelic principle the inheritance only passes to collaterals when no direct descendants, male or female, survive: see Figure 4.1(b). Collaterals belong to another (second) parentela, consisting of the descendants of the dead person's parents. Another characteristic of the parentela system is the *right of representation* that enables a child to inherit in place of its dead parent.

The gradual system is often combined with the principle that males exclude females, and the male line excludes the female line. This made it easier to keep land holdings intact, while the parentela system with the inclusion of female heirs facilitated their division.[11]

The medieval laws in Scandinavia present a very complicated picture of different inheritance rules (discussed below) showing that there must have been a long drawn-out tug-of-war between opposing principles: a free devolution of family property (during the owner's lifetime) *contra* legally fixed, individual shares in the inheritance; gradual *contra* parentela. The rights of collaterals, ascendants, and more distant descendants, of women, and of the female line were obviously matters of dispute for a very long time, and thanks to the runic evidence we can trace these issues and the different solutions adopted by Scandinavian landowners back to the eleventh and tenth centuries.

[10] B. Sawyer (1989) and (1991*b*). For a debate between Elsa Sjöholm and B. Sawyer see *Scandia*, 57.1 (1991), 121–32, and *Scandia*, 57.2 (1991), 327–34.

[11] Sjöholm (1988), 120–1.

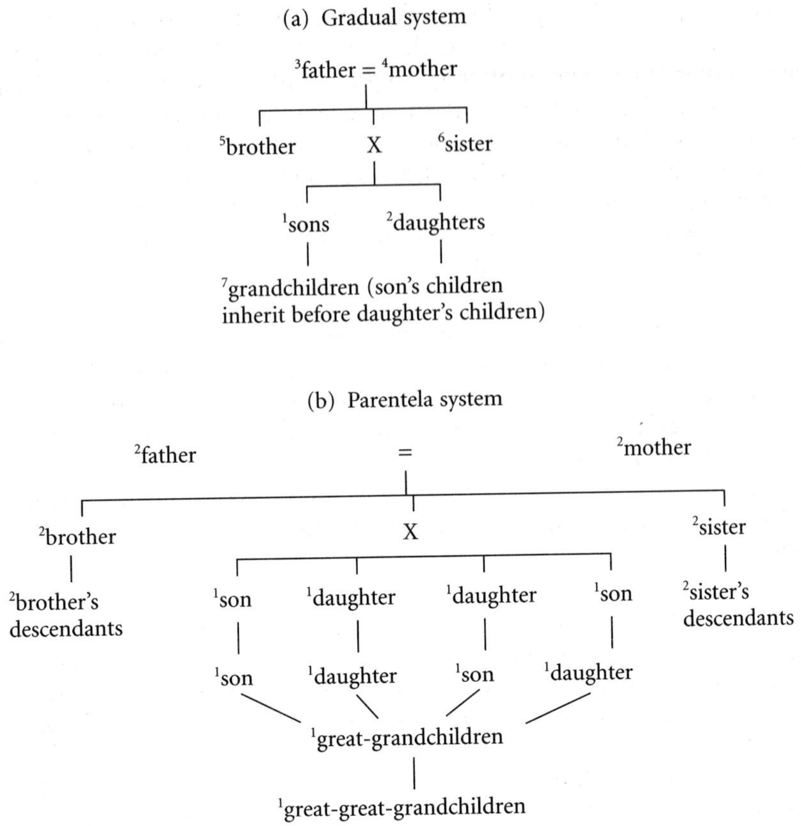

FIGURE 4.1. Inheritance systems

Note. In both the schemes above, X represents the deceased, and the numbers indicate the order of precedence among potential inheritors.

4.4. THE SPONSORSHIP PATTERNS

How would the different systems as described above be reflected on the rune-stones if they were practised consistently? Since the inheritance rights of parents and siblings are so strong in the *gradual* system, the proportion of reverse and collateral inheritances would be high, while, with no right of representation (see section 4.3 above, para. 2), inheritance by grandchildren would be exceptional. In combination with the preference given to men and the male line, the proportion of female heirs would be low, and inscriptions with additional references (see Ch. 3.1.2) to women and relatives through women would be unusual.

In the *parentela* system, however, such additional references were essential, since women were not excluded by men and inheritances could thus descend equally through them. The proportion of men and women sharing inheritances would be high, and thanks to the right of representation inheritances would often go to grandchildren or even more distant descendants. The fact that inheritances could descend through dead parents (grandparents etc.) made it crucial that all persons who could mediate their inheritance to the following generations of descendants were known and acknowledged. In the rune-stone period this could be achieved by carefully naming all sponsors/heirs, and this would partly explain the custom of multiple sponsorship.

In the gradual system this careful naming of all heirs was not necessary; if several brothers inherited after their father, it would often have been enough if one of them represented the others; if he lacked—or survived—any children, his brothers were his closest heirs and, again, they could all be represented by just one of them. This would partly explain the custom of single sponsorship.

The different ways that these systems of inheritance would be reflected on rune-stones can be summarized in a very simplified way as follows:

Proportion of:	*Gradual*	*Parentela*
collaterals and ascendants	high	low
men and women sharing inheritances	low	high
additional references to women/kin through women	low	high
multiple sponsorship	low	high
distant descendants	none	occur

As far as the rights of women and the female lines are concerned, there is a dividing line between, on the one hand, south and west Scandinavia and, on the other, eastern Sweden. In Denmark, Norway, Västergötland, Småland, and Östergötland daughters and sisters are rare among the sponsors (see Ch. 3.4.1–2) and references to women and their kin are exceptional, while in the East female sponsors often appear together with males, and references to women and their kin are quite common—references that were indeed essential where inheritances could descend through female relatives.[12] Is there the same dividing line as far as the rights of collaterals, ascendants, and distant descendants are concerned?

[12] In Uppland and Södermanland there are (99+40=) 139 inscriptions in which additional references are given; in (38+14=) 52 cases these are to women and in (2+1=) 3 to both men and women (=almost 40% of all additional references). In western Scandinavia references to women are very rare; they do not occur at all in Norway, Denmark, or Småland, and only 4 and 2 cases respectively are known from Östergötland and Västergötland.

4.4.1. South/West

Denmark and Norway have a comparatively high proportion of *fraternal* commemorations, always sponsored by men, most commonly acting alone (26.2% and 25%[13]), and no commemorations of grandfathers. This pattern, together with the low proportion of women both as sponsors and commemorated as deceased, and references to kin related through women, is consistent with the gradual system and with the principle that only one son at a time took responsibility for the inheritance—and, perhaps, was allowed to marry.

It is only in Denmark and Norway that the proportion of commemorations by male collaterals is higher than that of descendants; in Västergötland the proportion of collaterals is lower but together with the ascendants they by far outnumber the descendants.[14] This—together with the lack of commemorations by distant descendants and the comparatively low proportion of women and of references to kin related through women—suggest that the gradual system was common also in this Swedish province.

4.4.2. East

In contrast, the group of ascendants and collaterals as sponsors is comparatively low in the East, especially in Uppland and Öland, while (with only one exception) it is only here that we meet grandchildren commemorating their grandfathers.[15]

While in the South/West we meet mostly male sponsors, as a rule acting singly, in Uppland and Södermanland several heirs, often male and female together, commonly act jointly as sponsors, and there are also many references to female kin. Thus the pattern of the East is consistent with a system where it is necessary to name all the heirs who can mediate the inheritance to the following generations of descendants of both sexes. In Uppland, especially, many inscriptions include information that indicates the use of the parentela principle:

> Dan and Huskarl and Sven had this stone erected in memory of Ulvrik, their father's father. He had taken two 'gelds' [payments] in England. May God and God's mother help their souls. (U 241, Lingsberg)[16]

> Karl had this stone erected in memory of Viger, his father. He was Styvjald's son and Gullög's sister's son. (U 985, Hämninge)[17]

13 Cf. the proportion of descendants commemorating their fathers: only 21.5% and 10% respectively.

14 Collaterals and ascendants amount to 38.5%, compared with descendants at 24.8%.

15 The exception is Ög 152.

16 For this, and other religious formulas in inscriptions (e.g. U 37, Vs 18 and 19, Sö 8, on pp. 47, 52, 53, respectively), see Ch. 6 and Beskow (1994).

17 Another example is Sö 296, Skälby, Grödinge socken (parish): 'Åsgöt erected this stone in memory of Ärnfast, his mother's brother, Gyding's son . . .' In this case the sponsor is probably the only living descendant of Gyding, whose inheritance he now claims.

In both these examples we probably see the right of representation functioning; the reason why the three men commemorated their grandfather in U 241 must have been that since their father, Ulvrik's son, was dead, they stepped into his shoes. In U 985 a surviving son represents his dead father in inheriting both from his grandfather (Styvjald) and from his grandmother's sister (Gullög).[18]

In the whole of Scandinavia there are only nine inscriptions in which grandparents are commemorated, and (apart from U 241, Lingsberg (see above) eight of them are in the Mälar valley:

Björn and Åsger have this stone erected in memory of their father, and **lok** (a woman) in memory of her father's father, Orökja. (U 350, Frösunda)

Gillög, Ekenäv's daughter, had this stone erected in memory of Dragmal (?), her mother's father. (U 472, Knivsta)

(X had this stone erected in memory of) Östen, his father's father, and of Gudrik (?), his father, and of Gunna . . . (U 992, Funbo)

. . . had (the stone) carved in memory of himself. The England-traveller (**afi**) . . . **kunu-s.** (U 1181, Nora)

Åsmund carved these runes in memory of Sten, his father's father and father of Sibbe and Gerbjörn and Ulv. Here (is) a great memorial to a good man. (U N10, Lidingö)

Holmsten erected this stone in memory of Stenulv, his father's father, a good 'bonde', who lived in Brössike (?). God help his soul better than he had deserved. Hallbjörn cut the runes. (Sö 195, Ytterselö)

(X . . . in memory of his) father's father . . . (Sö 71, Västra Vingåker)

Illuge had this stone erected in memory of Sigsten, his father's father. May God give relieve his soul. (Ög 152, Furingstad)

In Småland (Sm 71) a man lists five ancestors, and in Hälsingland (Hs 14) another man also lists five ancestors and some ancestresses (see Pl. 15). In an inscription from Bromma, it can be deduced that there was an inheritance from a grandfather at stake:

Udd had this stone erected in memory of Björn, Ingrid's father. He was Vide's heir. (U 60, Bromma)

4.4.3. Between South/West and East—the Intermediate zone

As far as Småland, Östergötland, and Södermanland are concerned, the picture is less clear: in these provinces the proportion of sponsoring ascendants and collaterals together is slightly lower than that of descendants but is still comparatively high, which may suggest that the gradual principle was widely used. In Småland and Östergötland this is confirmed by the

[18] The fact that the grandfather, Styvjald, and the grandmother's sister, Gullög, are mentioned by name, but not the grandmother herself, has been interpreted by the editors of *SRI* as indicating that—in contrast to the latter—the two former were still alive.

PLATE 15. Hs 14, Malsta. In the inscription a man lists five ancestors and some ancestresses: 'Frömund erected these stones (this stone?) in memory of Rich-Gylfe, Bräse's son. And Bräse was Line's (?) son, and Line (?) was Unn's son, and Unn was Ofeg's son, and Ofeg was Tora's son. Groa was Rich-Gylfe's mother, and then . . . Gudrun. Frömund, Rich-Gylfe's son, cut these runes. We fetched this stone from Balsten in the north. Gylfe acquired this land and then lands in the north, in Vika (?), in three villages, and then in Lönnånger and then in Färdsjö.'

very low proportion of women sponsors. In Södermanland, however, the proportion of men and women sharing inheritances and the additional references to women, suggests that the parentela system had great influence there.

4.5. WHY WERE DIFFERENT INHERITANCE PRINCIPLES PREFERRED?

The real contrast is thus between on the one hand Denmark and Norway, with which Västergötland has much in common, and on the other hand Uppland and Öland, with which Södermanland has much in common. These contrasts only indicate that in these regions one of the systems dominated among the sponsors and should not obscure the fact that both systems—or principles from both systems—could have been used everywhere. The somewhat blurred picture presented by Södermanland, Östergötland, and Småland suggests that in these provinces neither system was dominant. There is no reason to expect the inheritance rules to have been the same inside whole regions; they may well have differed in different districts or even among different social groups.[19]

What makes the differences interesting is that the gradual system, with preference given to males, made it easier to keep land holdings intact, while the parentela system facilitated their division. In trying to understand why one system was preferred to the other, both the different economies and the different purposes of commemoration are relevant. The fact that the parentela system is found mainly in Uppland where most inscriptions are later than elsewhere, could indicate that parentela was a novelty. Even if that were the case, it would still be necessary to explain why in Sweden this system continued to be limited to the East; it is found in only two Swedish provincial law codes, of Uppland and Hälsingland.

The explanation must take account not only of the political situation but also of the social status of the sponsors in different areas. I have argued above that in regions where the gradual system dominated, landowners were anxious, as far as possible, to keep their inheritances intact by ensuring that they were succeeded by single adult males. It is significant that in west Scandinavia most of the rune-stones were erected by magnates. In contrast, the rune-stone fashion was more widespread in Uppland and was adopted by people who can be described, anachronistically, as 'gentry', and who constituted the local élites. In the absence of effective royal government the political, social, and economic strategies of these people were likely to be very different from those of the magnates of western Scandinavia. Although the parentela principle led to the division of inheritances, and could thus diminish a family's wealth, this could be

[19] Cf. Pollock and Maitland (1898), 255.

counteracted by strategic marriages that maintained power and status. To this end female inheritance rights were welcome; in choosing a promising son-in-law—with a good kin—a father could often forward the interest of the family better than by relying on his own sons (or other male relatives).

4.6. THE LAWS

The right of women (and the female line) to share inheritances with men (and the male line) which is associated with the parentela system made its way only slowly into the medieval Scandinavian laws, the majority of which (11 out of 17) follow the gradual system (see Table 4.1). Similarly, the right of representation gained ground only slowly; even in some of the parentela laws it remained limited.[20] The idea of *fællig* (joint ownership by the spouses) obviously met with resistance too; in the medieval laws the joint property of spouses never included inherited land. It is clear that when laws began to be written in Scandinavia inheritance rules were still a matter of dispute.

The provincial laws of Norway, the older Västgöta law, and the Dala and Guta laws (all gradual) do not regulate the division of property between sons and daughters (apart from rules governing the size of dowers and dowries). As heirs, men always took precedence over women of the same degree: for example, a son excluded a daughter, but if there was no son, the daughter was the next heir, excluding more distant male relatives.[21]

The introduction of legally fixed shares for both women and men obviously took time; a transitional stage is represented by the Östgöta and Västmanna laws (both gradual), where it was the right of *daughters* alone to share inheritances with sons that was accepted, while other female relatives were still postponed. The Danish laws (all parentela), the other Swedish provincial laws (two parentela, two gradual),[22] and the national laws of Norway and Sweden (both a compromise between gradual and parentela), however, provide for legally fixed shares for both women and men. This rule fixed a maximum for dowries and may thus have diminished some women's portion of the family property, but on the other hand it guaranteed unmarried women a legal share. All laws except the provincial laws of Norway and Gotland provided for property to be held jointly

[20] According to the Danish SL and VL, different generations of descendants could not inherit together.

[21] According to the Norwegian provincial laws, a daughter did not exclude her nephew; if her dead brother left a son, she had to share the inheritance with him.

[22] The Uppland and Hälsinge laws followed the parentela system; the Södermanna and younger Västgöta laws, the gradual.

TABLE 4.1. *Medieval Scandinavian Laws*

	Norway			Sweden										Denmark			
	GtL	FL	Nat.	VgL I	DL	GL	ÖgL	VmL	VgL II	SöL	UL	HL	Nat.	SL	VL	EL	JL
Gradual	×	×	×	×	×	×	×	×	×	×			×				
women postponed	×	×		×	×	×											
daughters only share							×	×									
all women share			×						×	×	×	×	×	×	×	×	×
Parentela											×	×		×	×	×	×

Norway:
GtL Gulathing law (fragments from *c.*1200)
FL Frostathing law (fragments from *c.*1220)
Nat. Magnus Lagabøte's national law, 1274

Denmark (SL, VL, EL, 1201–41):
SL Skåne-law
VL Valdemar's law (for Sjælland)
EL Erik's law (for Själland)
JL Jutlandic law, 1241

Sweden (all laws except VgL I and UL from the 14th century):
VgL I Västgöta law, older (fragments from *c.*1250)
DL Dala law
GL Guta law (Gotland)
ÖgL Östgöta law
VmL Västmanna law
VgL II Västgöta law, younger
SöL Södermanna law
UL Uppland law, 1296
HL Hälsinge law
Nat. Magnus Eriksson's national law, *c.*1350

by the spouses (including everything but inherited land), in which they had legally fixed shares.[23]

Even if legally fixed shares for both women and men, the right of representation, and the *fællig* were novelties in Scandinavia, the absence or presence of these principles cannot be used as criteria for dating the different laws. We know only the earliest date of the preserved or recorded manuscripts, not how old the inheritance regulations in them were. The Norwegian laws, preserved at least in fragments from the early thirteenth century and believed to be the oldest in Scandinavia (dating back to the eleventh century), have inheritance rules that are very similar to the rules in the later older-Västgöta law and the Dala law (from the thirteenth and the fourteenth centuries). Likewise the Danish laws, from the early thirteenth century, differ greatly from the Norwegian and most of the later Swedish laws but have many inheritance rules in common with the Uppland law of 1296. It is clear that the two national laws (of Norway, 1274, and Sweden, *c.*1350) are compromises between opposing inheritance rules that seem to have been used side by side over a long period of time.

4.7. SPONSORSHIP PATTERNS AND THE LAWS

The differences in sponsorship patterns in Scandinavia partly correspond to the different inheritance systems in the medieval laws: the parentela system in the Uppland law seems to have been very common among the sponsors in Uppland, while on the other hand the gradual system postponing women in the laws of Gulathing and Frostathing in Norway, in the older Västgöta law, and (with the exception of daughters) in the Östgöta law, seems to have been favoured by sponsors in Norway, Västergötland, and Östergötland. Further, the fact that wives do not act together with sons in Norway is consistent with absence of *félag* (*fællig*); when the provincial laws of Norway were compiled separate ownership was the normal marriage arrangement.

There is also a striking correspondence between the runic evidence of Gotland, particularly the Sjonhem monument (Ch. 3.1.5), and the Guta law. Three sons were commemorated on separate stones by their parents, and it is made clear that only one of them, Hailfos, had a surviving descendant, his daughter Hailvi. The reason why her great uncles are named (G 135) must be that, being a female descendant, she had to share inherited land with her closest male relatives, in full accordance with the later Guta law.

[23] In Denmark this joint property right extended also to the children; husband, wife, and sons had two shares each, daughters one each. In the other laws the joint property only concerns the spouses; the husband had two shares and the wife one.

The sponsorship pattern of Södermanland has many features in common with Uppland but some in common with the South/West zone. A natural explanation would be that inside this region the gradual principle was fairly common, but that the parentela system had strong influence. When the Södermanna law was compiled, it followed the gradual principle with the inclusion of women and the female line.

4.7.1. Denmark: a problem?

The inheritance systems of the medieval provincial laws correspond with those reflected by the rune-stones everywhere except in Denmark; here the laws follow the parentela principle, with the inclusion of females, while the runic evidence implies the gradual principle, with the postponement of females. According to the twelfth-century Danish historians Sven Aggesen and Saxo Grammaticus, the right of women to inherit together with men was introduced by Sven Forkbeard. This apparently supports the argument that Danish inheritance rules were changed between the rune-stone period and the time of the written laws. It is, however, possible, even likely, that in Denmark—as in other parts of Scandinavia—*both* systems were used in the tenth and eleventh centuries, and the reason why the parentela system is not reflected in the runic inscriptions is that the Danish *sponsors* preferred the gradual system.

Although all Danish laws follow the parentela principle, they show traces of another system, in which the right of collaterals was stronger, and the right of remote descendants was weaker; in two of the laws (the Skåne-law and the oldest redaction of Valdemar's law) the right of representation was limited: different generations of descendants could not share an inheritance; a surviving child took precedence over the children of a deceased sibling. These features are not necessarily traces of an *earlier* system,[24] they may simply reflect a compromise between contemporary, competing principles.

There is, however, one particular respect in which the runic evidence concerning inheritance and the later Danish laws correspond: they both show a marked reluctance to allow ascendants to inherit. In other parts of Scandinavia the proportion of ascendants sponsoring rune-stones varies between 17% and 25%, while it is much lower in Denmark (8%) and Öland (7.5%).

4.8. DIFFERENCES WITHIN UPPLAND

It is important to emphasize that different inheritance systems could have been used by sponsors in the same region. In Uppland, for example, the sponsorship pattern in the districts of Åsunda and Trögd (west of Sigtuna)

[24] As assumed in *KHL*, i, cols. 259–60 (s.v. 'arveret').

are in some respects closer to those of Västergötland, Norway, and Denmark than is the case in other parts of Uppland: most are sponsored by men (in Trögd mostly by single sponsors),[25] and the multiple sponsors rarely combine people with different relationships to the dead. Like Västergötland and Norway, Åsunda has a comparatively low proportion of sons commemorating their fathers but a very high proportion of reverse inheritances;[26] and, like Denmark, Trögd has a high proportion of men commemorating their brothers.[27]

Another feature that characterizes Åsunda and Trögd is the comparatively common occurrence of the 'dreng' title (probably denoting a warrior in a royal 'hird' or retinue);[28] together they have four of Uppland's ten examples. The concentration of dreng-stones in these two districts is all the more interesting in the light of the relatively high proportion of such stones in the neighbouring province of Västmanland, which has only thirty inscriptions, four of them naming 'drengs'. Finally it should be noted that Trögd and Åsunda together have as many as 29 of the 58 rune-stones in Uppland that are decorated with the four-legged beast, a motif that is likely to have been inspired by the great Jelling stone: see Plate 16.

The densest concentration of inscriptions in Uppland is in the districts around Sigtuna, which was founded in about 975, apparently by Olof Skötkonung's father, Erik. The mint that functioned there from *c.*995 to *c.*1030 shows that it was then a centre of royal power. Most runic inscriptions in Uppland are, however, of later date than that. It may be significant that the runic inscriptions that most clearly imply royal authority are found some distance to the west of Sigtuna, in the districts of Trögd and Åsunda. Apart from the high proportion of individual sponsors—unique in Uppland and reminiscent of the pattern in Denmark and Götaland—and the concentration of 'drengs' and stones depicting the four-legged beast, there is also a comparatively low proportion of *explicitly* Christian rune-stones in these districts.[29] This is also reminiscent of Denmark and Götaland, where Christianity was more firmly established and there was less need to demonstrate it. It is, therefore, arguable that Erik, whose son Olof had close links with Västergötland, founded Sigtuna as a base for a

[25] In Åsunda 24 out of 30 inscriptions in the Relationship Subgroup are sponsored by men, in Trögd 31 out of 41.

[26] In Åsunda there are 9 cases of son~father and 10 cases of reverse inheritance; in Trögd there are 13 cases of son~father and 7 cases of reverse inheritance.

[27] The figure is 10 out of 41, 9 being single sponsorships.

[28] See Ch. 5.4.

[29] In Trögd only 36%, and in Åsunda 40%, of the stones are explicitly Christian, compared with 65–70% in Uppland as a whole, and as many as 77% in the neighbouring districts of Håbo and Ärlinghundra, immediately around Sigtuna. While Trögd and Åsunda alone have 29 of Uppland's 58 four-legged beasts (Åsunda with 35 stones has 14 beasts, Trögd with 52 stones has 15), Håbo has none, and Ärlinghundra (with 71 rune-stones) has only one (U 428).

PLATE 16. Vg 181, Norra Åsarp. The main concentrations of 'dreng-stones' are in Denmark and Västergötland. On this stone we also have the four-legged beast, very similar to the one on Harald Bluetooth's stone in Jelling (DR 42), see Excursus. *Inscription*: 'Guve raised this stone in memory of Olav, his son, a very good dreng. He was killed in "Estland". Håvard (?) cut the stone.'

new type of Christian royal authority in Svealand, which was then in effect ruled by a number of independent chieftains and lords,[30] but that, sometime after 1030, resistance enforced a retreat to the west, which for a while served as the royal 'bridgehead'.[31] This is consistent with Adam of Bremen's report that in the 1060s pagan opposition forced Adalward to abandon the

[30] See Tesch (1989), 6–17.

[31] It should be added that neither in Trögd nor in Åsunda are there any commemorations of women.

attempt to establish a bishopric in Sigtuna and withdraw to Skara in Västergötland (Adam of Bremen, iii. 76, iv. 30).

4.9. CONCLUSION

The tentative conclusion of this discussion is that the different principles and systems of inheritance implied by the runic inscriptions reflect the different needs of magnates and 'gentry' in tenth- and eleventh-century Scandinavia; the former favouring principles that helped keep their estates intact, the latter favouring principles that helped build up networks of family alliances. Different stages of Christianization, different types of royal power, and the ways in which different landowning groups were affected, were each and concurrently factors in the contrasting patterns of inheritance/sponsorship. In social groups and areas most affected by growing royal power, male, adult heirs, normally one at a time, were preferred, but elsewhere and among groups less affected by the claims of kings, a system with individual shares for both women and men was practised. Everywhere, however, the kinship—and inheritance—system was *bilateral*; there is no trace of patrilinear lineages.

Bilaterality itself, however, did not favour women; they were only pawns in the game. In systems that postponed them as heirs their function, when necessary, was to preserve and hand on the family property to the next generation; in systems that included them their function was to enlarge the family and its resources by marrying and thus gaining the support of other families. There is nothing in the gradual system itself to prevent women from sharing inheritances with men (as the medieval laws show), but while division between all children and their descendants was inherent in the parentela system, a preference for men and the male line could more easily be combined with the gradual system.

It is no doubt this preference for men and the male line, a principle that was still current in many of the medieval laws, which has encouraged belief in an earlier patrilinear society in Scandinavia. Instead of interpreting this preference as a relic of an 'original stage', it is more fruitful to ask where, when, and why this preference was customary. It could possibly have been comparatively new in Scandinavia, serving the needs and purposes of an increasingly threatened class of magnates—a hypothesis that is consistent with our knowledge of developments in other parts of Europe at the time.[32]

It is not possible to determine which system, gradual or parentela, was the older in Scandinavia; they probably coexisted for a long time, and were adopted by different groups in society. The regional differences in spon-

[32] Cf. Hansen (1994), 103–54.

sorship patterns of the rune-stones can only indicate what system was dominant among those who sponsored them. The later development of inheritance law revealed by the provincial and national law codes is a fascinating subject for enquiry, but that lies outside the scope of the present study.

5

SOCIETY AND STATUS

SINCE a rune-stone was a sign of social and economic status we can assume that all sponsors were landowners, among whom different social strata can be distinguished. The various indications that a rune-stone was erected by or to commemorate a person of high status include titles and honorific epithets, as well as the number and (relative) size of the stones, the length of the inscription, the use of more than one face, and the elaborateness of the ornament. Individuals who sponsored or were commemorated by two or more inscriptions appear to have been unusually important, while rune-stones placed close to such prestigious monuments as large burial mounds or ship-settings (where stones are arranged in the shape of a ship) show even more clearly that they were the work of families of exceptionally high rank.

In western Scandinavia the relatively high proportion of rune-stones with one or more of these characteristics suggests that in that region the fashion of erecting such monuments was adopted mainly by families of high status. Families of similar status also erected rune-stones in east Scandinavia but there, especially in Uppland, many more were erected by or for landowners who were less distinguished. The custom was adopted by a wider range of landowners in that part of Scandinavia, partly because it lasted for much longer there than in the west, for reasons explained above (Ch. 1.3.2).

5.1. SPONSORS AND DECEASED

5.1.1. Multiple commemorations

In the Further Particulars sections of the Catalogue (e.g. pp. 206; 209; 233–6; 257–62), multiple commemorations are grouped under three headings: 1. *identical*, i.e. when the same sponsors commemorate the same individuals; 2. *in memory of the same individuals* by different sponsors; 3. *by the same sponsors* in memory of different individuals. In the following sections, groups 1 and 3 together are dealt with first, and thereafter group 2.

5.1.1a. Groups 1 and 3

The major sponsors of Scandinavia are found mainly in Denmark, Södermanland, and Uppland, but they are also found in other parts of Scandinavia.[1] Several of these sponsors of multiple monuments clearly belonged to ruling families. In Denmark Asfrid, widow of King Gnupa, sponsored two stones commemorating her and Gnupa's son, King Sigtryg.[2] Tue, descendant of Ravn, who sponsored four stones (three in memory of 'Queen' Thyre and one in memory of his mother) and also had a mound and other monuments (Sw. *kummel*) built, can, for reasons explained in the Excursus, be identified as a contender for royal power.[3] Ragnhild, the widow of a chieftain (*goði*), sponsored two large rune-stones in memory of two different men, one at Tryggevælde on Sjælland and one at Glavendrup on Fyn, both carved by the same rune-master (see Pls. 17 and 18).

According to the Tryggevælde inscription she also had a ship-setting made there, while at Glavendrup the stone was placed at the end of a Bronze-Age ship-setting.[4] Other people who sponsored double monuments in Denmark were Toke the smith (in memory of two different people), Esbern (in memory of his brothers), and Fader (in memory of a brother and a partner).[5]

In Södermanland, Holmfast sponsored a double monument on a rock face in Södertälje to commemorate his parents, for whom he also cleared a road and built a bridge; he further embellished the rock face with a carving of a beast.[6] Double monuments were made by Gudmund and Gisla in memory of their son, for whom they also built a bridge, and by Gudlög and her daughter Hjälmlög in memory of two sons/brothers.[7]

The greatest sponsor in Uppland was Jarlabanke, who sponsored no less than six stones in memory of himself. His high status is confirmed by his claim that he had established a *thing*-place at Vallentuna and that he 'owned' (?) the whole hundred,[8] presumably of Vallentuna (see Pl. 19). He also built a bridge (i.e. causeway) at Täby in that district, and claimed to own the whole of Täby.[9]

The widow Estrid, who, it will be argued below, was Jarlabanke's daughter, on her own or with relatives also sponsored six stones (one of them

[1] See Catalogue: Further Particulars, pp. 206; 209; 233–6; 257–62.

[2] DR 2 and 4.

[3] DR 26, 29, 30, and 34. See also Excursus.

[4] DR 209 (in memory of her husband, Alli) and 230 (in memory of her husband, Gunnulf).

[5] DR 58 and 91; 282 and 283; 334 and 335.

[6] Sö 311 (in memory of his mother), 312 (in memory of his father), and 313 (carving of a beast).

[7] Sö N10 and 134; 206 and 208. Another case is when Vigdjärv and Djärv raised a double monument, Sö 112 in memory of their father, and Sö 113 in memory of both their father and mother.

[8] U 212. The meaning of the word *atti*, here translated as 'owned', has been discussed at length, but there is no consensus about its implication.

[9] U 164, 165, and 212. See further below (Ch. 6.3). Cf. Gustavson and Selinge (1988).

Plate 17. DR 230, Tryggevælde. *Inscription*: 'Ragnhild, Ulv's sister, placed this stone and made this mound in memory of . . . and this ship-setting . . . her husband Gunnalv, a "clamorous" man, son of Nærve. Few will now be born better than he. May he become a *ræte* [outlaw, villain] who damages this stone or drags it from here.'

PLATE 18. DR 209, Glavendrup. *Inscription* (on three sides): A, 'Ragnhild placed this stone in memory of Alle . . . , *gode* [chieftain] of the "vier" [a people], honourable thegn of the hird [retinue].' B, 'Alle's sons made this monument in memory of their father, and his wife in memory of her husband, and Sote cut these runes in memory of his lord. May Thor hallow these runes.' C, 'May he become a *ræte* [outlaw, villain] who damages this stone or drags it (away to stand) in memory of someone else.'

PLATE 19. U 212, Täby. *Inscription* (on two sides): A, 'Jarlabanke had this stone raised in memory of himself while he was alive. Alone he "owned" the whole of Täby. (May God help) his soul.' B, 'Jarlabanke had this stone raised in memory of himself while he was alive, and he made this *thing*-place, and alone he "owned" the whole of this "hundare" (district).'

lost) in memory of her husband and sons (see Pl. 20).[10] The widow Inga on her own commemorated her husband with no less than four rune-stones, three at Snottsta and one at Vreta (see Ch. 2, Pl. 10, and Ch. 3 at pp. 49–51 above).[11]

Several important families, like Jarlabanke's, lived around Vallentuna lake in Uppland. The sons of Ulv of Skålhamra made three monuments to honour their father, one of them together with his widow.[12] Three of his sons erected a stone in memory of him on the west shore of the lake not far from Skålhamra, and together with their mother they erected a pair of stones on the other side of the lake at Bällsta, where they also established a meeting place for a *thing*. A cousin of Ulv's widow also commemorated him on a stone near Skålhamra.

About four kilometres north of the lake another Ulv, of Lindö, together with a son, was commemorated by four of his surviving sons, who erected four stones, two with runic inscriptions, marking the ends of a substantial bridge or causeway that they made in his honour.[13] About eight kilometres north-west of the lake, at Harg, Gunnar and Holmdis commemorated Holmdis's daughter with three stones (see Ch. 3.1.1, end), and their son with two stones and a bridge.[14]

The most impressive multiple monument in Gotland was sponsored by Rodvisl and Rodälv, commemorating three sons on three stones at Sjonhem (see Ch. 3.1.5).[15] Other great sponsors in Gotland were Liknat's sons, who sponsored one stone in memory of their father and another in memory of their mother.[16]

5.1.1b. Group 2

As we have seen, some of the major sponsors commemorated the same person(s) with multiple monuments, but there are also several cases where the same individual was commemorated by two or more *different* sponsors. This is of course an indication of status in itself, and in some cases it may even reveal a tug-of-war over the inheritance (as will be illustrated in the Excursus). So, for example, in Oppunda härad ('district') in Södermanland, Svarthövde was commemorated both by his brothers (Sö 57) and by his sons (Sö 58). Other examples are: Torkel and Styrbjörn, commemorated both by their brothers (Sö 34) and by their mother (Sö 35); Östen, commemorated both by his sons (U 135) and by his widow (U 136; see Pl. 20); Onäm, commemorated both by his daughters (U 328) and by his nephew (U 336).

[10] U 101, 136, 137, 143, 147(?), 310.
[11] U 329, 330, 331, 332.
[12] U 160, 225, and 226.
[13] U 236 and 237. On U 238 Ulv's widow commemorates her husband and their son Sven.
[14] U 312, 313, and 314; 315 and 316.
[15] G 134, 135, and 136.
[16] G 113 and 114.

Plate 20. U 136, Broby. *Inscription*: 'Estrid had these stones raised in memory of Östen, her husband, who went to Jerusalem and died away in Greece.'

It has been suggested that the deceased man Öpir, commemorated by his widow in Aspa (Sö 137), is the same Öpir who is commemorated by his sons in Viby, about two kilometres from Aspa (Sö N13).[17] This, however, creates a problem: Öpir in Viby was commemorated by at least two (probably more) sons, while Öpir in Aspa was obviously survived by only one son, who is described on another stone (Sö 138) as 'the good heir', in the singular. *If* we are dealing with the same Öpir in these three inscriptions, a possible explanation would be that he had been married twice, having had several sons by his first wife, but only one by his second wife, Tora. This solution is supported by the fact that the deceased son in Sö 138 is explicitly said to be the heir not only of Öpir but *also* of Tora. Especially in situations where there were children of two different marriages there must often have been disputes over sharing the inheritance.

While it is clear that some of these multiple monuments were sponsored by and commemorated people of exceptionally high status, including some rulers, it is likely that most of them commemorate members of local élites, although very few of them, or their kinsmen named in the inscriptions, are given titles.[18]

5.1.2. Shared monuments

At the other end of the scale of sponsors there are people who apparently could not afford to commemorate their relatives on separate rune-stones but, instead, shared the cost with other sponsors commemorating their own relatives. It is possible that the sponsors of some of these 'shared' monuments were related, but in the absence of any explicit indications of kinship that seems unlikely. Two examples of such 'low-budget monuments' are U 1032, where two men join forces to commemorate their fathers, and U 952, where one man commemorates his son Trygg and two other men commemorate their father, Stodbjörn. There are only twelve of these 'shared' monuments, eleven of them in Uppland, where the rune-stone fashion seems to have been adopted by families with relatively slender means.[19]

5.2. TITLE-BEARERS

Some 209 titles occur in 193 inscriptions,[20] that is 8.4% of the whole corpus; but the proportions in different regions vary greatly, being highest in Denmark (37.5%) and Västergötland (25.5%) but below the average else-

[17] Williams (1990), 186.

[18] Sö 34 and 112 commemorate 'thegns', and U143 commemorates a 'dreng', the meaning of which will be discussed below.

[19] In some cases it cannot be *proved* that the co-sponsors were unrelated, but the other possible 'low-budget monuments' are: Sö 237; U 91, 233, 277, 321(?), 749, 842, 1017, 1065, and 1069.

[20] The number of title-bearers is not the same as the number of inscriptions since some inscriptions contain more than one title.

where, with Uppland showing only 2.8%.[21] This confirms that the custom of erecting rune-stones was more 'aristocratic' in Denmark and Västergötland than elsewhere.

The titles can be grouped under four main headings: rulers, leaders, retainers, and others, as in the following list of title-bearers. (A detailed glossary of all individual titles is given in the first section of App. 6.)

Number of title-bearers	
1. Rulers (e.g. king, earl)	16
2. Leaders (e.g. captain, estate steward)	16
3. Retainers (e.g. 'hirdman', skipper, staller, thegn, dreng, sven)	153
4. Others	24
	209

The fourth group, 'Others', contains 24 individuals with titles such as *bryti* ('unfree steward'), smith, priest that cannot be treated as titles comparable with those in groups 1–3, although some clearly had high status.

Titles in group 1, indicating some kind of rulership, are most common in Denmark (10 individuals), and it is only here that *kings* appear as sponsors or deceased (see Pl. 21).

People acting as leaders (over districts and/or fleets), group 2, are found in Denmark (6 individuals), and in eastern Sweden (4 in Södermanland, 5 in Uppland, and 1 in Gästrikland).

In group 3, 132/?133 of the retainers were thegns, drengs, or svens;[22] both thegns and drengs (126 in all) are widely distributed—except in Norway where there is none. More than half of the other 21 retainers, e.g. 'hirdman', skipper, and staller, are found in Denmark.[23]

Most of the titles clearly denote persons of relatively high social status. It is significant that a title, often combined with an honorific epithet was considered sufficient indication of rank; very few rune-stones with a title have any of the other features associated with high status discussed above (p. 92), although in Denmark some have inscriptions that continue on two or more sides of the stones.

[21] Sö 7.4%, Sm 6%, Ög 5.2%, No 3.9%, and Öl 1.1%.

[22] There are 7 'svens' (probably young warriors): one in Denmark (DR 344), one in Östergötland (Ög 66), two in Västergötland (Vg 155 and 156), and three in Uppland (U 225, 323, 432).

[23] Twelve of these other retainers are in Denmark: DR 1, 3, 154, 155, 296, 297 ('retainer' or 'hirdman'); 411 ('follower'); N3 ('herald?'); 82, 218, 275, 363 ('skipper'). One is in Bornholm: DR 379 ('skipper'). Two are in Småland: Sm 42 ('ship's watch') and 76 ('staller'). There are three in Södermanland: Sö 171 and 335 ('skipper'); N1 ('ship's watch') and two in Uppland: U 479 ('follower') and 617 ('Viking watch'), and one is Östergötland: Ög 66 ('sven').

PLATE 21. DR 3, Hedeby. A Danish king is named as sponsor: 'King Svein set this stone in memory of his retainer (*heimþegi*) Skarde, who had gone to the west but now met his death at Hedeby.'

5.3. EPITHETS

A total of 330 people are given epithets—'good', 'able', 'generous', etc.—in 316 inscriptions: that is only 14% of the whole corpus, but 66% of the inscriptions with titles (128 out of 193). The number of occurrences of each epithet is given in Table 5.1 below, with an indication of their distribution; for more detailed data, see App. 7.

These epithets and their distribution are given in more detail, with references, in the list below. 'Noble', 'first' or 'foremost', *þróttr*, *frœkn*, and *hæfr*

TABLE 5.1. *Number and distribution of epithets*

Epithets	Number of occurrences	Distribution
1. 'good' (and variations) viz. 'good' (175), 'very good' (60), 'all-good' (7), best (16)	263[a]	widespread
2. (*a*) 'able', (*b*) 'bold', (*c*) 'strong' (*a*) *snjallr* (16), *nýtr* (11), *hæfr* (2), *snaar* (1) (*b*) *frœkn* (2) (*c*) *þróttr* (7)	39	not in Dk, No, and Born; most of group (*a*) and all of the rest are in the East
3. 'noble', 'first', 'dear'	4	Denmark only
4. 'wise' (e.g. eloquent, quick-minded, etc.)	9	Denmark and the East
5. 'generous' (e.g. with food)	15	mostly Småland and the East
TOTAL	330	

[a] The total is 263 'good people' in only 260 inscriptions, which include DR 230 'few will now be born better' than Ragnhild's dead husband, and Vs 24 praising the wife of a 'good bonde;' no better housewife will come to Hassmyra, where the stone was found.

were only used for men entitled thegn, dreng, or sven, and almost all those described as 'all-good' (6 out of 7) or 'very good' (57 out of 60) had the same titles. 'Good' and 'best', however, were used for a much greater variety of people. Most of the thegns and drengs are described as 'good', and the superlative 'best' is used for one thegn, three drengs, and eleven others, including two 'landmen' or landholders.

The following epithets are given only to men entitled thegn, dreng, or sven:

'noble' ('of high value'): used of only one thegn (DR 209)
'first', 'foremost': used of only one thegn (DR 277)
þróttr: used only of (7) thegns in Södermanland
frœkn: used only of (2) drengs (Ög 81 and Nä 18)
hæfr: used only of (2) drengs (Ög N18 and U 289)
'good': used more widely, though only of (31) thegns or drengs; the higher praise of being 'all-good', or 'very good' is only exceptionally used about others than members of this group
'all-good' (used in seven inscriptions): 6 title-bearers (1 thegn, 4 drengs, and 1 sven)[24]
'very good' (used of sixty individuals): 57 title-bearers (23 thegns, 27 drengs, 2 svens)[25]

[24] U 208 mentions 'all-good *sons*'.

[25] In the case of Vg 75 it is not clear who is 'very good', but it is probably the dead wife; Vg 92 and DR 338 mention a 'very good bonde'.

5.4. THEGNS AND DRENGS

There has been much debate about the meanings of 'thegn' and 'dreng', but no consensus has been reached. In 1927–8 Svend Aakjær argued that both thegns and drengs were royal servants, members of the king's attendant nobility and of his 'hird' or bodyguard. But, he added, 'as time went on . . . they [the titles] came to connote the possession . . . of certain moral qualities, especially nobility, generosity, chivalrousness and courage'.[26] The question is *when* such a change took place; some scholars argue that it occurred before the rune-stone period. John Lindow, for example, has argued that the drengs and thegns in the runic inscriptions belong to the sphere of 'the large, free middle class of farmers who made up the backbone of old Scandinavian society' and that they 'did not make up part of Nordic *comitatus* terminology',[27] and Jan Paul Strid, who concentrates on the drengs in the East, describes them as 'similar to English gentlemen in their variety of connotations' and goes on to approve of Fritzner's translation, 'a man who is as he should be', which he describes as 'rather ingenious'.[28]

The arguments put forward by Lindow and Strid are not convincing; if these terms only connote the 'free middle class of farmers', the question arises why they should be so few in Scandinavia at the time, and if 'dreng' only means that a man is 'as he should be' there was a serious lack of such men in Scandinavia, especially in the East where there are only nineteen.[29] See Plates 22 and 23.

John Gillingham has recently argued that in eleventh-century England we find a local élite ('thegns' and 'knights'), 'a broad land-owning class . . . many of them holding public office in a part-time and unpaid fashion, exercising social control over the populace, attending meetings both locally and nationally'.[30] It is difficult to see why there should not be an equivalent in Scandinavia, especially at a time when, thanks to Sven Forkbeard and Knut, English influence must have been very strong there.[31] Gillingham goes on to point out that even if some *milites* were not richer than ordinary farmers, they belonged to a different social group, namely the retainers of a lord. This seems consistent with the runic evidence; the monuments erected after thegns and drengs are not more spectacular than others; as pointed out above, it seems as if the titles themselves, with or without epithets, were enough to distinguish them.

As far as Denmark is concerned, there seems to be general agreement that thegn and dreng denoted retainers in the royal 'hird', and that the common epithet '(very) good' meant 'of high birth'. The interpretation of these titles and epithets in the Swedish material is more problematic; they

26 Aakjær (1927–8), 28 f. 27 Lindow (1975), 106. 28 Strid (1987), 313.
29 For another opinion, see Jesch (1993).
30 Gillingham (1995), 129–53, quotation from p. 134.
31 Compare the term *snjallr drengr* with *strenuus miles* in English sources.

PLATE 22. Vg 150, Velanda. Commemoration of a thegn: 'Tyrvi (Thorvi?) raised the stone in memory of Ogmund, her husband, a very good thegn. May Thor hallow (the stone or the runes).'

PLATE 23. Ög 64, Bjälbo. Drengs act as sponsors: 'Drengs raised this stone in memory of Grep, their guild-brother . . .'

are translated in very different ways in the standard edition of the inscriptions. It will be argued here that in both Denmark and Sweden, as in England, the word or title 'thegn' designated men who served a superior, normally a king. A 'dreng' was a young warrior, a member of a retinue, called a 'lið' or 'hird'. It can be assumed that the thegns and drengs named in Danish inscriptions were in the service of the Danish king and there are reasons to believe that some of the thegns and drengs named in Swedish inscriptions also served a Danish king.

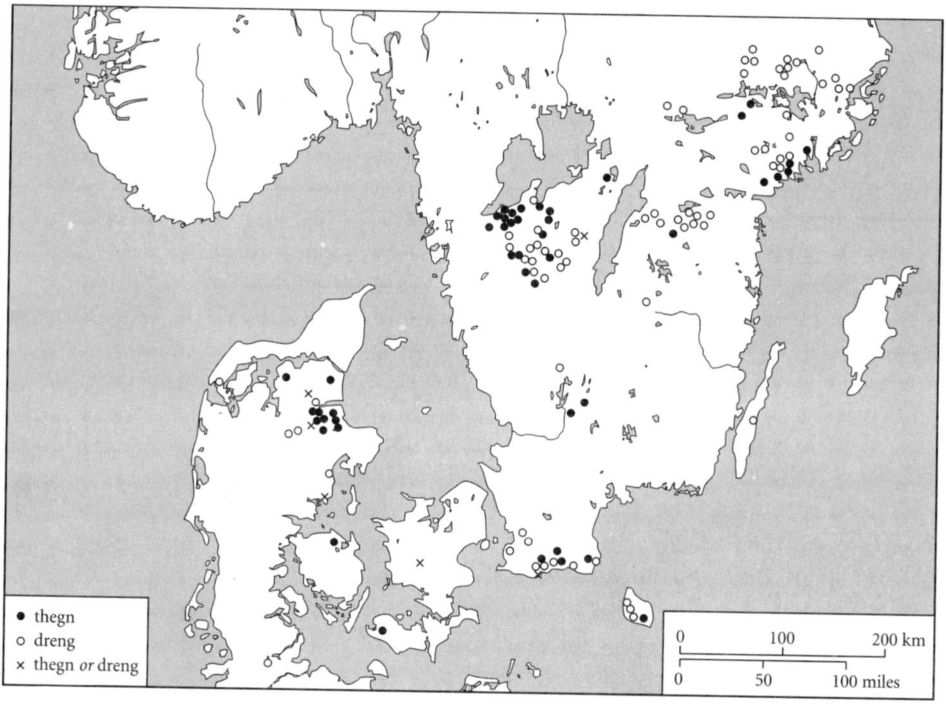

MAP 2. Distribution of 'thegns' and 'drengs'

The main concentration of inscriptions containing the titles thegn and dreng outside Denmark is in Västergötland (see Map 2) where, with one exception all drengs and thegns are described as 'good' or, more often, 'very good' (*góðr, allgóðr, harða góðr, mjǫk góðr*); in the exception a dreng is described as *beztr* ('best').[32] The same epithets are applied to most of the drengs and thegns in Danish inscriptions[33] but they are rarely used there or in Västergötland for anyone else, which suggests that they all belonged to a distinct group of men or families who acknowledged the Danish king as their lord.

[32] Drengs: Vg 32, 61, 81, 90, 112, 114, 123, 125 (*beztr*), 126–7, 130, 153–4, 157, 162, 179, 181, 184. Vg 81 is medieval and does perhaps not belong to the group discussed here. Thegns: Vg 8, 59, 62, 73–4, 101–3, 108, 113, 115, 137, 150–2, 157–8. Vg 82, 136, and 139 may be either drengs or thegns. A new find, ATA 5084/96, also contains the epithet *harða góðan þegn*.

[33] Drengs: DR 1, 68, 77–8, 127, 150, 262, 268, 276, 288–9, 295, 330, 339, 345. Thegns: DR 86, 98–9, 106, 115, 121, 123, 130, 143, 209, 213, 277, 293–4, 343, N5. DR 53, 94, 129, 228, 278 may be either drengs or thegns.

It is significant that, as Map 2 shows, the main concentrations of thegns and drengs are in the east of the territory that was apparently tributary to the Danish king in about AD 1000. The fact that numerous thegns and drengs are found in Skåning härad ('district'), in the heart of Västergötland, is consistent with evidence indicating that Sven Forkbeard was overlord of the Swedish king Olof Skötkonung, who established the first Swedish bishopric in Västergötland, initially at Husaby, but it was soon moved to Skara in the centre of Skåning härad.[34]

The fact that most of the thegns were commemorated by their sons, while most of the drengs were commemorated by parents or brothers, implies that drengs were young men and thegns were older. In one case we meet both titles in the same family, with a man commemorating both his father, a 'very good thegn', and his brother, a 'very good dreng'.[35] It further appears that while drengs were active warriors, the thegns were settled landowners. Drengs who fought for Sven or Knut and survived may well have continued, as thegns, to accept him as their royal lord after returning home. It is indeed possible that they had some special status as royal agents. Attention has been drawn to seven places named Tegnaby, or something very similar; these settlements are all situated in the coastal region between Oslo and Göteborg and their remarkably regular distribution suggests that they formed part of some organization.[36] The close similarity of the inscriptions in Denmark and Västergötland suggests that all the thegns and drengs named therein, whether Danes or Götar, were distinguished by their relationship to the Danish king Sven Forkbeard; they may also have been part of a royal organization by means of which the Danes tried to retain influence in the border territory that was already in the ninth century called 'Denmark', i.e. 'the march of the Danes'. The close connections between Denmark and Götaland are well illustrated by the fact that the same sponsor commemorated the same man, his *fælle* or partner, as a 'very good dreng', in two inscriptions, one in Jutland (DR 127) and the other in Västergötland (Vg 112).

The formulas *góðr, allgóðr, harða góðr, mjǫk góðr* that are so characteristic of the monuments commemorating thegns and drengs in both Denmark and Västergötland are also used for some of the eleven thegns and thirty-seven drengs in other parts of Sweden. Both the drengs named in Småland are 'good', as also are all four in Västmanland, eight of the ten in Uppland, six of the ten in Östergötland, and one of the eight in Södermanland.[37] The two thegns in Småland are described as *beztr* (Sm 35)

[34] See Introduction and Ch. 7. [35] Vg 157. [36] Löfving (1986), 168–75.

[37] Sm 48, 93; Vs 3, 18, 19, 22 (*beztr* ?); U 143, 610(?), 760, 767–8, 802 (*beztr*), 808, 972; Ög 60, 104, 122, 130, 201 and N18; Sö 167. The other dreng stones are: Ög 64, 81, 111, N19(?); Sö 4(?), 55, 137(?), 155, 163, 177, 320; U 166, 289; Nä 18, 23.

and *góðr* (Sm 37) respectively, and in Södermanland one of eight thegn-inscriptions (Sö 34) uses the epithet *góðr* (while the others use *þróttr*). It is possible that these twenty-one drengs and three thegns described as 'good' or 'best' had some special relationship with a Danish king. But what about the others?

Six of the drengs are given no epithet,[38] the others are variously said to be 'able'/'bold': *snjallr* (3); *frækn* (2); *nýtr* (2); *hæfr* (2); **ufilan** ? (1).[39] Of the eight remaining thegns, seven are *þróttr* (in Södermanland) and one *nýtr* (in Östergötland).[40] It is, of course, possible that these men, or some of them, served a Danish king, but as these words were not used in Danish inscriptions it is perhaps more likely that they served one or more Swedish leaders who commanded their own organizations, possibly modelled on that of the Danes. Whatever the explanation, it is significant that these adjectives are rarely or never used about others; *þróttr* is used only of thegns, *frækn* and *hæfr* only of drengs.

Of the six—possibly seven—sven-inscriptions, where the men were in all likelihood also young warriors, four have the same epithets as the thegns and drengs: one is 'all-good', two are 'very good' and one is *snjallr*.[41]

5.5. *BONI HOMINES*

As demonstrated above, most epithets qualify titles, but 'good' and 'best' are exceptions (see App. 7(c)): they are the most common epithets, with 263 examples (see Maps 3A–B), but less than half (105) refer to a title-holder. The people who are described as 'good' or 'best' can be grouped in the four categories shown in Table 5.2 below.

In Denmark, Västergötland, and Småland, where most of the 'good people' have titles, the epithet apparently reinforces the status indicated by the title and rank of the people in question, ranging from 'good' to 'best'. There are reasons for thinking that in eastern Sweden, where the majority of the 'good people' were described as relatives or 'bönder', the epithets were also used to mark status. In the first place, it is not likely that 'good' or 'best' refers to farming skill, excellence as a husband, or goodness of heart,[42] for if that were the case, there was a serious shortage of people with such qualities in Viking-Age Scandinavia (see App. 7(c)). I will return to consider what the epithet 'good' might mean, after first dealing with the 'Bönder' and the Relatives.

[38] Ög 64, 111, N19; Sö 4, 55, 137.

[39] For *snjallr* see Sö 155, 163, 320; *frækn*: Ög 81; Nä 18; *nýtr*: U 166; Nä 23; *hæfr*: U 289; Ög N18; **ufilan**: Sö 177.

[40] Sö 90, 112, 151, 158, 170, 367, N2 (*þróttr*); Ög 200 (*nýtr*).

[41] DR 344; Vg 155, 156; Ög 66; U 225, 323, 432.

[42] But cf. Wulf (1989).

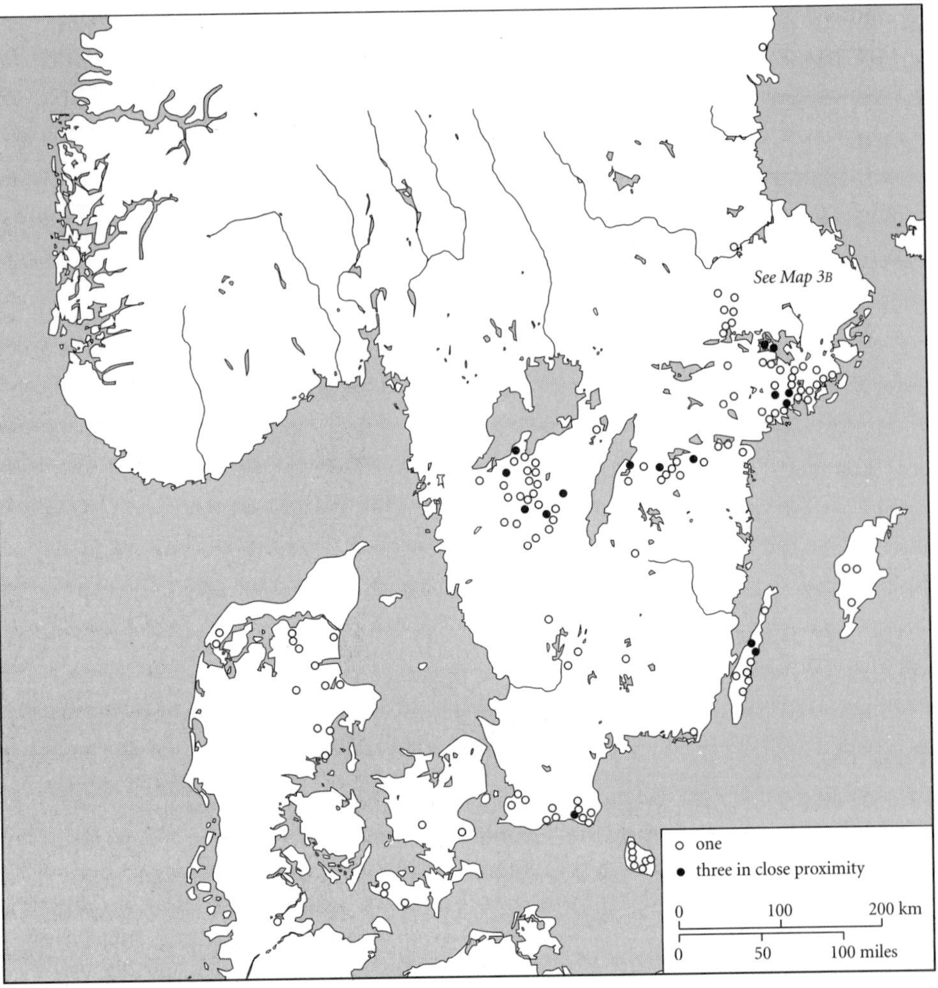

Map 3A. Distribution of 'good people' in Scandinavia, excluding Uppland

5.5.1. 'Bönder'

In 213 inscriptions we meet the word 'bonde', usually translated 'husband' when the sponsor is a woman, but in 34 inscriptions the sponsors are sons or other relatives,[43] and the question arises as to why, in these cases, the deceased is referred to as 'bonde' while so many others are not so termed (see App. 8). To be called a bonde obviously meant more than belonging to a landowning family; some inscriptions clearly show that the word

[43] e.g. Sö 72: 'Ulv and **maþur** raised this stone in memory of their kinsman (**friatr**) Styrman, their bonde . . .'; Sö 346: 'Slagve and Sven they raised this stone in memory of their bonde and brother'.

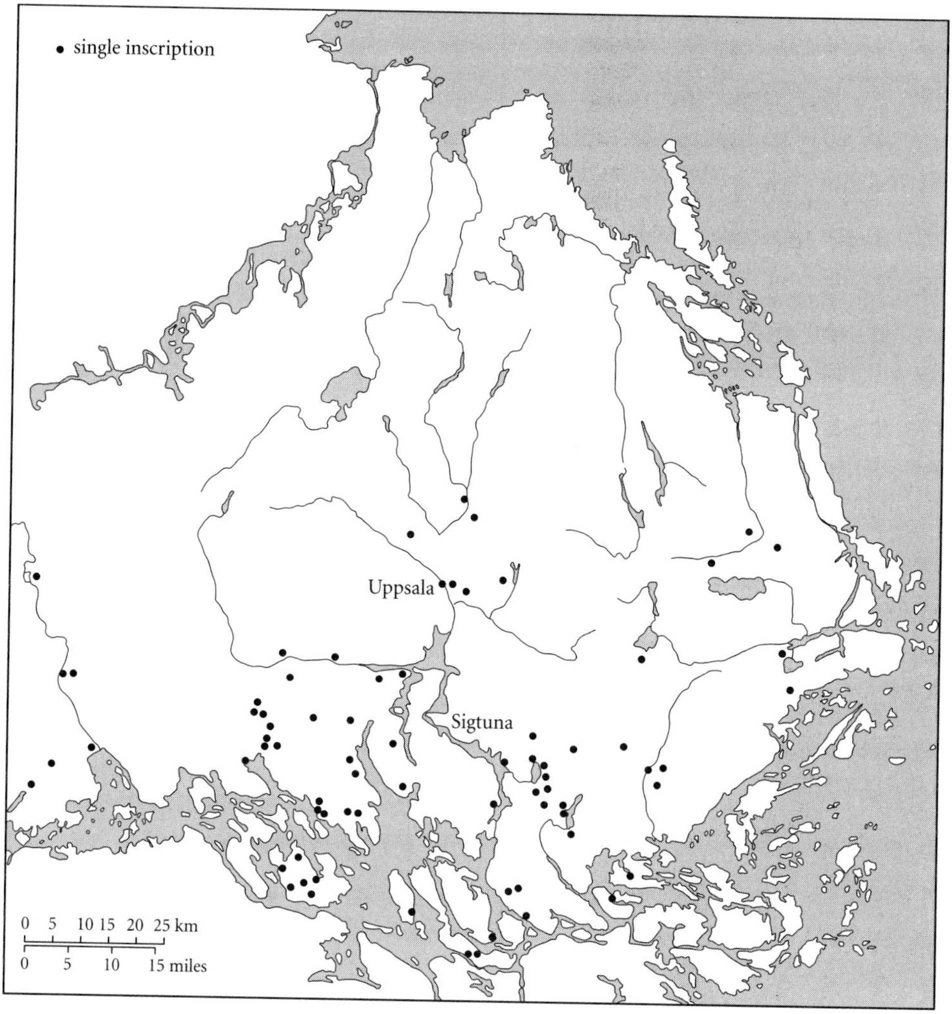

MAP 3B. Distribution of 'good people' in Uppland, Västmanland, and on Selö

implied responsibility for a family or household.[44] At Överselö, for example, a mother (together with her daughter) erected a stone in memory of two sons, only one of whom is referred to as a bonde and he is explicitly named as an heir.[45] In certain situations it was obviously important to state explicitly who had been the head of the family. For sons honouring

[44] See also Düwel (1975).

[45] Sö 208: 'Gudlög and Hjälmlög . . . they raised ——[b]ärn and in memory of Torsten, a good bonde, who lived in Fröslunda, Full[uges] heir, . . . who is Ännebrant's nephew (sister's son)'.

Table 5.2. *The four categories of* boni homines *(or 'good people')*

	'good', 'best'	Total	Percentage of total
Title-bearers	105	193	54.4
(*thegns, drengs, svens*[a]	*98*	*133*	*73.7*)
Relatives	101	1,559	6.5
(*male*[b]	*90*	*1,487*	*6.1*)
(*female*[b]	*11*	*72*	*15.3*)
'Bonde'			
='not husband'	25	34	73.5
='husband'	6	161	3.7
'Karl', 'man', 'the good', and unknown 'good'	26	360	
TOTAL	263[c]	2,307	11.4

[a] This group and the accompanying figures are subsumed in 'Title-bearers' above.
[b] This group and the accompanying figures are subsumed in 'Relatives' above.
[c] There are 263 'good people' in 260 inscriptions (cf. Table 5.1 above).

their father, however, it was unnecessary to refer to him as their bonde and they normally did so only when he could be called a 'good bonde'.

The connotation 'head of the family' is further abundantly evidenced by the 161 inscriptions in which a widow refers to 'her bonde' ('her' indicating that she had been formally married and was therefore lawfully under his power).[46] In only six cases is the bonde/husband said to have been 'good' and in one *nýtr*.[47] The fact that in fifteen inscriptions the widow used the epithet 'good' to qualify her husband's title or his role as a landowner, not his description as her bonde, supports the argument that 'good' referred to his social status, not to his quality as a husband.[48]

5.5.2. Relatives

The very small proportion of people commemorated as relatives who were described as 'good' (6.5%) would be remarkable if the word referred simply to character or disposition. A more plausible explanation for the relatively few 'good people' is that they, and their families, belonged to a distinct, well-respected social group. The interpretation of the epithet as a marker of status is further supported by the fact that several of the 'good people' are shown to have been important landowners by inscriptions that name

[46] In eighteen incomplete inscriptions it cannot be determined who the sponsor is—a wife, son, or other relative: Nä 9; Sö 314, 334; U 84, 526, 538(?), 568, 981, 1068, 1120; Ög 10, 140, N2; Öl 6, 32, 37, 113, 144.

[47] 'Good': Sö 94, 192; U 753; Ög 112, 160, 224. *Nýtr*: Ög 15.

[48] DR 277, 291; Sö 31, 157, 213, 338; U 20, 79, 143, 838, 873; Vg 150, 152, 154; Ög 200(?). Cf. Düwel (1975), 191–5.

the place where they lived, information that is relatively rare.[49] What is more, 'good people' were commemorated by relatively lavish monuments twice as often as those who were not so decribed.

Comparison of Maps 1A–B and 3A–B shows that the distribution of 'good people' in Denmark and Götaland is very much the same as that of the rune-stones in general. There is, however, no such correlation in Uppland and Södermanland. There are some concentrations: in Denmark and Västergötland, where almost all the 'good people' had titles, there are numerous districts in which over half the rune-stones commemorate 'good' men, but only four districts with more than four such monuments. And elsewhere in Scandinavia there are only eight districts with so many. The twelve districts and their totals are shown in Table 5.3.

It is remarkable that the proportion of 'good people' in Vallentuna hundred, the richest rune-stone district in Uppland, is only 6.9%, while that of Trögd hundred in south-west Uppland is 25%, a concentration that extends west into Västmanland and south into Södermanland on the island of Selö (Selebo district) in Lake Mälaren. It is even more remarkable that there is a dearth of 'good people' between the districts of Vallentuna and Trögd, i.e. around Sigtuna. The significance of these concentrations and contrasts is discussed in Chapter 7.3.5. The numerous 'good people' named on rune-stones elsewhere in Uppland and the East, where for most of the eleventh century kings had little power, show that this status was not conferred by kings. The 'good men' of the Scandinavian inscriptions are best understood as the equivalent of the *boni homines* familiar in other parts of early medieval Europe.[50] These were men acknowledged as trustworthy members of their communities who had a leading role in local affairs—for example, in assemblies, in making legal decisions, and as witnesses. The status was normally hereditary, passing from father to son, but it naturally affected the standing of the whole family, and it is therefore not surprising that the epithet 'good' could be given to sons, brothers, and even to sisters and daughters of 'good men'.

5.6. WOMEN AS LANDHOLDERS

The proportion of rune-stones commissioned by women serves to show how common it was for them to possess and dispose of property at that time. To raise a stone was a costly business, and women who did so on their own must have had adequate resources, whether inherited or acquired through marriage (as dowry or dower), and/or a share of the property they had held jointly with their husbands.

[49] Only in *c.*3% of *all* incriptions are there references to the place where people lived, while the proportion is almost 6% of the 'good-people inscriptions'.

[50] Niermeyer (1954–76), s.v. 'bono'.

TABLE 5.3. *'Good people': distribution in twelve districts where most often found*

District	Total no. of inscrs.	No. with 'good'	No. of 'good' with title
Denmark:			
Herrestad (Skåne)	7	6[a]	5
Västergötland:			
Skåning	7	6[b]	4
Kulling	7	6[c]	6
Åse	11	6[d]	5
Södermanland:			
Rönö	55	9[e]	2
Hölebo	26	8[f]	2
Selebo	37	7[g]	0
Sotholm	55	5[h]	0
Uppland:			
Trögd	52	13[i]	0
Vallentuna	101	7[j]	0
Åsunda	35	7 (6)[k]	3
Danderyd	54	5[l]	1
TOTAL	447	85 (86)	28

[a] Two are thegns (DR 293–4); three are drengs (DR 288–9, 339); one is an estate-holder (*búmaðr*, DR 291).

[b] Three are thegns (Vg 62, 73–4); one is a dreng (Vg 61); two are women (Vg 67 and 75).

[c] Two are thegns (Vg 151–2); two are drengs (Vg 153–4); two are svens (Vg 155–6).

[d] Four are thegns (Vg 101–3, 108); one is a dreng (Vg 112); one is either father or brother (Vg 110).

[e] Two have titles: one dreng (Sö 167), one captain (*stýrimaðr*, Sö 161); one is called 'the good' (Sö 130); the others are bönder and relatives (Sö 125, 136 ('best'), 138–9, 157, 374).

[f] One inscription mentions two thegns (Sö 34), the others bönder or relatives (Sö 19, 21–2, 28, 31, 38, 359).

[g] Sö 184, 192, 195, 208–9, 213–14. No titles.

[h] Sö 220, 231, 236, 252, 262. No titles.

[i] U 692, 697(?), 703, 707, 712, 714, 723, 727, 729, 733, 740, 751, 753.

[j] One inscription mentions a 'good man' (U 249), the others bönder or relatives (U 186, 191, 199=235, 208, 265, N17).

[k] Three inscriptions mention drengs (U 760=796, 767–8), the others relatives (U 763 and 764, both raised by the same men in memory of their father, and 770 raised by two daughters in memory of their father). U 781 is too incomplete to tell us who was 'good'.

[l] One dreng (U 143); the others are relatives (U 160–1, 171, N10).

Since almost 12% of all rune-stones were sponsored by women on their own, it appears that it was not unusual for women to have full social and economic responsibility. This proportion, however, is only a minimum; a further 15% of rune-stones were sponsored by women together with men (e.g. daughters, sisters, wives, or mothers together with sons or brothers of the deceased). Even if some of the women in this category were under male tutelage, at least half of them were widows and can be supposed to have been economically independent. The minimum figure for women's property ownership can, therefore, be raised to *c*.20%.

As an average, however, this figure is misleading since joint sponsorship is very unusual outside Uppland, Södermanland, and Öland. In Uppland *c*.24% of all rune-stones were jointly commissioned by men and women, but in Denmark the proportion is only *c*.2.5%, and in Norway there is no example of joint sponsorship. This regional variation is consistent with the other variations discussed in Chapter 4 (esp. 4.2 and 4.4). Where royal power was stronger, women normally appear as sponsors only when there were no husbands or kinsmen to take the responsibility, while in areas where it was weaker, as in large parts of Uppland, women could obviously present their claims and declarations together with kinsmen.

As already noted, women seldom inherited from their brothers, somewhat more often from their fathers, but as often as men from their children.[51] Half the mothers commemorating sons did so on their own, but many of the others who acted as sponsors together with their husbands were likely to survive them, and be left with the responsibility of looking after the family property. There are many good examples of this. An inscription at Högby in Östergötland was sponsored by Torgärd, who had probably lost her parents and had no surviving male relatives. She commemorated her maternal uncle and his four brothers (Ög 81; Pl. 24):

Torgärd raised this stone in memory of Assur, her mother's brother who died in the east in Greece.

The good man Gulle / got five sons:
At Fyris (?) Asmund fell / the unfrightened dreng
Assur died / in the east in Greece;
Halvdan was / **a Hulmi** killed,
Kare (killed?) **at Uddi** (?); / also Bue (is) dead.
Torkel carved the runes.

In Södermanland Sigrid commemorated her second husband Holmger on Ramsundsberget and built a bridge there for his soul (Sö 101: see Ch. 6.1 and Pl. 27). She had earlier been married to a certain Spjut (Sö 106), together with whom she had a son Alrik, who was apparently dead. With Holmger she had a daughter Ginnlög and a son Sigröd, but since Sigröd was not her co-sponsor, he was probably also dead.[52] Whether Sigrid also survived her daughter we will never know; what we do know, however, is that the daughter herself survived her husband, Assur (U 617). Elsewhere in Södermanland, in Ludgo parish, Tora survived both husband and son

[51] See Chs. 3 and 4. Women inheriting from their *brothers*: (*a*) alone, *c*.4.5%; (*b*) jointly with brothers, *c*.12% of the cases (=class 2 in the list at Ch. 3.4). Women inheriting from their *fathers*: (*a*) alone, *c*.6%; (*b*) jointly with brothers: *c*.17% of the cases (class 1). Women inheriting from their *children*: (*a*) alone, *c*.22.5%; (*b*) jointly with fathers, *c*.26.5% (class 3).

[52] Cf. Lindkvist (1997).

PLATE 24. Ög 81, Högby. Commemoration of five brothers by their sister's daughter, Torgärd (for the inscription, see text immediately above).

(Sö 137 and 138), and in Överselö parish Gudlög was left alone with her daughter Hjälmlög after the death of her husband and two sons (Sö 206 and 208).

The complicated case in Uppland of Gerlög and Inga, mother and daughter who both survived sons and husbands has been discussed above (pp. 49–51 and Fig. 3.1). There are many others, if simpler. In Spånga parish we meet another Inga who had inherited from her sons (U 72 and 73). After her death her brothers, Gärdar and Jorund, inherited from her, and—as in Gerlög's case—we can only speculate what happened to the inheritance after that. We can be fairly certain that Gerlög did not leave any heirs, and it is at least likely that neither Gärdar nor Jorund did so either. Since both the inscriptions describing these inheritance cases (U 29 and 73) are among the very few that do not state who sponsored them, it may well be that in these cases there was no claimant other than the Church, which then took responsiblity for the commemorations.

Other women who were left on their own are Holmlög, who survived her husband, son, and brother (U 285 and 286), and Holmfrid who commemorated her husband and two sons with both a stone and a bridge (U 854). Women in the Jarlabanke family met with similar fates: Estrid survived two husbands, Östen and Ingvar (U 136 and 310), and at least three sons (U 101 and 137); likewise both her daughter-in-law Jorun and her granddaughter-in-law Kättilö survived their husbands (U 143 and 142). There are many other examples.

Many of these women were obviously left with a considerable fortune, thus enabling them to sponsor grand monuments, and sometimes (as in some of the above examples) to build bridges. At Nordre Dynna in Opland (Norway) the widow Gunnvor commemorated her daughter with an elaborate rune-stone and a bridge (NIyR 68), and at Lösing in Östergötland the widow Afrid (?) also had a bridge built, honouring her two sons (Ög 157). During the missionary era to build a bridge and so improve communications was considered a meritorious act, earning divine favour. As will be shown in Chapter 6.3 women are over-represented among the bridge-stones (both as sponsors and commemorated), indicating their active interest in Christianity and readiness to respond to exhortations to support the Church with 'soul-gifts'. There is much to suggest that in Scandinavia, as elsewhere, women were among the first to accept and encourage the Christian faith. From the very beginning it was women who were particularly attracted by Christian teaching, and among the earliest Christians the proportion of women, especially of the upper classes, was larger than that of men.[53] It is probably significant that in describing Anskar's mission in ninth-century Sweden, Rimbert has women represent pious generosity.[54] And in Birka, the scene of the first known Christian mission to Sweden, the earliest objects that can be associated with the new faith, namely cross-shaped pendants, have all been found in women's graves.[55]

This is not the place to discuss the reasons for women's particular interest and involvement in Christianity; suffice it to say that in Viking-Age

[53] von Harnack (1908), 73; Brown (1961).
[54] *VA* ch. 20. See also B. Sawyer (1990), 278.
[55] Gräslund (1987*a*), 81–94, esp. 90–2.

Scandinavia there were many independent women who could exercise pious generosity if they wished, and we have seen that there were indeed many who did so. Apart from giving alms or improving communications, Christian charity could also be expressed by building a *seluhus* ('soul-house') or a *likhus*, apparently intended as a resting place for travellers (see Ch. 6.3)—an act that would benefit the builders' souls. It is interesting that in two of the three such enterprises mentioned in our material, women were involved; in one of them the *seluhus* is said to have been built by a husband in memory of his wife. We know about this thanks to the couple's two daughters, who commemorated their father by raising a stone and constructing a ford (U 996).

These road-improving sisters are an appropriate example with which to conclude this section. In a real as well as figurative sense they neatly symbolize the bridge-building functions of women in the runic material, both literally as bridge builders and figuratively as bridges between different families over which property passed by means of reverse inheritance.[56]

5.7. TRAVELLERS

The widely accepted view that it was Viking activity that gave rise to the fashion for erecting rune-stones to commemorate people who had died abroad (see Pl. 25) has been rejected above (Ch. 1.3.1). Another commonly held view is that these 'travellers' stones' can provide valuable information about Viking activity, showing what areas in Europe were most affected, what districts, or even villages sent out their men, and the social and economic status of the families of the travellers.[57] No doubt these travellers' stones do reflect Viking activity, but certainly not in a very representative way; their distribution is extremely uneven (see Table 5.4 and App. 9).

If we were to judge by the distribution of stones as shown in Table 5.4, Norway took part in hardly any plunderings or settlements abroad, and Denmark on only a very limited scale, while eastern Sweden, especially Södermanland, appears as the leading Viking province in Scandinavia. Since we know this was not the case the question arises as to what these stones reflect other than Viking activity; why are travels mentioned in these comparatively few inscriptions and not in others commemorating people who may well also have been abroad?

5.7.1. Who were the travellers?

According to Sven B. F. Jansson, 'the sensitive reader may catch in many of their inscriptions the Viking's love of adventure and exploits of boisterous daring'.[58] One has to be extremely sensitive indeed to catch this; it is only in a few inscriptions that we find echoes of pride, and praise of warlike qualities.

[56] B. Sawyer (1991*a*), 211–24. [57] See Larsson (1990). [58] Jansson (1987), 38.

Plate 25. Sm 101, Nävelsjö. Many of the 'travellers' stones' were cenotaphs, as here where the deceased had been buried in Bath. *Inscription*: 'Gunnkel raised this stone in memory of Gunnar, his father, Rode's son. Helge placed him, his brother, in a stone tomb in England, in Bath.'

The fact is that most of the travellers' inscriptions, like the others, are very brief, only stating that someone has gone and/or died abroad, often with a prayer that God will help his soul. It should also be pointed out that some of these inscriptions emphatically do not refer to Viking activity: in two of them we read about people whose function had been to organize

Table 5.4. *Travellers: distribution according to region*

Region	No. of travellers' stones	Regional total of inscrs.	Travellers as percentage of total
Denmark	16	168	9.5
Bornholm	1	31	3.2
Norway	3	51	5.9
Småland	9	116	7.8
Västergötland	10	156	6.4
Östergötland	14	212	6.6
Södermanland	64	352	18.2
Uppland	76	1,016	7.5
Gotland	6	30	20.0
Gästrikland	2	15	
Närke	1	19	
Västmanland	8	25	
Other regions	0	116	
TOTAL	210	2,307	9.1

the defence *against* Vikings (U 617; Sö N1); in two other cases the deceased were merchants (G 207; Sö 198); and in three inscriptions we meet people who went abroad for religious reasons (U 136, 605; Vg 81).[59]

A special group consists of those who are known to have served a (Danish) king—in one case King Sven Forkbeard, in five cases Knut the Great.[60] In six other cases it can be deduced that the deceased had been in royal service.[61]

There were other leaders besides kings; we meet one in Denmark (DR 117: Thore), one in Västmanland (Vs 5: Spjallbode), one in Östergötland (Ög 68: Väring), and several in Södermanland and Uppland (five different leaders in each province),[62] the most famous of whom was Ingvar (men-

[59] U 136 in memory of Östen, who went to Jerusalem (Ch. 5, Pl. 20); U 605 in memory of Ingerun, who wanted to go to Jerusalem; and Vg 81 sponsored by Benedikt 'the Rome-traveller'.

[60] Sven: DR 3; Knut: No 184; Sö 14; Ög 111 (**kuti** has also been interpreted as the name 'Göt'); U 194, 344.

[61] DR 66 and Vg 40, 'when kings fought'; DR 154, X's 'hirdman' (or 'retainer'); Sö 160, a man who died in England, *i liþi* ('in the retinue'); U 241, a man who had taken two *gälder* ('payments') in England; U 668, a man who sat in the west in *þikaliþi* ('in the *thing*-retinue').

[62] Sö 137, Öpir; 155, O(lev?); 217, Gudve; 260, Ulv; 338, Torsten. U 112, Ragnvald; 344, Toste and Torkel; 611, Fröger; also Ingvar: see next note.

tioned in twenty-five inscriptions![63]), who led an expedition to the East that ended in total disaster. It seems as if there were more opportunities for private enterprises in eastern Scandinavia than in western Scandinavia, probably because of the weaker royal power there. This is also indicated by the fact that 52.5% of the travellers' inscriptions mention people who went east, while only 27% mention people who went west.[64]

All these leaders—kings and others—must have had much larger bands of warriors than is indicated by the runic inscriptions. Why are travels mentioned in only the 210 cases listed in Table 5.4? The most likely explanation is that they reflect the concern of people at home rather than pride in foreign adventures; many serious questions about the ownership of property arose when a man, or woman, went far away from home. The medieval laws have regulations for such situations, but for the Viking period we can only deduce what was customary. It is, however, likely that after a certain period an official decision had to be made, presumably in a local *thing*, to allow the heir(s) to take over. Even if the traveller was reported as having died abroad, a formal recognition of the fact was probably necessary, even more so if nothing was known about his fate. Forty-eight inscriptions only state that the person 'was' or 'had gone' abroad, and these include nine of the twenty-five Ingvar-stones. We can be relatively sure that even travellers who were not explicitly said to have died abroad were regarded as deceased; if they had returned home this would have been stated, as in at least three inscriptions (DR 3; Sö 55; U 1016).

The following inscriptions illustrate some of the problems that had to be solved when travellers did not return.

1. When should the inheritance be divided?

Alve had this stone raised in memory of Arnfast, her son. He went east to Gårdarike. (U 636)

In this case the mother had obviously not heard conclusively that her son was dead, and we can deduce that after a certain period a decision was made at a *thing* to accept that he was, so that his heirs could inherit.

2. If someone was away for a long time, during which much could happen, who was then the rightful heir?

Kår had this stone raised in memory of Horse (?), his father, and Kabbe in memory of his relative-in-law. He went boldly, acquired property out in Greece for his heir. (U 792)

[63] Ingvar-stones: Vs 19; Ög 145(?), 155; Sö 9, 96(?), 105, 107, 108, 131, 173, 179, 254, 277, 281, 287, 320, 335; U 439, N32, 644 and 654 (double monument), 661, 778, 837, 1143.

[64] Proportion of inscriptions mentioning people who went both east and west, 1.6%; of people who went south, 3.3%; north, 0.5%; and who travelled inside Scandinavia, 14.8% (of 183 known cases).

If Kår had been an adult, he would most probably have sponsored this stone on his own, so the fact that a male relative (an in-law) acts as co-sponsor indicates that Kår was very young (perhaps even new-born) when his father left home. Considering the extremely high rate of infant mortality, there was a great risk that Kår might die before his father, in which case the inheritance would go to the paternal relatives. For the *maternal* relatives it would therefore be important to deal with the inheritance while the son was still alive, and—as in the former case—a formal recognition of his father's death is likely to have been made after a certain period, so that the son's inheritance could be rescued. An adult relative (most likely maternal!) helped by looking after the son's (and his mother's) interests. According to the older Västgöta law (of the thirteenth century) no one could inherit from an individual abroad other than the man or woman who was the heir when that individual left home.[65]

3. What if the heir himself was abroad?

Härtrud raised this stone in memory of her son Smed, a good dreng. Halvboren, his brother sits in Gårdarike [Russia]. Brand carved . . . (Öl 58; see Pl. 26)

Since the surviving brother, Halvboren, was far away in Russia, he was probably not allowed to inherit. According to the older Västgöta law an individual being far away from home, could not inherit from anyone at home.[66] Thus, Härtrud was the only heir after her son.

4. What if the heir was abroad—but returned home?

Ragnvald had the runes cut in memory of Fastvi, his mother, Onäm's daughter, she died in Ed. God help her soul. Ragnvald had the runes cut. He was in Greece, he was the chieftain of the following (*liðs forungi*). (U 112)

In this case the sponsor, Ragnvald, was eager to state that he had come home in time to look after his maternal inheritance.

5. Who survived whom?

Tora raised this stone in memory of Öpir, her husband.
This stone / stands in memory of Öpir
in the *thing*-place / in memory of Tora's husband.
In the west / he armed his men . . .[67] (Sö 137)

The end of the inscription (see note 67) is difficult to interpret, but it is likely that one of Öpir's sons had accompanied his father on this voyage.[68]

65 The older Västgöta law, see 'Ärvdabalken' ('Inheritance section') 12, in *SLL* v.

66 'Ärvdabalken' 12, *SLL* v. The formulation is 'sitting in Greece', which has been interpreted as meaning being far away from home.

67 *SRI* suggests the following interpretation of the last part of the inscription: 'the son saw it there. The dreng is now unfortunately dead, even if (as) praised (as here)', an interpretation that is, however, very uncertain.

68 For a discussion about Öpir and the possible connection between Sö 137, 138, and N13, see above, p. 99.

PLATE 26. Öl 58, Gårdby. The commemoration records that the deceased's heir is living abroad (for the inscription, see text above).

If so, it would be important to state who had survived whom, because that would decide to whom Öpir's inheritance would go. However the last part of this inscription should be interpreted, it seems that it was intended to show that the son survived his father. This explanation is supported by another inscription, commemorating the son:

> Here stands / the stone in memory of *the good*
> *heir of Öpir* / and of Torun (=Tora),
> of (?) Gylla's brother. / May God help his spirit. (Sö 138)

The issue was thus what would happen to Öpir's property: if it could not be decided who died first, or if the father had survived his son, the inheritance would go to the father's kin (both paternal and maternal), but if the son survived his father, he would inherit, *and after him, his mother, Tora.* There was perhaps yet another inheritance involved, namely from Öpir's sister Gylla, that would now also revert to Tora.[69]

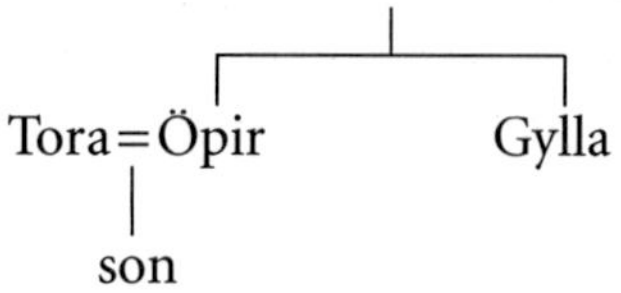

6. What if someone planned to go abroad?

Ingerun, Hård's daughter, had these rune cut in memory of herself. She wants to go east and out to Jerusalem. Fot carved the runes. (U 605)

As with those who wanted to enter a monastery or convent, people who planned a distant pilgrimage had to arrange for the division of their inheritance before leaving. This is obviously the reason why Ingerun sponsored a stone in memory of herself.

Thus, far from reflecting Viking expeditions in particular or travelling patterns in general the travellers' inscriptions first and foremost reflect the concerns of the relatives left at home.

5.8. CONCLUSION

The main arguments of this chapter are the following.

1. In western Scandinavia most sponsors represent a fairly restricted élite, while in the East they represent a broader section of the landowning group. In Denmark and Västergötland many sponsors and deceased are distinguished by titles and/or epithets of praise, showing their high status in society and indicating a political organization that was more developed than in the East.

2. The epithet 'good' has been interpreted as being used exclusively about people whose special status was recognized in their own

[69] Linguistically it is uncertain whether Gylla is Öpir's sister or daughter (i.e. the sister of the deceased son). Since it is stressed that the deceased was 'the heir' (in the singular), there are two possibilities; if Gylla was Öpir's daughter, she was probably already dead—otherwise she would have been another heir of Öpir and Tora—or, which is more likely, she was indeed Öpir's sister.

communities and who were the equivalent of *boni homines* elsewhere in Europe.

3. Women are generally well represented as sponsors, more so in the East than in western Scandinavia, but everywhere many were left on their own, often with considerable wealth, some of which was donated to the Church.

4. The travellers' stones do not reflect Viking expeditions or travelling patterns in general. The reason we hear about travellers is because of questions about their property and inheritance.

6

CONVERSION

It is clear that the erection of rune-stones answered religious and social needs in a period of transition; as pointed out in Chapter 1.3.2, the simple burial customs of the Christians broke dramatically with old traditions. Missionaries objected to the building of lavish constructions over the graves and to the rich furnishing of them; instead, they urged relatives to make gifts on behalf of the dead to them as representatives of the Church. Before churches and churchyards were built and became the natural places for memorials, ostentatious rune-stones in public places met the continued demand for the display of family wealth and status in a way that was probably also encouraged by the Church. The Christian rune-monuments of Scandinavia can be seen as an equivalent to the local shrines built by newly converted aristocrats on the Continent some five hundred years earlier; having made such provision for the memory of themselves and their kin, they were content with the humble Christian burial in nothing but a shroud.[1]

Another fundamental break with tradition was the Christian emphasis on the individual, the preoccupation with the world beyond death and each individual's soul. In pre-Christian society a person's status—in life as in death—reflected that of his/her family and kin, but the missionaries taught that all would be judged according to their actions, good and bad. People could improve their chances of salvation by almsgiving and gifts to the Church; in return the clergy would say prayers on their behalf. Thus people were urged to 'give for the sake of their souls', and great emphasis was placed on the need for a Mass to be said for the 'deliverance' of each individual soul from the purging fire.[2] On the Continent in the sixth century some new converts even took care of their pre-Christian ancestors, building chapels over the graves of pagan relatives to ensure that they too lay close to the saving Mass.[3] In Scandinavia, before the building of churches began, this is parallelled by the many converts who sought to help both their pagan relatives and themselves by supporting the missionaries and erecting rune-stones.

[1] Brown (1997), 164.

[2] It has been debated when the idea of a purging fire first developed, but since it was part of Pope Gregory the Great's teaching (in the 6th cent.), it seems safe to assume that it must have been firmly rooted and widespread in 11th-cent. Europe. See e.g. Brown (1997), 162 ff.

[3] Brown (1997), 164 ff.

Could tenth- and eleventh-century rune-stones have had these social and religious functions? The answer depends on the interpretation of the 'neutral' stones, i.e. the monuments that lack crosses and/or Christian prayers (on average 34%; in western Scandinavia the proportion is much higher—in Norway 70% and in Denmark 83%—while in Uppland it is as low as 20%).[4] Previously rune-stones without Christian symbols or prayers were regarded as pagan, while today most scholars agree that most of them are Christian monuments.[5] Some scholars go even further and suggest that the very act of erecting a rune-stone was designed to gain indulgence; even inscriptions without the prayer 'God help his/her soul' or the explicit formulation 'for X's soul' have been interpreted as meaning the same, the argument being that a cross or even the simple formulation 'in memory of X' was considered enough, meaning, in effect, 'for X's soul'.[6]

This interpretation is questionable; if 'in memory of X' was enough, why do so many sponsors add prayers for the soul? Instead of being facultative, the prayers ought to be seen as important additions, expressing the performative function of the rune-stones inscribed with them; they urge every passer-by to pray for the soul of the deceased! Further, it surely cannot have been enough to erect a rune-stone in order to gain indulgence; in exchange for indulgence the Church wanted financial support, be it money, land, other wealth, or enterprises like the building of churches and bridges. In demonstrating acceptance of the Christian faith, the rune-stones no doubt let us meet people who supported the Church in different ways, but it is only in about 150 cases that the nature of that support is explicit, and it generally took the form of bridge-building. It seems likely that in most cases donations were made to the Church, especially in eastern Sweden, where several family members are frequently named as sponsors; as in medieval wills, it was probably necessary to have the names of all potential heirs documented in the inscriptions, testifying to their consent.

6.1. TRANSITION: PAGAN AND/OR CHRISTIAN?

Even if many scholars agree that most rune-stones are Christian monuments, there is disagreement about the number that can be considered pagan, mainly because of the problematic interpretation of some depictions of pagan myths and apparently pagan formulas. Some pagan motifs were taken over by the Christians and reinterpreted. Scenes from the

[4] In the provinces north of Uppland, as well as on Bornholm, the proportion of 'neutral' stones is as low as *c.*10%; in Södermanland it is *c.*25%, while in Småland and Östergötland the proportion is *c.*40%, and in Västergötland as high as *c.*50%.

[5] Among earlier scholars should be mentioned Toni Schmid (1934), 52 and 108; for recent views, see Henrik Williams (1996*b*), 292 ff.

[6] So for example *SRI* ix. 347 f. (Elias Wessén). See also Peterson (1991), 341–51, and Williams (1996*b*), 293 ff.

Plate 27. Sö 101, Ramsundsberget (on a rockface). Carvings of scenes from the *Sigurd saga* (see also n. 7). *Inscription*: 'Si(g)rid, mother of Alrik, daughter of Orm, made this bridge for Holmger's soul, her husband and Sigröd's father.'

famous saga about Sigurd, who killed the dragon Fafnir, are common in medieval churches and occur at an early date on rune-stones in Södermanland (Sö 101 (see Pl. 27) and 327) and perhaps also in Gästrikland (Gs 2 and 9). Fafnir the dragon symbolizes Evil, and Sigurd, the triumphant Christ.[7] Similarly, the episode when Thor used the head of an ox to catch the World-serpent, a scene found on an Upplandic rune-stone (U 1161; see Pl. 28), has been interpreted as symbolizing God using Christ as a bait to catch Leviathan.[8]

The question is, however, how far we dare go in supposing that the use of pagan motifs and invocations prefigure Christian ideas; in current research there is a tendency to interpret most of them as so doing; even

[7] In the *Sigurd saga* (or more correctly the *Völsunga saga*), the king's son Sigurd is incited by his foster-father, Regin the smith, to recover the great gold treasure that his brother Fafnir/Favne, in the shape of a dragon, is jealously guarding. With the help of a sword that Regin has forged, Sigurd kills the dragon, and in the carving on Sö 101 we see him frying its heart. According to the saga he burns himself, and, when he puts his finger into his mouth, he suddenly understands the song of the birds, who tell him that Regin intends to deceive him. They advise Sigurd to kill the smith. To the the left we see Regin lying with his head cut off and with his tools beside him. To the right of Sigurd his horse stands loaded with the gold treasure. We cannot be certain how the inscription Sö 101 is related to the scenes depicted there; although it has been suggested that the connection is simply the close similarity between the names Sigurd and Sigröd, a deeper symbolism may be involved. If Sigrid's son Alrik is the same Alrik who had a stone erected nearby to commemorate his father, a Viking chieftain (Sö 106), her inheritance from them may have consisted of riches plundered abroad, a pagan 'gold treasure' she used for a pious—Christian—purpose, that is, to build a bridge close to this inscription for the soul of her second husband, the father of Sigröd.

[8] The motif with riders and women with drinking-horns on some Gotlandic stones (G 59, 77, 92, 110), traditionally interpreted as depicting Valhalla, has been reinterpreted by Michael Srigley, who suggests that, instead, the carvings represent scenes from Troy; see Srigley (1988–9), 161–87.

PLATE 28. U 1161, Altuna church. Thor using the head of an ox to catch the World-serpent. *Inscription*: 'Vifast, Folkad, **kuþar** had this stone raised in memory of their father Holmfast (and of their brother) Arnfast. Father and son were both burnt in. And Balle and Frösten, Livsten's retainers (carved).'

the so-called Odin's masks have been interpreted as depicting Christ's face.[9] I will treat the seemingly pagan features in three different groups: spells; invocations to Thor and Thor's hammer; masks.

[9] Hultgård (1992), 89–91. For the discussion on 'interpretatio Christiana' and 'praefiguratio', see Wamers (1997), 82–107.

6.1.1. Spells

In seven inscriptions (five in Denmark and two in Västergötland) we find spells, cursing anyone who disturbs the monument: for instance, 'May he become a *ræte* who damages this stone or drags it from here' (DR 230, see Ch. 5, Pl. 17); 'May he become a *ræte* and an *arg(r)* woman who cuts the stone to pieces' (Vg 67). The meaning of *ræte* is not clear; most scholars agree, however, that it is highly pejorative; suggested translations are 'outlaw', 'villain', 'miscreant/vandal'. *Arg(r)* denotes someone who is a coward, being 'un-manly', often in connection with sexual perversions. Since the use of magic and such pagan curses cannot have been acceptable to Christians, these seven inscriptions must be regarded as explicitly pagan.

6.1.2. Invocations to Thor and representations of Thor's hammer

In four or five inscriptions we meet invocations to Thor: 'May Thor hallow (these runes/this monument)!', three times in Denmark (DR 110, 209, and 220); once in Västergötland (Vg 150, see Ch. 5, Pl. 22), and possibly once in Södermanland (Sö 140). Some scholars hold that these invocations do not express pagan beliefs but are an adaptation of the Christian custom of blessing. It is argued that Thor, being a heavenly god who fights giants and monsters, that is the powers of Chaos, was more acceptable to the Christians than other pagan deities and symbolizes Christ fighting against Evil.[10] Other interpretations have been offered for Vg 150, in which **uiki** is translated not as 'hallow' but 'slay' ('may Thor slay . . .'), turning it into a threat against vandals, and for Sö 140, where the word **siþi** is said not to mean 'protect' (equivalent to 'hallow') but *sejdkarl*, implying that Thor was a magician, thus expressing Christian contempt for the old gods.[11]

If these interpretations of Vg 150 and Sö 140 are correct, it makes it more likely that the invocations to Thor are explicitly pagan—even if the formula was influenced by Christianity.

This has a bearing on the motif of Thor's hammer which is found on five rune-stones, in Denmark, Västergötland, and Södermanland.[12] It has been argued that the hammer could be interpreted as a cross, and the question is whether this ambiguity was intended, whether it expresses caution or syncretism—or should be interpreted as prefiguring the Christian cross.[13] Had there been more examples of Thor's hammer and invocations to Thor, the 'interpretatio Christiana' of these monuments would have been plausible, but since examples of both are so rare—and predominantly found in Denmark and Västergötland among the earliest inscriptions, it seems safer to regard them either as pagan or as reflecting uncertainty during a transitional period.

10 For a survey, see Wamers (1997), 85–7.
11 Williams (1996*b*), 299, 302–3.
12 DR 26, 120; Vg 113; Sö 86, 111.
13 Wamers (1997), 92–7.

6.1.3. Masks

Twelve rune-stones have facial masks: six in Denmark, three in Södermanland, and one each in Småland, Västergötland, and Närke.[14] These were formerly interpreted as depictions of Odin, but it has recently been suggested that the three from Södermanland depict Christ's face.[15] Since there is only one certain depiction of Christ on a rune-stone in this period—and then full-figure—on the Jelling stone erected by Harald Bluetooth (DR 42: see Excursus, Pl. 38 A–C), this suggestion is implausible; even if the faces on the three Södermanland stones are—to a modern eye—perceived as less terrifying than those in Denmark, it remains to be explained why we should find depictions of Christ's face in these three monuments only—and only in Södermanland. The stones with masks are all early. The four of them with crosses (DR 258 and 314; Sö 112 and 167) may be considered typical of the period of transition, but the others, one of which also has a spell (DR 81), ought to be treated as pagan. See Plate 29.

Although we can never be certain what function these formulas and pictures had—whether they were expressions of pagan beliefs, syncretism, or Christian thinking—it is best to treat them as non-Christian, expressing pagan belief or uncertainty. It should also be noted that most examples of these 'pagan features' are in Denmark and Västergötland, areas where Christianity was introduced by royal authority and where some manifestation of pagan reaction might be expected; in Uppland, where the Christianization was voluntary and thus a much slower process, there was a need for the assertion of Christian rather than pagan belief.

6.2. PAGAN FEATURES

6.2.1. Lamentations and revenge

An age-old and world-wide custom was to honour the dead by funeral lamentation; the dirge of lament could range from a formless outcry to a 'high order of poetic and musical expression approaching the lyric elegy and the epic lay'.[16] The Church opposed this custom, partly because it competed with its own funeral rituals, and partly because—in cases of homicide—it was an incitement to revenge. Carol Clover points out that the laments 'often combine praise for the dead persons with expressions of fear or self-pity at being left alone and perhaps unprotected'.[17] Lamentational poems are known in Icelandic literature, where there is much to indicate that the care of family honour was largely the responsibility of

[14] DR 62, 66, 81, 258, 314, 335; Sm 103; Sö 112, 167, 367; Vg 106; Nä 34.
[15] Hultgård (1992), 84 ff., 89.
[16] Clover (1986), 163. The quotation is from Brakely (1950), 755.
[17] Clover (1986), 163.

PLATE 29. Sö 112, Kolunda, Stenkvista parish. Rune-stone with both a mask and a Christian cross. *Inscription*: 'Vigdärv and Djärv raised this stone in memory of Torkel, their father, a strong thegn (*þróttr þiagn*)'.

women.[18] This corresponds well with what is known about women's leading role in the funeral rituals of many pre-Christian cultures. It is, therefore, interesting that women are well represented among inscriptions in poetic form; in one case it is explicitly said that the wife had produced (or commissioned) a lament for her husband: on two of the Bällsta rune-stones in Uppland (U 225 and 226) we read:

18 Clover (1986), 175–83. Cf. Mundal (1983), 11–25, and (1992), 69–84, esp. 77 f.

May there be no mightier / memorials
than those Ulv's sons / made in memory of him,
snjallir svæinar, ['able warriors'] / in memory of their father.

They raised the stones / and made the staff
also, the mighty one, / as marks of honour (?).
Likewise Gyrid / loved her husband;
thus in a lament / he will be commemorated.[19]
Gunnar cut the stone.

In Aspa Tora was left alone after the deaths of her husband and son; the following two inscriptions may well have been part of her lament (Sö 137 and 138):

. . . . .
This stone / stands in memory of Öpir
in the *thing*-place / in memory of Tora's husband.
In the west he / armed his men . . .

Here stands / the stone in memory of the good
heir of Öpir / and (of) Torun (=Tora),
(of ?) Gylla's brother. / May God help his spirit.

Likewise, the widow Tola in Gripsholm was left alone and commemorated her son Harald in the following terms (Sö 179):

Tola had this stone raised in memory of her son Harald, Ingvar's brother.
They fared *drængila* ['in a warlike manner'] / far for gold
and in the east / gave the eagle (food).
(They) died in the south / in Serkland.

Torgärd in Högby (Östergötland) probably survived parents, siblings, and all her maternal kin. The following inscription may have been part of her lament (Ög 81, see Ch. 5, Pl. 24):

Torgärd raised this stone in memory of Assur, her mother's brother who died in the east in Greece.
The good man Gulle / got five sons:
At Fyris (?) Asmund fell / the unfrightened dreng
Assur died / in the east in Greece;
Halvdan was / **a Hulmi** killed,
Kare (killed?) **at Uddi** (?); / also Bue (is) dead.
Torkel carved the runes.

[19] U 226 (Bällsta): 'ok Gyriði gats at veri, þy man i *grati* getit lata' has traditionally been translated: 'Gyrid too loved her husband; thus she will think of him *in tears*.' According to Jón Helgason the preposition *i* does not allow the translation 'tears', and, instead—by analogy with the Eddic titles *Oddrunargratr* and *Mariugratr*—he translates the noun *grátr* with 'lament', a translation enthusiastically endorsed by the Swedish runologist Sven B. F. Jansson. See Helgason (1944), 160 f., and Jansson (1963), 127 f., 136 f.

Kättilö in Turinge was not left alone after her husband's death, but she may still have been responsible for the following poem (Sö 338, see Ch. 1, Pl. 5):

Kättel and Björn they raised this stone in memory of Torsten, their father, Anund in memory of his brother, and *huskarla* (the 'housecarls') in memory of *iafna* ('the just one' ?), Kättilö in memory of her husband:

> The brothers were / among the best men
> in the land, / and out in the host (*liþi*)
> treated their / retainers well.
> He fell in battle / east in Russia
> the host's captain (*liðs forungi*) / of 'landmen' the best.

Whether or not the Vallentuna widow Ingeberg's little poem could be called a lament, it is at least the oldest example of end-rhyme in Swedish literature (U 215 and 214):

[U 215] Ragnhild and Ulvhild had this stone raised in memory of their father and brother . . . [U 214] and Ingeberg in memory of her husband:

> He drowned in the Holm's sea,
> his ship sank bodily;
> those who lived were only three.[20]

In Norra Härene the widow Åsa raised a rune-stone in memory of her husband, together with her four sons (Vg 59):

Rävning, Gälle, Brynjulv, and Gävulv set this stone in memory of Fot, their father, a very good thegn.

> Åsa her husband's / memory has honoured
> in a way that a wife / will hereafter never do.
> Hjälm and Hjälle carved the runes.

What did Åsa mean by saying that she has honoured her husband in a way that no wife will do hereafter? Åsa may have been aware that she was living in a period of transition and may simply have meant that 'hereafter' the dead would not be honoured by rune-stones but by grave-slabs in churchyards; on the other hand, the poetic form of the inscription may indicate that she had honoured her husband with an 'old-fashioned' lament.

As pointed out above, laments could serve the purpose of reminding relatives and friends of their duty to take revenge, a characteristic of the pre-Christian mentality described in Old Norse literature. It has been argued that revenge does not necessarily mean a pagan way of thinking; the Old Testament talks about God as vengeful, and thus such a prayer as in G 134, 'May God fail those who failed him', should not be considered typical of continued pagan values but, rather, as in full accord with Christian teaching.[21] This may have been be so, but as this is the only example of a prayer for revenge, and we do not know what role the Old

[20] Jansson (1987), 142 (translated by P. Foote).

[21] Williams (1996*b*), 297.

Testament played in the missionaries' teaching, it seems more likely that we are here dealing with yet another example of 'transitional mentality'. Another example of vengeful feeling is:

> Torsten and Ragnfrid they raised this stone in memory of Björn in Granby, Kalv's brother. *Vigmund killed him.* May God help his spirit and soul better than he deserved. (U 338, Granby)

6.3. CHRISTIAN FEATURES

6.3.1. Three 'baptismal certificates'

Three Scandinavian monuments mark the official acceptance of Christianity, the so-called 'baptismal certificates' of Denmark, Norway, and the (now Swedish) province of Jämtland. On the biggest and most magnificent rune-stone in Scandinavia, King Harald Bluetooth claims to have made the Danes Christian (DR 42, Pl. 38 A–C), and this stone will be further discussed in the Excursus. Sweden's northernmost rune-stone stands on the island of Frösön in Jämtland, and its inscription reads:

> Östman, Gudfast's son, had this stone raised and this bridge built, and he had the whole of Jämtland Christianized. Åsbjörn built the bridge. Tryn and Sten cut the runes.

Unfortunately we do not know who Östman was; a widespread view is that he was a native chieftain, perhaps 'law-speaker', the leader of an assembly, knowledgeable in the law. The closeness to Tröndelag and St Olav's shrine in Nidaros (Trondheim) leads some scholars to stress the importance of western influences,[22] while the stylistic features of the stone (and Östman's very name) lead others to stress the Christian influences from the East.[23] We must probably reckon with both, but a clear indication of very strong eastern influence over Jämtland is the fact that this province came to belong to the Swedish archdiocese of Uppsala and continued to do so even after the Norwegian king took *political* control over it.

In Norway the inscription on the Kuli stone (NIyR 449: Ch. 1, Pl. 2) has recently been reinterpreted by Jan Ragnar Hagland on the basis of Jan O. H. Swantesson's technique of micro-mapping. According to Aslak Liestøl's reading the inscription says:

> Tore and Hallvard raised this stone in memory of X. (?). Twelve winters Christianity had been (**uirit**) in Norway

but Hagland, dismissing the question of the deceased's name as insoluble, reads **um rit** (instead of **uirit**) and gives the following interpretation of the second sentence: 'Twelve winters had Christianity *improved* (things) in

[22] e.g. Sandnes (1996). [23] e.g. Vikstrand (1996).

PLATE 30. U 164 and 165, Täby. Jarlabanke's bridge at Täby in Uppland. Jansson (1987) writes: 'As far as we can tell, Jarlabanke put up four rune stones by his bridge, two facing each other at the north end and two at the south end. The bridge was also flanked by smaller standing-stones (ON *bautasteinar*), without runes on them. The length of the causeway was about 150 m., its width 6.5 m.' *Inscriptions*: U 164, 'Jarlabanke had these stones raised in memory of himself while he was still alive, and he built this bridge for his soul, and alone he owned the whole of Täby. May God help his soul.' U 165 has the same inscription (with a few words now missing).

Norway' (or perhaps even: '. . . had Christianity *secured law and order* . . .'). There has also been an attempt to date the inscription on the Kuli stone; assuming that a bridge close to the stone was contemporary, a dendrochronological test was made on its wooden remains. The result was the year 1034, implying that the formal acceptance of Christianity occurred in 1022, i.e. in Olav Haraldsson's (St Olav's) time.

6.3.2. Bridge-building

The missionaries objected to the old ways of honouring the dead, and, instead, exhorted the relatives to pray and give gifts for the soul. One, very prestigious, soul-gift was the building of a bridge, an enterprise that also honoured the builder. To build a bridge and so improve communications was considered a meritorious act that earned divine favour, and was thus encouraged by the Church. Early in the eleventh century Wulfstan, archbishop of York, urged anyone who had the means, to build and endow a church and, among other deeds for the love of God (*Godes Þankes*), 'to facilitate the people's journeying by bridges over deep waters and foul

TABLE 6.1. *Bridge-inscriptions: incidence by region*

Region	No. of bridge-inscrs./regional total	Bridge-inscrs. as percentage of regional total
Denmark	3/168	1.8
Norway	2/51	3.9
Småland	11/116	9.5
Västergötland	8/156	5.1
Östergötland	10/212	4.7
Södermanland	19/352	5.4
Uppland	81/1,016	8.1
Öland	1/87	1.1
Gotland	2/30	
Hälsingland	1/11	
Jämtland	1/1	
Västmanland	6/25	
TOTAL	145/2,225	

ways'.[24] In many cases the sponsors declare that they have done it for the sake of their dead relative's soul. Some 145 inscriptions report the building of a bridge. Over half of them are in Uppland (see Pl. 30) but, as Table 6.1 shows, the others are widely distributed throughout Scandinavia (see also App. 10).

There are remarkable concentrations. In Västergötland, for example, six of the eight such inscriptions are in two districts in the west of the province (three each in the districts of Vadsbo and Redväg). Similarly six of the eleven inscriptions in Småland are in two central districts (three each in Västra and Östra härader). In Uppland half are in four adjacent districts: Seminghundra (15), Danderyd (11), Vallentuna (9), Sollentuna (6).

These bridge-stones tend to be relatively early. Of the 81 in Uppland, 64% are earlier than 1070, and over a third are before 1050. The sponsors seem to be a representative cross-section of the types of people who erected rune-stones, and few of the stones show any indication of high status. One significant feature of this group, however, is the relatively high proportion of women involved, confirming their active role in the Conversion process. While women (alone or jointly) sponsored only 28% of the inscriptions in Uppland, they were responsible for

[24] *Be dædbetan*, cl. 14 from the so-called *Canons of Edgar*, compiled by Wulfstan (see D. Bethurum (1957), p. 2), cited by Liestøl (1972: 73) from Thorpe (1840: 282–3). On the high proportion of women among bridge-builders, see B. Sawyer (1991*a*); on the role of women in the Conversion, see also Gräslund (1989).

over half of the bridge-stones there. The frequency of women among those commemorated by bridges is even more remarkable; less than 5% of all inscriptions commemorate women, but 19% of the bridge-stones do so.[25]

6.3.3. Self-commemorative stones

Another distinct and significant group of stones are those by which people commemorated themselves. There are thirty-three, all but two in the Mälar region.

Uppland	28 (6 erected by Jarlabanke)[26]
Västmanland	2 (Vs 17 and 32)
Södermanland	1 (Sö 55)
Västergötland	1 (Vg 76)
Denmark	1 (DR 212a)

It was predominantly men who commemorated themselves; only five women did so (U 11, 133, 605, 652, 1093); in two inscriptions women are commemorated by their self-commemorating husbands (Vs 17 and U 347).

These monuments are sometimes called 'boasting stones', but that is an unsatisfactory term, since the focus on the sponsor is hardly something that distinguishes them. Since it would have been a greater honour to have one's posthumous reputation proclaimed by others, as happened in most cases, self-commemoration must have been an exceptional measure that was apparently made necessary for lack of close relatives or by the fear that surviving relatives would not sponsor a monument or, more seriously, might fail to execute bequests. This is consistent with the fact that most of these monuments are relatively early. It was indeed in Uppland, where royal power was weak and many people were unconverted, that such fears were most likely to be justified. It was there that some people may have had good cause not to trust their kinsmen to make suitable gifts to the missionaries to ensure that prayers were offered for their souls, and they therefore took the precaution of making such gifts while they were alive. Since most of the self-commemorative stones are explicitly Christian (eight of them mention bridge-building, and one refers to a pilgrimage to Jerusalem), it seems reasonable to regard them as sponsored by people who wished to ensure that they would be properly commemorated by the Church.

Some of these inscriptions clearly imply that the sponsor had no heir. The widows Gudlög and Gunnhild, for example, commemorated

[25] Cf. Gräslund (1989), 223 ff. and (1996), 327.

[26] U 11, 123, 133, 171, 194, 308, 345, 347, 433, 605, 652, 734, 739, 766, 803, 962, 1011, 1040, 1093, 1114, 1181, N27; Jarlabanke: U 127, 149, 164, 165, 212, 261.

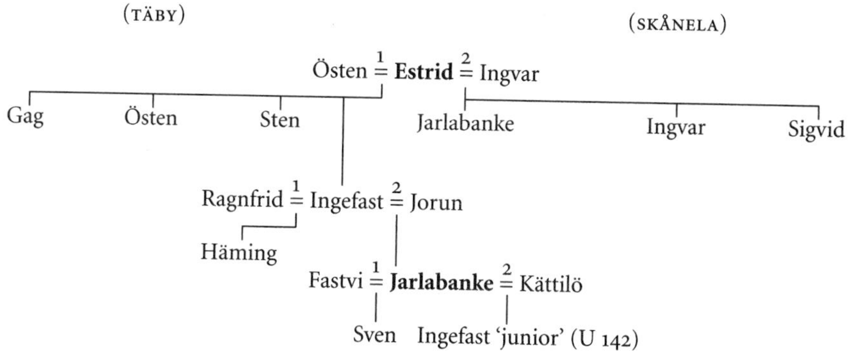

FIGURE 6.1. Traditional view of Jarlabanke's family

Note. Estrid was married twice: first to Östen in Täby, with whom she had four sons, secondly to Ingvar in Skånela, with whom she had three sons. Estrid's son Ingefast was also married twice: first to Ragnfrid and secondly to Jorun. According to the traditional interpretation, Ingefast's son Jarlabanke was married twice, but see discussion in text.

both their sons and themselves,[27] and so did Torsten and Gudfast,[28] while Livsten commemorated not only his three sons but also his wife.[29] Another good example is Björn Finnvidsson, who on one stone commemorated his brother Olev, stating that they were both the rightful heirs of Älgesta, and then commemorated himself as he obviously lacked other heirs.[30]

6.3.3a. *Jarlabanke*

The most remarkable of the self-commemorators is Jarlabanke of Täby, a man of high status who erected no fewer than six monuments in his own memory (see Ch. 5, Pl. 19, and above, Pl. 30) Numerous rune-stones in that part of Uppland name people who were connected with him by kinship or marriage.[31] The traditional interpretation of his family connections, presented in *Sveriges runinskrifter*, is shown in Figure 6.1.

According to the *SRI* stemma the self-commemorator Jarlabanke was married twice and was the father of Ingefast ('junior'), who commemorated him by a stone and a bridge (U 142). This appears to contradict the interpretation of the self-commemorating stones advanced here. The identification of the self-commemorating Jarlabanke with the father of Ingefast is, however, open to objections on both linguistic and stylistic grounds that have been discussed by Sune Lindqvist and developed by James Knirk.[32] Knirk argues that since the name Jarlabanke was given both

[27] U 133 and 652. [28] Sö 55 and U 766. [29] U 347.
[30] U 130 (see Ch. 4, Pl. 14) and U 433.
[31] The relevant stones are listed in the Catalogue: Further Particulars (p. 261).
[32] Lindqvist (1923); letter from Knirk to B. Sawyer, 21 Aug. 1994 (=Knirk (1994)).

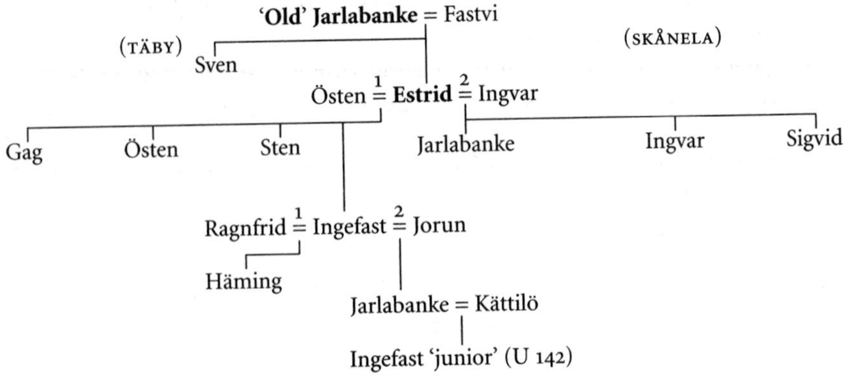

FIGURE 6.2. Knirk's view of Jarlabanke's family

to a son and grandson of Estrid, by two marriages, that was probably her father's name, and that *he* ('Old' Jarlbanke) was the self-commemorator (i.e. the great-grandfather of Ingefast junior's father, Jarlabanke). Knirk's reconstruction of the family relationships is as shown in Figure 6.2.

This is more consistent with the stylistic and linguistic dating of the stones than the traditional interpretation, and it also make it easier to understand why 'Old' Jarlabanke felt the need to commemorate himself. His rune-stones manifest his enthusiasm for Christianity, but his only surviving child was Estrid, whose first husband, Östen, had died on pilgrimage to Jerusalem apparently while his father-in-law was yet living (U 136, 140). At that early stage of the Conversion Jarlabanke may well have doubted that he would be commemorated as he wished, and feared that his donations to the Church would not be respected.

Signe Horn Fuglsang has made the following comment on Knirk's interpretation:

> This theory would explain the close similarities of motif between the stones raised in memory of Östen and those raised by Jarlabanki in memory of himself, and would establish a more straightforward stylistic evolution for the runestone ornament of the Jarlabanki family. This in turn would imply that the Jarlabanki who is commemorated on U 142 could not be identical with the man who raised stones in memory of himself and made the bridge and the assembly place. From a morphological point of view the theory is tempting.[33]

Nevertheless she continues to accept the traditional interpretation because U 142 'plainly states that Jarlabanki was the son of Jorun'.[34] This, however, is no obstacle if Jorun's son was not the self-commemorator. The fact that Ingefast found it necessary to explain that his father Jarlabanke was the

[33] Horn Fuglsang (1998), 203–4 n. 18.

[34] Ibid. 204 n. 18.

son of Jorun suggests that there were other Jarlabankes, and that he wished to avoid a misunderstanding.

It is generally assumed that most rune-stones were erected while their sponsors were alive, but it is worth considering the possibility that at least some were erected after the sponsor's death and that the signature of a rune-master, which was not a normal feature of inscriptions, was in effect a guarantee that the sponsor's wishes concerning the disposal of his wealth had been fulfilled (see Ch. 7.3.3).

6.3.4. Churches and other buildings for pious purposes

The building of churches is mentioned in only three runic inscriptions: NIyR 210 (Oddernes in West Agder) names Øyvind, 'the godson of St Olav', who built a church on his *odal* (hereditary land); DR 315 (Lund in Skåne) names Toke, who 'had the church built'; and the medieval DR 347 (Norra Åsum in Skåne) reports that Archbishop Absalon and Esbern Mule built 'this church'.

The Swedish inscriptions do not mention churches, but other buildings for pious purposes do occur: U 996 (Karberga), erected by two daughters in memory of their father, reports that their father, Tore, had had a *seluhus* ('soul-house') built in memory of his wife, Ingetora. This could have been either a hostel for travellers or a hospital for the sick. Two other references to buildings for pious purposes are more problematic: both Sö 174 (Aspö church in the district of Selebo) and U 818 (Gryta in Kulla parish, Lagunda härad) refer to the building of a *likhus*, a word that has been interpreted as 'hostel' by Erik Brate,[35] and as 'sarcophagus' by Sven B. F. Jansson.[36] Henrik Williams has pointed out that although grave-monuments shaped like houses are known from this period, as far as we know the name *likhus* was never applied to them. Further, since Sö 174 reports that the commemorated man had been killed in Gotland, it is unlikely that he was buried at home, in which case, Williams argues, *likhus* can hardly mean a sarcophagus but should be interpreted as meaning hostel or hospital.[37] What is more, both these inscriptions also report that a bridge was built, manifestly a pious act.

6.3.5. Pilgrimage

Other indications of piety are stones commemorating pilgrims: U 136 (Broby) in memory of Östen who died in Greece on his way to Jerusalem (see Ch. 5, Pl. 20), and U 605 (Stäket), by—and in memory of—Ingerun who planned to go to Jerusalem. Significantly, both these stones were sponsored by women.[38] We will never know whether Ingerun began her pilgrimage, but the fact that a woman could even plan such an enterprise

[35] *SRI* iii. 136. [36] *SRI* viii. 435. [37] Williams (1996*a*), 60 f.
[38] Sawyer and Sawyer (1993), 198 f. Cf. Gräslund (1996), 328.

at this early date is remarkable. Probably Ingerun—like all other pilgrims—had to deal with the division of her property before she set out on such a long journey.

6.3.6. Baptism

Seven Uppland monuments commemorate people who died in 'white clothing', that is immediately after having been baptized.[39] It is perhaps significant that most of these monuments, commemorating death-bed converts, were sponsored by women: three of them by women acting on their own—two mothers and a widow[40]—and two by mothers acting together with their husbands.[41]

6.3.7. Prayers

All the prayers in the inscriptions are concerned with the soul of the deceased and are based on the funeral liturgy of the Western Church. The most common are: 'May God help his/her soul/spirit' and 'May God and God's mother help his soul'; but there are more elaborate formulations, for instance: 'May God help his soul and forgive him his guilt and sins' (U 323), 'May God and God's mother help his spirit and soul. Give him light and paradise' (U 160). 'God' must refer to Christ; this is indicated partly by the formula 'God's mother', and partly by the fact that neither the Father nor the Holy Ghost is ever mentioned. The reason for the absence of references to the Trinity has been much discussed; according to Per Beskow missionaries had to emphasize the unity of God in contrast to pagan polytheism. To avoid the misunderstanding that the Christians had three Gods, the missionaries simplified their teaching by identifying God with Christ.[42]

No saints are invoked on the rune-stones; apart from Christ, we meet only Mary and the archangel Michael. It is perhaps significant that Mary is never invoked as a virgin but always as a mother; this may have been due to the high esteem in which fertility had been held in pagan Scandinavia and possibly facilitated the acceptance of the new faith. Britt-Marie Näsström has even suggested that Mary may have replaced the fertility goddess Fröja; many of Fröja's functions were taken over by Mary, in rites connected with childbirth, weddings, and fertility of the soil.[43] In pagan Scandinavia women had played an important role in Fröja's cult, and it is plausible that Mary's popularity was especially great among female converts. Anne-Sofie Gräslund has pointed out a clear correlation between female sponsors and the use of the prayer to 'God and God's mother'; while less than one third of the shorter 'May God help' inscriptions involve

[39] U 243, 364, 613, 699, 896, 1036, N40.
[40] U 613, 1036 (mothers); U 699 (widow).
[41] U 243 and (perhaps) 364. U 896 may also have been sponsored by the parents, while it is impossible to decide about the relationship of U N40. Cf. Gräslund (1989), 230 f.
[42] Beskow (1994), 22.
[43] Näsström (1996), 335–48.

women as sponsors or deceased, women are represented in almost half of the 'God's-mother' inscriptions.[44]

Another prayer, found in fifteen cases (and only in the Mälar valley), is: 'May God help his soul better than he deserved'.[45] Apart from expressing Christian humility, it is perhaps worth considering whether this explicit addition was felt to be needed where the dead person had converted very late in life—or, indeed, had not converted at all!

According to Anne-Sofie Gräslund's chronology, prayers in Uppland are more common on the older rune-stones than on the younger, where Christian ornaments prevail instead. The reason for this has recently been discussed by Torun Zachrisson, who argues that the older stones were sponsored by people who were already Christian and could understand the meaning of the prayers, while the younger stones were sponsored by new converts who did not understand them but had to be taught by pictures rather than words. Zachrisson treats the younger stones as a 'second wave' of rune-stone erection, interpreting it as a result of missionary activity initiated and led by the episcopal see of Sigtuna.[46] Apart from the fact that we have no evidence for such an organized Sigtuna mission during the second half of the eleventh century, Zachrisson's argument is not convincing; first, it is hard to see why highly sophisticated, symbolic ornaments would have been so much easier to understand than words, and secondly, it is more likely to have been the older stones, rather than the younger ones, that were sponsored by new converts.

It seems more fruitful to look at Uppland against the Scandinavian background as a whole and to remember that even the older stones in Uppland are young compared with those in the southern and western regions. What has to be explained is why prayers are more common in eastern Sweden than in other parts of Scandinavia.[47] The most plausible reason is that in the East Christianity was not imposed from above; conversion was a voluntary act, and was demonstrated by sponsoring explicitly Christian rune-stones. That prayers are less common in the younger inscriptions of Uppland is only to be expected, since Christianity had already gained ground. The function of the prayers—to exhort passers-by to pray for the deceased's soul—was no longer so necessary when representatives of the Church began to be numerous enough to take over that responsibility.

[44] Gräslund (1996), 327. The figures given are 31% and 47% respectively.

[45] Sö 195, 197, 210, 212, 321, N17; U 69, 338, 371, 512, 539, 586, 726, 758, 759.

[46] Zachrisson (1998), 129–36, 155–9.

[47] An exception is Småland, where prayers are as common as in Uppland, occurring in *c.*21% of the inscriptions. The percentages for Södermanland and Öland are *c.*19%, for Östergötland 14%, for Västergötland 11%, for Norway 8% (four inscriptions), and for Denmark 5.5% (nine inscriptions).

6.3.8. Mentality

It is not easy to trace the change of mentality due to conversion in the rune-stone material—apart from the prayers; most inscriptions are stereotyped, short, and matter-of-fact. It has been suggested that, at least in the East, the adjective 'good' denoted Christian qualities, but, as argued in Chapter 5.5, it is more likely to refer to a special status in society, as it does

PLATE 31. U 595, Harg. This picture has been interpreted as a bell-tower; if this is correct, it is the earliest picture of a Swedish church building. *Inscription*: 'Gudleif and Sigvid, Aldulv's heirs, had this stone carved in memory of their father and of Sigborg, his mother.'

PLATE 32. U 529, Sika (on a rock face). The inscription yields no clear meaning, but the picture has given rise to two different interpretations. According to one, it depicts a Mass, with the congregation divided into two groups—perhaps, as suggested by Bertil Nilsson, one group of women and the other of men (see Williams (1996*a*), 56). According to the other interpretation, it depicts the stable at Bethlehem, with Mary handing Jesus over to Joseph, who is to show him to the Three Wise Men waiting outside, i.e. the same scene as on the Norwegian Dynna stone (NIyR 68).

PLATE 33. U 901, Håmö (now at Umeå University). The picture shows three individuals, probably men, who, according to Elias Wessén (*SRI* viii. 621), are fighting each other. A more likely interpretation has been presented by Bengt Hult (1992: 107–16), who suggests that it depicts a Christian burial with one man attending to the dead person and another carrying the cross. *Inscription*: '. . . Karl and Igulbjörn had these stones raised and this bridge built in memory of Jovur, their father . . . help his soul.'

in western Scandinavia. Further, it has often been remarked that the inscriptions show no sign of grief for the dead. This, of course, does not mean that grief was not felt and expressed in other ways;[48] it was obviously not normal to exhibit personal feelings on this kind of monument. There may have been exceptions, expressing emotions, but two of the four examples cited by Henrik Williams are not among them; the Bällsta inscription, discussed above (p. 131: U 226) does not say that the dead man will be remembered with 'tears' but that a lament will be produced in his

[48] Cf. Williams (1996*b*), 297 f.

Plate 34. U 631, Kalmar church. The picture shows a Christian couple, and here the interpretations vary greatly: are they a couple entering Paradise—or setting out on a pilgrimage? Does it depict Mary and Elisabeth—or the women around the sepulchre? According to Hans Christiansson, the figure holding the cross is a man, leading a woman on to the right—Christian—path. What casts doubt on this interpretation, however, is that we cannot be sure which is the man and which the woman! On the basis of the types of clothing the couple are wearing Else Roesdahl interprets the figure holding the cross as a woman and the other figure as a man. The implication of this interpretation is interesting in that it would give us yet another indication of women's active role in the Conversion. Since, however, both interpretations are possible, it cannot be decided what this scene actually means. See Williams (1996*a*: 51–3); Gräslund (1996: 313). *Inscription*: 'Nigulas had these stones raised in memory of **syhsa**, his father.'

honour, and the reason the sponsor of the Ardre inscription (pp. 55–6: G 111) added that his wife had died young, leaving infant children, must have been the legal importance of this fact; had she died without any children, her property would have reverted to her own family.

6.3.9. Christian depictions

Christian depictions (*bildframställningar*) are rare, and most of them are found in the Mälar valley and the province of Gästrikland.[49] The interpretation of some of them is still debated (see Pls. 31–4).[50]

[49] U 529, 595, 631, 901, 1161; Sö 101, 286, 327; Gs 2, 7, 9, 18c, 19; Vg 80, 129; NIyR 68; DR 42. (18c contains an uninterpreted inscription and therefore does not appear in the catalogue.)

[50] For a survey of the Upplandic motifs, see Williams (1996*a*), 51–7.

6.4. CONCLUSION

Even if most of the rune-stones of the tenth and eleventh centuries are Christian monuments, a few can be be interpreted as expressing pagan belief or uncertainty, particularly the inscriptions containing spells and invocations to Thor. Other inscriptions illustrate the transition from pagan to Christian thinking and burial customs, for example funeral lamentations and prayers urging God to take revenge. The transition is also illustrated by the small group of self-commemorative stones, characteristic of a stage when Christians could not be sure that their provisions *mortis causa* would be carried out by their, perhaps still pagan, relatives.

Apart from crosses, Christianity is most commonly manifested in prayers; references to baptism, pilgrimages, and the building of churches or hostels are rare. References to to the building of bridges for the sake of the soul of the deceased are, however, fairly common. This bridge-building activity in Viking-Age Scandinavia is perhaps the best illustration of a transitional stage, when many new converts tried to bridge the gap between their, and their kin's, pagan past and their own—Christian—era.

7

CONCLUSION AND FUTURE RESEARCH

7.1. THE RUNE-STONE FASHION

This study is based on 2,307 runic inscriptions on stone (some fragmentary) that were made in Scandinavia between the middle of the tenth century and the beginning of the twelfth. They are all in the Nordic language and with very few exceptions they all have the same basic formula: 'X raised this stone' or 'had this stone raised in memory of Y' (or variations giving the same information).[1] Most inscriptions state the relationship between X and Y, and many give additional details. This remarkable uniformity justifies treating these monuments as the result of a fashion that began in Denmark and spread to Västergötland and Norway before the end of the tenth century, and—at the latest—by 1020 had reached what is now eastern Sweden. The individual monuments cannot be closely dated but it appears that relatively few were made in Denmark or Västergötland after the 1020s. In Norway most are earlier than 1050 although a few may be later. In eastern Sweden, however, the fashion flourished until the early twelfth century, even later on the islands of Bornholm and Gotland.

Although the main purpose of this study has been to discover what these inscriptions can reveal about Scandinavian society, in particular its inheritance customs, it was first necessary to explain their purpose, distribution, and chronology or, in other words, why the fashion spread as it did and why it ended.

These runic monuments had three obvious functions. In the first place they commemorated dead individuals but, unlike later gravestones, they were also memorials to the living, the sponsors, most of whom were closely related to the people they commemorated. They also displayed publicly the wealth and status of the people concerned. The dead had previously been honoured and their status demonstrated in various ways, by elaborate funeral rituals and by burial mounds or stone settings, sometimes in the shape of a ship. Christian missionaries rejected these pagan customs in favour of simple burials in consecrated churchyards and new, liturgical,

[1] Since my corpus includes many fragments it is impossible to give an absolute figure, but of the sufficiently complete inscriptions only five lack the formula: J 1; U 29, 73, 541, 558. Four others (Sö 138; U 316, 344, and 348) are paired with stones that have the formula.

ways of commemorating the dead. In the transition period, before churches and churchyards were easily accessible, converted families could commemorate their dead and display their status by runic monuments placed in traditional cemeteries, by roads or bridges, in places of assembly, or near the homes of the dead. In most cases it was the heir, or heirs, who had the main responsibility and appear as sponsors in the inscriptions.

The formula in the inscription on Harald's Jelling stone (see DR 42) had been used by others in Denmark earlier, but he combined it with a proclamation that he had 'made the Danes Christian'. This, together with his success in 'winning all Denmark for himself' and reasserting Danish overlordship in Norway, led others to follow his example and so spread the fashion for this type of monument. The fashion was further extended by the even greater prestige of his son Sven, who, from 1000 to his death in 1014, was acknowledged as king in Norway and was overlord of the first Christian king in Sweden, Olof Skötkonung.

In Denmark itself, the political and religious transformation wrought by Harald and Sven created a need among the leading men, *old* magnates and *new royal agents*, to defend old and new rights to land, titles, and power, and to resist the changes or acknowledge their acceptance of the new situation. King Harald's own runic monument provided the model for such declarations of religious and political affiliation, combined with assertions of rank, and claims to titles as well as land.[2] The distribution of rune-stones reflects the degree of political and religious change, with the main concentrations where the change was greatest. Thus South Jutland and Fyn, which had long been the core of the Danish kingdom in which royal power was well established, have few rune-stones of this type. Mid- and northern Jutland, Sjælland, and Skåne, where the majority of Danish rune-stones are to be found, were the areas that were most affected by the extension of direct royal authority by Harald and his son, a process reflected by the so-called Trelleborg forts, and the creation of new towns, episcopal sees, and royal mints.[3]

This is not to say that all sponsors were driven by the same—political—need, but once the fashion was set, it spread fast, thanks to the prestige of the Danish kings. Also, outside Denmark many rune-stones were a response to religious and political change. In Västergötland, exposed as it was to Danish influence, many rune-stones seem to mark loyalty to the Danish king, but here, as elsewhere, there are also signs that they reflect the development of the authority of native rulers. In Götaland, as in Denmark, central areas with few rune-stones were apparently the bases from which Swedish kings attempted to extend their power. The contrast between Kinnekulle in Västergötland, where the few rune-stones are all

[2] Cf. Randsborg (1978).

[3] P. Sawyer (1988), 276–7, 291–333.

late, and the surrounding area suggests that it was under royal control at an early stage, a conclusion reinforced by the fact that the first episcopal see in Sweden was established there. What is more, the earliest, west, part of Husaby church is clearly modelled on royal or imperial churches in Germany, which also influenced the earliest royal churches in Denmark.[4] (See Pls. 35 and 36.)

The lack of late Viking-Age rune-stones in Vestfold and Østfold is probably to be explained in the same way. This part of Norway had been under Danish overlordship in the ninth century and was a key centre of Danish power under Harald Gormsson and Sven Forkbeard. It is significant that the main concentration of Norwegian rune-stones of this period is in Rogaland, which in the 1020s was controlled by Erling Skjalgsson, an ally of the Danish king Knut, and an opponent of Olav Haraldsson. The fact that the rune-stone fashion did not have much influence in other parts of Norway may have been in part due to the rejection of Danish claims after 1035. It is, however, worth pointing out that the distribution of rune-stones in Denmark and Norway is less dramatic than the distribution map (Map 1) suggests. Unlike Denmark, the greater part of Norway was uninhabited. Later evidence suggests that the population of Norway was about a third of Denmark's. If, as seems likely, this was true in the tenth and eleventh centuries, the number of rune-stones in relation to the population is much the same in both countries. It is, therefore, remarkable that rune-stones were erected in the far north of Norway.

In eastern Sweden it appears that one of the main functions of the rune-stones was to declare the acceptance of Christianity by individuals or families. The fundamental changes reflected by the inscriptions seem to have begun later and lasted longer in Uppland than elsewhere. The large number of rune-stones there suggests that the custom was more popular and more broadly based than in Denmark and Götaland; sponsors did not come from only the very highest social strata. Unfortunately, little is known about the political situation in Uppland during the eleventh century, but it is clear that kings had considerable difficulty in asserting their power there. Olof Skötkonung and his son Anund, successively kings of the Svear, issued coins from their mint in Sigtuna from *c.*995 to *c.*1030. There are other indications that Sigtuna, which was founded *c.*975, apparently by Olof's father, Erik, served as the base from which they and later kings attempted to enlarge their authority in Mälardalen. They were, however, unable to impose Christianity on the whole region until the end of the century. Conversion was, therefore, a long drawn-out process, achieved by various individuals, chieftains, and magnates, who had influence and could persuade local assemblies at least to tolerate converts. Even if we cannot exclude a certain degree of enforcement, conversion in

[4] Johansson (1986), 387–542; Claesson (1989), 21–5, 69.

Plate 35. Vg 55. *Inscription*: 'Ulv and Ragnar, they both raised this stone in memory of Fare, their father . . . Christian man. He had good faith in God.'

Plate 36. Vg 56. *Inscription*: 'Styråke raised this stone in memory of **kaur**, his father.'

The time of transition is well illustrated by these two rune-stones near Kinnekulle (Källby ås) in Västergötland; Vg 56 is certainly pagan—with its big 'dog-headed' man dominating the surface, while Vg 55 is an explicitly Christian stone.

Uppland seems to have been largely voluntary, and the many explicitly Christian inscriptions provide some valuable hints about the way it came about. (See Pl. 37.)

Without the support of a strong central power, missionaries had not only to rely on local chieftains and magnates for protection, but were also entirely dependent on gifts from believers. By commissioning rune-stones,

PLATE 37. J 1, Frösön. *Inscription*: 'Östman, Gudfast's son, had this stone raised and this bridge built, and he had the whole of Jämtland Christianized. Åsbjörn made the bridge. Tryn and Sten carved these runes.' Östman takes credit for having Christianized the whole of Jämtland. It is a matter of debate who this Östman was; was he a law-speaker or just a very powerful chieftain? Was he from Jämtland, or had he come from outside the province? (See *Jämtlands kristnande*, 1996).

individuals as well as entire families could proclaim their faith along with the implication that they also actively supported the clergy. At the same time, this must often have been an acknowledgement of the authority of the missionaries' secular patrons. Since the support given to the missionaries will frequently have been economic, it was in the interest of all that claims to inheritances and property should be clearly stated. If any property that had belonged to the deceased was donated to the Church, heirs who had claims to the inheritance must have assented, and by acting as sponsors in commemorating such a donor they could, in effect, publicly proclaim their approval of his or her actions. This would help explain the custom of multiple sponsorship, which was especially common in Uppland. It is also revealing that it was in Uppland that some people found it necessary to commemorate themselves while they were still alive, apparently fearing that their heirs would not do so and might revoke gifts made to the Church, or fail to implement bequests.

A religious motive for sponsoring rune-stones does not, however, exclude a political one; in fact, the stones seem also to have been a response to attempts that were made in the eleventh century to increase royal authority in the Mälar region. The acceptance and promotion of Christianity by leading Upplanders may sometimes have been an act of loyalty to a king, but, alternatively, it could have been a reaction to the claims by kings that they were the exclusive sponsors of the new religion. Two Uppland inscriptions which mention the creation of a new place of assembly, or *thing*, may reflect such reactions. Assemblies of local communities presupposed the acceptance by all of a common, traditional, religious cult. Conversion resulted in exclusion from the traditional assembly and created the need for an alternative, Christian one, and, as Torun Zachrisson has suggested, some new (Christian) assemblies may have been instituted not by the king but by local magnates.[5]

Most of the rune-stones in Uppland were made after about 1020, that is at least two generations after the foundation of Sigtuna. That would have been time enough for royal influence to have had the effect that can be discerned in the neighbouring districts of Trögd and Åsunda (see Ch. 4.8). It is uncertain how quickly and effectively this new form of royal power was accepted in other parts of Uppland, but it is arguable that the remarkable vitality of the rune-stone fashion in this province was in part a reaction to the attempts by kings based in Sigtuna to extend their authority, a development that local lords and their followers either welcomed or resisted.

If rune-stones were indeed a symptom of crisis, their uneven distribution in Scandinavia (few in the South/West, many in the East) is a good

[5] See U 212 (Jarlabanke) and U 225 (Ulvkel, Arnkel, and Gye), both in Vallentuna *härad*. Cf. Zachrisson (1998), 154.

reflection of the political and religious transition that took place during the tenth and eleventh centuries. The period of transition was brief in some areas, notably Denmark and Västergötland, but prolonged in others, especially Uppland, where there was persistent resistance to the new kind of centralized royal power that had its roots in Götaland.

This hypothesis explains why the rune-stone fashion did not last longer. When the transitional period was over, and churches and churchyards began to be widespread, such monuments were no longer needed. It should, however, be emphasized that the change was not abrupt. There are many examples of 'transitional' memorials in churchyards, in the form of recumbent gravestones with runic inscriptions of the same type as on the upright stones. There are also some pairs of erect stones that appear to have marked the head and foot of graves which may have also been covered by horizontal slabs, possibly inscribed, that have not survived.[6]

7.2. LATE VIKING-AGE SOCIETY

Rune-stones do not cast much light on Viking activity (Ch. 5.7). The relatively few that commemorate 'travellers' reflect the concerns of their families when they did not return home. The few that refer to Viking expeditions, successful or not, have received a disproportionate amount of attention. It is more rewarding to consider what can be learned about the society that these voyagers left behind.

Sponsors were nearly always landowners, but there is an important difference between west and east Scandinavia; in the west most sponsors belonged to a fairly restricted élite, in the east they came from a much broader range of landowners. In all parts of Scandinavia, however, we can discern a hierarchical society: some people, being magnates and leaders with big retinues, held high offices and dominated the assemblies; others, albeit less exalted but comprising local élites, sponsored lavish monuments and built bridges; while further down the social scale, especially in the East, many people were content to erect simpler monuments, commemorating their dead relatives with inscriptions that were much the same as those used by the rich and powerful.

Women are generally well represented as sponsors, more so in eastern than in western Scandinavia, but everywhere many were left on their own, sometimes with considerable wealth, part of which was donated to the Church. The inscriptions show that in tenth- and eleventh-century Scandinavia a woman did not sever all links with her own family when she married. Moreover, in the new family that she and her husband created, both partners, together with their children, shared in property rights or

6 Hagenfeldt and Palm (1996), 59; see e.g. U 23, 296, 545, 546, 549, 631, 959, 1,013.

expectations from the family so formed, as well as from both partners' families. There is no proof that wives actually owned a share of the household property at that time as they did later, but it does seem likely that they did. The fact that many inscriptions were sponsored by widows, either on their own or together with other members of the family, suggests that as wives they had a leading role in their families, most probably as co-owners. With some regional exceptions it seems to have been the widow's task to sponsor her husband's memorial if his sons, brothers, or father did not survive him, or if his sons were too young. In such a situation the widow apparently took over the headship of the household, guardianship of minors, and control of the property, suggesting that she had well-defined rights as co-owner when her husband was alive. The many memorials sponsored jointly by a widow and sons confirm the nuclear character of families and indicate the existence of *félag* (Dan. *fællig*) or joint ownership.

The inscriptions also show that families were formed by monogamous marriages. A man may have had relationships, and children, with several women, but when he died, only one wife was acknowledged. We do not know what the rituals of marriage were, but there is no doubt that then, as later, they were based on contracts between families. Reciprocally binding agreements were needed, especially between wealthy families, for reverse inheritance could result in the transfer of large estates from one family to another. Contracted marriages were not the only form of partnership. Concubinage, or informal relationships without legal consequences, was common later, and, although the inscriptions do not provide any evidence for the custom, there is no doubt that it was a common practice.

The inscriptions also provide some information about the size and composition of families in parts of eastern Sweden, where men and women jointly acted as sponsors. Inscriptions mentioning more than three or four children are rare, but as a high rate of infant mortality can be assumed, many more children must have been born. Daughters are significantly fewer than sons. In Upplandic inscriptions with both, the ratio of sons to daughters is 2:1. This circumstance cannot be explained by the exclusion of married daughters, for they are sometimes named. It was probably a result of a deliberate attempt to control the size of the population by limiting the number of girls who were allowed to survive.[7] Christian missionaries objected to infanticide, and in Iceland it was prohibited soon after the conversion. Christianity was certainly responsible for many other changes that affected families, but too little is known about the pre-Christian situation to say much about the immediate consequences of conversion.

[7] See Sawyer and Sawyer (1993), 40–2.

Thanks to the emphasis on the sponsors and their relationship with the deceased, the runic inscriptions can cast light on inheritance and property rights in this period. The main conclusion of this investigation is that we can discern two different patterns of inheritance, reflecting the different needs of magnates and 'gentry' in tenth- and eleventh-century Scandinavia; one helped keep family estates intact, the other helped to build up networks of family alliances (Ch. 4.9). As the later provincial and national laws show, these different customs were a matter of dispute for a very long time.

7.3. FUTURE RESEARCH

The corpus of inscriptions on which this study is based provides abundant material for further research. Many questions remain, and some topics certainly merit fuller discussion than has been possible here; several examples are noted below.

7.3.1. Personal names and genealogies

It would be instructive to take account of personal names as possible indicators of status and compare that evidence with the other criteria discussed above (Ch. 5).[8]

It is sometimes possible, especially in Uppland and Södermanland, to identify several members of a single family over three or more generations. A systematic study of these family trees would make it possible to discover more about marriage alliances, the extent of family connections, and different conventions of name-giving.

7.3.2. Administrative and/or ecclesiastical districts

As shown in Chapter 4.8 the rune-stones in south-west Uppland are in many respects very different from those in other parts of Uppland. Similarly, the three deaneries (*prosterier*) in the diocese of Strängnäs have different types of runic inscriptions.[9] It has been suggested that these could reflect the activity of different missionaries, but it is perhaps more likely that the deaneries represent lordships or confederations that existed in the eleventh century.[10] It would be rewarding to investigate whether there are other districts in which rune-stones have common characteristics that distinguish them from those in neighbouring areas. This could cast light on the antiquity of some administrative or ecclesiastical districts, or, alternatively, indicate the existence of different groupings in the eleventh century.

Another worthwhile investigation would be to study areas around places that appear to have been important power centres in the eleventh and

[8] Wessén (1927). [9] Ståhle (1950), 100. [10] P. Sawyer (1987), 76.

twelfth centuries to see if, as at Kinnekulle in Västergötland, rune-stones of the type studied here are rare, or entirely absent. Neill and Lundberg have shown that in Västergötland and Östergötland some such districts have different types of monument, misleadingly known as 'Eskiltuna sarcophagi'.[11]

The hypothesis advanced here that the rune-stone fashion flourished when there were few churches and churchyards needs to be tested by a systematic investigation of the evidence for the erection of the first churches and the creation of churchyards.

7.3.3. Signed and unsigned inscriptions

Many inscriptions name the men who were responsible for making, carving or cutting, or painting them. Some of these craftsmen appear to have executed designs prepared by others who in more recent times have been called 'rune-masters' or 'runographers', but in many cases the carver was perhaps also the 'master'. The reason why some inscriptions name the 'master', while others do not has only been touched upon above (Ch. 4.2), where it is suggested that the 'master's' signature functioned as an authorization, confirming that alms had been given and promising spiritual—as well as secular—support. There are of course other possibilities: some people might not have lived to see the completion of the stones they sponsored, in which case the signature could indicate that the sponsors had commissioned the rune-masters to take responsibility for seeing the work through.

Is there actually a practical explanation for the fact that while some sponsors use the active form 'raised', 'cut', 'carved', etc., others use the formulation 'had this stone raised'; is it possible that the former were still alive and responsible at the time of the erection, while the latter were not? These are just suggested answers, but it is clear that the question needs further study. It is particularly puzzling that many *unsigned* inscriptions have confidently been attributed to known rune-masters.[12]

7.3.4. The inscriptions: contents, design and ornament

The placing of personal names on the monuments needs further investigation. So, for example, on one of the Sjonhem stones (G 135) the names of the four paternal uncles, important in the order of inheritance, are placed centrally, immediately under the Christian cross (Ch. 3.1.5). As far as women are concerned, it may be significant that, even if they are mentioned last, they are sometimes centrally placed on the stone itself: for

[11] Neill and Lundberg (1994). No explanation can be offered here for the dearth of late Viking-Age rune-stones in Halland and Bohuslän in contrast to their relative abundance in neighbouring parts of Denmark, Sjælland, and Skåne, and in Västergötland.

[12] The best discussion of the possibility of making such attributions is Thompson (1975). For a list of signed and attributed inscriptions, see Axelson (1993). See also Åhlén (1997), 138–41.

example, U 908 (Fiby), where Kättilvi is placed at the top, immediately under the cross; U 957 (Vedyxa), where Arnfrid is placed centrally under the cross; and U 961 (Vaksala church), where the name of the widow, Runfrid, crosses the name of her husband, Kättilbjörn, on the centre of the stone.

One relevant topic that has not been discussed here is the possible relationship between the content of an inscription and its design. It is, for example, interesting that the complicated chain of inheritance cases in the Hillersjö inscription (U 29), has been visualized by the rune-master in an extremely convoluted 'serpent' (see Ch. 2, Pl. 10). Also, the inscription U 337 (Granby), with its complex information about the relatives of the deceased, has a very elaborate design. In both these cases, the design might of course have been chosen for practical reasons; the rock face at Hillersjö is after all fairly small, and lots of information had to go into a confined space. But a possible correlation between content and design might still be present, as, for example, on the stone where Inga tells us that her husband, Ragnfast, owned Snottsta after his father, Sigfast (U 331); the inscription is arranged in two separate serpents. Does this signal that we are here dealing with two separate declarations? The inscription informs us (1) about Inga's status as an independent widow, implying her right to administer Ragnfast's property, and (2) what this property consisted of and how it had come into Ragnfast's possession.

A related question is the possible relationship between the content of an inscription and its *ornament*; so, for example, it has been suggested above (Ch. 6 n. 7) that the scenes from the *Sigurd saga* on Ramsundsberget (Sö 101, Pl. 27) illustrate what its sponsor, Sigrid, had in mind, namely the acquisition of a great treasure.

7.3.5. 'Good people' in Scandinavia

The distribution of the 263 'good people' named in runic inscriptions (see Maps 3 A–B, App. 7(c)) needs further study. It has been argued above (Ch. 5.5) that the 'good men' are equivalent to the *boni homines* familiar in other parts of early medieval Europe. They were leading members of local communities whose status depended on recognition within those communities; it was not conferred by rulers. Kings did, however, rely on them as their agents when they attempted to extend their authority. References to such people in runic inscriptions can therefore provide clues to the extent of royal authority in late Viking-Age Scandinavia. There is, for example, little doubt that the 'good' thegns and drengs in Denmark and Västergötland had a special relationship with the Danish king Sven Forkbeard and possibly with his son Knut (Ch. 5.4). The concentrations of 'good' thegns and drengs in east Skåne and Västergötland can be seen as marking the eastern boundary of Danish overlordship in the early eleventh century.

The distribution in *eastern* Sweden is more difficult to interpret. It is likely that the concentration in south-west Uppland, in the districts of Trögd and Åsunda, which extend south to Selö and west into Västmanland, reflects the importance of that area as a base for royal power in eleventh-century Svealand. If so, the scatter of 'good people' in other parts of Uppland, especially east of Sigtuna and around Uppsala, may reflect the extension of that authority before the end of the rune-stone period, that is before the early twelfth century. The relatively large number of 'good people' in south-east and east Södermanland suggests that the eleventh-century Swedish kings were more successful in extending their authority south of Mälaren than in Uppland. If this argument is sound, the evidence confirms that eleventh-century Swedish kings had little influence north of Uppland or south of Bråviken, although they may have had more success in Öland.

The most remarkable anomaly is the dearth of 'good people' immediately around Sigtuna. In the districts of Håbo and Ärlinghundra, with 138 inscriptions, there are only three 'good people' (U 430, 634, 641; U 610 is very doubtful), but over 77 per cent of these inscriptions are Christian. The explanation is perhaps that many of the local élite in the vicinity of Sigtuna accepted Christianity but *not* the authority of the Christian kings, an interpretation consistent with the evidence of Adam of Bremen noted in Chapter 4.8.

7.3.6. Comparisons with other stone monuments

A comparison of Scandinavian runic inscriptions with stone monuments erected elsewhere and at other periods may contribute to a better understanding of their function, or functions. Roman tombs and early Christian monuments in the British Isles clearly ought to be brought into the discussion, and not only because they may have influenced the development of stone monuments in Scandinavia. Less obvious, but no less potentially instructive, are the deeds of foundation and donation that were recorded in the form of monumental inscriptions carved in stone in Armenia under the rule of the Bagratid dynasty (AD 861–1045).[13]

The Catalogue of the corpus, given below, will facilitate the study of these, and many other, questions. Much additional information will be found in the corpus, which (shortly after the publication of the present volume) will be available as a data-base deposited in Runverket (Stockholm).

[13] Davies and Fouracre (1986), 207.

EXCURSUS

THE TUG-OF-WAR OVER THYRE

The main purpose of this excursus is to argue that King Gorm did not raise a rune-stone in memory of Queen Thyre; it was his son, King Harald, who had a rune-stone raised in Gorm's name in order to rewrite history and justify his claims.

For centuries the two Jelling stones (DR 41 and 42: Pls. 1 (Ch. 1) and 38 A–C below) have been the subject of lively discussion. Various problems have been debated, but, as far as I know, nobody has hitherto asked why two Danish kings in succession were so careful to honour Thyre, the wife of Gorm and mother of Harald.

The original wording of the inscriptions on the two stones is as follows[1]:

Gorm's stone (DR 41: Ch. 1, Pl. 1)
(side A) **kurmR kunukR k(ar)þi kubl þusi a(ft) þurui kunu** (side B) **sina tanmarkaR but**

King Gorm made this monument in memory of Thorvi (Thyre), his wife, Denmark's adornment.

Harald's stone (DR 42: Pl. 38)
(side A) **haraltr kunukR baþ kaurua kubl þausi aft kurmfaþursin aukaft þąurui muþur sina sa haraltr ias sąR uan tanmaurk** (side B) **ala auk nuruiak** (side C) **auk t(a)ni (karþi) kristną**

King Harald commanded this monument to be made in memory of Gorm, his father, and in memory of Thorvi (Thyre), his mother—that Harald who won the whole of Denmark for himself, and Norway, and made the Danes Christian.

DR 41 has younger orthographic and linguistic features than DR 42; while DR 41 consistently uses dividing marks between the words, some words in DR 42 are run together (**kurmfaþursin**; **aukaft**), and where DR 41 has monographic spelling, probably denoting a monophthong (**þusi**; **þurui**), DR 42 has digraphic spelling, probably denoting a diphthong (**þausi**; **þąurui**). These features, together with others noted below, suggest that the inscription on Gorm's stone is later than that on Harald's.

One problem that engaged scholars during the 1930s and 1940s was whether the epithet **tanmarkaR but** on Gorm's stone referred to Thyre

[1] Translations from Moltke (1985), 206–7.

Face A.

Face B.

Face C.

PLATE 38. DR 42, Jelling (three faces). Face A has most of the inscription (see main text for transcription and translation), while face B shows the 'Jelling beast', symbol of royal power, wreathed round by a serpent. In the bottom left-hand corner is the sacred triquetra, symbol of the Trinity. Face C has Scandinavia's oldest portrayal of Christ.

or Gorm.[2] It is now generally accepted that it is Thyre who is referred to in her capacity as 'Denmark's adornment' or 'Danebod'.[3] Quite apart from the linguistic arguments supporting this interpretation, one wonders how the alternative interpretation ever gained ground; if the praise had not concerned Thyre, why was she honoured at Jelling in such prestigious ways? The question is justified, since it is very unusual for women to be commemorated with rune-stones. Among Denmark's 177 Viking-Age rune-stones only twelve were raised in memory of women (ten in memory of women on their own; two in memory of women together with men).[4] Further, it is exceptional for a king to sponsor rune-stones; these two in Jelling and one stone in Hedeby, sponsored by a King Svein (probably 'Forkbeard') in memory of his 'hirdman' (Dk 3: Pl. 21), are the only examples.

Since it is unusual for women to be honoured with rune-stones, we can assume that we are dealing with unusual women. The importance of Thyre 'Danebod' is confirmed by Saxo Grammaticus, Sven Aggesen, and their Icelandic colleagues—even if they give very different accounts of her role in Danish history. It is clear that these medieval authors had not seen Gorm's stone; according to Saxo, Thyre survived her husband, and in Sven Aggesen's work it is impossible to decide who survived whom.[5] Neither of them knew that it was Gorm who should have commemorated Thyre; they both report that Harald wanted to honour his mother (not both parents) with a big stone, an enterprise that, according to Sven Aggesen, had to be interrupted because of a rebellion against Harald, while, according to Saxo, it was the direct cause of the uprising.[6] Tradition had obviously preserved the memory both of a stone commemorating Thyre that was never erected, and of the epithet that honoured her, the real meaning of which had, however, been forgotten. Both Sven and the author of the *Jómsvíkinga saga* render her name 'Denmark's ornament' (*Decus Datie*; *Danmarkar bót*), but while Sven explains it by saying that she had rescued the Danish kingdom from being conquered by the German emperor, the author of the

[2] Moltke (1976: 167, and 1985: 207) rejects the argument, accepted in *DR* (col. 77), that the epithet referred to Gorm (the 'framing theory'). Lange (1982–3) tries to revive the debate in support of the 'framing theory', arguing that **but**, which he interprets as 'bøt', i.e. 'strong', must refer to Gorm, 'the greatest military leader and first sole king of the country' (p. 217); his argumentation is far from convincing.

[3] The meaning of the epithet has also been debated; a general interpretation has been 'the one who mended Denmark': see *DR*, cols. 78–80; K. M. Nielsen (1974), 156 ff.; Moltke (1976), 167, and (1985), 207. Since other translations of **but** are possible, the interpretation will doubtless be the object of further discussions.

[4] In memory of women only: DR 26, 29–30, 34, 40–1, 55, 114(?), 134, and 188; in memory of women together with men: DR 42 and 143.

[5] Saxo Grammaticus (1931 edn.), I, IX. xi (p. 268); Aggesen (1917 edn.), VII (pp. 116–17).

[6] Saxo Grammaticus (1931 edn.), X. viii (p. 276); Aggesen (1917 edn.), VII–VIII (pp. 116–21).

Jómsvíkinga saga has her rescue the Danes from a famine.[7] According to Saxo, who calls her 'the head of the Danish sovereignty' (*Danicae maiestatis caput*) she defended the southern border of Denmark by building a fortification (*Danevirke*).[8]

Critical historians have rejected these late stories as fantasies, but it is hardly justifiable to let Thyre completely disappear from Danish history—as Lauritz Weibull did.[9] We will return to these medieval stories, but first there is other evidence to be considered.

If only 'unusual' women were honoured by rune-stones, who were they? Most seem to have belonged to the very highest strata of society; so, for example, Viborg was the mother of a prominent chieftain in Bække (DR 20), and there is little doubt that Asbod was the wife of a *landhirþir* or 'estate steward' (DR 134).[10] Like Thyre Danebod a certain Thyre without a surname had two, perhaps even three, rune-stones raised in her memory, confirming her importance and high status:

DR 26 (Læborg, with a 'Thor's hammer'): (side A) **rhafnukatufi hiau runaR þasiaft** (side B) **þurui trutnik sina** (Tue, Ravn's descendant, carved these runes in memory of Thyre, his queen).

DR 29 (Bække 1): **rafnuka tufi auk futin auk knubli þaiR þriR kaþu þuruiaR hauk** (Tue, Ravn's descendant, and Funden and Gnyble, those three made Thyre's mound).

DR 34 (Horne): . . . **fnukatufikaþihaukþ**—— . . . (Tue (Ravn's) descendant, made (Thyre's or this ?) mound).

DR asserts that the Horne stone, raised by the same man who honoured Thyre in Læborg and Bække, does not commemorate anyone called Thyre. The only trace left of the deceased's name is þ and a following rune that cannot be **u**, but was plausibly **a**. Since in Læborg and Bække the name Thyre is spelled with a **u** directly after **þ**, the editors state that the name in the Horne inscription cannot have been Thyre. They admit that on Harald's stone (DR 42) the name is spelt **þąurui**, with an **a** before **u**, but since they presuppose that the Horne inscription is using the same formula as Bække 1 (**kaþu þuruiaR hauk**), they state that the missing word cannot have been Thyre but possibly **þansi** ('this'). This argument, however, is weak; even if the same formula had been used, we cannot assume consistency in the spelling.

Although the name of the woman commemorated in at least two of the above inscriptions is Thyre and her stones belong to the same

7 Aggesen (1917 edn.), VI (pp. 114–15); V–VII (pp. 108–17); *Jómsvíkinga saga* (1962 edn.), Ch. 3, pp. 3–4.

8 Saxo Grammaticus (1931 edn.), x. vi (p. 274); x. iii (p. 272).

9 Weibull (1948), 225–43.

10 See discussion below, cf. n. 21.

period as the Jelling stones, the editors of *DR* did not identify her as Thyre 'Danebod'.[11] It is, however, most unlikely that, in a period when women were seldom commemorated by rune-stones, two contemporaries in Jutland, both named Thyre, were honoured by two (one of them possibly by three) rune-stones, a distinction that was only once bestowed on a man.[12]

The reasons given for *not* identifying the Thyre of the inscriptions from Læborg and Bække with King Gorm's wife require some discussion. First, the *DR* editors' argument is that 'since Thyre was one of the most common names at the time, the identification of Thyre on the Bække–Læborg stones with Gorm's Thyre must be considered highly uncertain' (DR col. 52). As the claim that the name was common at that time largely depends on its occurrence in seven (possibly eight) inscriptions, four or five of which are in question here, the argument is circular. Even if this name *was* common, the fact that the only additional information given to identify the Thyre in the Læborg and Bække stones—which are close to Jelling—is that she was Tue's queen makes it more likely that she was the same person, and very well known. It is significant that the other three women called Thyre who are named in runic inscriptions are identified as the widows or mother of named individuals (DR 97, 133, 217).[13]

Secondly, the Bække and Horne inscriptions refer to Thyre's *mound*, but, according to Moltke, Queen Thyre never had a mound of her own but was buried together with King Gorm, in the mound that he had himself made.[14] We now know that this was a false assumption; Thyre was *not* buried together with Gorm.[15] The place of her burial remains unknown.

Thirdly, while, in *DR*, the Læborg, Bække, and Horne stones are dated as 'pre-Jelling', Moltke later changed his mind and accepted that they must be later than Gorm's stone and at least contemporary with Harald's.[16] The arguments in favour of their dating before Gorm's time were the—wrongly placed—**h** in **rhafnukatufi** (DR 26), indicating a knowledge of the original spelling of the name *hrafn*, together with the type of word-divider on the Læborg stone,[17] while, on the other hand, the arrangement of the band around edge of the face of the Horne stone led Moltke to think that it should be dated *c.*1000.[18]

Despite these revised datings Moltke continued to reject the identification of Ravninge-Tue's Thyre with Thyre Danebod. There is, however, no

[11] See *DR*, col. 52; but cf. K. M. Nielsen (1974), 172–9. [12] DR 2 and 4 (Sigtryg).

[13] DR 97: Thyre, the wife of Vigot; DR 133: Thyre, the mother of Odinkar and Gudmund; DR 217: Thyre, the wife of Krog.

[14] Moltke (1976), 200. [15] Krogh (1982), 188.

[16] Moltke (1976), 185. [17] See n. 19 below.

[18] In Bække 1 the sponsor of these three stones spells his name **rafnuka tufi**, without an **h** and with a word-division before **tufi**.

reason to suppose that rune-stones were erected immediately after the death of the people being commemorated. Harald's stone at Jelling, for example, must have been erected some time after his parents' death. What is more, there is no reason to suppose that all Ravninge-Tue's stones were strictly contemporary. To judge by the dating criteria used by Moltke, they must have been erected over a period of years.[19] It is, therefore, worth considering the implications of identifying the Læborg–Bække Thyre with the Thyre Danebod of Jelling.

In the debate about the meaning and significance of **tanmarkaR but** there has been no discussion of the reasons for erecting rune-stones, and why the fashion flourished for only a relatively short time. As I have tried to demonstrate, rune-stones were not merely memorials to the dead but reflect the claims of surviving relatives or partners.

What, then, were the claims reflected in the Jelling inscriptions? I suggest they concerned the very important inheritance that Harald claimed after his father's death. If the Thyre commemorated by Ravninge-Tue was indeed the same person as the Thyre commemorated by Gorm and Harald, what was he claiming? Moltke argued that when Ravninge-Tue stated that he had cut the runes in memory of his **trutnik**, *drottning* ('lady'/'queen'), he was in effect declaring that he was subordinate to an unnamed lord, and that Thyre was his lord's wife. This is highly questionable. Why should an inferior sponsor two, perhaps three, rune-stones to commemorate the wife of his superior, and who was this superior lord, if not Gorm himself?[20] It is much more likely that **trutnik**, *drottning*, simply denoted his own wife, and that by commemorating her he declared his right to administer the inheritance she left.[21]

A possible interpretation of this evidence is that during the first half of the tenth century Ravn and Gorm competed for Danish royal power and that one of the main objectives in their conflict was control of 'Denmark', the boundary territory east of the Store Bælt (Great Belt).[22]

[19] This brings us to the question of whether the Bække 2 stone might also have been sponsored by Ravninge-Tue. It has previously been argued that the Bække 2 stone was sponsored by 'Revne and Tobbe (?)' in memory of 'their mother Vibrog (Viborg?)', but I wonder if the spelling **hribna ktubi** may instead be a variant of the spelling **rhafnukatufi**, i.e. 'Ravninge-Tue'. If this is so, he sponsored *two* stones in Bække, one in memory of his mother Vibrog and the other in memory of Thyre (in Læborg referred to as his **trutnik**= 'queen'). Cf. DR 30 (Bække 2): **hribna ktubi**; DR 26 (Læborg): **rhafnukatufi**; DR 29 (Bække 1): **rafnuka tufi**; DR 34 (Horne): . . . **fnukatufi** . . .

[20] It is generally very rare for rune-stones to be sponsored by inferiors in memory of superiors; apart from the Karlevi stone (in Öland) there are only four examples in Denmark: DR 58, 131, 295, and 363—in all cases commemorating *men*.

[21] Like Asser, who honoured his wife (**trutnik**), Asbod, DR 134.

[22] For this interpretation of Denmark, see P. Sawyer (1988), 22–3. Albrectsen (1994: 17–26) is willing to interpret *mark* as a border area when it comes to Slesvig but obviously not

The description of Thyre as **tanmarkaR but** signified not only that she came from that area, but had inherited a claim to authority there, making her a very attractive marriage partner. If we assume that, like Ragnhild who commemorated two husbands, either side of the Store Bælt, Thyre subsequently married both Gorm and Ravninge-Tue,[23] the many monuments honouring her are understandable as a manifestation of the political tug-of-war. As excavations at Jelling have shown that the south mound lacked a grave-chamber, and that the north mound contained only the remains of Gorm, which were removed by Harald to the church he built there,[24] we cannot any longer suppose that Thyre was buried there. If, as seems likely, she was in fact buried by the Ravn family who, according to the Bække 1 stone 'made Thyre's mound', it was even more important for Harald to prove that he was her son and heir, as he did on the huge Jelling stone. It is moreover possible that he built the south—empty—mound in Jelling, in order to obscure the fact that Thyre had been buried by another, competing, family about thirty kilometres from Jelling. The remarkable similarity between the monuments at Bække and Jelling, both of which incorporated a Bronze-Age mound at the end of a stone ship-setting, is another indication of competition between the two families.[25]

This interpretation leaves several questions open.

1. We know that Harald's stone at Jelling has always stood exactly halfway between the two mounds—but where was Gorm's stone placed originally?
2. If Harald was responsible for completing both the mounds at Jelling, what was the form of Gorm's monument in honour of Thyre? The word **kubl** ('memorial') in Gorm's inscription may refer to something more than the rune-stone itself.
3. Why did Gorm commemorate Thyre? In a period when wives were very rarely honoured by rune-stones, we can safely assume that it was because the husband needed to publicize the alliance, whether its importance was social or political. But why did Gorm as king of the Danes need to do so? Was his power questioned?
4. Why does Harald not refer to his father as king, although Gorm is

when it comes to areas east of the Store Bælt. He argues against a view that, during the 10th cent., the Danish kingdom was divided into two parts, only one of which was called 'Denmark', a view that is held by nobody, so far as I know. There is no question of a divided kingdom but of border areas, subordinated to Danish kings that were not yet fully integrated in the kingdom.

[23] Cf. Ragnhild, who had also been married twice, once in Fyn, once in Sjælland, and who commemorated both husbands, in Glavendrup and Tryggevælde respectively (DR 209 and 230).

[24] Cf. Krogh (1982), 183–216.

[25] See also K. M. Nielsen (1974), 190.

called that in his own inscription? Can it be that Gorm was never called king during his own lifetime?

5. Why does Gorm's inscription show younger features than Harald's?[26]

The later traditions about Gorm, Harald, and Thyre provide some clues to answer these questions. Both Saxo's and Sven Aggesen's versions of events were of course coloured by their contemporary circumstances, with distortions and errors, but they do have several significant features in common.

Neither Saxo nor Sven reports that Gorm survived Thyre, although that is the message of Gorm's stone! Both writers depict Gorm as a shadowy figure, while Thyre is a politically active woman who, according to Sven, outwitted the German emperor and, according to Saxo, did the same to her husband. According to both authors, Harald was faced by a rebellion when he wanted to honour his mother with a stone. It is only Saxo who makes this the direct cause of the uprising that led Harald to abandon any attempts to honour his mother. According to Saxo, Thyre only accepted Gorm's proposal of marriage on condition that he gave her 'Denmark' as dower or morning-gift. Whatever 'Denmark' meant in this context, the condition is clearly so unreasonable that Saxo must have misunderstood what he had heard or read. The tradition reported by Saxo that the marriage was made on certain conditions is probably correct, that was normal practice, but the condition is more likely to have been that Thyre brought 'Denmark' as her dowry in return for certain undertakings by Gorm, who as a result had the opportunity to extend his power beyond the Store Bælt. The elements in the traditional account presented by Sven and Saxo that are relevant here are: (1) Thyre, whose epithet ('Danebod') was well-known but misunderstood, came from 'Denmark', east of the Store Bælt; (2) she survived Gorm (who had in some way been outwitted by her); and (3) Harald wanted to honour her memory with a stone that, because of a rebellion and Harald's loss of power, was never erected and was unknown until it was discovered in the sixteenth century.

In the light of these traditions it is possible to modify the reconstruction of events put forward above in the following ways: Gorm, by marrying Thyre from 'Denmark', extended his power, but faced competition from the family of Ravn, based in Bække (and probably from others as well). After Gorm's death, Thyre married Tue, a descendant of Ravn. Harald buried his father with pagan rites in a large mound raised over a

[26] See Pls. 1 (beginning of Ch. 1) and 38 A–C. Cf. Palm (1992), 33. The existence of a serpent's head (to the right—an ornamental detail to which Erling Johansen and Aslak Liestøl (1982–3: 210) have drawn attention) argues in favour of a later dating for Gorm's stone. It should also be observed that on Gorm's stone Thyre is referred to as Gorm's **kuna**, a word for wife that occurs in only one other inscription of the same period (DR 209). In other cases the words used are **lika** (DR 40), **trutnik** (DR 26), and **trunik** (DR 134).

Bronze-Age burial, at Jelling, not far from Bække. When Thyre died, Tue and his kinsmen buried her in a mound and erected two or three rune-stones in her honour. Harald gained the upper hand, sooner or later, and in order to conceal the fact that his mother, Thyre, was buried elsewhere and to assert his claim to his maternal inheritance he built an empty mound in her memory.

When Harald was converted to Christianity, he also 'converted' the monuments in Jelling. Between the mounds he not only built a church, in which he reburied his father's remains, but also set up his impressive rune-stone. In order to strengthen his position as king and legitimate heir of Gorm and Thyre Harald sponsored another stone in Gorm's name in order to emphasize (1) that Thyre had been Gorm's wife, and (2) that she, as 'Denmark's adornment', had enabled him to extend his power. It also proclaimed (3) that his father, Gorm, had been *king*, and (4) that Gorm had been responsible for certain, probably pagan, memorials in Jelling, while Harald, as a Christian, was responsible for the church and the huge, manifestly Christian, rune-stone.

This was to rewrite history, and when Harald tried to erect this stone (according to Saxo, on his mother's mound) there was a rebellion that led to his fall. When his son Sven finally triumphed, he abandoned Jelling and moved the centre of gravity of the kingdom eastwards to 'Denmark', with Roskilde and Lund as the new centres. The 'Jelling dynasty' was therefore only based in Jelling for a very short time.

APPENDIX 1

Distribution of Rune-stones

Distribution of rune-stones according to region

Region	Main corpus of inscriptions	Relationship subgroup[a]
Bornholm	31	26
Denmark:		
Blekinge	4	4
Fyn	7	6
Halland	1	1
Lolland-Falster	8	8
Nørrejylland	80	70
Sjælland	9	7
Skåne	53	47
Sønderjylland	5	5
Öland	1[b]	1
SUBTOTAL	168	149
Norway:		
Agder	7	6
Buskerud	3	1
Hordaland	5	3
Mon and Jæren	1	0
Møre and Romsdal	1	1
Nordland	2	2
Opland	9	8
Rogaland	18	15
Sogn and Fjordane	2	1
Telemark	1	1
Troms	1	1
Trøndelag	1	1
SUBTOTAL	51	40
Sweden:		
Gotland	30	22
Gästrikland	15	11
Hälsingland	11	9
Jämtland	1	0
Medelpad	15	13
Närke	19	11
Småland	116	82
Södermanland	352	273
Uppland	1,016	791
Värmland	2	0
Västergötland	156	117
Västmanland	25	16
Östergötland	212	180
Öland	87	36
SUBTOTAL	2,057	1,561
GRAND TOTAL	2,307	1,776

[a] The 'Relationship Subgroup' is defined on p. 43.
[b] DR 411, a very early rune-stone—before Öland became Swedish.

APPENDIX 2

Categories of Sponsors and Deceased

(a) *Distribution of the Relationship Subgroup (of 1,776 inscriptions) according to region and sex* (m = men; w = women)

	No. of inscrs.	Sponsors (%)			Deceased (%)		
		m	w	m+w	m	w	m+w
Dk	149	83.9	12.8	3.4	90.7	7.4	2
No	40	90	10	—	90	10	—
Sm	82	86.5	4.9	8.6	95	2.5	2.5
Vg	117	82.4	12.6	5	89.9	8.4	1.7
Ög	180	79.4	15.6	5.1	93.3	4.5	2.3
Sö	273	72.8	11.3	15.8	94.8	2.9	2.2
U	791	63.6	12.4	24.1	93.3	2.7	4.1
Öl	36	83.8	5.4	10.8	81.1	13.5	5.4
Other regions	108	82.4	8.3	9.3	84.2	5.6	10.2
TOTAL	1,776	72.9	11.7	15.3	92.3	4.2	3.4

(b) *Regional distribution of the main categories A–EF shown as percentages of the Relationship Subgroup*

	Scand.	South/West		Intermediate			East			*Deceased*
		Dk	No	Sm	Vg	Ög	Sö	U	Öl	
Male sponsors:										
A	66.6	75.2	82.5	81.5	72.3	73.2	69.2	58.9	64.9	*m*
B	3.6	6.7	7.5	2.5	8.4	4.5	1.8	1.9	13.5	*w*
AB	2.7	2	—	2.5	1.7	1.7	1.8	2.8	5.4	*m+w*
TOTAL	72.9	83.9	90	86.5	82.4	79.4	72.8	63.6	83.8	
Female sponsors:										
C	11.1	12.1	7.5	4.9	12.6	15.6	10.6	11.5	5.4	*m*
D	0.4	0.7	2.5	—	—	—	0.7	0.4	—	*w*
CD	0.2	—	—	—	—	—	—	0.5	—	*m+w*
TOTAL	11.7	12.8	10	4.9	12.6	15.6	11.3	12.4	5.4	
Male+female sponsors:										
E	14.6	3.4	—	8.6	5	4.5	15	22.9	10.8	*m*
F	0.2	—	—	—	—	—	0.4	0.4	—	*w*
EF	0.5	—	—	—	—	0.6	0.4	0.8	—	*m+w*
TOTAL	15.3	3.4	—	8.6	5	5.1	15.8	24.1	10.8	

APPENDIX 3

Frequency of Relationships

Percentage incidence of the 2,280 relationships in the Relationship Subgroup, according to zone and region

Relationship	Total	South/West			Intermediate				East			
		Dk	No	Average	Sm	Vg	Ög	Average	Sö	U	Öl	Average
son~father	31.5	18.8	10	(14.4)[a]	31.8	21.9	30.1	27.9	34.9	33.4	41.3	36.5
brother~brother	14.8	23.2	25	(24.1)	19.1	14.3	15.8	16.4	16.4	12	13	13.8
father~son	10.4	4.3	15		19.1	16.5	11.3	(15.6)	12.1	9.3	4.3	(8.6)
wife~husband	8.0	7.9	5	(6.5)	2	7.5	8.4	(6.0)	5.6	10	10.9	(8.8)
man~man	7.6	11.6	22.5		8.3	9.9	6.4	8.2	5	6.5	6.5	6.1
mother~son	7.2	2.4	—		5.2	4.5	3.5	4.4	9	9	4.3	(7.4)
daughter~father	3.8	—	—		2	0.7	4.9	(2.5)	5.1	4.8	—	(3.3)
kinsman~kinsman	3.4	3.7	7.5	(5.6)	4.3	7.4	7.9	6.5	2.6	2.4	—	(1.7)
sister~brother	1.2	—	—		1	—	2.5	(1.2)	2.2	1.3	—	(1.2)
male partner~ditto	1.1	9.8	—		—	2.3	1	(1.1)	0.3	0.3	—	(0.2)
all others	11.0	18.3	15.0		7.2	15.0	8.2		6.8	11.0	19.7	

Note. The greatest differences within the three zones are as follows.

South/West. The greatest correspondence between Denmark and Norway is the high proportion of brother~brother. Both regions also share a low proportion of son~father: Norway has the lowest proportion in the whole of Scandinavia, while the proportion in Denmark is nearer to that in Västergötland. Wife~husband has a low proportion in both Norway and Södermanland, but an even lower one in Småland, while in Denmark it is again nearer to that in Västergötland. There is a big difference in the proportion of father~son; while this is quite common in Norway, it is very rare in Denmark (cf. Öland).

Intermediate. In some cases Östergötland is more similar to Södermanland than to Västergötland and Småland, as follows: brother~brother, Ög 15.8/Sö 16.4; father~son, 11.3/12.1; man~man, 6.4/5.0; daughter~father, 4.9/5.1; sister~brother, 2.5/2.2.

East. In Öland neither daughters, kinsmen, sisters, nor male partners sponsor memorials to men. Also, Öland is similar to Denmark in having a very low proportion of father~son.

[a] When there are great differences within the three areas, the average proportion is shown in brackets, or—for Denmark and Norway—not given at all.

APPENDIX 4
Inheritances

The tables below show the regional distribution of different types of inheritance in the Relationship Subgroup of 1,776 inscriptions.

(a) *Regional grand totals*

Scandinavia	1,776
Dk	149
No	40
Vg	117
Sm	82
Ög	180
U	791
Sö	273
Öl	36
Other regions	108

Note. Since many of the inscriptions contain more than one type of inheritance, the total number of inheritances is greater than the number of inscriptions.

(b) *Types of inheritance by region*

Type of inheritance	Scand.	Dk	No	Vg	Sm	Ög	U	Sö	Öl	Other regions
1. *Paternal*										
no. of inscrs.	772	32	4	29	35	71	398	137	20	46[a]
% of total	43.5	21.5	10	24.8	42.7	39.4	50.3	50.2	55.5	
2. *Fraternal*										
no. of inscrs.	355	39	10	18	19	36	139	67	7	20
% of total	20	26.2	25	15.4	23.2	20	17.6	24.5	19.4	
3. *Reverse*										
no. of inscrs.	339	11	7	27	21	31	157	60	3	22
% of total	19.1	7.4	17.5	23.1	25.6	17.2	19.8	22	8.3	
4. *Maternal*										
no. of inscrs.	55	7	1	2	0	2	23	9	2	9
% of total	3.1	4.7	2.5	1.7	0	1.1	2.9	3.3	5.5	

[a] No percentages are given for 'Other regions' (Bornholm, Gotland, Gästrikland, Hälsingland, Jämtland, Medelpad, and Västmanland).

(c) *Heirs and heiresses by region*

Type of inheritance	Scand.	Dk	No	Vg	Sm	Ög	U	Sö	Öl	Other regions
1. *Paternal*										
no. of inscrs.	772	32	4	29	35	71	398	137	20	46
% men	87.6	100	(4)[a]	(28)	94.3	85.9	83.9	86.9	(20)	(45)
% women	6.2	0	0	(1)	2.9	12.7	6.5	8	0	0
% men+ women	6.2	0	0	0	2.9	1.4	9.5	5.1	0	(1)
2. *Fraternal*										
no. of inscrs.	355	39	10	18	19	36	139	67	7	20
% men	92.7	100	(10)	(18)	(18)	86.1	91.4	88	(7)	(20)
% women	4.5	0	0	0	(1)	11.1	4.3	7.5	0	0
% men+ women	2.8	0	0	0	0	2.8	4.3	4.5	0	0
3. *Reverse*										
no. of inscrs.	339	11	7	27	21	31	157	60	3	22
% men	51	(7)	(6)	(21)	(16)	77.4	36.9	45	(2)	(14)
% women	29.5	(4)	(1)	(5)	(2)	19.4	37.6	26.7	(1)	(3)
% men+ women	19.5	0	0	(1)	(3)	3.2	25.5	28.3	0	(5)
4. *Maternal*										
no. of inscrs.	55	7	1	2	0	2	23	9	2	9
% men	90.9	(6)	(1)	(2)	0	(2)	(22)	(7)	(2)	(8)
% women	5.5	(1)	0	0	0	0	0	(2)	0	(1)
% men+ women	3.6	0	0	0	0	0	(1)	0	0	0

[a] Where there are less than 30 inscriptions in a region no percentages are given; instead, the *number of inscriptions* is given in brackets.

(d) *Divided inheritances by region*

Type of inheritance	Scand.	Dk	No	Vg	Sm	Ög	U	Sö	Öl	Other regions
1. *Paternal*										
no. of inscrs.	772	32	4	29	35	71	398	137	20	46
div. inheritances	488	8	0	13	11	29	292	94	15	26
% of total[a]	63.2	25		44.8	31.4	40.8	73.4	68.6		
2. *Fraternal*										
no of inscrs.	355	39	10	18	19	36	139	67	7	20
div. inheritances	172	4	2	1	2	8	99	44	3	9
% of total[a]	48.5	10.3				22.2	71.2	65.7		
3. *Reverse*										
no of inscrs.	339	11	7	27	21	31	157	60	3	22
div. inheritances	111	0	0	1	4	1	73	26	1	5
% of total[a]	32.7					3.2	46.5	43.3		
4. *Maternal*										
no. of inscrs.	55	7	1	2	0	2	23	9	2	9
div. inheritances	24	0	0	1	0	1	9	6	2	5
% of total[a]	43.6									

[a] Where there are less than *c*.30 inscriptions in a region no percentages are given.

APPENDIX 5

Unspecified Relationships Implying Inheritance

In the Relationship Subgroup (of 1,776 inscriptions) there are 199 inscriptions with unspecified relationships, of which 132 nevertheless *imply* inheritance. These 132 inscriptions are grouped in the following way (see Ch. 3.5):

I now lost or damaged that are likely to have included specified relationships, e.g. Gs 15: 'Roald and Udd had this stone raised in memory of Ärnmund . . . [damaged part] May God help his spirit'

II complete, specifying some relationships but not all, e.g. U 126: 'Forkunn had this stone and this bridge made in memory of Torger, his son, and in memory of Åsgisl. May God and God's . . . help their spirit'

IIIa complete, without specifying any relationships but *suggesting* close relationship, e.g. Sö 250: 'Gynna raised this stone in memory of Saxe, Halvdan's son' (women normally act as sponsors only when they are closely related to the deceased)

IIIb complete, without specifying any relationships but stressing the identity of the deceased, e.g. Ög 94: 'Asgöta and Gudmund they raised this monument in memory of Oddlög(?), who lived in Haddestad. He was a good bonde, died in Greece(?)'

Regional distribution of 132 unspecified relationships implying inheritance

Region	Group and identification nos.			
	I	II	IIIa	IIIb
Dk[a]	6, 53, 63, 90, 106, 115, 129, 365	149	120, 188, 239	29, 81, 91, 110, 345, 359
Born[a]	370, 397	377	—	—
No[b]	226, 259	—	66, (247)[c]	186, 413, N5, N6
G	59, 188, 200, 207	113	—	—
Gs	8, 14, 15	9	—	—
Hs	2	—	—	—
M	—	—	—	4
Ög	41, 74, 107	23	238; N6	82, 94, 151, 177
Öl	92	—	27	—
Sm	—	—	—	10
Sö	228, 321, 323	115, 124, 149, 254, 262, 265	165, 250, 276	69, 160, 277; N18
U	111, 115, 140, 319, 476, 498, 590, 719, 773, 827, 909, 1020, 1062; N7, N25	126, 437, 454, 508, 514, 585, 622, 753, 854, 920, 922, 932, 938, 1036, 1053, 1069, 1107	4, 322, 361, 757, 775, 1172, 1177	16, 121, 419, 518, 524, 540, 721, 755, 818, 824, 905
Vg	2, 177, 180	33	9, 30, 66, 165	95, 127, 135, 141
Vs	11; N1	—	—	—
TOTAL OF INSCRS.	47	29	21	35 (= 132)

[a] Identification numbers refer to *DR*.
[b] Identification numbers refer to *NIyR*.
[c] No 247 does not belong to the subgroup since we do not know if the sponsors were men, or women, or both. The inscription says: 'Members of the ale-guild raised this stone in memory of Skarde when they drank his "inheritance ale"', thus a clear indication of an inheritance being at stake.

APPENDIX 6
Titles

In the main corpus of 2,307 inscriptions there are 209 occurrences of titles. The glossary below lists these titles and their meanings, and the tables that follow show (*a*) their regional distribution, and (*b*) their individual identification numbers.

Glossary of titles

Note. With some exceptions I have followed the English translations in 'Samnordisk runtextdatabas', made by Mindy Macleod. The exceptions are: *goði*, *rinkr*, *skipari*, *stallari*, *drengr*, *sveinn*, *dróttning*, and *karl*.

Rulers	
konungr	king
dróttinn	lord
goði	chieftain
hersir	chieftain
(rinkr)	(chieftain)
jarl	earl
Leaders	
stýrimaðr	captain
landhirðir	estate-steward
liðs forungi	commander of the retinue
landmaðr	landholder
landborinn maðr	man born to landed property
búmaðr	estate-holder
Retainers	
heimþegi	retainer, 'hirdman'
liði	retinue
tiðenda maðr	herald?
skipari	skipper
skipvǫrðr	ship's watch
víkinga vǫrðr	viking watch
stallari	staller
þegn	thegn
drengr	warrior (dreng)
sveinn	warrior? (sven)
Others	
bryti	steward
húskarl	housecarl
smiðr	smith
dróttning	lady; 'queen'
karl	ceorl?
gildi	guild-brother
víkingr	viking
skald	skald
lækir	doctor
prestr	priest

(a) *Inscriptions with titles: proportions and types*

Region	No. of inscrs.	% of total	Rulers	Leaders	Retainers[a]	Others	No. of titles
Dk	63	37.5	10	6	12+37=49	7	72
Born	5	16.1	—	—	1+4=5	—	5
No	2	3.9	1	—	— —	2	3
Sm	7	6.0	2	—	2+4=6	1	9
Vg	40	25.6	—	—	0+40=40	2	42
Ög	11	5.2	—	—	1+11=12	—	12
Sö	26	7.4	1	4	3+16=19	2	26
U	28	2.8	2	5	2+13=15	7	29
Öl	1	1.1	—	—	0+1=1	—	1
G	2	6.7	—	—	—	2	2
Gs	2	(15)[b]	—	1	—	1	2
Nä	2	(19)[b]	—	—	0+2=2	—	2
Vs	4	(25)[b]	—	—	0+4=4	—	4
TOTAL	193	8.4	16	16	21+132=153	24	209[c]
% of 209 titles			7.7	7.7	73.2	11.5	100.1

[a] In this column the second figure is the number of thegns, drengs, and svens.

[b] Where there are less than 30 inscriptions in a region no percentages are given; instead, the *number of inscriptions* is given in brackets.

[c] Some inscriptions have more than one title.

(b) *Inscriptions with titles: distribution and identification numbers*

	Dk+Born[a]	No[b]	Sm	Vg	Ög	Sö	U	Öl	Other regions
Rulers									
konungr	3, 4, 41–2		42				11		
dróttinn	131, 209, 295	252							
goði	190, 192, 209								
hersir						136			
(rinkr)							(907)[c]		
jarl			76						
Leaders									
stýrimaðr	1					161	922, 1011, 1016, N39		
landhirðir	107, 134								
liðs forungi						338	112		Gs 13
landmaðr	133, 314					338			
landborinn maðr						54			
búmaðr	291								
Retainers									
heimþegi	1, 3, 154–5, 296–7								
liði	411						479	(1)[d]	
tiðenda maðr	N3								
skipari	82, 218, 275, 363; Born 379		42			171, 335			
skipvǫrðr						N1[e]			
víkinga vǫrðr							617		

þegn	86, 98–9, 106, 115, 121, 123, 130, 143, 209, 213, 277, 293–4, 343, N5; Born 372		35, 37	8, 59, 62, 73–4, 101–3, 108, 113, 115, 137, 150–2, 157–8	200	34, 90, 112, 151, 158, 170, 367, N2			
drengr	1, 68, 77–8, 127, 150, 262, 268, 276, 288–9, 295, 330, 339, 345; Born 380, 387, 389		48, 93	32, 61, 81, 90, 112, 114, 123, 125–7, 130, 153–4, 157, 162, 179, 181, 184	60, 64, 81, 104, 111, 122, 130, 210, N18, N19	4?, 55, 137?, 155, 163, 167, 177, 320	143, 166, 289, 610, 760=796, 767–8, 802, 808, 972	58	Nä 18, 23; Vs 3, 18, 19, 22
þegn or *drengr*	53, 94, 129, 228, 278			82, 136, 139					
sveinn	344			155–6	66		225, 323, 432		
Others									
bryti	40					42	11		
húskarl						18	330, 335		
smiðr	58, 91, 108								Gs 14
dróttning	26, 134								
karl							659		
unknown title	217								
gildi							379, 391		
víkingr			10						G N1
skald		239					951		
lækir									G 138
prestr				91					

[a] Identification numbers in this column refer to *DR*.
[b] Identification numbers in this column refer to *NIyR*.
[c] I originally interpreted the word **rinkia** in U 907 as a form of **rinkr* (= warrior), but Lena Peterson has informed me that this is linguistically impossible. The title has, however, been kept (bracketed) in this survey, since the meaning of **rinkia** does not seem to be clear.
[d] Öl 1 is the same inscription as DR 411.
[e] Sö N1: *gerðu skipvorð* = 'kept ship's watch'.

APPENDIX 7
Epithets

In the main corpus of 2,307 inscriptions there are 330 occurrences of epithets. The glossary below lists the epithets and their meanings, and the tables that follow show (*a*) their regional distribution, (*b*) their individual identification numbers, and (*c*) their regional distribution and identification numbers according to status of bearer.

Glossary of epithets

Note. I have followed the English translations in 'Samnordisk runtextdatabas', made by Mindy Macleod.

1. 'good', etc.

góðr	good
allgóðr	all-good
mjǫk góðr	very good
harða góðr	very good
betri	better
beztr/betzti	best

2. 'able'; 'bold'/'strong'

hæfr	competent
nýtr	capable
snarr	quick
snjallr	able
frœkn	brave
þróttr[1]	strong

3. 'noble', 'first', etc.

dróttinfastr	loyal to his lord
dýrr	valued
fyrstr	first
heiðverðr	honourable

4. 'wise', 'eloquent', etc.

hugsnjallr	able-minded
ráðspakr	quick-witted
rýnastr	most rune-skilled
málrisinn	eloquent
málspakr	eloquent
spár	foresighted
úheimskr	wise
jafn	just

5. 'generous'

góðr matar	free with food
mildr matar	free with food
maðr matar	free with food
óniðdingr[2]	unvillainous

[1] *þróttr* is not an adjective but a noun, meaning 'power', 'strength'; *þróttar þegn* should thus be translated 'thegn of strength'.

[2] *óniðdingr* is a noun meaning 'generous person' (or rather: 'a not ungenerous person').

(a) *Inscriptions with epithets: incidence and types*

Region	No. of inscrs.	Epithets						No. of epithets[a]
		1. good, etc.	2a. able	2b/c. bold/ strong	3. noble, first, dear	4. wise, eloquent, etc.	5. generous	
Dk	47	42			4	3	1	50
Born	7	7						7
No	2[b]	1						2
Sm	12	5	1				7	13
Vg	44	44						44
Ög	32	27	5	1/0			2	35
Sö	64	42	14	0/7		3	2	68
U	78	70	6			3	3	82
Öl	13	13						13
G	4	3	1					4
Gs	2	1	1					2
Nä	3		2	1/0				3
Vs	7	7						7
Hs	1	1						1
TOTAL	316	263	30	2/7	4	9	15	330
% of 330 epithets		79.7		11.8 (=2a+b/c)	1.2	2.7	4.5	

[a] Some inscriptions contain more than one epithet.
[b] Including NIyR 68: a 'most accomplished' maiden (*honnurst*).

(b) *Inscriptions with epithets: distribution and identification numbers*

Epithet	Dk + Born[a]	No[b]	Sm	Vg	Ög	Sö	U	Öl	Other regions
1. good, etc.									
góðr	53, 55, 98, 127, 129, 143, 150, 154, 212b, 262, 298, 314, 339, 365, 411; Born 372, 380, 387, 390, 394, 402		16, 37, 93	8, 81, 92, 101, 103, 110, 128	10, 17, 60, 66, 81, 94, 112, 119, 122, 130, 154, 172, 180, 190, 201, 207, 220–1, 224, 239(×2), N1, N2, N9	*38 inscrs.*[c]	*64 inscrs.*[d]	33, 56, 58, 66, 70, 73–4, 76, 118, 130, 146, 159, 170	G 59, 138, 188; Hs 21; Vs 3, 4, 11, 18, 19
allgóðr	293; Born 389			32	N18		143, 208		
mjǫk góðr	94, 99			73, 108, 123, 137, 150					
harða góðr	1, 68, 77, 86, 106, 115, 123, 127, 130, 213, 228, 268, 276, 278, 288–9, 294, 338, 343	244	48	59, 61, 62, 74–5, 82, 90, 92, 102, 112–15, 126, 130, 136, 139, 151–8, 162, 179, 181, 184	60, 104		610?		
betri	230								
beztr/betzti	133, 217, 291, N5		35	67, 125		64, 136, 213, 338	16, 527, 802		Vs 24; Gs 14; Vs 22
2. (a) able, (b) bold, (c) strong									
(a) *hæfr*					N18		289		
nýtr			157		15, 21, 105, 200	7, 314	56, 166		Nä 23, 34
snarr									G 113
snjallr						11, 70, 88, 140, 144–5, 147,	225, 960, 1163		Gs 2

(b) *frækn*			81	155, 163, 166, 320, 344		
(c) *þróttr*				90, 112, 151, 158, 170, 367, N2		Nä 18
3. noble, first, etc.						
dróttinnfastr	81					
dýrr	81					
fyrstr	277					
heiðverðr	209					
4. wise, eloquent, etc.						
hugsnjallr				136		
ráðspakr	161					
rýnastr				56		
málrisinn					703, 739	
málspakr					1146	
spár	294					
úheimskr	56					
jafn				338		
5. generous						
góðr matar		39, 44		130	805	
mildr matar	291				739	
maðr matar					703	
óniðingr		2, 5, 37, 131?, 147	77, 217	189		

[a] Identification numbers refer to *DR*.
[b] Identification numbers refer to *NIyR*.
[c] The individual identification numbers are: Sö 4, 10, 18–19, 21–2, 28, 31, 34, 38, 62, 94, 125, 130, 138–9, 157, 161, 167, 184, 192(×2), 195, 208–9, 214, 220, 231, 236, 252, 262, 287, 300, 311, 331, 349–50, 359, 374.
[d] The individual identification numbers are: U 1, 42, 57, 69, 79, 160–1, 171, 186, 191, 199=235, 208, 249, 265, 300, 323–4, 349, 425, 430, 435, 508, 512, 524, 530, 585–6, 634, 641, 692, 697, 703, 707, 712, 714, 723, 727, 729, 733, 740, 751, 753, 760=796, 763–4, 767–8, 770, 781, 808, 828, 838, 873, 926, 972, 999, 1032(×2), 1033, 1098, N10, N17, N35, N39.

(c) *Regional distribution of 'Good (better, best) people'*

Region	No. of 'good'	Title-bearers	'Bonde'	Man, etc.	Husband	Wife	Father	Brother	Son	Daughter/ sister	Other women
Dk[a]	42	1, 53, 68, 77, 86, 94, 98, 99, 106, 115, 123, 127, 129–30, 133*, 143, 150,154, 213, 228, 262, 268, 276, 278, 288–9, 291*, 293–4, 314, 339, 343, N5*	298, 338	55, 127, 217*, 230*, 365, 411		212b					
Born[a]	7	372, 380, 387, 389	402				390	394			
No[b]	1			244							
Sm	5	35*, 37, 48, 93		16							
Vg	44	8, 32, 59, 61–2, 73–4, 81–2, 90, 101–3, 108, 112–15, 123, 125*, 126–7, 130, 136–7, 139, 150–8, 162, 179, 181, 184	92, 128			75?	110?				67*
Ög	27[c]	60, 66, 104, 122, 130, 201, N18	94, 119, 207, 221	81	112, 160, 224	239	17, 154, 172, 180, 220		N9	dau. 239, sr. N1	
Sö	42	4, 34, 161, 167	19, 157, 195, 208, 213*	64*, 136*, 338*	94, 192		10, 21–2, 28, 31, 38,	184, 209, 252, 287	62, 138, 192, 236, 331		139, 300, 311[d]

Sö (cont.)							125, 130, 214, 220, 231?, 262, 349–50, 359, 374				
U	70[e]	143, 610?, 760=796, 767–8, 802*, 808, 972, N39	1, 16*, 57, 199=235, 425, 435, 527*, 641, 999	249, 300, 323, N10	753		*26 inscrs.*[f]	712, 740	*14 inscrs.*[g]		
Öl	13[h]	58	76				33, 56, 66, 70, 74, 118, 146	73, 170	159		
G	3[i]			59, 188							
Gs	1[j]										
Hs	1										
Vs	7	3, 18–19, 22*	24[k]	11		(24*)[k]			4	(sr. 24)[k]	21

* Inscriptions marked with an asterisk contain the forms 'better' or 'best'.
[a] Identification numbers refer to *DR*.
[b] Identification numbers refer to *NIyR*.
[c] The number includes three inscriptions in which it is uncertain what 'good' refers to: Ög 10, 190, N2. [d] Sö 300 and 311 mention 'good mothers'.
[d] Sö 300 and 311 mention 'good mothers'.
[e] In U 714 and 781 it is uncertain what 'good' refers to. In U 18 and 161 male in-laws are referred to, and in U 524 an heir.
[f] U 79, 160, 186, 191, 349, 508, 512, 530, 586, 634, 692, 697, 707, 723, 727, 729, 751, 763–4, 770, 828, 838, 873, 1032(×2), 1033, 1098.
[g] U 42, 69, 79, 171, 208, 265, 324, 430, 585, 703, 733, 926, N17, N35.
[h] In Öl 130 it is uncertain what 'good' refers to.
[i] Includes G 138: 'good' doctor? (*lækir*).
[j] Includes Gs 14: 'the best of smiths'.
[k] Vs 24 contains 'good bonde', 'better housewife', and 'good sister', but has still been counted once only, i.e. as an example of 'good bonde'.

APPENDIX 8

'Bönder'

Regional incidence and status of 'bönder'

Region	No. of 'bönder'	Status: Head of household	Uncertain	Husband
Dk[a]	5	298, 338		277, 291, 317
Born[a]	2	402		399
No	0	—		—
Sm	3	1		64, 124
Vg	10	92, 128		18, 118, 150, 152, 154, 170–1, 178
Ög	23	94, 105, 119, 207, 221	10, 140, N2	15, 29, 93, 112, 128, 150, 160, 192, 194, 200, 205–6, 212, 224, 228, N10
Sö	30[b]	6, 19, 72, 157, 195, 208, 213, 346	314, 334	8, 14, 23, 31, 94, 96, 101, 116, 137, 157, 192, 198, 205, 213, 242, 288, 297, 306, 328, 338
U	125[c]	1, 16, 57, 199=235, 355, 425, 435, 512, 527, 641, 805, 859+860, 999	84, 526, 538, 568, 981, 1068, 1120	20, 25, 30, 35–8, 43–4, 50, 62, 79–80, 114, 121, 131, 136, 142–4, 146, 151–2, 158?, 173, 193, 210–11, 214, 238–40, 253=264, 277, 294, 310, 317–18, 328–9 (+330–2), 351, 376, 390, 412, 421, 445, 460–3, 478, 485, 517, 532, 545, 572, 606, 617–18, 621, 633, 637, 647, 687, 699, 716, 721, 744, 753, 789, 793, 819, 821, 829, 838, 846, 854, 871, 873, 875, 878, 908, 919, 935, 956–7, 961, 963–4, 977, 986, 1035, 1044, 1083, 1095, 1097, 1111, 1116, 1151–2, 1154, 1162, N5, N8, N19
Öl	9	76?	6, 32, 37, 113, 144	31, 68–9
Gs	2			1, 4?
Nä	3		9	28, 32
Vs	1	24		
TOTAL	213	34 inscrs.	18 inscrs.	161 inscrs.

[a] Identification numbers refer to *DR*.

[b] In both Sö 157 and 213 the word 'bonde' is used twice, once meaning 'head of household', once meaning 'husband'.

[c] In U 330–2 the word 'bonde' is used as meaning 'husband', but since they are sponsored by the same woman as U 329, they have not been counted in the total here.

APPENDIX 9
Travellers

Travellers: regional distribution and identification numbers

Region	Travellers' stones/ regional total	Identification nos. of travellers' stones
Dk[a]	16/168	3, 6, 37, 66, 108, 154, 177, 216, 220, 259, 266, 279, 295, 330, 334, 337
Born[a]	1/31	380
No[b]	3/51	62, 184, 239
Sm	9/116	5, 27, 29, 46, 48, 51, 77, 101, 104
Vg	10/156	20, 40, 61, 81, 135, 178, 181, 184, 187, 194
Ög	14/212	8, 30, 68, 81, 83, 94, 104, 111, 145, 155, 181, 213, N7, N12
Sö	64/352	9, 14, 16, 33–4, 39, 46–7, 49, 53, 55, 62, 65, 82–3, 85, 92, 96, 105–8, 126, 130–1, 137, 148, 155, 159–60, 163–6, 170–1, 173–4, 179, 198, 207, 216–17, 254, 260, 277, 279, 281, 287, 308, 319–20, 333, 335, 338, 345, 348, 351, 360, N1, N11–12, N18–19
U	76/1,016	73, 104, 112, 130, 133, 136, 140–1, 153–4, 158, 180, 194, 201, 209, 214+215[c], 240+241[c], 258, 270, 283, 324, 343+344[c], 346, 349, 356, 358, 363, 366, 374–5, 414, 431, 439, 446, 504, 518, 533, 539–40, 577, 582, 605, 611, 614, 616–17, 636, 643+644[c], 654, 661, 668+669[c], 687, 698–9, 778, 785, 792, 812, 837, 890, 896, 898, 922, 925, 948, 954, 956, 978, 1016, 1028, 1048, 1087, 1143, 1181, N7, N32
G	6/30	134–5, 138, 207, 220, N1
Gs	2/15	8, 13
Nä	1/19	29
Vs	8/25	1+2[c], 5, 9+10[c], 18–19, 22, 27, N1
TOTAL	210/2,307 (=9.1%)	

[a] Identification numbers refer to *DR*.
[b] Identification numbers refer to *NIyR*.
[c] Paired stones.

APPENDIX 10
Bridge-builders

(a) *Bridge-inscriptions: regional distribution and identification numbers*

Region	Bridge-inscriptions/ regional total	Identification nos. of bridge-inscriptions
Dk[a]	3/168	229, 238, 269
No[b]	2/51	68, N4
Sm	11/116	15, 17, 72?, 73, 80, 96, 99, 100, 130, 137, 157
Vg	8/156	2, 4, 17, 30, 76, 173, 182, 183
Ög	10/212	10, 45, 68, 132, 147, 157, 162, 212, 214, N3
Sö	19/352	see table (b) below
U	81/1,016	see table (b) below
Öl	1/87	74
G	2/30	203, N5
Hs	1/11	12
J	1/1	1
Vs	6/25	9+10[c], 13, 17, 28, 31, N1
TOTAL	145 inscrs.	

[a] Identification numbers refer to *DR*.
[b] Identification numbers refer to *NIyR*.
[c] Paired stones.

(b) *Bridge-inscriptions in Södermanland and Uppland: distribution and identification numbers by district*

District	Bridge-inscriptions/ district total	Identification nos. of bridge-inscriptions
Södermanland		
Hölebo	2/26	22, 30
Oppunda	2/28	71?, 74
O. Rekarne	1/30	101
Rönö	6/55	122, 127, 141–2, 149, N10
Selebo	2/37	174, 178
Sotholm	1/55	252
Svartlösa	2/28	299–300
Öknebo	2/22	311–12
Åker	1/22	328
Uppland		
Färentuna	2/44	36, 45
Sollentuna	6/61	69, 92, 101–2, 114, 118
Danderyd	11/54	126–7, 135, 142–3, 145–6, 149, 164–5, N7
Vallentuna	9/101	200, 212?, 217, 224, 236, 261, 267, 272, 279
Seminghundra	15/83	311, 315+316[a], 317, 323, 327, 330, 335, 345, 347, 353, 363, 376, 377–8, N23
Ärlinghundra	5/71	456, 462, 475–6, N32
Långhundra	3/27	489, 497, 505
Sjuhundra	1/9	514
Lyhundra	2/27	565, 572
Närdinghundra	1/4	586
Bro	1/23	617
Håbo	1/61	638
Åsunda	1/35	791
Lagunda	3/31	818, 828, 839
Hagunda	5/41	854, 856, 859, 861, 867
Ulleråker	1/27	901+904[a]
Vaksala	1/37	947
Rasbo	3/19	993, 995–6
Norunda	7/49	1017, 1020, 1031, 1033, 1041, 1046, N47
Bälinge	2/49	1108, 1114
Oland	1/13	1133

[a] Paired stones.

CATALOGUE

EXPLANATORY NOTES

All inscriptions are listed by number under the following regions: Denmark with Bornholm; Norway; the Swedish provinces in alphabetical order (see Map 4), but with Uppland last (see Map 5). The 'Further Particulars' section at the end of each main region gives additional details of ornaments, multiple commemorations, and connected monuments.

Following the standard editions, the Danish and Norwegian inscriptions are listed under the main administrative districts that were current at the time of their publication. The Danish inscriptions are listed under the headings 'amt', or, for the now Swedish provinces of Skåne and Halland, under 'län', and the Norwegian under 'fylke'. (These main disctricts correspond roughly to counties or shires in England.) Under each *amt*, *län*, and *fylke* the inscriptions are listed under subdistricts in the column headed 'herred'.

The Swedish inscriptions are listed under provinces (Sw. 'landskap') that have not been administrative districts in historic times but are generally accepted as regional units. In the provinces of Närke, Östergötland, Småland, Södermanland, Uppland, Västergötland, and Västmanland the inscriptions are listed under subdistricts, headed 'härad', and in Gotland under 'ting'.

Place-names are normally given in the forms used in the standard editions. The numbered footnotes give further references for certain stones, and/or indicate (by an asterisk) the present location of stones that have been moved.

Column headings in the Catalogue

id. Identification number in the standard editions, or (for new finds) the new numbers used here, preceded by 'N' and the abbreviated region/province: Dk (Denmark), No (Norway), G (Gotland), etc. Numbers may have the following suffixes:

- # 'lost'
- m 'multiple monuments', indicating that two (or more) rune-stones were sponsored by, or erected in memory of, the same individuals (see 'Further Particulars')
- c 'connected monuments', indicating that individuals mentioned in several inscriptions are related to, or otherwise connected with, each other (see 'Further Particulars')

herred This column appears in the tables for Denmark, Bornholm, and Norway only. In Denmark the stones are named after the parish (see the 'place column'); in Norway the parish sometimes corresponds to the 'herred', but where this is not the case, the parish will be given in the place column. For towns, the word 'town' follows the name, e.g. 'Århus town'.

parish For the Swedish stones the subdistricts (Sw. plur. *härader* or (major) towns) do not have a column but are given as headings, and, instead, the names of the parishes have a special column. For smaller towns the word 'town' follows the name, e.g. 'Visby town'.

place — Location of stone when it was first recorded; for abbreviations used in place-names (and a glossary of Scandinavian words), see pp. 197–8 below. If a stone has been moved, this is indicated in a footnote, but if the new location is close to the place where it was first recorded, this is indicated only by a semicolon in the column entry (e.g. 'ch.; ch.yd.'= 'moved from the church into the churchyard').

type — This column appears in the tables for Sweden and Uppland only, where an entry is shown only if the stone is other than upright:

- rec. recumbent stone
- rock inscribed on a rock face

rel.sh. — Relationship between sponsors and deceased (see 'Keys to Codes' below, § 1).

s/m — Single sponsor or multiple sponsors.

dat. — Date=period (see 'Keys to Codes' below, § 2).

fsp. — Find-spot (see 'Keys to Codes' below, § 3).

state
- dam. damaged
- fr. fragment(s)
- h. hidden (for example behind a wall, pillar, etc.)
- ph. partly hidden
- pt/s. part(s), i.e. bigger than fragments
- 2s/3s inscription on two/three sides

height — Height in centimetres; shown in brackets for fragments, parts, and partly hidden stones.

design — Layout style of inscription—in bands or serpents (see Cat. Fig. 1 below). The number of rows/bands is shown in brackets. Where the design is uncertain, this is indicated by a solidus, e.g. 7/9=*either* design 7 *or* design 9. The + sign after the design code indicates additional bands or serpents that have not been classified. Note also:

- fr front
- bk back
- sd side
- xbd bands shaped like a cross
- mbd band on the middle of the stone
- sp spiral
- go Gotlandic style, see Pl. 6
- öl Ölandic style, see Pl. 7

cross — Type of cross carved on stone (see Cat. Fig. 2 below); the word 'cross' indicates that the stone is shaped like a cross. The number of crosses is shown in brackets. Where the cross type is uncertain, this is indicated by

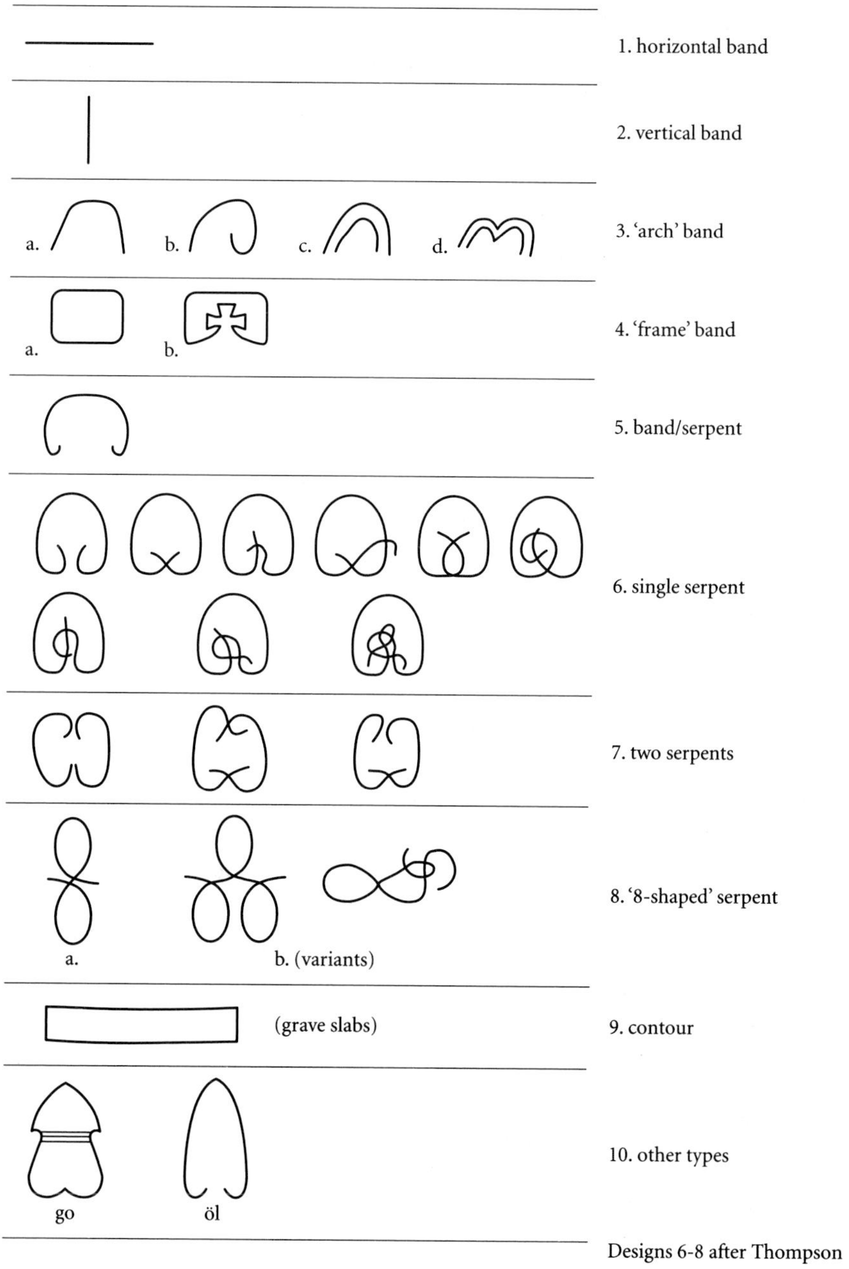

CATALOGUE FIGURE 1. Layout styles of inscriptions

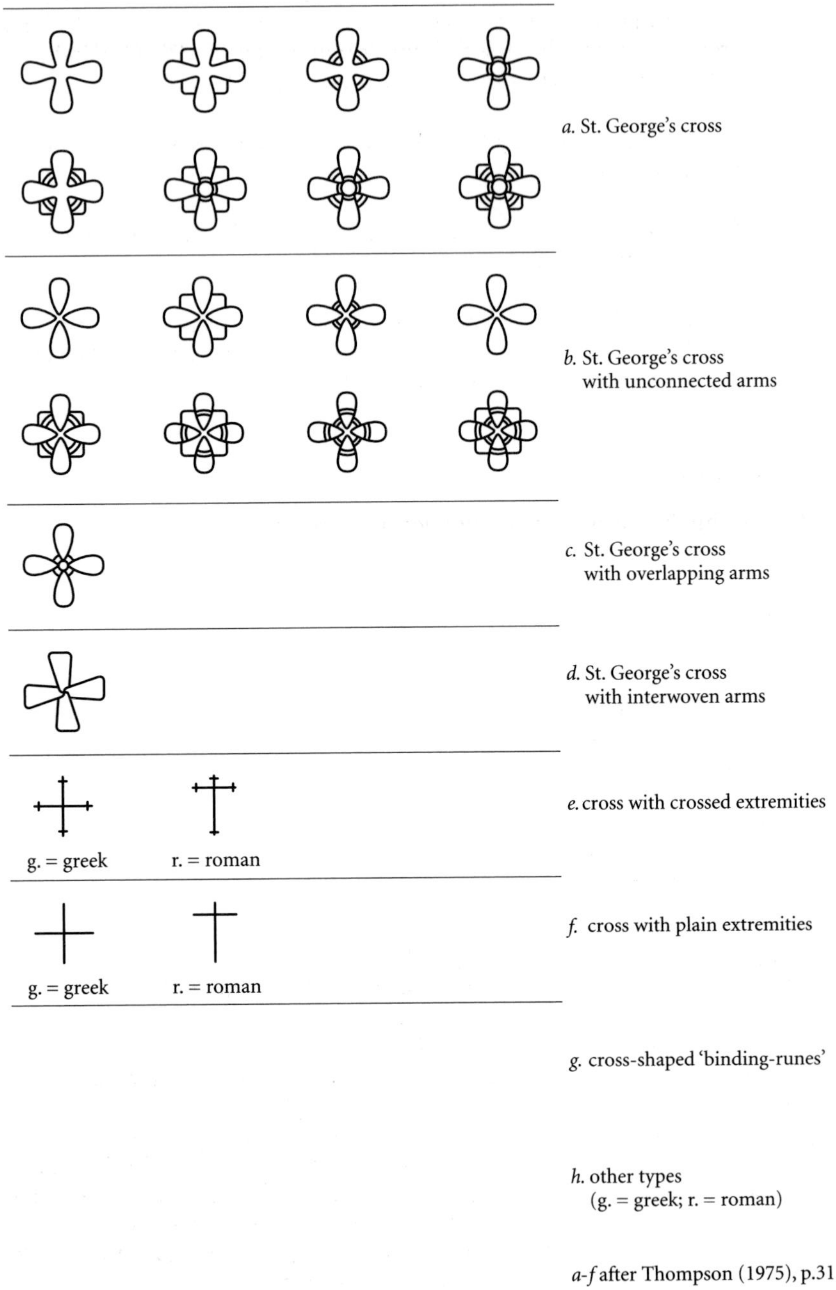

a. St. George's cross
b. St. George's cross with unconnected arms
c. St. George's cross with overlapping arms
d. St. George's cross with interwoven arms
e. cross with crossed extremities
g. = greek
r. = roman
f. cross with plain extremities
g. = greek
r. = roman
g. cross-shaped 'binding-runes'
h. other types (g. = greek; r. = roman)
a-f after Thompson (1975), p.31

Catalogue Figure 2. Types of cross

a solidus, e.g. A/B: *either* cross type A *or* cross type B; or, if there are more than two possibilities, by a dash, e.g. A–C: cross type A *or* B *or* C. If the cross type cannot be classified, this is indicated by a +(?). 'Chr.' indicates a depiction of Christ crucified (see plate 38 A–C).

orn.	Ornament, indicated by +; see 'Further Particulars' sections for details of individual ornaments.
rel.	Religious expression or image, or Christian/pagan invocations; a Christian prayer is indicated by +.
sign.	Signature of the rune-carver. If the name is unreadable, this is indicated by 'X'. If it is uncertain whether there is a signature or not, and whether there is a cross or not, this is indicated by +(?).

Keys to Codes

1. Relationship between sponsors and deceased (rel.sh.)

Main categories (~ means 'commemorating')

A	men~men
B	men~women
AB	men~men+women
C	women~men
D	women~women
CD	women~men+women
E	men+women~men
F	men+women~women
EF	men+women~men+women
X	uncertain relationship
0	no relationship

Subcategories	*Examples*
1. child~parent	A 1=son~father, C 1=daughter~father; E 1=son+daughter~father
2. sibling~sibling	B 2=brother~sister
3. parent~child	C 3=mother~son; F 3=parents~daughter
4. kin~kin*	A 4=(sometimes) nephew~uncle
5. partner~partner	in category A=trading partners or comrades-in-arms; in other categories=spouses. In these cases the sponsor and deceased were not blood relations but may have had property in common.
6. unspecified relationships	i.e. when names only are mentioned and only the sexes can be determined
7a. superior~inferior	A 7a=king~'hirdman'
7b. inferior~superior	A 7b=man~leader
8. person~him/herself	i.e. the 'self-commemorative' inscriptions

* This category contains both consanguinity and affinity and many different terms of kinship, e.g. nephew (brother's or sister's son) grandson (son's or daughter's son), uncle (father's or mother's brother), unspecified consanguinity (*frændi*) and affinity (*magR*), i.e. son/brother/father-in-law.

Complex relationships

(i) When sponsors commemorate people with whom they have different relationships, these are separated by a solidus: A 1/2=a man commemorates both his father and brother.

(ii) Two (or more) sponsors with different relationships to the deceased are indicated and separated by a full point: A 1.2=a son *and* a brother commemorate a man together.

(iii) Where the sponsors are of both sexes (categories E and F) and have different relationships with the deceased, their sex is shown by combining the digit with a zero (0), *before* for a woman, *after* for a man, e.g. 01=daughter, 10=son. E 10.05 therefore means that a man is commemorated by his son and his wife.

(iv) In inscriptions commemorating two or more people of both sexes with whom the sponsor has different relationships (categories AB and CD), zero is used in the same way as in (iii) above, e.g. AB 20/01=a man commemorates both his brother and his mother.

(v) In the few cases where there are different relationships between sponsors and deceased of both sexes (category EF), this is explained in combinations of the other categories, e.g. EF: CD 3+AB 2: a mother commemorates her son and daughter and a man his brother and sister.

2. Date=Period

1 before *c.*960
2 960–1050
2a 960–1020
2b 1020–1050
3 1050–1100
3a 1050–1070
3b 1070–1100
4 after 1100

3. Find-spot

1 countryside
2 field, meadow
3 farm/messuage
4 dump
5 river, lake, sea
6 bridge
7 roadside
8 ancient grave(s)
9 *thing*-place
10 church, churchyard, vicarage

Abbreviations used in the Catalogue

br.	bridge
Ch.	church
ch.host.	church hostel
ch.yd.	churchyard
des.	deserted; not in use
f.d.	Sw. 'före detta'=formerly
g.	Sw. 'gård'=farm, e.g. Norreg.=Norregården=North farm
h.	hidden (see also ph. below)
kv.	Sw. 'kvarter'=quarter (in towns)
L.	Sw. 'lilla'=little
med.	medieval
mon.	monastery or nunnery
N.	Dan. 'nord/nørre'; Norw. 'nord/nordre'; Sw. 'norr/norra'=north
Ø.	Dan. 'øst(er)/østre'; Norw. 'øst/østre'=east
Ö.	Sw. 'öst(er)/östra'=east
p.	parish
ph.	partly hidden
S.	Dan. 'syd/søndre'; Norw. 'sønna/søndre'; Sw. 'syd/söder/södra'=south
St.	Sw. 'stora'=great, e.g. St. Västölet
S:t	saint
v.	Sw. 'väg'=road, e.g. Turingev.=Turinge road
V.	Dan. 'vest/vestre'; Norw. 'vest/vestre'; Sw. 'väst(er)/västra'=west
vic.	vicarage

Glossary of Scandinavian words used in the Catalogue

ägor	property
allmänning	common
amt	Dan. 'county'
äng	meadow
ärkebiskopsgård(en)	(the) archbishop's residence
ås	ridge
backe	slope
bruk	factory
by	village
bygdegård	community centre
domkyrka(n)	(the) cathedral
folkhögskola(n)	(the) folk high school
friluftsmuseum	outdoor museum
fylke	Norw. 'county'
gamla	old
gård	farm
gata(n)	(the) street
härad	Sw. regional (administrative) district
hed	heath
hembygdsgård	old homestead museum

hembygdsmuseum	old homestead museum
herred	Dan. and Norw. regional (administrative) district
klockaregård(en)	(the) church servant's cottage
klockar(e)stuga(n)	(the) church servant's cottage
krog	inn
kvarn	mill (water *or* wind)
län	Sw. 'county'
länsmuseum	regional ('county') museum
malm	hill
nedre	lower
skog	forest
skola(n)	(the) school
slottsskolan	the castle school
Stifts- och landsbibliotek(et)	(the) Diocese and County Library
tä	cattle-path
ting	Gotlandic (administrative) district
torg(et)	(the) market-place

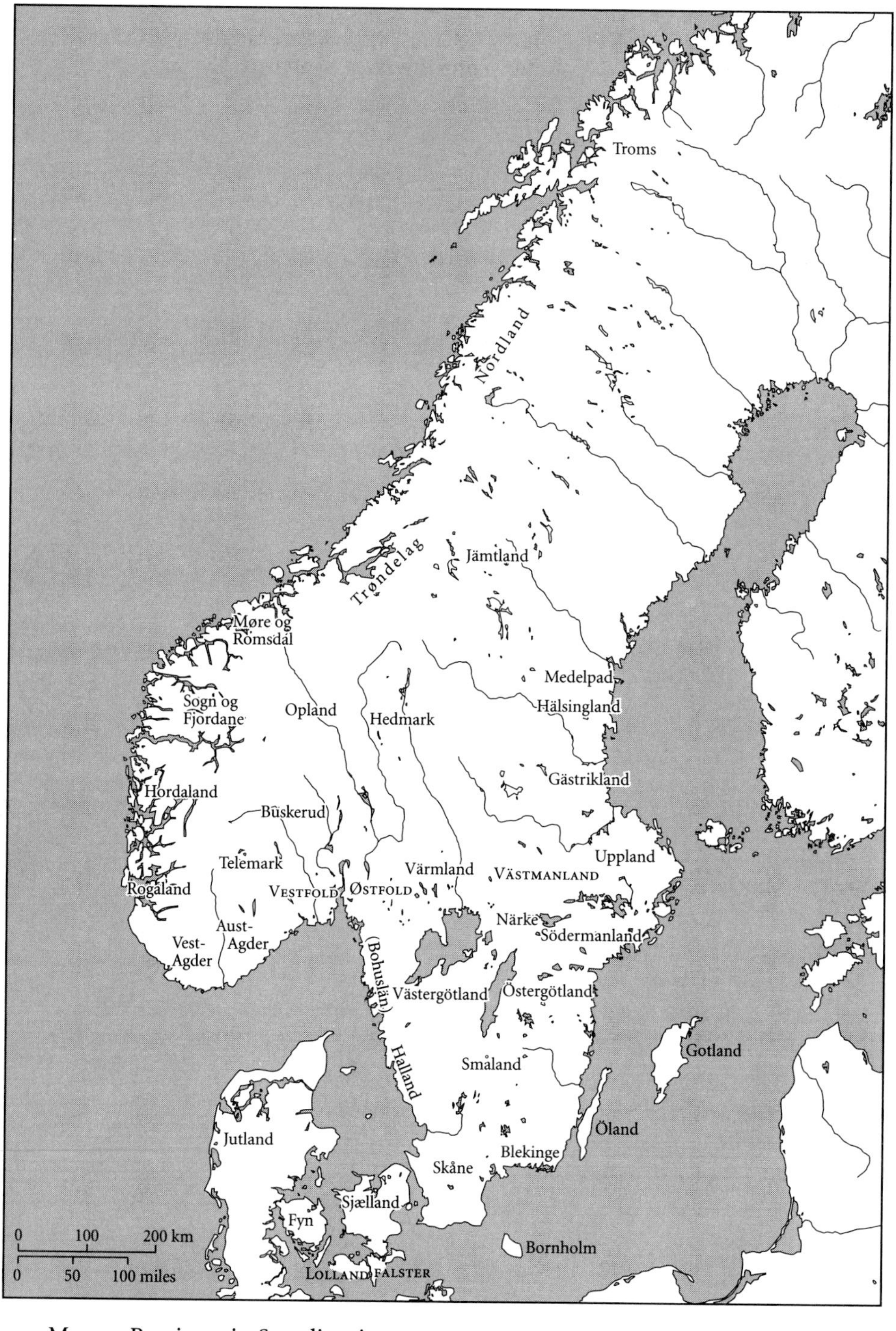

MAP 4. Provinces in Scandinavia

DENMARK (DK) AND BORNHOLM (BORN)

(Total no. of inscriptions: Dk, 168 + Born, 32)

id.	herred	place	rel.sh.	s/m	dat.	fsp.	state	height	design	cross	orn.	rel.	sign.
Sønderjylland													
Gottorp amt													
1[1]	Hedeby (medieval town)		A 5	s	2	8	2s	210	2	—	—	—	—
2m[2]	Hedeby		C 3	s	2	5,7	2s	214	2(2+3)	—	—	—	—
3	Hedeby	Oxevejen	A 7a	s	2	7,8	2s	158	2(4+1)	—	—	—	—
4m[3]	Hedeby	Gottorp	C 3	s	2	3	3s	124	2(3+ 2+1)	—	—	—	Gorm
6	Slesvig town	Sles.cathedral	A 6	s	2	10	4s	68	2(1+ 3+1)	—	—	—	Gudmund
Nørrejylland													
Ribe amt													
26mc	Malt	Læborg	B 5?	s	2	7,10	2s	236	2	—	+	—	—
29mc	Anst	Bække ch.	B 5?	m	2	10	—	164	2(3)	—	—	—	—
30c	Anst	Bække	B 1	m	2	8	—	125	2(2)	—	—	—	—
34mc[4]	Ø.Horne	Horne ch.	B 5?	s	2	10	—	70	3a	—	—	—	—
Vejle amt													
36	Brusk	S.Vilstrup	X	s	2	1	—	188	2	—	—	—	—
37	Jerlev	Egtved ch.yd.	A 2	s	2	10	—	80	2(3)	—	—	—	—
40	Tørrild	Randbøl	B 5	s	2	7	—	185	2(3)	—	—	—	—
41mc	Tørrild	Jelling ch.yd.	B 5	s	2	10	2s	139	2(3+1)	—	—	—	—
42mc	Tørrild	Jelling ch.yd.	AB 1	s	2	10	3s	243	1(4+ 1+1)	Chr.	+	—	—
44[5]	Slaug	Grindsted ch.	X 60		2	10	fr.	?	?	—	—	—	—
Århus amt													
53[6]	Had	Gylling	A 6/2	s	2	3	3s,fr.	(137)	2	—	—	—	—
55c[7]	Tyrsting	S.Vissing ch.yd.	D 1	s	2	10	—	245	2(4)	—	—	—	—
56	Tyrsting	S.Vissing ch.yd.	A 1	s	2	10	—	157	2(3)	—	—	—	—
58mc	Hjelmslev	Hørning	A 7b	s	2	6	—	157	3a+ mbd2	A	—	—	—
62	Framlev	Sjelle ch.	A 5	s	2	10	—	163	2(5)	—	+	—	—
63[8]	Århus town	Frue ch.	A 6	s	2	10	pt.	(65)	2(5)	—	—	—	—
65c[9]	Århus town	cathedral school	X		2	3,10	—	100	2(2)	—	—	—	—
66[10]	Århus town	watermill	A 5	m	2	5	3s	160	3b	—	+	—	—
67[11]	Århus town	Frue ch.	A 1	s	2	10	—	196	2	—	—	—	—
68[12]	Århus town	Frue ch.	A 5	m	2	10	2s	157	3a+2	—	—	—	—
69[13]	Hasle	Vejlby	A 4	s	2	8	dam.	150	3a	Er	—	—	—
N1[14]	Gjern	Sporup ch.	A 1	s	2	10	dam.	135	5	—	—	—	—

[1] DR 1: *Museum vorgeschichtlicher Altertümer, Kiel (the asterisk here and at nn. 2, 3, etc. below indicates the present location of the stone).
[2] DR 2: *Museum vorgeschichtlicher Altertümer, Kiel. [3] DR 4: *Museum vorgeschichtlicher Altertümer, Kiel.
[4] DR 34: *Nørholm manor (garden). [5] DR 44: *Grindsted Museum, G. 270. [6] DR 53: *Gylling church.
[7] DR 55: *S.Vissing church. [8] DR 63: *Århus Museum. [9] DR 65: *Århus Museum. [10] DR 66: *Århus Museum.
[11] DR 67: *Århus Museum. [12] DR 68: *Århus Museum. [13] DR 69: *Århus Museum. [14] Dk N1: Moltke (1985), 265.

id.	herred	place	rel.sh.	s/m	dat.	fsp.	state	height	design	cross	orn.	rel.	sign.
Viborg amt													
77	Middelsom	Hjermind	A 2	s	2	8	2s	165	2+1	—	+	—	—
78#	Middelsom	Hjermind	C 3	s	2	2	—	126?	2(2) +1	—	—	—	—
79#	Middelsom	Le	X	m?	2–3	10	—	(200)	3b	+(?)	—	—	—
80	Middelsom	Skern; ch.yd.	X		2	10	—	96	?	—	—	—	—
81	Middelsom	Skern; ch.yd.	C 6	s	2	3	—	193	3c(sp) +1	—	+	—	—
82[15]	Middelsom	S.Vinge	A 7a	s	2	5,7	—	164	2(4)	—	—	—	—
83	Middelsom	S.Vinge ch.	A 2	s	2	10	—	180	2(7)	—	—	spell	—
84#	Middelsom	Langå	X	?	2	5	fr.	(125)	2(3)	—	—	—	—
85#	Middelsom	Langå	A 1/2	s	2	5	—	400	2(3)	—	—	—	Thore?
86	Middelsom	Langå; ch.yd.	A 2	s	2	5	—	158	2(3)	—	—	—	—
87	Middelsom	Langå ch.	X	?	2	10	fr.		?	—	—	—	—
90#	Middelsom	Torup ch.	A 6	s	2	10	—	160?	2(2)	—	—	—	—
91mc	Middelsom	Grensten ch.yd.	A 6	s	2	10	—	143	2(5)	—	—	+	—
94	Sønderlyng	Ålum; ch.	A 3	s	2	10	—	133	2(5)	—	—	—	—
96c	Sønderlyng	Ålum	A 3	s	2	10	2s	205	3b	—	+	+	—
97c	Sønderlyng	Ålum ch.yd.	C 4	s	2	10	—	150	3c(sp)	—	—	—	—
98	Sønderlyng	Bjerregrav ch.	C 5	s	2	10	—	215	2?(3)	—	—	—	—
99	Sønderlyng	Bjerregrav ch.	C 5	s	2	10	2s	140	2(4+1)	—	—	—	Thord
N2[16]	Rind	Klejtrup	X 40	?	2	5	—	165	2	—	—	—	—
N3[17]	Nørlyng	Asmild ch.	C 5	s	2	10	2s	120	2	—	—	—	—
Randers amt													
106#	Galten	Ørum	A 6	m	2	8	—	156	?	—	—	—	—
107[18]	Ø.Lisbjerg	Egå	A 4	m	2	8?	—	108	3a(2)	+(?)	—	—	—
108	S.Djur	Kolind ch.	A 2	s	2	10	—	198	2(4)	—	—	—	—
109	S.Hald	Ø.Alling ch.	A 6	s	2	10	—	139	2(3)	—	—	—	—
110	S.Hald	Virring ch.	A 6	s	2	10	—	155	2(5)	—	—	—	—
114[19]	N.Djur	Rimsø; ch.	B 1	s	2	8,10	2s	226	3b+2	—	—	Tor	—
115	Støvring	Randers	A 6	s	2	3	2s,dam.	120	3a+2	—	—	—	—
116[20]	Støvring	Randers	A 2/1	s	2	3	—	118	2(5)	—	—	—	—
117[21]	Støvring	Mejlby	A 3	s	2	7	—	138	2(4)	—	—	—	—
N4[22]	Støvring	Lem ch.	X 20	s	2	10	dam.	(106)	3a	—	—	—	—
N5[23]	Støvring	Borup ch.	A 1	s	2	10	dam.	170	2	—	—	—	—
118	Rovsø	Stenalt	A 3	s	2	8,3	2s,fr	(60)	?	—	—	—	—
120[24]	Nørhald	Spentrup	C 6	s	2	5,6	—	132	3a?	—	+	—	—
121[25]	Nørhald	Asferg	A 2	s	2	8	—	150	3a+2	—	—	—	—
122	Nørhald	Glenstrup; ch.yd.	A 1	s	2	8,10	—	150	4a	—	—	—	—
123	Nørhald	Glenst.; Handest ch.	A 1	s	2	10	3s	147	3a+2	—	+	—	—
124	Nørhald	V.Tørslev; ch.yd.	A 2	s	2	7	—	154	2(3)	Fr	—	—	—
125	Gerlev	Dalbyover ch.	A 5	s	2	10	—	156	2(3)	—	—	—	—
127[26]	Onsild	Hobro ch.yd.	A 5	s	2	10	—	152	4a	—	—	—	—
N6[27]	Onsild	Svenstrup ch.	X 10	s	2	10	—	100	3b	—	—	—	—
Ålborg amt													
129[28]	Gislum	Durup ch.	A 6	s	2	10	—	78	2?(2)	Fr?	—	—	—
N7[29]	Gislum	Farsø ch.	A 2	m	2	10	—	180	3a+ mbd	—	+	—	—
130	Års	Giver ch.	A 1	s	2	10	—	102	2(4)	—	—	—	—
131	Års	Års ch.yd.	A 7b	s	2	10	2s	160	3a(2) +2	—	—	—	—
132	Års	Flejsborg ch.	A 1	s	2	10	—	150	3a	—	—	—	—
133	Års	Skivum ch.	E 05 ?.10	m	2	10	—	198	2(6)	—	—	—	—
134	Års	Ravnkilde ch.	B 5 or 7?	s	2	10	—	132	2(4)	—	—	—	—
135[30]	Års	Ravnkilde	A 2	s	2	5,8	—	140	3a+ mbd	—	—	—	—

Continued

[15] DR 82: *Ulstrup manor. [16] Dk N2: Moltke (1985), 307 f. [17] Dk N3: Moltke (1985), 306.
[18] DR 107: *Nationalmuseet. [19] DR 114: Moltke (1985), 538. [20] DR 116: Moltke (1985), 537; *Randers Museum.
[21] DR 117: *Randers Museum. [22] Dk N4: Moltke (1985), 531. [23] Dk N5: *NOR* 1996, 6 f. [24] DR 120: M. L. Nielsen (1997*a*), 54.
[25] DR 121: Moltke (1985), 318; *Nationalmuseet. [26] DR 127: *Hobro Museum. [27] Dk N6: Moltke (1985), 312.
[28] DR 129: *Nøragersgård (garden). [29] Dk N7: Moltke (1985), 523. [30] DR 135: *Ravnkilde vicarage (garden).

id.	herred	place	rel.sh.	s/m	dat.	fsp.	state	height	design	cross	orn.	rel.	sign.
138	Hornum	Suldrup ch.yd.	A 2	s	2	10	—	127	3b	—	—	—	—
143	Fleskum	Gunderup; ch.	AB 1	s	2	8	2s	246	2(2+2)	—	—	—	—
144	Fleskum	Gunderup ch.yd.	A 1	s	1	10	—	225	2	—	—	—	—
145	Fleskum	Ferslev ch.	A 3	s	2	10	—	106	2(2)	—	—	—	—

Tisted amt

id.	herred	place	rel.sh.	s/m	dat.	fsp.	state	height	design	cross	orn.	rel.	sign.
149#[31]	Refs	Ydby	A 6.1	m	2	8?	3s	(126)	2(1+ 1+2)	—	—	—	—
150[32]	Refs	Hurup ch.yd	A 1 or 2?	s	2	10	2s	106	2(1+4)	—	—	—	—
154#[33]	Hundborg	Torup ch.	C 5	s	2	10	—	187	3a(2)+ mbd2	—	—	—	—
155	Hundborg	Sjørind ch.yd.	C 5	s	2	10	—	63	3a(2)	—	—	—	—

Hjørring amt

id.	herred	place	rel.sh.	s/m	dat.	fsp.	state	height	design	cross	orn.	rel.	sign.
160	Hvetbo	Jetsmark	A 2	s	2	3	—	118	2(2)	—	—	—	—
161	Hvetbo	Hune ch.yd.	A 1	m	2	10	—	149	3a+ mbd(2)	—	—	—	—

Fyn

Svendborg amt

id.	herred	place	rel.sh.	s/m	dat.	fsp.	state	height	design	cross	orn.	rel.	sign.
188#	Vindinge	Ørbæk	B 6	s	1	8	—	?	?	—	—	—	—
189#	V.Vindinge	Avnslev ch.yd.	X	s	1	10	2s	?	2(2+2)	—	—	—	—

Odense amt

id.	herred	place	rel.sh.	s/m	dat.	fsp.	state	height	design	cross	orn.	rel.	sign.
190c	Båg	Helnæs	A 4	s	1	8	—	205	2(4)	—	—	—	Åver
192c[34]	Båg	Flemløse ch.yd.	A 1	m	1	10	2s	225	2(3+1)	—	—	—	Åver
201#	Åsum	Allerup ch.	AB 1	s	3	10	—	?	3a(2)	—	—	—	—
202	Åsum	Rønninge	A 2	s	2	6,8	—	104	2(3)	—	—	—	—
209m[35]	Skam	Glavendrup	E 05.10	m	2	8	3s	188	2(4+ 6+2)	—	—	Tor; spell	Sote

Lolland-Falster

Maribo amt

(212 bears two different inscriptions)

id.	herred	place	rel.sh.	s/m	dat.	fsp.	state	height	design	cross	orn.	rel.	sign.
212a	Sønder	Tillitse ch.yd.	A 8	s	3	10	3s	143	2(4+2)	A	+	+	—
212b	Sønder	Tillitse ch.yd.	B 1	s	3		—		2(2)	—	—	—	—
213[36]	Sønder	Skovlænge	A 1	s	2	6,8	—	140	2(4)	—	—	—	—
220[37]	Sønder	S.Kirkeby ch.	A 2	s	2	10	dam.	79	2(4)	—	—	Tor	—
216[38]	Fuglse	Tirsted ch.yd.	A 4	m	2	10	2s	254	2(4+3)	—	—	—	—
217[39]	Fuglse	Sædinge	C 5	s	2	5,7	4s	174	2(3?+2+ 3?+2)	—	—	—	—
218	Fuglse	Tågerup; ch.	A 2	m	2	2	—	156	2(4+)	—	—	—	—
219m[40]	Musse	Bregninge ch.yd.	C 3	s	2	8,10	—	163	2(4+)	—	—	—	—

(220 follows 213)

Sjælland

Præstø amt

id.	herred	place	rel.sh.	s/m	dat.	fsp.	state	height	design	cross	orn.	rel.	sign.
221[41]	Vordingborg town		X 60	s	1–2?	3	2s	144	3a+2	—	—	—	—
227#	Tybjerg	Sandby ch.	A 2	s	2	10	fr.	?	1(2)	—	—	—	—
228	Tybjerg	Sandby ch.	A 2	s	2	10	2s	110	2(3+1)	—	—	—	—
229	Tybjerg	Sandby ch.	A 1/2	s	3	10	2s,fr.	144	3a(2+1) +2(2)	—	—	—	—

[31] DR 149: Moltke (1985), 547.
[32] DR 150: Moltke (1985), 528.
[33] DR 154: Moltke (1985), 544.
[34] DR 192: *Jægerspris.
[35] DR 209: Moltke (1985), 226.
[36] DR 213: *Maribo Museum.
[37] DR 220: Moltke (1985), 230.
[38] DR 216: *Nationalmuseet.
[39] DR 217: Moltke (1985), 292, 300; *Maribo Museum.
[40] DR 219: *Nationalmuseet.
[41] DR 221: *Nationalmuseet.

id.	herred	place	rel.sh.	s/m	dat.	fsp.	state	height	design	cross	orn.	rel.	sign.
230m[42]	Fakse	Tryggevælde	C 5	s	2	3	2s	325	2(5)+ 3(sd)	—	—	spell	—
Sorø amt													
237	Alsted	Alsted ch.	A 1/2?	s	2	10	—	140	3a	A	—	—	—
238	Alsted	Fjenneslev ch.yd.	A 8?	s	2	10	—	220	2	Fg	—	—	—
Holbæk amt													
239	Løve	Gørlev ch.	C 6	s	1	10	2s	315	2(2+2)	—	—	—	Gunne, Armund
N8[43]	Løve	Gørlev ch.	X 10	s	2	10	—	160	2+	—	—	—	—
Skåne													
Malmöhus län[44]													
Skytt härad													
258[45]	Bösarp		X	s	2	3,6	4fr.	?	?	Fg	+	—	—
259	Fuglie	Fuglie ch.yd.	A 2	s	2	8,10	—	105	2(4?)	—	—	+	—
260	Fuglie	Toftegården	A 3	s	2	3,8	—	121	2	—	—	—	—
Oxie													
262	Fosie	Fosie; vic.	A 5	s	2	3	—	172	3a+?	—	—	—	—
Bara													
264	Hyby	Vissmarlöv	X	s	2	2	3s	108	2+1	Er(2)	+	—	—
265#	Hyby	Vissmarlöv	X 6	s?	2	3	—	(126)	3b	—	—	—	—
266[46]	Uppåkra	Hjärup	A 2	s	2	?	2s	138	2(2+ 1+)	—	—	—	—
Vemmenhög													
268	Ö.Vemmenhög	Dybäck	A 2	s	2	6,7	—	140	3a	—	—	—	—
269[47]	Källstorp	Jordberga	A 2	s	2	2	3s	111	2	E?	—	—	—
270[48]	Skivarp	Skivarp ch.yd.	A 5	s	2	10	—	105	3a	—	—	—	—
271	Tullstorp	Tullstorp ch.	E 6	m	2	10	—	204	5?	—	+	—	—
272#	Svenstorp	Svenstorp old ch.	X	s?	2	10	—		?	—	—	—	—
275[49]	Solberga	Torsjö	A 2	s	2		—	157	3a+ 2(2)	—	—	—	—
276	Örsjö	Örsjögården	A 2	s	2	3	—	162	4a	—	—	—	—
Ljunit													
277	S.Villie	Rydsgård	C 5	s	2	2	—	180	3(2)	—	—	—	—
278	V.Nöbbelöv	V.Nöbbelöv vic.	A 2	s	2	10	—	234	4a	—	—	—	—
(279: stone bears two different inscriptions)													
279a	Skivarp	Skivarpsv.	A 5	s	2	6,10	dam.	154	4a+3a+ mbd(2)	—	—	—	—
279b	Skivarp	Sjörup old ch.											
280[50]	Skårby	Skårby	A 2	m	2	8	—	240	3a	—	+	—	—
281	Skårby	Skårby ch.yd.	A 6	s	2	10	—	116	3a	—	—	—	—
282m[51]	Skårby	Hunnestad	A 2	m	2	2	—	153	3a(2)	—	+	—	—
283m[52]	Skårby	Hunnestad	A 2	s	2		—	109	3a+2	D	—	—	—
Herrestad													
287	Bjäresjö	Bjäresjö ch.yd.	X 6	s	2	10	—	127	3a	—	—	—	—
288[53]	Bjäresjö	Bjäresjö	A 2	s	2	2,8	—	170	3b	—	—	—	—
289[54]	Bjäresjö	Bergsjöholm	A 4	s	2	2	—	238	3a+ mbd2	—	—	—	—
291[55]	Sövestad	Krageholm	E 05.10	m	2	5	—	148	3a+ mbd2	—	—	—	—
293#	St.Herrestad	Herrestad	C 5	s	2	3	—	?	4a?	—	—	—	—
294	Baldringe	Baldringe ch.yd.	A 1	s	2	10	—	141	3a(2)+ mbd2	—	—	—	—

Continued

[42] DR 230: *Nationalmuseet. [43] Dk N8: Moltke (1985), 239. [44] Now part of Skåne *län*.
[45] DR 258: *Historiska museet in Lund. [46] DR 266: *Stenshöggård. [47] DR 269: *Jordberga manor. [48] DR 270: *Kulturen in Lund.
[49] DR 275: *Torsjö manor. [50] DR 280: *Kulturen in Lund. [51] DR 282: *Kulturen in Lund. [52] DR 283: *Kulturen in Lund.
[53] DR 288: *Kulturen in Lund. [54] DR 289: *Bjärsjöholm manor. [55] DR 291: *Krageholm manor.

id.	herred	place	rel.sh.	s/m	dat.	fsp.	state	height	design	cross	orn.	rel.	sign.
339	St.Köpinge	St.Köpinge ch.yd.	A 5	m	2	10	—	162	3a(2)	—	—	—	—
Torna													
295c	Hällestad	Hällestad ch.	A 7b	s	2	10	3s,ph.	133	2(4+2 +1)	—	—	—	—
296c	Hällestad	Hällestad ch.	A 2	s	2	10	ph.	122	2(4)	—	—	—	—
297c	Hällestad	Hällestad ch.	A 2	s	2	10	ph.	138	3a	—	—	—	—
298[56]	Dalby	Sjöstorp	A 1	s	2	6	—	174	2(3)	—	—	—	—
314c[57]	Lund	Allhelgona ch.	A 2	s	2	10	4s	396	2(1+1)	Fg	+	—	—
316[58]	N.Nöbbelöv	N.Nöbbelöv ch.	A 5	s	2	10	—	134	3a?	—	—	—	—
317[59]	Valkärra	Valkärra	E 05.10	m	2	2	—	173	3a+2	—	—	—	—
318[60]	Håstad	Håstad ch.	A 1.5?	m?	2	10	fr.	(70)	3c(sp?)	—	—	—	—
Harjager													
321	V.Karaby	Ålstorp	A 5	m	2	7	2s	121	2(2+2)	—	—	—	—
323#	L.Harrie	L.Harrie	X 60		1	2	—	250	2	—	—	—	—
324	St.Harrie	St.Harrie ch.	A 4	s	2	10	ph.	(89)	2(3)	Hr	—	—	—
325[61]	Dagstorp	Dagstorp	A 1	s	2	2	—	158	3a	—	—	—	—
328	Holmby	Holmby ch.	A 1	s	2	10	—	113	3a+1	+(?)	+	—	—
Frosta													
329[62]	Gårdstånga	Gårdstånga	A 5	m	2	8	—	218	3a	+(?)	—	—	—
330[63]	Gårdstånga	Gårdstånga	A 5	m	2	8	2s,fr.	100	3a(1+ 1)+2	—	—	—	—
331[64]	Gårdstånga	Gårdst. ch.	A 6	s	2	8	—	128	2(2+)	—	—	—	—
Onsjö													
334m	V.Strö	V.Strö	A 2	s	2	8	—	170	3a(2)	—	—	—	—
335m	V.Strö	V.Strö	A 5	s	2	8	3s	205	3b	—	+	—	—
Kristianstads län[65]													
Ingelstads härad													
337[66]	Valleberga		A 6	m	2	3	2s	157	fr:3a+ mbd2(2); bk:3a	D	—	+	—
338	Glemminge	Glemminge ch.yd.	A 1	s	2	10	—	112	3a+4a	—	—	spell	—
(339 follows 294)													
343	Ö.Herrestad	Ö.H'stad ch.yd.	A 1	m	2	10	—	150	3a	—	+	—	—
344	Simris	Simris ch.yd.	A 2	s	3	10	—	171	6	—	—	—	—
345	Simris	Simris ch.yd.	A 6	s	2	10	—	150	6	—	—	+	—
Villand													
N9[67]	Åhus	Elleköpinge	A 6	s	2	10	dam.	319	2	—	—	—	—
unknown													
351#	?		A 2	s	2				3a	—	—	—	—
Halland													
(Halmstad län)													
354[68]	Kvibille	Kvibille ch.	A 6	m	3	10	ph.	(168)	4a	—	—	+	—
Blekinge													
Listers härad													
356	Sölvesborg	Sölvesborg ch.	A 3	s	1	10	—	140	2(2)	—	—	—	—
359[69]	Mjällby	Istaby	A 6	s	1		2s	180	2(2+1)	—	—	—	—

[56] DR 298: *Kulturen in Lund. [57] DR 314: *outside the University library. [58] DR 316: *Runstenskullen in Lund. [59] DR 317: *Runstenskullen in Lund. [60] DR 318: *Historiska museet in Lund. [61] DR 325: *Kulturen in Lund. [62] DR 329: *Röllebacken, Holmby parish. [63] DR 330: *Runstenskullen in Lund. [64] DR 331: *Runstenskullen in Lund. [65] Now part of Skåne *län*. [66] DR 337: *Runstenskullen in Lund. [67] Dk N9: Moltke (1985), 377; *FV* 1966, 105. [68] DR 354: recumbent. [69] DR 359: *SHM 6249.

Östra

id.	herred	place	rel.sh.	s/m	dat.	fsp.	state	height	design	cross	orn.	rel.	sign.
363	Sturkö	Grytö	A 7b	s	2	5	—	145	3a?	—	—	—	—
365#	Lösen	Lösen ch.	C 6	s	3	10	—	125	6?	Fg	—	—	—

Öland

id.	herred	place	rel.sh.	s/m	dat.	fsp.	state	height	design	cross	orn.	rel.	sign.
411	Vickleby	Karlevi	A 7b	m	2	5,8	2s	137	2(12?)	+(?)	—	—	—

Bornholm

Sønder herred

id.	herred	place	rel.sh.	s/m	dat.	fsp.	state	height	design	cross	orn.	rel.	sign.
369#	Poulsker		X	s	3	3	fr.	?	3a?	—	—	—	—
370[70]	Åker	Grödby	A 6	m	3	6	—	255	3a	—	—	+	Sart
371[71]	Åker	Møllegård	A 1	m	3	6	—	228	3a+ mbd2	—	—	+	—
372[72]	Åker	Bjælke	A 6	s	3	7	fr.	(285)	9	+(?)	—	—	—
376	Bodilsker	Bod.ch.	A 1	m	3	10	pt.	(84)	3a	A	—	—	—
377	Bodilsker	Bod.ch.	A 2.6	m	3	10	—	195	3a+ mbd(2)	—	—	—	—
378	Bodilsker	Bod.ch.	B 5	s	3	10	—	357	6	A	—	+	—

Vester herred

id.	herred	place	rel.sh.	s/m	dat.	fsp.	state	height	design	cross	orn.	rel.	sign.
379	Ny Larsker	Ny Lar.ch.	A 1	s	3	10	—	260	6+xbd	+	—	+	—
380	Ny Larsker	Ny Lar.ch.	A 3	s	3	10	—	186	5	D	—	+	—
383	V.Marie	V.Mar.; ch.yd.	A ?/2	m	3	3	—	167	3a(2)	—	—	+	—
384	V.Marie	V.Mar.; ch.yd.	A 1/2	m	3	3	—	190	3b	—	—	+	—
385	V.Marie	V.Mar.; ch.yd.	A 2	s	3	5,7	pt.	(107)	3b?	—	—	+	—
386[73]	V.Marie	V.Mar.ch.yd.	X		3	10	frag.		9?	—	—	—	—
387[74]	V.Marie	V.Mar.ch.	A 2	s	3	10	—	210	6	—	—	—	—
389	Nyker	Nyker ch.	A 3	s	3	10	2fr.	(179)	6+xbd	Hr	—	+	—

Øster herred

id.	herred	place	rel.sh.	s/m	dat.	fsp.	state	height	design	cross	orn.	rel.	sign.
390[75]	Ø.Marie		A 1	s	3	5	—	300	3a	—	—	—	—
391	Ø.Marie	Ø.Mar.ch.ruin	A 1	m	3	10	2s	145	2(2)	—	—	+	—
392	Ø.Marie	Ø.Mar.ch.	A 2	m	3	10	2s	170	5	Hp[76]	—	+	—
393	Ø.Marie		A 6	s	3	6	—	225	2	—	—	—	—
394[77]	Ø.Marie	Ø.Mar.ch.yd.	AB 20/01	m	3	10	—	151	3b	—	—	—	—
397[78]	Ø.Larsker	Ø.Lar.ch.	A 6	s	3	10	—	150	3a	A	—	—	—
398	Ø.Larsker	Ø.Lar.ch.	A 1	m	3	10	3s	163	3b(2)+ 3	—	—	+	—
N10[79]	Ø.Larsker	Ø.Lar.ch.	A 2	m	2?	10	—	197	3b	—	—	—	—

Nørre herred

id.	herred	place	rel.sh.	s/m	dat.	fsp.	state	height	design	cross	orn.	rel.	sign.
399	Klemensker		C 5	s	3	5	4s,dam.	274	3a(2)+ 3b(2)	—	—	+	—
400[80]	Klemensker		A 1/2	m	3	7	—	106	3b(2)	—	—	—	—
401	Klemensker	Brogård	AB 1/2	s	3	8?	—	267	5	—	—	—	—
402[81]	Klemensker	Marevad	A 1	s	3	6	—	200	6	A	—	+	—
403[82]	Klemensker	Kuregård	A 1	m	3	3	pt.	(190)	2+?	—	—	—	—
404	Klemensker	Klem.ch.	A 2	s	3	10	2s,3fr.	(126)	3a+2	D	—	+	——kil, Svenne
406[83]	Klemensker	Klem.old ch.	X	m	3	10	2fr.	(148)	5	—	—	—	—
408	Rutsker	Rut.ch.	X		3	10	fr.	(39)	2(4?)	—		+	—
409	Rø	Rø ch.	X 1		3	10	fr.	(118)	?	A/D?	—	—	—

411 follows 365 (under Öland)

NEW FINDS

	amt/hd.	follows DR		amt/hd.	follows DR		amt/hd.	follows DR
N1	Århus	69	N5	Randers	N4	N8	Holbæk	239
N2	Viborg	99	N6	Randers	127	N9	Villands	345 (below Ingelstads hd)
N3	Viborg	N2	N7	Ålborg	129	N10	Øster	398 (below Bornholm)
N4	Randers	117						

[70] DR 370: *Åkirkeby church. [71] DR 371: *Åkirkeby church. [72] DR 372: a part of the stone is now in S.Åkirkeby; Moltke (1985), 550.
[73] DR 386: recumbent. [74] DR 387: Moltke (1985), 332. [75] DR 390: *Svaneke churchyard.
[76] DR 392: 'Hp': the cross is shaped like a propeller. [77] DR 394: Moltke (1985), 549. [78] DR 397: Moltke (1985), 318.
[79] Dk N10: Moltke (1985), 343; see also M. L. Nielsen (1997*a*), 50. [80] DR 400: *Allinge old churchyard. [81] DR 402: *Hasle churchyard.
[82] DR 403: *Klemensker churchyard. [83] DR 406: *Klemensker church.

Denmark and Bornholm: Further Particulars

Ornaments (indicated by + in column headed 'orn.')

NØRREJYLLAND		SKÅNE	
26	hammer	258	mask
42	Christ and beast	264	deer
62	mask	271	beast; ship
66	mask	280	beast
77	ship	282	man; axe
81	mask	284–6	see 'Multiple Commemorations' below, group 3
96	rider	314	two masks; beasts
120	hammer	328	ship
123	two deer	335	mask; human couple
N7	ship	343	leaf

Multiple Commemorations

1. Identical

2+4, in memory of Sigtryg by his mother Asfrid.
26+34, in memory of Thyre by her husband (?) Tue.

2. In memory of the same individual(s) (by different sponsor(s))

26+29+34+41+42, in memory of Thyre: 26+34 by Tue (her husband?); 29 by Tue, Funden, and Gnyble (husband and sons?); 41 by Gorm (her husband); 42 also in memory of Gorm by their son Harald.

3. By the same sponsor(s) (in memory of different individuals)

58+91, by Toke the smith: 58 in memory of Troels, Gudmund's son, who gave him gold and freedom; 91 in memory of Revle, son of Esger Bjørn's son.

209+230, by Ragnhild; 209 together with Alle's sons in memory of her husband Alle; 230 in memory of her husband Gunnulv.

282–6, by Esbern: 282 together with Tomme in memory of their brothers Ro and Legfrød, Gunne Hånd's sons; 283 in memory of his brother Tomme; 284 ornament: woman, riding on a wolf-like animal: 285 ornament: beast; 286 ornament: animal and mask.

334+335, by Fader: 334 in memory of his brother Asser; 335 in memory of Bjørn (with whom he jointly owned a ship).

Connected Monuments

26+29+30+34: 26+29+34 Tue in memory of Thyre; 30 Tue in memory of his mother Vibrog.

41+42+55: 41 Gorm in memory of his wife Thyre; 42 Harald in memory of his parents Gorm and Thyre; 55 Tove in memory of her mother (= Harald Gormson's wife?).

58+65+91+314: 58 Toke the smith in memory of Troels; 65 Esger Bj(ørn's son?) sponsor or deceased?; 91 Toke the smith in memory of Revle, son of Esger Bjørn's son; 314 Troels, son of Esger Bjørn's son, in memory of his brothers Olav and Ottar.

91: see this section above, at 58+65, etc.

96+97: 96 Vigot in memory of his son Esge; 97 Thyre, Vigot's wife, in memory of Thorbjørn, Sibbe's son.

190+192: 190 Roulv in memory of his brother's son Gudmund; 192 in memory of Roulv by his sons.

295+296+297: 295 Eskil in memory of Toke Gormson, his 'drott' (lord); 296 Asgot in memory of his brother Ærre, Toke's 'hirdman' (retainer); 297 Esbern, Toke's 'hirdman' in memory of his brother Toke.

314: see this section above, at 58+65, etc.

NORWAY (NO)

(Total no. of inscriptions: 51)

id.	herred	place	rel.sh.	s/m	dat.	fsp.	state	height	design	cross	orn.	rel.	sign.
Opland fylke													
59[1] (61+62 = same stone)	Fåberg	Fåberg ch.	A 1	s	3	3	—	304	2	—	—	—	—
61	Ø.Toten	Hof p., Nedre Alstad	C 5	s	2	3	2s	270	2	—	+	—	—
62	Ø.Toten	Hof p., Nedre Alstad	A 3	s	2–3	3	—		1(3)	—	—	—	—
N1[2]	Kolbu	Kol. p., Haugset	A 2	s	3	3	—	162	2	—	—	—	—
63	Gran	Gran p.ch.	A 2	m	3	10	—	135	3 or 4?	—	—	+	—
64#	Gran	Gran p.ch.	X		3		fr.h.			?	?	?	?
66[3]	Gran	Gran p.ch.	C 6	s	2	10	3fr.	(132)	2(sd)	—	+	—	—
68	Gran	Gran p., N.Dynna	D 3	s	2	3	—	282	2(sd)	—	+	—	—
84	Vang	Vang p.ch.	A 4	m	2	10	—	215	2(sd)	—	+	—	—
Buskerud fylke													
96#	Norderhov	Tanberg p.	A 2	s	2–3	10	—		2(sd)	—	—	—	—
97#	Norderhov	Tanberg p.	X 10		2	10	—		1+2	—	—	—	—
N2[4]	Haug	Haug p., Klekken Nedre	X	s	3–4	4	2s,fr.	(49)	2	—	—	—	—
Telemark flylke													
163	Mo	Skafså p.ch.	A 2	m	3	10	—	190	2(2,sd)	—	—	—	Gudmund, Ondott
Aust-Agder fylke													
180#	Åmli	Åmli p.ch.	X		2–3	10	—		2	—	—	—	—
184	Evje	Evje p., Galteland	A 3	s	2	3	7fr.	(189)	2(2)	Hg	—	—	—
186#	Bygland	Bygl.p.vic.	A 6	s	2	10	—	150	2(2)	—	+	—	—
Vest-Agder fylke													
208	Tveid	Tveid p., Ryen	A 2	s	2	3	8fr.	(380)	2	—	—	—	—
211	Søgne	Søgne p.vic.	A 3	s	3–4	10	—	200	2(2)	—	—	—	—
213[5]	Lister and Mandal	Vanse p., Skollevoll	C 5	s	2	6	—	200	2	—	—	—	Skog
214[6]	Herad	Framvaren	A 6	s	3	1	—		2	—	—	—	—
Rogaland fylke													
222		Eigersund	X		2–3		fr.		2(2)	—	—	—	—
223#	Nærbø	Nær.p., Njærheim	A 2	s	2?	10	—		2(2)	cross	—	—	Ulvrek

Continued

[1] NIyR 59: *NOR* 1990, 20. [2] No N1: Knirk (1987), 195 (archive no.: A 23).
[3] NIyR 66: *Oldsaksamlingen (the asterisk here and at nn. 4, 5, etc. below indicates the present location of the stone).
[4] No N2: (Knirk 1987), 191–202 (A 231); *Oldsaksamlingen, 36687.
[5] NIyR 213: *Oldsaksamlingen, 3612. [6] NIyR 214: rock.

id.	herred	place	rel.sh.	s/m	dat.	fsp.	state	height	design	cross	orn.	rel.	sign.
224	Nærbø	Njærheim p.	A 2	s	2?	3	fr.		3	B/C?+Fg	—	—	—
225	Klepp	Klepp p.ch.	B 5	s	1–2	10	2s	215	3+2(sd)	—	—	—	—
226	Klepp	Klepp p.ch.	A 6	s		10	fr.		2(2)	—	—	—	—
228	Klepp	Klepp p., Tu	A 2	s	1–2	3	2s	215	2(sd)	—	+	—	—
233[7]	Klepp	Bore p.ch.	X		10		fr.		2?	—	—	—	—
237	Klepp	Bore p., Sele	A 4	s	1–2	8	2s,fr.	(240)	2(2+2)	cross	—	+	Ulvrek
239	Høiland	Højl. p., Stangeland	A 3	s	2	2,5	dam.	265	2(2)	—	—	—	—
244	Sola	Sola p., Helland	A 3	s	2	3,8	—	200	2(2)	Fg	—	—	—
245	Sola	Sola p., Helland	A 3	s	2		—	295	3	—	—	—	—
247[8]	Sola	Sola p., Skadberg	X 60	m	2–3	3,8	—	310	2	—	—	—	—
251	Stavanger town	Mariakirken	B 5	s	2	10	4fr.	(360)	2(sd)	Fg	—	—	—
252	Stavanger town	Breia-vatnet	A 7b	s	2	7	2s		1+2	cross+Fg(2)	—	—	—
259[9]	Rennesøy	Sørbø p.	A 6	m	2	10	—	c.240	2(2)	—	—	—	—
260[10]	Rennesøy	Sørbø p.	A 2	s	2–3		3fr.		2	—	—	—	—
N3[11]	Rennesøy	Sørbø p.ch.	A 2	s	2a	10	—	240	2	—	—	—	—
N4[12]	Sokndal	Sok. p., Eik vic.	B 1	s	2	5,6	2pts.	150	2(3)	—	—	+	—

Hordaland fylke

id.	herred	place	rel.sh.	s/m	dat.	fsp.	state	height	design	cross	orn.	rel.	sign.
271	Etne	Gjerde p.ch.	A 1	s	2	10	2s	200	2(sd)	Fg(2)	—	—	—
272	Etne	Gjerde p.ch.	A 4	s	3	10	—	225	2(sd)	+(?)	—	—	—
273	Etne	Grindheim p.ch.	A 1	s	2	10	—	330	2(sd)	Fg	—	—	—
300[13]	Hamre	Hamre p., Eikeland	X		2	3	fr.	—	2	—	—	—	—
301[14]	Manger	Manger p.ch.	X	s	3–4	10	dam.	196	2(2)	—	—	—	—

Sogn og Fjordane fylke

id.	herred	place	rel.sh.	s/m	dat.	fsp.	state	height	design	cross	orn.	rel.	sign.
413#	Vik	Kvamsøy p., Kvamme	A 6	s	2	3	—	440	2(2)	Fg(2)	—	—	—
417	Kinn	Svanøy p.ch.	X	s	2	10	—	200	2	cross	—	—	—

Møre og Romsdal fylke

id.	herred	place	rel.sh.	s/m	dat.	fsp.	state	height	design	cross	orn.	rel.	sign.
449	Edøy	Edøy p., Kuli	A 6	m	2	3,6	—	c.240	2(2,sd)	Fg+Hr	—	—	—

Sør-Trøndelag fylke

id.	herred	place	rel.sh.	s/m	dat.	fsp.	state	height	design	cross	orn.	rel.	sign.
453	Rissa	Rissa p., Hårberg	A 1	s	2	3,8	2pts.	345	2	Fg?	—	—	—

Mon-Jæren fylke?

id.	herred	place	rel.sh.	s/m	dat.	fsp.	state	height	design	cross	orn.	rel.	sign.
543[15]	uncertain		X		2		2s,fr.		2	—	—	—	—

Nordland fylke

id.	herred	place	rel.sh.	s/m	dat.	fsp.	state	height	design	cross	orn.	rel.	sign.
N5[16]	Vågan	Våg.p., Gimsøy	A 6	s	1–2a	8,7	dam.	170	2	—	—	—	—

[7] NIyR 233: *Oldsaksamlingen, 14746. [8] NIyR 247: *Stavanger Museum. [9] NIyR 259: Liestøl (1964), 32 ff.
[10] NIyR 260: *Stavanger Museum. [11] No N3: Liestøl (1964), 29, 35–9 (A 13).
[12] No N4: Liestøl (1972), 45–66, 67–76 (A 53). [13] NIyR 300: *Bergen Museum.
[14] NIyR 301: *Bergen Museum. [15] NIyR 543: *Universitetets historiske museum, Bergen.
[16] No N5: *NTS* 18 (1958), 290; Knirk (1994), (A 11); *Tromsø Museum.

id.	herred	place	rel.sh.	s/m	dat.	fsp.	state	height	design	cross	orn.	rel.	sign.
N6[17]	Steigen	Steig.p., Lauvøy	A 6	s	2a	1	dam.	240	2	—	—	—	—

Troms fylke

id.	herred	place	rel.sh.	s/m	dat.	fsp.	state	height	design	cross	orn.	rel.	sign.
N7[18]	Trondenes	Trond.p., Ervik	A 6	s	3–4	4	4s,fr.	(47)	2	—	—	+	—

NEW FINDS

	fylke	*follows* NIyR		*fylke*	*follows* NIyR
N1	Opland	62	N5	Nordland	543
N2	Buskerud	97	N6	Nordland	N5
N3	Rogaland	260	N7	Troms	N6
N4	Rogaland	N3			

[17] No N6: *NTS* 20 (1965), 263; Knirk (1994), (A 17).

[18] No N7: Knirk (1994), (A 222).

Norway: Further Particulars

Ornaments (indicated by + in column headed 'orn.')

OPLAND

61 bird, dog/wolf?, rider, falcon, spear, horse, weapons

66 rider, man, animal's head

68 three (wise?) men on horses; Christ, star, house/church/stable with people

84 beast; stylized tree

AUST AGDER

186 figure

ROGALAND

228 man

SWEDEN (EXCLUDING UPPLAND)

Gotland (G): 30 inscriptions[1]

id.	parish	place	type	rel.sh.	s/m	dat.	fsp.	state	height	design	cross	orn.	rel.	sign.
Grötlinge ting														
37	Grötlingbo	Grötl.ch.		B 1	m		10	fr.		go	—	—	—	—
Hemse														
52[2]	Rone	Rone ch.		X 03? 02?			10	fr.		go	—	—	—	—
Hablinge														
59	Hablingbo	Habl.ch.		A 6 (or 1?)	m		10	2s,dam.	102	go	—	+	—	—
N1[3]	Hablingbo	Habl.ch.		A 1	m		10	—	190	go	A–C?	—	—	—
Fardhem														
77[4]	Levide	Lev.farm		AB 1	s		10	fr.		go	—	+	+	—
Bur														
92[5]	Närs	Bosarve		X 30			8	2s,fr.		go	—	+	—	—
Garda														
109	Alskog	Ollaifs		X 10			6	dam.	180	go	—	+	—	—
110[6]	Alskog	Tjängvide		X 20			3	dam.	175		—	+	—	—
Kräklinge														
111[7]	Ardre	Ardre ch.		B 5	s		10	—	76	go	—	—	—	—
112[8]	Ardre	Ardre ch.		B 3	s		10	2s	73	go	—	—	—	—
113m[9]	Ardre	Ardre ch.		A 1.6	m		10	2s	84	go	—	—	—	Likraiv
114m[10]	Ardre	Ardre ch.	rec.	B 1	m		10	—		3	—	—	—	—
116[11]	Kräklingbo	Smiss		X 30			7	fr.		go	—	—	—	—
Halla														
134mc[12]	Sjonhem	Sjonh.ch.		E 3	m		10	—	167	go	B	—	+	[13]
135mc[14]	Sjonhem	Sjonh.ch.		E 3	m		10	—	163	go	B	—	—	[15]
136#mc	Sjonhem	Sjonh.ch.		E 3	m		10	—		?	—	—	—	Dan, Botbjärn
138	Halla	Halla ch.		C 5/3	s					go	—	—	+	—
141[16]	Halla	Unsarve		X			2	fr.		go	—	+	—	—
188	Mästerby	Mäst.ch.		E 6	m		10	fr.			+(?)	—	+	—
Stenkumla														
200	Atlingbo	Atl.ch.		A 6	m		10	fr.		8?	—	—	+	Audvald
203[17]	Hogräns	Hogr.ch.		A 2/1	s		10	—	254	go	A	—	+	Rodbjärn, Gairlaiv
207	Stenkumla	Stenk.ch.		A 6	m		10	fr.	250	go	—	—	—	—
208	Stenkumla	Stenk.ch.		A 1	m		10	fr.	200	go	C?	—	+	—
Dede														
218	Follingbo	Foll.ch.		X 20			10	fr.			—	—	—	—
220[18]	Follingbo	Hallfrede		X 60			3	fr.			—	—	—	—
Endre														
N2[19]	Visby town		rec.	A 1?	s		10	—	200	7/9?	A?	+	+	X, Torlaif
N3[20]	Visby town	S:t Hans ch. ruin		A 1	m		10	—	136	go	—	—	—	—
Bro														
N4[21]	Lokrume			E 10.05?	m		10	dam.	120		—	+	—	—

[1] In notes 2 and 19–23 the new finds are given their official number (brackets) in the forthcoming publication of Gotland's inscriptions,
[2] G 52: *SHM, 15095 (the asterisk here and at nn. 4, 5, 6, etc. below indicates the present location of the stone).
[3] G N1: *FV* 1990, 23 f. (G 370). [4] G 77: *GF, C 398. [5] G 92: *GF, C 1874. [6] G 110: *SHM, 4171.
[7] G 111: *SHM, 11458. [8] G 112: *SHM, 11118. [9] G 113: *SHM, 11118. [10] G 114: *SHM, 11118.
[11] G 116: *GF, C 1875. [12] G 134: *GF, B 1061. [13] G 134: the same as G 136. [14] G 135: *GF, B 1062.
[15] G 135: the same as G 136. [16] G 141: *GF, C 399. [17] G 203: *GF, C 10645. [18] G 220: *GF, C 8161.
[19] G N2: *FV* 1983, 224 f (G 343). [20] G N3: Lindqvist (1942), 144 (G 342). [21] G N4: *SHM, 14342 (G 252).

id.	parish	place	type	rel.sh.	s/m	dat.	fsp.	state	height	design	cross	orn.	rel.	sign.
Forsa														
N5[22]	Hangvar			A 1/2+?	s			2fr.			D	—	—	—
Rute														
N6[23]	Rute			C 3	s			3fr.	116		—	—	—	—

NEW FINDS

	ting	*follows* G		*ting*	*follows* G
N1	Hablinge	59	N4	Bro	N3
N2	Endre	220	N5	Forsa	N4
N3	Endre	N2	N6	Rute	N5

Gästrikland (Gs): 15 inscriptions

id.	parish	place	type	rel.sh.	s/m	dat.	fsp.	state	height	design	cross	orn.	rel.	sign.
1	Österfärnebo	Öst.ch.		C 5	s	3	10	—	195	8a	A	—	—	Önjut
2	Österfärnebo	Öst.ch.		A 1	m		10	fr.	—	6	A+Fg	+	+	—
4#	Hedesunda	Hed.ch.		E 05.40?	m		10	—	225	8a	A	—	—	Öpir
6	Hedesunda	Hade		X 01			2	fr.	—	?	Fr	—	—	—
7	Torsåker	Tors.ch.		X 20	s		10	fr.	210	4a+	A	+	—	—
8[24]	Torsåker	V.Hästbo		A 6	s		10	fr.	—	4a+	—	—	—	—
9	Årsunda	Års.ch.		AB 20/ 03/60	s		10	dam.	210	6	A	+	—	—
11	Valbo	Järvsta		A 1	m		7	—	205	7	A	—	+	Åsmund
12[25]	Valbo	Lund		C 3?	s		2	dam.	300	7	A	—	+	Åsmund
13[26]	Valbo	Söderby		A 2	s		2	dam.	225	7	—	—	+	Sven, Åsmund
14	Ovansjö	Ov.ch.		A 6	m		10	fr.	(178)	7/8?	—	—	—	—
15[27]	Ovansjö	Ov.vic.		A 6	m		10	dam.	106	7	A	—	+	—
16a[28]	Ovansjö	Ov.vic.	rec.	X 60		3–4	2,10	fr.	—	?	—	—	—	Björn
19#	Ockelbo	Ock.ch.		A 3	s		10	—	230	6	—	+	—	—
21[29]	Hamrånge	Axmar		X 60			2	fr.	—	?	—	—	—	—

Hälsingland (Hs): 11 inscriptions

(id. nos from M. Åhlén, 'Runinskrifter i Hälsingland', *Bebyggelsehistorisk tidskrift*, 27 (1994), 33–50)

id.	parish	place	type	rel.sh.	s/m	dat.	fsp.	state	height	design	cross	orn.	rel.	sign.
2[30]	Norrala	Norr.ch		A 6	m		10	—	175	6	A/Hr?	—	+	X
6[31]	Järvsö	Järvsö vic.		AB 1	s		10	—	260	10(sp)	A/Hg?	—	—	—
8#[32]	Hudiksvall town	Hud.ch.		A 2	s						—	—	—	—
9[33]	Hälsingtuna	Häls.ch.		X 30?			10	fr.	(125)		—	—	—	—
10[34]	Hälsingtuna	Häls.ch.		A 3	s		10	—	350	8a	C	—	—	Bruse?
11	Hög	Hög ch.		A 1	s		10	—	190	5	H	—	+	Alver, Brand
12	Hög	Hög ch.		A 2	s		10	—	152	3b	Hr	—	—	—
14m[35]	Rogsta	Malsta		A 1	s		2	2s	256	5	A/Hg?	—	—	—
15m[36]	Rogsta	Sunnå		A 1	s				183	2(2)	+(?)	—	—	+(?)
18[37]	Delsbo	Delsbo ch.		X 60			10	fr.			—	—	—	X
21	Jättendal	Jätt.ch.		E 10.05	m		10	—	196	3a	Hg	—	—	Gunnborga

Jämtland (J): 1 inscription

id.	parish	place	type	rel.sh.	s/m	dat.	fsp.	state	height	design	cross	orn.	rel.	sign.
1[38]	Frösö	Östsundet		0						6	A	—	+	Tryn, Sten

Continued

[22] G N5: *GF, C 183 (G 309). [23] G N6: *Bunge hembygdsmuseum (G 325). [24] Gs 8: *Torsåker church.
[25] Gs 12: *Valbo church. [26] Gs 13: *Heliga Trefaldighetskyrkan (Holy Trinity Church), Gävle. [27] Gs 15: *Ovansjö church.
[28] Gs 16a: *Ovansjö church. [29] Gs 21: *SHM, 19984. [30] Hs 2: ATA 4661/72. [31] Hs 6: *FV* 1952, 99.
[32] Hs 8: Peterson (1994), 240. [33] Hs 9: L 1066. [34] Hs 10: Peterson (1994), 234.
[35] Hs 14: Jansson (1985), 25; Peterson (1994), 223; *Hälsingland Museum, Hudiksvall.
[36] Hs 15: Jansson (1985), 10; Peterson (1994), 223; *Hälsingland Museum, Hudiksvall.
[37] Hs 18: This stone is a part of Hs 16, see Owe (1996), 135. [38] J 1: Otto von Friesen, *Runorna i Sverige*, Uppsala, 1928.

Medelpad (M): 15 inscriptions

(id. nos from A. Hellbom, *Medelpads runstenar* (Sundsvalls Museum, 1979))

id.	parish	place	type	rel.sh.	s/m	dat.	fsp.	state	height	design	cross	orn.	rel.	sign.
1	Njurunda	Nolby		A 1	m		7	—	160	7	A	—	—	Fardägn
3	Njurunda	Berga		EF 1	m		7,8	—	170	5	A?	—	—	—
4	Attmar	Attmar ch.		A 6	s		7	dam.	110	5	—	—	+	X
5	Attmar	Attmar ch.		AB 20/01	s		2,10	—	225	7	A	—	+	—
6	Tuna	Målsta		A 1	s		7?	—	155	5	—	—	—	—
7	Tuna	Tuna ch.		A 1	s		10	part	(105)	5	A	—	—	Håkan
8[39]	Tuna	Sköle		A 3	s		8	dam.	165	5	A	—	—	—
9#	Selånger	Sel.old ch.		A 1	m		10	—		8a	A	—	—	—
10	Selånger	Sel.old ch.		A 1 or 2?	m		10	dam.	105	5	—	—	—	—
11[40]	Selånger	Högom		E 3	m		3	—	130	4a+2	A	—	—	—
13	Selånger	Oxsta		X			5,6,7	pt.	(65)	6?	—	—	—	X
14	Sättna	Byn		A 1	m		8?	pt.	(150)	6	A	—	—	—
15	Skön	Skön ch.; ch.yd.		A 3	s		10	—	125	5	D	—	—	—
16	Skön	Skön ch.; ch.yd.		A 1 or 2?	s		10?	—	105	5	—	—	+	X
17	Skön	Skön ch.		X 60	s		10	fr.		6?	B?	—	—	X

Närke (Nä): 19 inscriptions

id.	parish	place	type	rel.sh.	s/m	dat.	fsp.	state	height	design	cross	orn.	rel.	sign.
Edsberg härad														
4[41]	Edsberg	Riseberga mon.	rec.	X 10	s		2,10	fr.		4a?	—	—	—	—
Hardemo														
8[42]	Kräcklinge	Väsby		X	m		7	dam.	210	6	—	—	—	—
Kumla														
9	Kumla	Övre Vesta		C 5 or A 7?	s		7	—	165	3a	—	—	—	—
Asker														
11[43]	Asker	Tälje br.		A 1	m		9	—	125	6	—	—	+	—
12	St.Mellösa	St.Mell.ch.; ch.yd.		C 3	s		10	—	167	3a	—	—	—	—
13	St.Mellösa	St.Mell.ch.	rec.	X			10	fr.	—	6?	—	—	—	—
14	St.Mellösa	Bärsta		C 3+?	s		2	—	127	6	B+Fg	—	—	—
15	St.Mellösa	Åsby		A 1	s		1,7	—	300	6	—	—	—	—
Örebro town														
16[44]	Almby	Ormesta		X	s		3	dam.	120	3a	—	—	—	—
18[45]	Hovsta	Kumla by		X 40			?	fr.		3a?	—	—	—	—
20[46]	Vintrosa	Granhammar ch.	rec.	X 60			10	dam.	185	3a	—	—	+	Åvid
Glanshammar														
23[47]	Glanshammar	Glansh.ch.		A 3	s		10	dam.	230	7	—	—	—	—
25#	Glanshammar	Glansh.ch.		X			10	fr.			—	—	—	X
26	Glanshammar	Glansh.ch.		AB 1	m?		10	dam.	160	6	—	+	—	—
28#	Glanshammar	Glansh.ch.		A 1	s		10	dam.			—	—	+	—
29	Glanshammar	Apelboda		A 2	s		2	—	215	6	—	—	—	—
31	Götlunda	S.Lunger		A 2	m		8	—	115	6	—	—	—	—
32	Götlunda	Urvalla		A 1	m		7	2s,dam.	72	7	—	—	—	—
34	Rinkaby	Nasta		C 3	s		7		193	3a	—	—	—	—

Småland (Sm): 116 inscriptions

id.	parish	place	type	rel.sh.	s/m	dat.	fsp.	state	height	design	cross	orn.	rel.	sign.
Allbo härad														
1	Alvesta (Aringsås)	Ar.ch.yd		A 1	s		8	—	163	6	C	—	+	Åsmund or Åsgöt?
2#	Alvesta (Aringsås)	Ar.ch.yd.		A 6	s		10	—		3a	—	—	—	—

---

[39] M 8: *Torkarlsberget. [40] M 11: Åkerberg Norberg (1997), 59 ff. [41] Nä 4: *Örebro länsmuseum, 6223.
[42] Nä 8: *Kräcklinge church. [43] Nä 11: *Hummelsta, Stora Mellösa parish. [44] Nä 16: *Örebro länsmuseum, 7561.
[45] Nä 18: *Örebro länsmuseum, 430. [46] Nä 20: *Örebro länsmuseum, 20879. [47] Nä 23: *FV* 1978, 221.

id.	parish	place	type	rel.sh.	s/m	dat.	fsp.	state	height	design	cross	orn.	rel.	sign.
5	Hjortsberga	Transjö		A 3	s		8	3s	250	2	—	—	—	—
7	Skatelöv	Enet		E 6? A 6?	m		7,8	—	210	3b	Fg	—	+	—
Kinnevald														
8	Dänningelanda	Dänn.by		E 3	m		7	dam.	130	3b	C?	—	—	—
9#	Vederslöv	Nöbbele by		X 60	s?		3	—		4a?	—	—	—	—
10	Växjö town	Domkyrkan		A 6	s		10	—	110	5	—	—	+	—
Konga														
11	Furuby	Kårestad		A 1/2	m		8	—	383	3a	—	—	—	—
13	Uråsa	Högmalöv		A 3	s		5,7,8	—	125	3b	—	—	—	—
15	Ö.Torsås	Kåragården		X 60	s ?		10	dam.	(75)	3a	—	—	—	—
16	Ö.Torsås	Nöbbele		A 1	m		8	2s	135	3a	C	—	—	—
Norrvidinge														
17[48]	Asa	Kråketorp		A 2	s		7	fr.		3a?	—	—	+	—
19	Gårdsby	Stojby		AB 6	s		8	—	207	3a	—	—	+	—
20#[49]	Söraby	Rottnekvarn		X	m?		5	2s		2	—	—	—	—
Sunnerbo														
27	Berga	Berga ch.yd.		X 60	s		10	dam.	208	3a	A–C?	—	—	—
28	Berga	Berga ch.yd.		X 60			10	dam.	100	3/4?+mbd	C?	—	—	—
29	Berga	Ingelstad		X 10	s		5,7	—	150	3a+	Hg	—	—	—
30	Berga	Trotteslöv		X 30			6,8	dam.	175	3a?	Hr	—	—	—
31	Dörarp	Toftaholm		X 20	s?		2	—	175	5	A	—	+	—
32[50]	Hamneda	Hamn.old ch.		X 10			10	dam.	147	3a+	C?	—	—	—
33m[51]	Hamneda	Hamn.old ch.		X 20			10	—	185	3a+	—	—	+	—
34#	Ljungby	Ljungby old ch.		X 40			10	dam.		?	—	—	—	—
170	Ljungby	Skansen		B 2	s		3,10	dam.	110	3a?	—	—	—	—
35	Ljungby	Replösa		A 1	s		7,8	—	178	3b(sp)	—	—	—	—
36c	Nöttja	Bolmaryd		A 6	m		2	—	220	3a	A+Eg	—	—	—
37c	Nöttja	Bolmaryd		A 1	s		6	—	185	3b(sp)	A?Hr?	—	+	—
39[52]	Ryssby	Ryssby ch.		A 1	s		10	—	220	3a+2	A?	—	—	—
40#m	Ryssby	Ryssby ch.yd.		A 6?			10?	fr.		3a	+(?)	—	—	—
41m	Ryssby	Ryssby ch.yd.		A 6?	s?		10	fr.	(70)	3a+mbd	—	—	—	—
42	Ryssby	Tuna Lunnag.		A 2	s		5,8	—	200	2 (sd)	Hg	—	—	—
43	S.Ljunga	S.Ljunga ch.		A 3/?	s		10	fr.	(82)	3b(sp)	Hr	—	—	—
44	S.Ljunga	Ivla Ytterg.		A 2	s		7,8	2s	130	3a+4a	—	—	—	—
45	Tutaryd	Bräkentorp		A 2	s		7	—	85	3b(sp)	A	—	—	—
46#	Vittaryd	Eriksstad		C 3?	s		6	—		3a+mbd	Hr	—	—	—
Västbo														
48	Bredaryd	Torp Norreg.		A 3	s		5	—	184	3a+mbd	D	—	—	—
51	Forsheda	Forsh.ch.yd.		A 4	s		10	—	325	3a+mbd	—	—	—	—
52	Forsheda	Forsh.-allmänning		A 1	m		6,7,8	dam.	200	3a+mbd	—	—	—	—
53	Reftele	Ölmestad by		A 3	s		7,8	dam.	120	3a(2)	—	—	+	—
Östbo														
59[53]	Rydaholm	Horda		A 2	s		6	dam.	130	3a	—	—	—	—
60	Rydaholm	Skaftarp		A 1	m		8	2s	167	3b+2	A	—	—	—
61	Tånnö	Runstensholm		A 3[54]	m		7,8	—	144	3a(2)+mbd	—	—	+	—
62	Voxtorp	Ed		A 3	s		7,8	—	180	3a	—	—	—	—
64	Värnamo	Västhorja		C 5/3	s		7,8	—	320	3a	—	—	+	—
65	Åker	Åker vic.		X			7,8	dam.	237	1(6)(cross)	Fr	—	—	—
Västra														
69	Fröderyd	Fröd.ch.yd.		A 2	s		10	—	150	3a	A	—	—	—
71	N.Sandsjö	N.Sandsjö vic.		A 1/4	s		5	—	250	3a+mbd	—	—	—	—
72	Ramkvilla	Ramkv.ch.		X 60			10	dam.	(86)	3a	—	—	+	—
73	Skepperstad	Terle; ch.yd.		A 1	s		6	—	143	3a	Hr	—	—	—
75	Svenarum	Morarp		A 1 or 2?	s		7	—	206	3a+mbd	—	—	+	—
76c	f.d.N.Ljunga	Sävsjö Komstad		C 1	s		5,7	fr.		5	—	—	—	—

Continued

[48] Sm 17: *Asa church. [49] Sm 20: Johnsen (1968), 163. [50] Sm 32: *Hamneda vicarage.
[51] Sm 33: *Hamneda vicarage. [52] Sm 39: *FV* 1964, 227. [53] Sm 59: *Upplid.

id.	parish	place	type	rel.sh.	s/m	dat.	fsp.	state	height	design	cross	orn.	rel.	sign.
77c	f.d.N.Ljunga	Sävsjö Västerg.		A 2	s		5,8	—	297	3a+mbd	—	—	—	—
78	f.d.Vallsjö	Sävsjö Uppåkra		A 3	s		2	—	178	3a	Hr	—	—	—
79#	Vallsjö	Vall. old ch.	rec.	A 3	s		10	fr.	(135)	3a	A	—	—	—
80[55]	Vallsjö	Sävsjö		A 1	m		6	dam.	133	3a(2)	—	—	—	—
83[56]	Vrigstad	Vrig.ch.yd.	rec.	E 3	m		10	—	158	1	—	+	+	—
84#	Vrigstad	Biskopsbo		X 20			8?	—	210	3a?	—	—	—	—
Östra														
85	Alseda	Alseda ch.yd.		A 1	m		10	—	159	5	—	—	—	—
86#	Alseda	Holsby		A 2	m?		8?	fr.	(110)	?	—	—	—	—
87#	Alseda	Repperda		A 2	s		3	fr.	(105)	3a?	+(?)	—	—	—
89	Alseda	Repperda		A 2	s		7	—	170	3/4?	D	—	—	—
91[57]	Alseda	Slättåkra		A 3	s		5	dam.	129	3a	—	—	—	—
92	Björkö	Björkö ch.yd.		A 1	s		10	2s,dam.	173	3a+2	A	—	+	—
93	Björkö	Nömme		A 3.1	m		5,7	—	200	3b	—	—	—	—
94	Lannaskede	Lann.ch.	rec.	B 3	s	3	10	fr.	(107)	3/9?	—	—	—	—
95	Lannaskede	Lann.ch.	rec.	X 60	m		10	dam.	162	7/9?	B	—	—	—
96	Lannaskede	Brobyholm		AB 30/ 20/05	m		5	2s	134	5+3a	—	—	—	—
97	Myresjö	Myr.old ch.		X 10	s		10	dam.	138	2	—	—	—	—
98	Myresjö	Myr.old ch.		X 60	?		10	fr.	(59)	3b	—	—	—	—
99	Myresjö	Nederby		A 1	m		5	—	157	3b(sp)	D	—	—	—
100	Nävelsjö	Glömsjö		A 3	s		5	—	252	5	A	—	+	—
101	Nävelsjö	Nöbbe-lesholm		A 1	s		7	2s	260	3a+2	A	—	—	—
103#	Skede	Rösa		X	s?		7	—	200	3a?	—	+	—	—
104	Vetlanda	Vetl.ch.		X 60?	?		10	fr.	(87)	?	—	—	—	—
105	Vetlanda	Vetl.ch.		C 2	s		10	—	134	3a	—	—	—	—
106	Vetlanda	Vetl.ch.yd.		A 2	s		10	—	230	3a+	—	—	—	—
107#	Vetlanda	Vetl.ch.yd.		A 6	s		10	—	160	4a+	Hr	—	+	—
109#	Vetlanda	Vetl.-klockarstuga		A 2	s		10	—	185	4a	Fg	—	—	—
110[58]	Vetlanda	Torget		A 1/2	s		7	—	172	3a	+(?)	—	—	—
111	Vetlanda	Fageräng		A 2	s		6	—	169	3a+	—	—	+	—
113	Vetlanda	Tångerda		A 3	s		3	—	114	3a	A	—	—	—
Tveta														
121	Rogberga	Rog.ch.yd.		A 4	s		10	—	200	3a	—	—	—	—
Vista														
122	Gränna	Uppgränna		A 2/4	s		7	—	171	4a+	C	—	—	—
124[59]	Visingsö	Kumlaby ch.	rec.	E 10.05?	m		10	—	147	7/9?	—	+	+	—
125[60]	Visingsö	Kumlaby ch.	rec.	X 60	s?		10	dam.	149	9	A	—	—	—
126#	Visingsö	Kumlaby ch.		A 1	m		10	—			—	—	—	—
N.Vedbo														
128	Linderås	Göberga		X 60			3	dam.	84	3?	A	—	—	—
129#	Säby	Säby ch.		A 1	s		10	—	200	3/4b?	—	—	—	—
130	Eksjö	Eksjö ch.		A 2	s		10	—	207	6	—	—	—	—
S.Vedbo														
131	Flisby	Hjortholmen		X 20	s		7,8	dam.	104	6	—	—	—	—
132	Flisby	Rickelstorp		A 1	s		6,7	—	131	3b	—	—	—	—
133	Flisby	Sunneränga		A 3	s		7	2s	215	3a+2	B	+	—	—
134	Hult	Sandshult		A 1	s		7	—	136	3b(2)	—	—	—	—
136#	Hult	Österby		X	s		2	—	160	3/4?	A–C?	—	—	—
137[61]	Höreda	Kvarnarp		X 30	?		7	dam.	156	5	—	—	+	—
138#	Höreda	Markestad		A 1	s		6	—	165	3a	—	—	—	—
139[62]	Höreda	Markestad		A 2+?	s		2	fr.	120	5?	—	—	—	—
140#m?	Höreda	Ryningsholm		A 1	s		8	—	100	3b	A?	—	—	—
N1m[63]	Mellby	Mellby ch.		A 6+A 1	m			—	225	?	—	—	+	—
141	Mellby	Medalby		X 20	s		8	fr.	(74)	5	—	—	—	—

[54] Sm 61: Two fathers commemorate one son each. [55] Sm 80: *Vallsjö manor. [56] Sm 83: *SHM, 3450.
[57] Sm 91: *Jönköping town park. [58] Sm 110: *Apoteksparken. [59] Sm 124: *Braheskolan (school).
[60] Sm 125: *Braheskolan (school). [61] Sm 137: *Eksjö (park). [62] Sm 139: *Jönköping länsmuseum.
[63] Sm N1: SVS, 4.

id.	parish	place	type	rel.sh.	s/m	dat.	fsp.	state	height	design	cross	orn.	rel.	sign.
142[64]	Mellby	Värneslätt		A 1	s		7	—	130	5	A	—	—	—
143m	Mellby	Värneslätt		A 1	s		7	—	110	5+	—	—	+	—
N.Tjust														
146#	Ukna	Kolsebro		A 1	s		3	—	235	3a	—	—	—	—
147	V.Ed	V.Ed ch.		A 6	s		10	—	139	5	—	—	—	—
148#	V.Ed	L.Hälleberg		E 1	m		3	2s	175	5+	A	—	—	Arnfast+X
149[65]	V.Ed	L.Hälleberg		E 3	m		2	fr.	(87)	3a	—	—	—	—
Aspeland														
150#	Mörlunda	Mörl.ch.	rec.	X	m		10	—	140	9	—	—	—	—
151#m	Mörlunda	Mörl.ch.		X	m		10	—	112	9	—	—	—	—
152[66]	Mörlunda	Sinnerstad		X 10/6?			8	fr.	(183)	3a	C?	—	—	—
Handbörd														
153#	Högsby	Högsby ch.		A 1	m		10	—	111	3a+	—	—	—	—
154[67]	Högsby	Högsby ch.		A 1	s		6	—	215	2	—	—	+	—
155	Långemåla	Bötterum		A 1	s		2	dam.	102	2/3?	+	—	—	+
N.Möre														
157#	Ryssby	Ryssby old ch.		A 1 or 2?	s		10	—		6	A–C?	—	—	—
161	Kalmar town	Slottet		X	m		3	fr.	(77)	?	—	—	—	—
S.Möre														
163[68]	Arby	Arby ch.yd		X 60			10	dam.	155	3a	A?	—	—	—
166	Hossmo	Hossmo ch.	rec.	X			10	fr.	(65)	9	B	—	+	—
169	Ljungby	Ljungby ch.		E 6?	m		10	—	143	6	A	—	—	—
170	follows Sm 34													

NEW FIND

	härad	*follows* Sm
N1	S.Vedbo	140

Södermanland (Sö): 352 inscriptions[69]

Daga härad

id.	parish	place	type	rel.sh.	s/m	dat.	fsp.	state	height	design	cross	orn.	rel.	sign.
1#	Björnlunda	Björnl.ch.		X	m		10	—	275	6?	—	—	—	—
2m	Björnlunda	Axala	rock	E 3	m	2		—	159	4b	A	—	+	—
3	Björnlunda	Vänga		E 3	m	2b	3	—	153	6	B	—	—	—
4#	Björnlunda	Vänga		X 60				fr.	(57)	5	—	—	—	—
6#	Björnlunda	Vänga		X 10 or 20?=70b[70]				fr.	(55)	5	—	—	—	—
7	Björnlunda	Öja		E 1	m	2–3	6	—	410	7	B	—	+	—
354[71]	Dillnäs	Dill.ch.		X	s		10	fr.		?	—	—	—	—
8	Dillnäs	Nybble		C 1	m	2b		—	235	6	—	—	+	—
9	Dillnäs	Lifsinge		E 3	m	2b	8	7fr.	205	6	A	—	+	—
10	Frustuna	Frust.ch.yd.		A 1	m	2b	10	—	195	6	A	—	+	—
11	Gryt	Gryt ch.		E 3	m	2b	10	—	187	7	D	—	+	Öpir
12#	Gryt	Gryt ch.		X 10/?			10	—	135	?	—	—	—	—
13mc[72]	Gryt	Gatstugan		E 3?	m		3	—	138	6	A	—	—	—
14m?	Gåsinge	Gås.ch.		C 5.1	m		10	—	196	7	Er	—	+	—
15m?	Gåsinge	Gås.ch.yd. (cf. 14)		D 1?	m?	2b	10	fr.	(39)	3a	—	—	—	—
16	Kattnäs	Katt.ch.yd.		X 60			10	—	100	8a	—	—	+	—
17#	Kattnäs	Norrtuna		X	m		3	fr.	(61)	5?	A–C?	—	—	—

Continued

[64] Sm 142: SVS, 9. [65] Sm 149: *V.Ed church. [66] Sm 152: *Mörlunda church.

[67] Sm 154: *FV* 1971, 205. [68] Sm 163: *FV* 1974, 209.

[69] In order to place inscriptions in the correct districts the strict sequence of id. nos. has to be violated; the following inscriptions are to be found after the numbers given in brackets: 276–81 (after 328 in Åker), 307–12 (after 336 in Öknebo), 314 (after 80 in V.Rekarne), 354 (after 7 in Daga), 355–7 (after 120 in Ö.Rekarne), 359 (after 39 in Hölebo), 360 (after 55 in Oppunda), 362–3 (after 84 in V.Rekarne), 367 (after 45 in Jönåker), 370 (after 134 in Rönö), 374 (after 173 in Rönö), 377 (after 208 in Selebo), 381 (after 306 in Svartlösa), and 382 (after 329 in Åker).

[70] Sö 6: Fragmentary commemoration of a father or brother, who is at the same time the 'bonde' of the sponsor(s).

[71] Sö 354: *SHM, 9377. [72] Sö 13: *Ånhammar park. For a new interpretation see Stille (1996).

id.	parish	place	type	rel.sh.	s/m	dat.	fsp.	state	height	design	cross	orn.	rel.	sign.
Hölebo														
18#	Hölö	Hölö ch.		X 7a	m		10	fr.	(71)	6	—	—	—	Hakon
19	Hölö	Lida		A 1	s	3a	3	—	212	6+mbd	—	—	+	—
20	Hölö	Smedsta		A 1?	s		7	—	122	3a	—	—	—	—
21#	Mörkö	Hörning-sholm		A 1	m		3	—			—	—	—	—
22	Mörkö	Håga		A 1	m	2b	6,7	5fr.	200	7?	B	—	—	—
23#	Mörkö	Skälby	rock	E 05.20?	m		?	—	150	6	A	—	+	—
25	Trosa Vagnhärad	Långbro		A 1	m		7	—	137	6	—	—	—	—
26[73]	Trosa V'hd.	Ytter-Stene		A 2	m	2	2,5	4fr.	160	4b	A	—	—	—
27	Trosa V'hd.	Söder-Husby, Åby		E 2	m	2	5	fr.	(110)	4b	A	—	+	—
28#	Trosa V'hd.	Nora		A 1	s	2a	5,7	—	151	3a	—	—	—	—
29#	Trosa V'hd.	Nora		A 2	s	2a	5,7	—	191	3a	—	—	—	—
30	Trosa V'hd.	Nora		E 3	m	2b	5,7	fr.	(92)	6	B	—	+	—
31[74]	Trosa V'hd.	Nora		A 1	m	2b	3	fr.	(53)	6	—	—	—	—
32	Trosa V'hd.	Skåång		E 1	m	2b	7	—	145	6+	—	—	+	—
33[75]	Trosa V'hd.	Skåång		A 2	s	2b	7	—	160	6	D	—	—	—
34m	Trosa V'hd.	Tjuvstigen		A 2	m	2	7	—	203	4b	A	—	—	—
35m	Trosa V'hd.	Tjuvstigen		X 30	s	2b	7?	—	160	6	—	—	+	Torer
36	Trosa V'hd.	Trosa br.		A 1/2	m	2	7	—	138	4b	A	—	—	—
37	Trosa V'hd.	Vappersta		E 3.20?	m	2b	7	—	160	6	A	—	—	—
38#	Trosa V'hd.	Åby		A 1	s	2a	7	—		3a?	—	—	+	—
39	Trosa V'hd.	Åda	rock	A 2	s	3a	7	—	122	6	—	+	—	—
359	Trosa V'hd.	Åda	rock	A 1	m	3a	5	—	104	6	B	—	—	—
40[76]	Västerljung	Väst.ch.		A 1	s	2b	10	3s	295	6	D	+	—	Skamhals
41	Västerljung	Björke	rock	A 1	s	3a	7,8	—	120	6	A	—	—	Tate?
42	Västerljung	Gillberga		A 7a	s		7?	—	116	5?	C	—	—	—
43[77]	Västerljung	Skälberga		X 10			8	3fr.		5?	A?	—	+	—
Jönåker														
44#	Bergshammar	Berg.ch.		C 3	s		10	fr.	(73)	4a	A–C?	—	—	—
N2[78]	Lunda	Lunda vic.		A 1/2	s	2b	10	—	232	5	A	—	—	—
N1[79]	Lunda	Giberga		X 60			3	fr.	(67)	3a?+	—	—	—	—
45c	S:t Nikolai	Släbro		A 1/2	m	2b	5	—	138	6	A	—	—	—
367	S:t Nikolai	Släbro		E 10.05	m	2a	5	—	174	2?	—	+	—	—
46[80]	Nykyrka	Hormesta		A 2	m	2a	2	—	284	3a+	A/C?	—	—	Kättil, Stack
47	Nykyrka	Vålsta		A 3	s		8	—	143	3a+	C	—	—	—
48	Stigtomta	Stigt.ch.		A 6	m	3a	10	—	107	6+	—	—	—	—
49	Stigtomta	Ene		A 1	m	2b	2	—	185	6+	A?	—	—	—
50	Tuna	Jogersta		E 3	m	2b	5	—	168	6	—	—	—	—
51	Nyköping town	Allhelgona ch.yd.		A 2	m		10	—	91	4b+mbd	—	—	—	—
Oppunda														
52	Bettna	Märing br.		A 1	s	2b	?	—	159	6+	—	—	—	—
53#	Bettna	Valstad		A 3	s	2a	8,10?	—	250	3a?	—	—	—	—
N3[81]	Bettna	Åkra		X 01			8	fr.	(109)	3a?	—	—	—	—
54	Blacksta	Bjudby		A 2	m	2a	7,9?	—	295	6	A?	—	—	Stenkil
55	Blacksta	Bjudby		A 8/3	s	2b	2	10fr.?	295	6	A?	—	+	Brune, Slode
360	Blacksta	Bjudby		A 2	s	2a	2	—	180	3a(2)	A–C?	—	—	—
56	Blacksta	Fyrby	rock	A 1	m	2a	7	—	225	3b	—	—	—	—
57#m	Blacksta	Trinkesta		A 2	m	2b	7,8	—		6+	—	—	—	—
58m[82]	Floda	Stav		A 1	m		2	fr.	(95)	6?	—	—	—	—
59	Husby-Oppunda	Flåsta		A 1	m	2b	5	—	90	6	—	—	—	—
60[83]	Husby-Opp.	Ramsta		C 5.1/3.2	m	2	7	—	205	4b+	A–C?	—	—	—
61	Husby-Opp.	Ösby		A 3.2 (?)	m	2b	7	—	134	6+	—	—	—	—
N5[84]	Julita	Julita gård		A 1	s		10	—	190	3a	A?	—	—	—
62	Lerbo	Hässlö		A 3	s		8?	—	280	6	A	—	—	—
63#	St.Malm	St.Malm ch.		A 1?/2	s	2b	10	—	183	6	—	—	—	—
64#	St.Malm	Fågelö	rec.	A 1	m		3	—	225	6	A	—	—	—

[73] Sö 26: *FV* 1978, 222.
[74] Sö 31: *one fragment in SHM, 19224, another fragment in Björksta, see ATA 6735/59.
[75] Sö 33: *Fredriksdal.
[76] Sö 40: *FV* 1959, 266.
[77] Sö 43: *FV* 1986, 220.
[78] Sö N2: *FV* 1948, 295.
[79] Sö N1: *FV* 1948, 291.
[80] Sö 46: *Nykyrka churchyard.
[81] Sö N3: *FV* 1984, 253.
[82] Sö 58: *Floda church.
[83] Sö 60: *Husbygård.
[84] Sö N5: *FV* 1973, 189.

id.	parish	place	type	rel.sh.	s/m	dat.	fsp.	state	height	design	cross	orn.	rel.	sign.
65[85]	St.Malm	Djulefors		C 3 or 4?	s	2a	3	—	150	6	A	—	—	—
66	Sköldinge	Sköld.ch.yd.		X 60	m	3b	10	—	99	3a	—	+	+	—
67#	Sköldinge	Häringe		A 1	m		7	—	200	6+	—	—	+	—
68#	Sköldinge	Remmeröd		A 1	s	2b	6	—	183	6	—	—	—	—
69	Sköldinge	Valla		A 6	m		?	fr.	(123)	6	—	—	—	—
70	Vadsbro	Hedenlunda		A 2	m	2a	7	—	140	3a+	A	—	—	—
71	V.Vingåker	Hansta		X 40			7	dam.	255	3a+mbd	A	—	—	—
72#	V.Vingåker	Kjesäter		A 4=7b[86]	m	2b	7	—	504?	5+2mbds =cross[87]	—	+	—	
73	V.Vingåker	Lyttersta		D 6	s	2a	5,8	—	123	3a	A	—	—	—
74	V.Vingåker	Ålsäter		A 3	s	2a	5?	—	197	6	A	—	—	—
75	Vrena	Vrena ch.yd.		A 2	m	2b	10	—	150	6+	—	—	—	—
N4[88]	Vrena	Vrena ch.		X 10						?	—	—	+	—
V.Rekarne														
76#	Lista	Lista ch.		C 1	s	2b	10	—	188	7	A	—	+	—
79	Torshälla	Hällby	rock	X 10/20	m		7	dam.	215	8	C	—	—	—
80#	Torshälla	Rambron		X			6	—		6	—	+	—	—
314[89]	Torshälla	Torsh.ch.		X 60		2a	10	2pts.	(162)	?	—	—	—	—
82	Tumbo	Tumbo ch.		A 2	s	2b	10	dam.	118	6	A	—	—	Tule
83#	Tumbo	Tumbo ch.	rec.	X 60			10	fr.	(103)	1	—	—	—	—
84	Tumbo	Tumbo ch.; ch.yd.		A 2	s	2	10	—		4b	C	—	+	—
362	Tumbo	Tumbo ch.		A 2	m	2	10	—	185	4b	C	—	—	—
363	Tumbo	Tumbo ch.		A 1	s	2	10	—	150	4b	C	—	+	—
N6[90]	Tumbo	Tumbo ch.		A 6	m	2	10	—	205	4b	C	—	—	—
N7[91]	Tumbo	Tumbo ch.		E 2	m	2	10	—	153	4a?	D	—	—	—
85	Tumbo	Västerby		A 1	m	2	5	4fr.	(123)	4b	C	—	—	—
86	Öja	S.Åby	rock	A 1	m		7	—	177	4a	—	+	—	—
88[92]	Öja	Valby		A 1/4	m	2b	2	—	230	6+	—	—	—	—
Ö.Rekarne														
90	Hammarby	Lövhulta		A 1	s	2b	2	—	182	5	—	—	—	—
91#	Hammarby	Tidö		A 6	m	2b	2	—	320	6	C	—	+	—
92	Husby-Rekarne	H.-R. ch.yd.		X 20	s		10	—	164	(sd)	—	—	—	Balle
94#	Husby-Rek.	Berga		C 5?	s			—		?	—	—	+	—
96	Jäder	Jäder ch.		X 10	s	2b	10	—	171	6/7?	—	—	—	—
97	Jäder	Jäder ch.		A 1	s		10	2s	185	6+sd	C	—	—	—
98	Jäder	Jäder ch.		X	s?		10	—		10(circle)	—	—	—	—
101c	Jäder	Ramsunds-berget	rock	C 5	s	2a	7	—	(470)	7	—	+	+	—
102	Jäder	Vävle		C 3	s	2b	8	—	137	6	—	—	+	—
103	Jäder	Vävle		A 1/2	s		7,8	—	132	6+3a	B	—	—	—
N8[93]	Kjula	Kjula ch.		X 20			10	fr.	(120)	3a	A	—	—	—
104	Kjula	Berga		A 1	s	2a	8	—	176	6	C	—	—	Ulv
N9[94]	Kjula	Harby		X 60			2	—	277	5	—	—	—	—
105	Kjula	Högstena		A 3	s	2b	7	2s	190	5+	C	—	—	—
106c	Kjula	Kungshållet		A 1	s	2a	7,8	—	330	4b	D	—	—	—
107	Kloster	Balsta, Gredby		A 1	s	2a	6?,7	—	170	6	B	—	—	—
108	Kloster	Gredby		A 1	s	2b	7	—	139	5	B	—	—	—
109	Kloster	Gredby br.		E 3.20	m	2b	6	—	314	7	A–C?	—	—	—
110#	Kloster	Grönsta		X 10	s	2b	2	—	188	6	B?	—	—	—
N21[95]	Kloster	Årby		A 2	m	2	3,7,8	dam.	170	4b	B	—	—	—
111	Stenkvista	Sten.ch.yd.		A 1	m	2b	10	—	220	5	—	+	—	—
112m	Stenkvista	Kolunda		A 1	m	2b	7,8	—	190	5	A–B?	—	—	—
113m	Stenkvista	Kolunda		AB 1	m	2a	10	—	100	2(4)	—	—	—	—
115[96]	Stenkvista	Kolunda		E 1.60?	m	2b	6	fr.	(81)	7?	—	—	—	—
116	Sundby	Sundby ch.	rec.	E 10.05	m	3a	10	—	196	7/9?	—	—	—	—
118	Sundby	Ostra		A 6	s	2a	7,8	dam.	217	6	C	—	+	—
120	Ärila	Skogshall	rock	AB 20/01	s	3a	7	—	123	6	A	—	+	—
355[97]	Eskilstuna town	Fors ch.	rec.	X	m		10	fr.	(80)	1	—	—	—	—
357	Eskilstuna	E.slottskolan		X 02		3a	10	—	157	6/7?	—	—	—	—
N22[98]	Eskilstuna	Fors ch.	?	X 30			?			?	—	—	—	—

Continued

[85] Sö 65: *Eriksberg. [86] Sö 72: two men commemorate their relative, who is also their 'bonde'.
[87] Sö 72: the two bands in the middle make up a cross. [88] Sö N4: *FV* 1954, 19; Owe (1996), 116. [89] Sö 314: *FV* 1958, 245.
[90] Sö N6: *FV* 1958, 242. [91] Sö N7: *SB*, 12. [92] Sö 88: *Stora Sundby. [93] Sö N8: *FV* 1969, 298.
[94] Sö N9: *FV* 1986, 218; M. L. Nielsen (1997*b*), 59–82. [95] Sö N21: *FV* 1993, 229. [96] Sö 115: *FV* 1992, 154.
[97] Sö 355: *FV* 1948, 313. [98] Sö N22: *FV* 1973, 187; *Djurgårdsmuseet.

id.	parish	place	type	rel.sh.	s/m	dat.	fsp.	state	height	design	cross	orn.	rel.	sign.
Rönö														
122m	Helgona	Skresta		A 3	s		7,8	—	194	5	A	—	—	—
123m	Helgona	Skresta		A 3	s	2a	7,8	2s	160	1	—	—	—	—
124	Bogsta	Bog.ch.		A 1/6	m	3b	10	—	162	6	—	—	—	—
125	Bogsta	Bog.ch.		A 1	s		10	—	160	5?	A	—	+	—
126	Bogsta	Fagerlöt	rock	A 1	m	2b	7	—	178	7	A	—	—	—
127#	Bogsta	Rossbäck		X 20			5?	—	159	5?	—	—	—	—
128	Lid	Lid ch.		F 01.50	m	2a	10	—	153	6	A	—	—	Kar
130	Lid	Sparsta		A 1	s	2b	8	2s	182	5+	Er	—	—	—
131	Lid	Lundby		A 2	m	2a	7	—	158	2	B	—	—	—
132	Lid	Sanda		C 1	s	2	2,5	—	120	4b	B	—	—	—
133	Lid	Väringe		X 6?	s		5,8	—	130	5?	G	—	—	Äsbjörn
134m	Ludgo	Ludgo ch.		X 30		2a	10	—	118	2(6)	—	—	+	—
370	Ludgo	Ludgo ch.		X			10	fr.	(50)	2?	—	—	—	—
N10m[99]	Ludgo	Ludgo ch.	?	E 3	m	2	10	—	120	4b	B	—	+	—
135#	Ludgo	Ludgo vic.		X 60		2	10	fr.	(48)	?	—	—	+	—
136#	Ludgo	Aspa		A 1	m	2a	6	—	258	5	A?	—	—	—
137mc	Ludgo	Aspa		C 5	s	2a	7,9	2s	185	3a+2	—	—	—	—
138c	Ludgo	Aspa		0		2b	7,9	—	165	5+3a	—	—	+	—
N11[100]	Ludgo	Aspa br.		C 3	s	2b	6,7	—	198	5+2	—	—	—	—
139	Ludgo	Jursta, Korpbron		B 4	s	3a	7	—	148	6+3a	A	—	+	Kjul, Finn
140	Ludgo	Jursta, Korpbron		A 4	s	2b	5,7	—	167	5	G	—	—	—
141m[101]	Ludgo	Löta		E 3	m		6	—	166	3b	—	—	—	—
142	Lästringe	Kalkbron		A 2	m		6	—	109	6	—	—	—	—
143	Runtuna	Run.ch.; ch.yd.		A 3	s	2	10	—	97	4b	B	—	+	—
144	Runtuna	Broby	rock	A 1	m	2b	7	—	140	6	A	—	—	—
145#	Runtuna	Eneby		A 1	m		5	2s	140	4+5	B	—	—	—
147#	Runtuna	Glåttra		C 1	m		3	—	135	4	A	—	—	—
148	Runtuna	Innberga		A 1	m		5	—	240	5	A?	—	—	—
149[102]	Runtuna	Kungsberga		E 3.(60)	m	2	2	2s,dam.	120	3b+1	B?	—	+	—
150	Runtuna	Kungsberga		X 60			2	fr.	(60)	3a?	A	—	—	—
151	Runtuna	Lövsund		A 2	s	2a	7	2s	130	5+	A	—	—	—
152[103]	Runtuna	Membro		A 1	s	2a	7	—	209	4b	B	—	—	—
153#	Runtuna	Skarpåker		X	m		3	fr.	(79)	3a	A	—	—	—
154	Runtuna	Skarpåker		A 3	s	2a	3	—	190	6	A	—	+	—
155[104]	Runtuna	Söderby		A 1?	m		8	—		6	—	+	—	—
N12[105]	Runtuna	Sörby		X 10			2	fr.	(94)	4a?	A–C?	—	—	—
157#	Runtuna	Ärsta		E 10.05	m		6	—	203	5?	A?	—	—	—
158[106]	Runtuna	Österberga		A 1	m		2	—	160	5+mbd	—	+	—	—
159	Runtuna	Österberga		A 1	m	2a	6	—	250	3a+	A	—	—	Rörik, Gudmund, Boe, Gunnlev
160[107]	Råby	Råby ch.		A 6	s	2a	10	—	110	1+2 =cross[108]	+	—	—	—
161[109]	Råby	Råby ch.		X 20	s	2a	10	—	95	3a+	—	—	—	—
162[110]	Råby	Råby ch.		A 6	m	2a	10	—	95?	2	—	—	—	—
163[111]	Råby	Ryckesta		A 3	s	2b	7	—	122	6+	A	—	—	—
164	Råby	Spånga		A 1	m	2a	8	—	196	4	A/B?	+	—	—
165	Spelvik	Grinda		C 6	s	2a	8	—	161	2+3a	—	—	+	—
166	Spelvik	Grinda		A 1	m	2a	2	—	175	4a	A/B?	—	—	—
167	Spelvik	Lands-hammar		A 3	s	2b	7	2s	157	5	A	+	—	—
168[112]	Spelvik	Lands-hammar		X 40?				fr.	(64)	3/4?+	Eg	—	—	—
N13mc[113]	Spelvik	Viby		A 1	m	2	8	—	155	4b	A	—	—	—
169#	Svärta	Ekeby		A 6	s			fr.	(74)	3b?	—	—	—	—
170	Svärta	Nälberga		A 1	m	2?	7	—	185	3a+mbd	A	—	—	—
171[114]	Säterstad	Esta	rock	A 1	s	2	2	3pts.	160	4b	B	—	—	—
172	Tystberga	Tyst.ch.		A 3	s	2	10	fr.?	(75)	?	—	—	+	—
173mc	Tystberga	Tystberga		E 2/1	m	2	2	—	120	7?	—	—	—	—
374c	Tystberga	Tystberga		X 40.10?	m?	2a	2	—	215	4/7?	A	—	—	—

[99] Sö N10: *FV* 1948, 282. [100] Sö N11: *FV* 1948, 289. [101] Sö 141: *Ådala. [102] Sö 149: *Runtuna church.
[103] Sö 152: *Runtuna church. [104] Sö 155: ATA 6888/59; *NOR* 1994, 25. [105] Sö N12: ATA 6163/61.
[106] Sö 158: *FV* 1981, 196. [107] Sö 160: *Täckhammar. [108] Sö 160: the bands make up a cross. [109] Sö 161: *Täckhammar.
[110] Sö 162: *Täckhammar. [111] Sö 163: *Täckhammar. [112] Sö 168: *FV* 1948, 304; *Trossbobacken.
[113] Sö N13: *FV* 1982, 235. [114] Sö 171: *SHM, 24015; three parts.

id.	parish	place	type	rel.sh.	s/m	dat.	fsp.	state	height	design	cross	orn.	rel.	sign.
Selebo														
174	Aspö	Aspö ch.		A 3	s	2a	10	—	207	6	B	—	+	—
175	Aspö	Lagnö	rock	E 6	m	3a	2	—	150	7	—	+	—	—
176[115]	Kärnbo	Kärn.des.ch.		X 8/20	s	1?	10	fr.	(103)	4a?	—	—	—	—
177	Kärnbo	Kärn.des.ch.		C 3?	s	2	10	—	158	4b?	B	—	—	—
178	Kärnbo	Gripsholm		AB 20/01	m	3a	6,7	—	206	7?	B	—	—	Brune
179	Kärnbo	Gripsholm		C 3	s	2	3	—	200	6	—	—	—	—
180	Kärnbo	Harby	rock	X			2	dam.		3a	A	—	+	—
181[116]	Kärnbo	Helanda		X			7	fr.	(120)	?	—	—	+	—
182#[117]	Kärnbo	Läggesta		X 30			7	fr.		?	+(?)	—	—	—
183	Kärnbo	Viggeby		A 1	m	2b	7,8	—	110	5	—	—	—	—
184	Kärnbo	Årby		A 2	s	2	7,8	—	138	4b	Fg/r?	—	+	—
187	Toresund	Harby		A 1	m	2b	7	—	178	6	A–C?	—	+	—
188	Toresund	Åkerby	rock	E 06.20	m	2a	8	dam.	150	6	—	—	—	—
189	Toresund	Åkerby		A 1	s	2a	2	2s	235	4a	D?	—	—	—
190	Ytterenhörna	Ytt.ch.		A 1.2	m	2b	10	dam.	194	6	—	+	+	Torbjörn
192	Ytterselö	Berg		C 5/3	s	3a	7,8	—	167	6	A	+	+	—
194	Ytterselö	Brössike		A 1	m	2b	8	—	133	6	—	—	—	—
195	Ytterselö	Brössike	rock	A 4	s	3a	7	dam.	125	6	—	—	+	Hallbjörn
196	Ytterselö	Husby, Kolsundet		C 1	s	2b	5	—	165	6+	A	—	—	Assur
197m	Ytterselö	Husby, Kolsundet	rock	A 2	m	3a	5	—	169	8	—	—	+	—
198	Ytterselö	Mervalla		C 5	s	2b	8	—	110	6+	B	—	—	—
199	Ytterselö	Ullunda	rock	X	m	2b	2	dam.	128	8a?	A?	—	—	—
200	Ytterselö	Åsa		A 1	m	2b	8	—	185	6	A?	—	—	—
202	Ytterselö	Östa		A 1	s	2b	8	—	138	5+mbd	—	—	—	—
203m	Ytterselö	Östa		A 2	m	3a	7	—	210	6	B	—	—	Balle
204	Överselö	Överselö ch.		A 4	s	3a	10	—	150	7	—	—	—	—
205	Överselö	Överselö ch.		E 10.05. 03.20	m	3a	10	—	210	7	—	+	—	Äsbjörn, Tidkume, Orökja
206m	Överselö	Överselö ch.		C 3.2	m	3a	10	—	111	7	—	—	—	—
207	Överselö	Överselö ch.; ch.yd.		A 1	s		10	dam.	146	6	B	—	+	—
208m	Överselö	Överselö ch.		C 3.2	m	3a	10	fr.	(107)	7	—	—	—	—
377	Överselö	Överselö ch.		X 30			10	dam.	232	?	A	+	—	—
209	Överselö	Fröberga		A 2	m	2b	7		151	5	B	—	—	—
210	Överselö	Klippinge		A 2	s	2b	2	dam.	143	6	B	—	+	Balle
211	Överselö	Ljunga		A 1	m	2b	7	—	136	6	—	—	—	—
212	Överselö	L.Lundby		A 2	s	2b	7	—	175	6	B	—	+	—
213	Överselö	Nybble		E 05.10	m	3a	8	—	136	7	—	+	—	—
214	Överselö	Årby		A 1	s	2b	8	dam.	245	7?	D	—	—	Balle
Sotholm														
215#	Sorunda	Sor.ch.		A 1?/2	m	2b	10	—		6	D	—	—	Amunde
216#	Sorunda	Aska		X 60	m?		7	—		?	—	—	—	—
217	Sorunda	Berga		A 1	m	2b	7	—	140	6	D	—	—	—
218	Sorunda	Billsta	rock	A 1	m	3a	7	dam.	127	6	A	—	—	—
(219–221 = same rock)														
219	Sorunda	Blista	rock	A 2	s	3a	7	—	168	6	C?	—	—	Hägvid
220	Sorunda	Blista	rock	A 1	m	3a	7	—	160	6	—	—	—	—
221	Sorunda	Blista	rock	A 1	s	3a	7	—	160	7	—	—	+	—
222	Sorunda	Frölunda	rock	A 3	s	3a	7	dam.	160	6	—	—	—	—
223#	Sorunda	Fullbro		A 3	s	2b	6	fr.	(135)	6?	—	—	—	—
224	Sorunda	Grödby		A 1	m	2b	7	—	120	6	—	—	—	—
226	Sorunda	N.Stutby		A 1	m	2b	7	—	160	6	—	+	—	—
227	Sorunda	Sundby	rock	A 2	s	3a	3	—	159	6	B/C?	—	—	—
228#	Sorunda	Nedre Söderby		A 6?	s			—		6	—	—	—	—
229	Sorunda	Torp		A 1	m	2b	7	—	175	6	D	—	—	—
231	Sorunda	Trollsta	rock	X 10? 20?	m?		7	dam.	123	5	A	—	—	—
232	Sorunda	Trollsta		A 1.2	m	2	3	—	103	4b	A	—	—	—
233[118]	Sorunda	Trollsta		A 1	m	2b	2	2pts.	120	5	D?	—	—	Amunde
234	Sorunda	Trollsta		A 1	m	2a	3	fr.	(155)	8a	—	—	—	—
235	Sorunda	Västerby		A 1	m	3a	7	fr.	(100)	6?	—	+	—	—
N17[119]	Tyresö	Tyresö ch.		X	s		2	fr.	(100)	5	—	—	+	—

Continued

[115] Sö 176: *SHM, 10173.
[116] Sö 181: *Mariefred church.
[117] Sö 182: *Mariefred church, now lost.
[118] Sö 233: *FV* 1948, 307.
[119] Sö N17: *FV* 1971, 207.

id.	parish	place	type	rel.sh.	s/m	dat.	fsp.	state	height	design	cross	orn.	rel.	sign.
236	Västerhaninge	Alvsta		E 3	m		8	—	151	5	A	—	—	—
237	V'haninge	Fors		A 1+ A 3 (?)	m	2b	5,7	—	179	7	—	+	—	—
238#	V'haninge	Fors		A 1	m		?	—		6	A	—	—	—
239	V'haninge	Häringe		A 2	s	2b	5	fr.	(129)	6	—	+	—	—
240	V'haninge	Ribby		A 1	s	2b	7	—	136	6	D	—	—	—
241	V'haninge	Skogs-Ekeby		A 2	m	2b	5,8	—	170	6	A	—	—	—björn
242	V'haninge	Stav		C 5.1	m	2	2	—	194	4b	D	—	—	—
244	V'haninge	Tuna		X	s?	2a	8	—	155	8(2)	D	—	—	—
246	V'haninge	Vreten		X	m		8	fr.	111	5?	—	—	—	—
247#	V'haninge	Ålsta		X	m		?	fr.	(105)	?	C	—	—	—
248	Ösmo	Björsta	rock	A 1	m	3a	2	—	150	6	—	—	—	—
250	Ösmo	Jursta		C 6	s	2b	7	—	161	6	A	—	—	—
251	Ösmo	Klastorp		C 1	m	2b	7,8	—	100	6	D	—	—	—
N15mc[120]	Ösmo	Säby		E10/05?	m		2	—	150	5	Eg	—	—	—
252[121]	Ösmo	Säby		X 20		2b	2	—	117	5	—	—	—	—
253#	Ösmo	Vansta		A 1	m		7,8	—		6	A	—	—	—
254	Ösmo	Vansta		A 1/6	m	2b	5	—	149	6	D	—	—	—
255	Ösmo	Vidby	rock	A 2	s	3a	7	—	122	6	C	—	+	—
N14[122]	Ösmo	Ådala		A 1	m	2a	2,7	—	195	5	—	—	—	—
256	Ösmo	Älby		A 1	m	2a	8	—	180	8a	A	—	—	—
257#	Ösmo	Älby		X 40	s		8	—		6	A–D?	—	—	—
258	Ösmo	Älby		A 3	s	2b	8	—	155	6	A	—	—	—
259	Österhaninge	Alby		X 20			2,5	fr.	(50)	6?	—	—	—	—
260	Ö'haninge	S.Betby		X 30			2	—	205	5?	A	—	—	—
262	Ö'haninge	Blista		A 1/6	s	3a	2	—	263	6	A–D?	—	—	—
263#	Ö'haninge	Broby		C 1	m	2b		—		6	A	—	—	—
265	Ö'haninge	Högsta		A 3/6	s	2b	5,8	—	140	6	D	—	—	—
N16	Ö'haninge	Lövhagen		C 2	m	2b	6,7	—	200	7	—	—	—	—
266	Ö'haninge	Sanda		C 3	s	2b	7	—	120	6	D	—	—	Asbjörn?
268	Ö'haninge	Söderby		A 3	s	2a	2	—	180	7	—	—	—	Amunde
269	Ö'haninge	Söderby malm		A 1	m	2a	7	—	170	8a	C	—	—	—
270	Ö'haninge	Tyresta	rock	A 3	s	3a	7	—	168	6	C	+	—	Halvdan
271#	Ö'haninge	Täckeråker		A 1	s	2b		—		6	D?	—	—	Amunde
272	Ö'haninge	Upp-Norrby		A 3	s	2a	2	—	170	8	—	+	—	—
273	Ö'haninge	Valsta		X 10	s	2b	2	—	118	6	D	—	—	—
Svartlösa														
274[123]	Stockholm town	Södersluss		E 1	m	2b	3	fr.	(135)	8a	C	—	—	—
(276–281 follow Sö 328)														
282#	Botkyrka	Bot.ch.		A 1/2	m		10	—	160	7	—	—	—	—
283	Botkyrka	Bot.ch.		X	m		10	—	154	?	—	—	—	—
284	Botkyrka	Bot.ch.		X 20?			10	fr.	(100)	5?	—	+?	—	—
285	Botkyrka	Bot.ch.		E 3	m	3a	10	—	137	6	—	—	—	—
286[124]	Botkyrka	Bot.ch.	rec.	E 40.03	m		10	—	168	1	—	+	—	—
287#	Botkyrka	Hunhammar		A 2.1	m		8	—	330	6+3a	A–C	—	—	?
288	Botkyrka	Hågelby		E 1.05	m	2a	7	—	180	6	—	—	+	—
289	Botkyrka	Hamra, Spåntorp		X 10	m	2b	7	—	180	6	A	—	+	—
305[125]	Botkyrka	Söderby		A 1	m	3a	5	—	260	7	A	—	—	—
290	Brännkyrka	Farsta		A 2	m	2b	7	—	127	8	C	—	—	—
291	Grödinge	Gröd.ch.; ch.yd.		A 1	m	2a	10	—	125	6	—	—	—	—
292mc	Grödinge	Bröta		A 4=5[126]	s	3a	7	—	260	8a	C	—	—	—
293[127]	Grödinge	Eldtomta		A 1	m		3	2fr.		?	—	—	—	—
294#	Grödinge	Hallsveden		A 1	m	3a	?	—	180	6	—	—	—	—
N18[128]	Grödinge	Nolinge		A 6	s		6,7	—	133	4a	—	—	—	Björn
295#	Grödinge	Skälby		X 60			7	—		?	—	—	—	—
296	Grödinge	Skälby		AB 40/05	s	2b	7	—	155	6	A	—	—	—
297[129]	Grödinge	Uppinge	rec.	C 5.1?	m	2b	2	—	150	8a(2)	C/D?	—	—	—
298c	Grödinge	Uringe malm		A 1	m	2b	7	—	220	6	C	—	—	—
299	Huddinge	Hudd.ch.	?	B 1	m	2b	10	—	100	5?	—	—	—	—
300	Huddinge	Glömsta	rock	B 1	s	2	7	—	102	(circle)	A	—	—	—
301	Huddinge	Ågesta br.		A 1	m	2b	6	—	186	8a	—	+	—	—
302	Salem	Bergaholm		B 2.1	m	3a	8	—	175	6	B	—	—	—

[120] Sö N15: *FV* 1971, 208. [121] Sö 252: *FV* 1948, 310. [122] Sö N14: *FV* 1948, 298. [123] Sö 274: *Skansen.
[124] Sö 286: *SHM, 3481. [125] Sö 305: *Lindhov. [126] Sö 292: a man commemorates his relative-in-law, who is also his partner.
[127] Sö 293: *Grödinge church. [128] Sö N18: *FV* 1954, 20. [129] Sö 297: *Grödinge bygdegård.

id.	parish	place	type	rel.sh.	s/m	dat.	fsp.	state	height	design	cross	orn.	rel.	sign.
303[130]	Salem	Bornö		E 3	m	2b	6	2pts.	(115)	5	—	+	—	—
304	Salem	Oxelby		A 3	s	2b	2,7	—	162	6	A–D?	+	—	—
(305 follows Sö 289)														
306	Salem	Söderby krog		A 1	m		7,8	—	150	7?	+(?)	—	—	—
(307–312 follow Sö 336)														
(314 follows Sö 80)														
381	Salem	Ladvik		X 10			2	fr.	(112)	?	—	—	—	—
Villåttinge														
315	Dunker	Sundby		X	m		3	fr.	(65)	?	—	—	+	—
316#	Dunker	Vadsbro		X 60	m?	2b	2	fr.		?	—	—	—	—
317#	Flen	Öja backe		A 3	s	2b	2	—	150	6	—	—	—	—
318	Helgesta	Sund		AB 10.02	m	2b	5	2s	274	6+3b	A	—	+	—
319[131]	Årdala	Sannerby		A 1	s	2a	2	—	80	4	A+Eg	—	—	—
320	Årdala	Stäringe park		A 2	m	2b	5	—	223	6	—	—	—	—
Åker														
321	Fogdö	Kråktorp		A 6	m	2b	5,8	—	245	6?+	—	—	+	—
N19[132]	Vansö	Lagnö		X 60	s		8,9?	—	140	5?	A	—	—	—
N20[133]	Helgarö	Rällinge		X 60			8	—	157	?	—	—	—	—
323#	Helgarö	Åsby		A 6	m	2a	8	—		?	—	—	—	Skammhals
324	Helgarö	Åsby	rock	X 60	m?		7	—	160	7?+	C?	+	—	—
325	Härad	Här.ch.; ch.yd.		A 1	s	2a	10	—	143	7?	—	—	—	—
326	Härad	Här.ch.		X	m		10	fr.	(92)	?	—	—	—	—
327	Härad	Göksten	rock	X		2a	7	—	150	6	B	+	—	—
328mc	Strängnäs town	Tynäs		E 1	m	2a	2	—	140	6+	—	—	—	—
276	Strängnäs	Domkyrkan		E 6	m	2b	10	—	254	6	A	—	—	—
277	Strängnäs	Domkyrkan		E 6	m	2a	10	fr.	194	6?	—	—	—	—
278	Strängnäs	Domkyrkan		X	s		10	—	100	6/7?	—	—	—	—
279	Strängnäs	Domkyrkan		X 60		2b	10	—	65	6?	—	—	—	—
280c	Strängnäs	Domkyrkan	rec.	E 05/03. 10/20	m		10	—	198	5	A	—	—	—
281	Strängnäs	Domkyrkan		C 3?	s	2a	10	fr.	(100)	6?	—	—	—	—
329#	Åker	Åker ch.		X 60	s	2a	10	fr.	(75)	6?	—	—	+	—
382#	Åker	Åker ch.		X 10	m		10	—		6?	C	—	+	—
331m	Åker	Skämby	rock	EF 3	m	2b	3,10	—	215	7	—	—	+	—
332	Åker	Skämby	rock	A 3	s	2b	3,10	—	140	6/8?	A	—	—	—
333	Åker	Ärja des.ch.; ch.yd.		A 3/2	s	2b	10	—	159	6?+	—	—	—	Eskil
334[134]	Åker	Ärja des.ch.		X 60			10	fr.	(61)		+(?)	—	—	—
335	Åker	Ärja des.ch.		A 2	s	2b	10	—	150	6	B	—	—	—
Åkerbo														
336	Kung Karl	Kungsör	rock	A 2	s	2a	7	—	140	6	—	—	+	—
Öknebo														
307[135]	Södertälje town	Igelsta kvarn		A 1	m	2a	7	—	116	3b	—	—	—	—
308	Södertälje	Söd.station		E 3	m	3b	7	—	185	6	—	—	—	Öpir
309[136]	Södertälje	Söd.ch.yd.	?	X 60			10	fr.	(42)	6	—	—	—	—
310#	Södertälje	Gneta vic.		A 1			10	fr.		?	—	—	—	—
311c	Södertälje	old Turingev.	rock	B 1	s	3a	7	—	120	6	—	—	—	—
312c	Södertälje	old Turingev.	rock	A 1	s	3a	7	—	155	6	A?	—	+	Östen
338	Turinge	Tur.ch.		E 10.20. 70.05	m	3a	10	—	209	6	B+ Fg(8)	—	—	—
339#	Turinge	Tur.ch.		A 1	s		10	—		3b?	—	—	—	—
340[137]	Turinge	Ö.Kumla		A 2	s	2b	2	—		5	B/C?	—	—	—
341#	Turinge	Stavsta?		A 2	s		?	—		6	A	—	—	—
342#	Turinge	Ströpsta		X	m		?	—		?	—	—	—	—
343	Tveta	Tveta ch.		A 1	m	2	10	—	102	4b	A	—	—	—
344	Västertälje	Kiholm	rock	A 1	m	3a	5	—		6	A	—	—	—
345[138]	Ytterjärna	Ytt.ch; ch.yd.		X 60			10	4fr.	157	?	—	—	—	—
346[139]	Ytterjärna	Gerstaberg		A 7b=2[140]	m	2b	3	dam.	142	5	A?	—	—	—

Continued

[130] Sö 303: *FV* 1948, 302. [131] Sö 319: *Stäringe park. [132] Sö N19: *FV* 1954, 22; *SHM, 30415.
[133] Sö N20: ATA 6491/60. [134] Sö 334: *Mariefred church. [135] Sö 307: *Torekällberget museum, Södertälje.
[136] Sö 309: *Torekällberget museum, Södertälje. [137] Sö 340: *Torekällberget museum, Södertälje.
[138] Sö 345: *FV* 1958, 246. [139] Sö 346: *FV* 1948, 313. [140] Sö 346: two men commemorate their 'bonde', who is also their brother.

id.	parish	place	type	rel.sh.	s/m	dat.	fsp.	state	height	design	cross	orn.	rel.	sign.
347	Ytterjärna	Gerstaberg	E 05/03. 10/20		m	3a	2	—	235	?	—	—	+	Esbjörn, Ulv
348	Ytterjärna	Kjulsta	A 4		s			fr.	(105)	?	—	—	—	—
349	Ytterjärna	Lideby	A 1		m	3a	7,8	—		6	B	—	+	—
350	Ytterjärna	Valsta	A 1		m	2b	7	—	188	5	Er	—	+	—
351	Överjärna	Öv.ch.	X 10		s		10	—	165	5+	Er	—	—	—
352[141]	Överjärna	Linga	E 40.02		m	2b	8	—	148	7	Er	—	—	—
353	Överjärna	Tällby	X		m	2b	10	fr.	(70)	5?	A–D?	—	—	—

354 follows Sö 7, above
355 and 357 follow 120
359 follows 39
360 follows 55
362–3 follow 84
367 follows 45
370 follows 134
374 follows 173
377 follows 208
381 follows 306
382 follows 329

NEW FINDS

	härad	*follows* Sö		*härad*	*follows* Sö		*härad*	*follows* Sö
N1	Jönåker	N2	N9	Ö.Rekarne	104	N16	Sotholm	265
N2	Jönåker	44	N10	Rönö	134(+370)	N17	Sotholm	235
N3	Oppunda	53	N11	Rönö	138	N18	Svartlösa	294
N4	Oppunda	75	N12	Rönö	155	N19	Åker	321
N5	Oppunda	61	N13	Rönö	168	N20	Åker	N19
N6	V.Rekarne	84(+362–3)	N14	Sotholm	255	N21	Ö.Rekarne	110
N7	V.Rekarne	N6	N15	Sotholm	251	N22	Ö.Rekarne	120(+355, 357)
N8	Ö.Rekarne	103						

Uppland (U): see separate section, beginning on p. 238.

Värmland (Vr): 2 inscriptions

id.	parish	place	type	rel.sh.	s/m	dat.	fsp.	state	height	design	cross	orn.	rel.	sign.
2	Väse	Rör	X 20				7	—	148	2(sd)	—	—	—	—
3	Hammarö	V.Hovlanda	A 4		s		7	—	87	2	—	—	—	—

Västergötland (Vg): 156 inscriptions

Vadsbo härad

id.	parish	place	type	rel.sh.	s/m	dat.	fsp.	state	height	design	cross	orn.	rel.	sign.
2	Ullervad	Torstentorp	B 6+?		s		7	2s,dam.	120	2	—	—	—	—
3	Bällefors	Armeneby	A 1		m		2	—	108	4a	—	—	—	—
4	Ek	St.Ek	A 3		s		7	2s	165	2	—	+	—	—
6	Fägre	Fägremo	X		m		7	dam.	205	3a?	—	—	—	—
7	Götlunda	Vallby, Sörg.	A 4		s		8	—	175	5	—	—	—	—
8	Hjälstad	Hjäl.ch.yd.	A 2		s		10	3s	160	5	A(2)	—	+	—
9c	Leksberg	Lek.ch.yd.	C 6		s		10	dam.	174	3a	—	—	—	—
11m	Leksberg	Lek.backe	A 3		s		2?	dam.	295	5	—	—	—	—
12c	Leksberg	Hindsberg	X		s?		3?	2s,fr.	(95)	3a+2	—	—	—	—
106	Leksberg	Karleby	X 01				2	fr.	(115)	2(sd)	—	+	—	—
13m	Leksberg	Karleby	AB 30/04		s		7	—	195	5	—	—	—	—
14	Lyrestad	Rogstorp	A 1		m		2	2s,dam.	330	3a	A	+	—	—
15	Mariestad	Sunnevad	A 3		s		7	—	275	5	—	—	—	—
16	Tidavad	Frölunda	A 1		m		2	—	150	3a	—	—	—	—
17#	Torsö	Skeberga	AB 3/ 20/40		s		3?	2s	130	5	Er	—	—	—

Kålland

id.	parish	place	type	rel.sh.	s/m	dat.	fsp.	state	height	design	cross	orn.	rel.	sign.
18	Gösslunda	Göss.ch.yd.	C 5		s		10	—	173	2	—	—	—	—
20	Gösslunda	Västanåker	X 30		s		6	dam.	215	4a	—	—	—	—

[141] Sö 352: *Skansen.

id.	parish	place	type	rel.sh.	s/m	dat.	fsp.	state	height	design	cross	orn.	rel.	sign.
21#+22	Häggesled	Hägg.ch.yd.	rec.	A 1	s		10	fr.		3a	—	—	+	—
23	Häggesled	Hägg.ch.yd.	rec.	A 1	s		10	—	60	4a	—	—	—	—
24[142]	Häggesled	Hägg.ch.yd.	rec.	B 1	s		10	fr.	(59)	4a	—	—	—	—
25#	Häggesled	Hägg.ch.yd.	rec.	X 40?	s		10	fr.	(55)	?	—	—	—	—
26[143]	Häggesled	Hägg.ch.yd.	rec.	X 60			10	fr.	(55)	3/4?	A	—	+	—
27	Häggesled	Hägg.ch.yd.	rec.	X 60	s		10	fr.	(37)	4a?	A?	—	—	—
30	Järpås	Järpås ch.		B 6	m		10	—	125	3a	—	—	—	—
32	Kållands-Åsaka	Käll.-Ås. ch.yd.		E 6	m		10	—	173	4a	A	+	—	—
33	Mellby	Stommen		E 3?	m		6	—	160	3a	A	—	—	—
34	Mellby	Tolsgården		X	s		6,8	fr.	160	2(sd)	—	—	—	—
35	Otterstad	Läckö		A 4	s		7	—	180	3a	—	—	—	—
37	Rackeby	Rack.ch.yd.		A 3	s		10	dam.	165	2	Fr	—	—	—
39	Rackeby	Åkersberg		A 3	s		8	6fr.	175	3a	Fr	—	—	—
40	Råda	Råda ch.		A 3	s		10	—	203	4a	—	—	—	—
41	Råda	Råda ch.yd.	rec.	X	s		10	fr.	(95)	3/4?	—	—	—	—
42#	Råda	Råda ch.yd.	rec.	X 10			10	fr.	?	7/9?	—	—	—	—
44	Skalunda	Skal.ch.yd.	rec.	C 3?	s		10	dam.	107	3/4?	—	—	—	—
45	Skalunda	Skal.ch.yd.		A 1	m		10	—	175	4	—	—	—	—
47	Strö	Strö ch.		X 40	s		10	fr.	(80)	2	Hr	—	—	—
48	Strö	Strö ch.yd.		X	s		10	dam.	(85)	2	—	—	—	—
49#	Uvered	Brokvarn		X	m		7	—	200	3	—	—	—	—
Kinnefjärding														
50	Husaby	Hus.ch.yd.	rec.	B 1	m		10	—	235	5	—	—	+	—
51[144]	Husaby	Hus.ch.yd.	rec.	A 3	s		10	—	210	4	A	+	—	—
52	Husaby	Hus.ch.yd.	rec.	X	s		10	fr.	(90)	9	—	—	—	—
53[145]	Husaby	Hus.ch.	rec.	X 60			10	fr.	(124)	7/9?	—	—	—	—
55	Källby	Källby ås		A 1	m		7,8	—	440	5	Hr	—	+	—
56[146]	Skälvum	Skälv., stream		A 1	s		6	—	310	3	—	+	—	—
58#	Lindärva	Lind.ch.	?	X			10	fr.	120	3?	—	—	—	—
59[147]	N.Härene	N.Här.ch.		E 10.05	m		10	—	338	4+2	—	—	—	Hjälm, Hjälle
Skåning														
61	Edsvära	Härlingstorp		C 3	s		6,7	dam.	114	4+3	—	—	—	—
62	Edsvära	Ballstorp		A 6	s		6	—	220	3+mbd	—	—	—	—
66	N.Vånga	Postgården		C 6	m		10	dam.	160	3	—	—	—	—
67[148]	Saleby	Sal.ch.		B 5	s		10	—	262	4+2+	—	—	—	—
73	Synnerby	Synn.ch.yd.		A 1	m		10	—	257	3b	A	—	—	—
74	Vinköl	Vin.old ch.yd.		A 1	s		10	dam.	232	4	A	—	—	—
75	V.Gerum	V.Ger.ch.	rec.	B 5	s		10	—	228	4	A	—	—	—
Valle														
76	Bolum	Backgården		A 1/8	s		8	dam.	115	3+2	A?	—	+	—
77	Eggby	Egg.ch.yd.		X 30	s		10	—	215	3b	—	—	—	—
78#	Stenum	Stenums gata		A 2	s		7?	—	200	5	A		—	—
79[149]	Varnhem	Varn.mon.	rec.	B 5	s		10	—	165	9	Hr	—	—	—
Gudhem														
80#	Bjärka	Härlunda ch.	?	A 2	s		10?	—	200	2	C?	+	—	—
81[150]	Broddetorp	Brodd.old ch.yd.	rec.	A 6	s		10	dam.	180	9	—	—	+	—
82[151]	Broddetorp	Fjällåkra		X	s		3	fr.	(73)	2?	—	—	—	—
83#	Broddetorp	Brodd.vic.	?	X 30?			10	fr.		?	—	—	—	—
85	Dala	St.Dala	?	X				fr.	(35)	1/2?	—	—	—	—
87	Gudhem	Gud.ch.	rec.	A 1	m		10	fr.	200?	9	A–C?	—	—	—
88	Gudhem	Gud.ch.	rec.	X	s		10	dam.	195	1	—	—	+	—
90	Håkantorp	Torestorp		A 3	s		8	—	200	3	Hr	—	—	—
91[152]	Högstena	Hög.ch.yd.	rec.	B 5?	s		10	dam.	153	1	—	—	—	—
92	Högstena	Hög.ch.		A 1	m		10	fr.	164	4	Hr?	—	—	—

Continued

[142] Vg 24: *SHM, 15310. [143] Vg 26: *SHM, 15310. [144] Vg 51: *SHM, 11645. [145] Vg 53: *SHM, 11645.
[146] Vg 56: ATA 7543/74; *Källby ås, Källby parish. [147] Vg 59: *Dagsnäs, Bjärka parish.
[148] Vg 67: *Dagsnäs, Bjärka parish. [149] Vg 79: *Varnhem monastery, museum.
[150] Vg 81: *Skaraborg länsmuseum. [151] Vg 82: *Broddetorp church. [152] Vg 91: *Skaraborg länsmuseum.

id.	parish	place	type	rel.sh.	s/m	dat.	fsp.	state	height	design	cross	orn.	rel.	sign.
93	Rådene	Råd.old ch.yd.	rec.	A 1	s		10	—	162	3	Hg	—	—	—
95[153]	Ugglum	Ugg.ch.yd.	rec.	A 6	s		10	—	179	1	—	—	—	Harald
97#	S.Kyrketorp	S.Kyrk.ch.yd.	rec.	A 4	s		10	—	170	1	Hg	—	+	—
Kåkind														
98[154]	N.Kyrketorp	N.Kyrk. ch.yd.	rec.	C 3+?	s		6,10	fr.	(84)	9	?	—	?	—
Åse														
100	Flo	Flo ch.yd.		A 2	s		10	—	212	3	Hg	—	—	—
101	Flo	Bragnum		X 10	s?		2	dam.	147	3	—	—	—	Asbjörn
102	Håle	Håle des. ch.yd.		A 1	s		10	—	240	3+mbd	—	—	—	—
103	Håle	Håle des. ch.yd.		A 1	m		10	2s	157	3	A	+	—	—
104	Sal	Sal ch.yd.		X 40	s		10	—	200	5	—	—	—	—
105	Särestad	Sal ch.yd.	rec.	A 3	s		10	—	190	5	H	—	+	—
(106 follows Vg 12)														
107	Tun	Tun ch.		X 60	s		10	fr.	220	3?	Hr	—	—	—
108	Täng	Täng des. ch.yd.		A 1	s		10	—	175	2(sd)	—	—	—	—
109	Täng	Täng des. ch.yd.		A 1	s		10	dam.	232	6	A	—	—	Eskil
110	Vänersnäs	Näsbyholm		C 3/1?	s		7	2s,fr.	(110)	2	—	—	—	X
112c	Ås	Ås ch.		A 5	s		10	dam.	275	3	—	—	—	—
Viste														
113	Bjärby	Töfta, Lärkegapet		A 4	s		2,5	—	250	2	—	+	—	—
114	Bjärby	Töfta, Börjesg.		A 2	s		5	—	250	3	—	—	—	—
115	Tängene	Grästorp, St.Västölet		C 5	s		6	4pts.	240	5	—	—	—	—
116	Hyringa	Hyr.des.ch.yd.		X	s		10	fr.	252	2	—	—	—	—
117	Levene	Lev.ch.yd.		A 3	s		10	—	460	4	H	—	+	—
118	Slädene	Släd.ch.yd.		C 5	s		10	—	200	5	—	—	—	—
(119 bears two different inscriptions)														
119a	Sparlösa	Spar.ch.yd.		A 6	s		10	4s	177	2+3	—	+	—	X
119b	Sparlösa	Spar.ch.yd.		A 2	s					sd				
120#	Sparlösa	Spar.ch.		X	m		10	fr.	(80)	3–4?	—	—	—	X
Barne														
122[155]	Barne-Åsaka	Abrahams-torp		A 5	s		3	—	255	6	—	—	+	—
123	Barne-Åsaka	Västerg.		A 3	s		7	—	181	4+2	—	—	—	—
124	Ryda	Ryda ch.		A 1	s		10	—	220	2+1=cross	—	—	—	—
125	S.Kedum	S.Ked.ch.yd.		A 2	s		10	—	244	3+	—	—	—	—
Laske														
126#	Larv	Larv ch.		A 3	s		?	—	140?	3?	—	—	—	—
127	Larv	Larvs hed		E 6	m		7	—	267	6	A	—	+	—
128	Ö-Bitterna	Per Jonsg.		A 1	m		2	—	223	3b	D	—	—	—
Vilske														
129[156]	Grolanda	Skärvum ch.yd.	rec.	X	s		10	—	193	1	—	+	+	—
130	Grolanda	Skånum		A 2	s		7	—	250	6	Hr	—	—	Tryggve?
131#	Vilske-Kleva	Sjögerås	rec.	A 6	s		3	—	180	1	Hg	—	—	—
133	Marka	Skyberg		A 2	s		7	—	240	3+	—	—	—	—
Frökind														
135#	Kinneve	Hassla by		A 6	s		2,3?	2s	150	2	—	—	—	—
136	Kinneve	Svenstorp		A 2	s		2	dam.	230	5	A	—	—	—
137[157]	Kinneve	Sörby		A 1	m		5	—	212	3	—	—	—	—
139	Vårkumla	Vår.ch.yd.		A 1	s		10	—	150	5	Hr	—	—	—
149[158]	Vårkumla	Grännarp		A 1+?	s		3	fr.	(75)	3b	—	—	—	—

[153] Vg 95: *SHM, 3276. [154] Vg 98: *Skövde Museum. [155] Vg 122: *Dagsnäs, Bjärka parish. [156] Vg 129: *Skaraborg länsmuseum.
[157] Vg 137: *Alarp. [158] Vg 149: *Åsaka torp (a crofter's holding), Vartofta-Åsaka parish.

id.	parish	place	type	rel.sh.	s/m	dat.	fsp.	state	height	design	cross	orn.	rel.	sign.
Vartofta														
140	Baltak	Madängsbro		X 60	s		5	dam.	184	3	—	—	—	—
141	Mularp	Mul.ch.	rec.	A 6	s		10	—	130	1	—	—	+	—
146#	Slöta	Slöta ch.	rec.	B 5	s		10	—	150	1	—	—	—	—
147#	Slöta	Slöta ch.	?	X 10	?		10	—	?	2?	—	+	—	—
148#	Slöta	Slöta ch.	?	X 30	?		10	—	120	2	Hg	—	—	—
(149 follows Vg 139)														
Väne														
150	Väne-Åsaka	Velanda		C 5	s		7	—	190	3	—	+	—	—
Kulling														
151	Eggvena	Egg.ch.yd.		A 6	s		10	dam.	135	3	H	—	—	—
152	Eggvena	Håkansg.		C 5	s		7	—	236	4	A?	—	—	—
153	Fölene	Föl.ch.yd.		A 3	s		10	dam.	155	4	—	—	—	—
154	Fölene	Föl.ch.yd.		C 5	s		10	—	158	3+2	—	—	—	—
155	Hol	Hol ch.yd.		X 30	s		10	dam.	(95)	3	—	—	—	—
156	Remmene	Remm.ch.yd.		A 4	s		10	2s	161	3+2	H	—	—	—
257[159]	Tumberg	Tum.med.ch.		X 40	s		10	fr.	(51)	3?	D	—	—	—
Gäsene														
157	Hov	Fröstorp		A 1/2	s		7,8	—	170	5	—	—	—	—
Ås														
158[160]	Fänneslunda	Fänn.ch.		A 4	s		10	—	170	5?	+(?)	—	—	—
159[161]	Hällstad	Hagahult		X	s		2	fr.	(60)	?	A–C?	—	—	—
160	Hällstad	Väby, Väby g.		A 1	s		2	—	220	2	—	—	—	—
161	Härna	Härna by		A 4	s		8	—	385	2	—	—	—	—
162	Möne	Rävicke, Bengtsg.		A 3	s		6	2s	170	6?	D?	—	—	—
165	S.Ving	S.Ving ch.yd.	rec.	C 6	s		10	—	180	1	—	—	—	Harald
166	S.Ving	S.Ving ch.yd.		X	s		10	dam.	100	3	—	—	—	—
168	S.Ving	Hökerum		X 40?	s		7,8	dam.	202	3	—	—	—	—
169	S.Ving	Svedjorna		E 3	m		8	—	335	5	—	—	—	—
Redväg														
170	Blidsberg	Blid.ch.; ch.yd.		C 5/3	s		10	dam.	195	3b	—	—	—	—
171	Blidsberg	Blid.ch.; ch.yd.		C 5	s		10	—	215	3+mbd	—	—	—	—
172	Blidsberg	Storeg.		A 1 or 2?	s		8	—	125	3b	—	—	—	—
173	Böne	Böne vic.		A 2	s		8	—	172	3b	—	—	—	—
197	Dalum	Dal.ch.; ch.yd.		A 2	m		10	—	180	3b	C	—	—	—
198	Dalum	Dal.ch.; ch.yd.		A 3	s		10	—	165	3	—	—	—	—
174	Dalum	Nöre		A 3	s		7	—	230	3b	—	—	—	—
175	Dalum	Silarp br.		A 1	m		6	—	170	2	H	—	—	—
176[162]	Dalum	Vedåsla		X 20	s		3	dam.	(110)	3	Hg	—	—	—
177	Humla	Hum.ch.; ch.yd.		B 6	s		10	fr.	(140)	4?	—	—	—	—
178	Kölaby	Köl.ch.; ch.yd.		E 40.05	m		10	—	185	5(sp)	D	—	—	—
179	Kölaby	Lillegården		A 2	s		8	—	185	5	H	—	—	—
180[163]	Kölaby	Stommen; Köl.ch.yd		A 6	s		2	fr.	(140)	5	Hg	—	—	Funnen
181	N.Åsarp	Frug.		A 3	s		8	—	210	5	A	+	—	Håvard?
182	N.Åsarp	Hög, Skatteg.		A 5	s		8	—	140	5	—	—	—	—
183#	N.Åsarp	Hög		A 2	s		8	—	150	3+	—	—	—	—
184[164]	Smula	Smula ch.		A 4	s		10	—	148	5	H	—	—	—
186[165]	Timmele	Timm.ch.		A 6	s		10	—	205	5	Fg	+	+	—
187	Viste	Viste ch.yd.		A 2	s		10	—	185	3b	D	—	—	—
Kind														
189	Länghem	L.Svenstorp		X	s		7	dam.	160	5?	—	—	—	—
190	Månstad	Månstads-kulle		A 3	s		6	—	197	3	D	—	—	—
192	Nittorp	Gölingstorp		A 3	s		2	—	235	3	—	—	—	—

Continued

[159] Vg 257: *Kullings-Skövde church. [160] Vg 158: *Fänneslunda manor.
[161] Vg 159: *Borås Museum. [162] Vg 176: *Blidsberg's church. [163] Vg 180: *Kölaby churchyard.
[164] Vg 184: *Dagsnäs, Bjärka parish. [165] Vg 186: *Dagsnäs, Bjärka parish.

id.	parish	place	type	rel.sh.	s/m	dat.	fsp.	state	height	design	cross	orn.	rel.	sign.
193	Svenljunga	Sven.ch.; old ch.yd.		X 60			10	dam.	170	3b	H	—	—	—
194	Svenljunga	Herrekvarn		A 3	s		5,7	—	290	5	—	—	—	—
195	Tranemo	Normanslid		A 2	s		7	dam.	200	3	Hg	—	—	—

Göteborg town

id.	parish	place	type	rel.sh.	s/m	dat.	fsp.	state	height	design	cross	orn.	rel.	sign.
196[166]	Göteborg	Älvsborg	rec.	A 2	s		?	—	181	10	Hg	+	—	—

197 and 198 follow Vg 173
257 follows 156

Västmanland (Vs): 25 inscriptions

Snevringe härad

(1+2m = paired stones)

id.	parish	place	type	rel.sh.	s/m	dat.	fsp.	state	height	design	cross	orn.	rel.	sign.
1	Ryttern	St.Ryttern ch.		A 3	s	2b	10	—	170	6	—	—	—	—
2	Ryttern	St.Ryttern ch.		—				dam.	115	—	C	—	—	—

Tuhundra

id.	parish	place	type	rel.sh.	s/m	dat.	fsp.	state	height	design	cross	orn.	rel.	sign.
3#	Dingtuna	Kävlinge		C 3	s		7	—		3b	H	—	+	—
4	Dingtuna	Vändle, Norrg.		E 3	m	4	3	fr.	—	?	—	—	+	—
5	Dingtuna	Vändle, Sörg.		X 60	s	2b	3	dam.	145	?	—	—	+	Siggi

Västerås town

(9+10m = paired stones)

id.	parish	place	type	rel.sh.	s/m	dat.	fsp.	state	height	design	cross	orn.	rel.	sign.
9	Lundby	Saltäng br.		A 3	s	3a	7	—	215	6	A	—	+	—
10	Lundby	Saltäng br.		—				—	162	—	—	+	—	—
11#	Västerås town	Smäcken		A 6	m		6	fr.	—	?	—	—	—	—
12[167]	Västerås	Stora gatan	rec.	X	s?	3a	10	fr.	—	2(sd)	—	+	—	—
13	f.d. Badelunda	Anundshög area		A 1	s	2	8	—	310	4a	—	+	—	Vred

Siende härad

id.	parish	place	type	rel.sh.	s/m	dat.	fsp.	state	height	design	cross	orn.	rel.	sign.
N1[168]	Hubbo	Jädra		A 6	m?		7	—	227	5	A–C?	—	—	—

Yttertjurbo

id.	parish	place	type	rel.sh.	s/m	dat.	fsp.	state	height	design	cross	orn.	rel.	sign.
15[169]	Björksta	L.Kyringe		AB 10/04	s	3b		2s	285	7+6	—	+	—	Balle
16	Tortuna	Tor.ch.		X	s	3a	10	dam.	199	6?	H	—	—	X
17	Tortuna	Råby		AB 05/80	s	2b	6	—	142	6	—	+	—	—

Norrbo

id.	parish	place	type	rel.sh.	s/m	dat.	fsp.	state	height	design	cross	orn.	rel.	sign.
18m[170]	Skultuna	Berga		A 3	s	2b	3	—	150	6	—	—	+	—
19m[171]	Skultuna	Berga		A 3	s	2b	3	dam.	137	6	—	—	+	—
20[172]	Romfartuna	Romf.vic.		A 1	m	2b	10	—	128	6	H	—	—	Litle
21[173]	Romfartuna	Äs		X 60		2b	3	fr.		?	+(?)	—	—	—
22[174]	Haraker	Ulvsta		X 20		3a	2	dam.	100	6	H	—	—	—
23	Fläckebo	Gussjö		X	s		7	dam.	150	4a?	—	—	—	—
24[175]	Fläckebo	Hassmyra		B 5	s	3a	5	—	215	6+	—	+	—	Rödballe

Övertjurbo

id.	parish	place	type	rel.sh.	s/m	dat.	fsp.	state	height	design	cross	orn.	rel.	sign.
27	Kila	Grällsta		A 1	m	2	7	—	175	6	H	—	—	Litle
28#	Kila	Grällsta		X	s?		7	fr.		?	—	—	—	—
29	Sala	Sala ch.		A 1/2	m	3	10	—	395	7	—	+	—	Livsten
30[176]	Möklinta	Forneby		X	s		8	fr.	—	?	—	—	—	—
31	Möklinta	Öster-bännbäck	rock	A 4/3	s	2	7	dam.	125	6	H	—	—	—

Vangsbro

id.	parish	place	type	rel.sh.	s/m	dat.	fsp.	state	height	design	cross	orn.	rel.	sign.
32[177]	Västerfärnebo	Väst. vic.		X 8/?	s	3	10	fr.	—	?	H	+	—	—

NEW FIND

	härad	*follows* Vs
N1	Siende	13

[166] Vg 196: *Göteborg Museum, 367. [167] Vs 12: *Västerås länsmuseum. [168] Vs N1: *FV* 1988, 36; see also Strid (1988), 9.
[169] Vs 15: *Målhammar. [170] Vs 18: *Skultuna bruk. [171] Vs 19: *Skultuna bruk. [172] Vs 20: *Romfartuna church.
[173] Vs 21: *Västerås länsmuseum. [174] Vs 22: *Svanå bruk. [175] Vs 24: *Hembygdsgården.
[176] Vs 30: *Gammelgården. [177] Vs 32: *Gammelgården.

Öland (Öl) 87 inscriptions[178]

(id. nos. according to B. Nilsson, *The Runic Inscriptions of Öland* (Univ. Michigan, 1973))

id.	parish	place	type	rel.sh.	s/m	dat.	fsp.	state	height	design	cross	orn.	rel.	sign.
(1[179]	Vickleby	Karlevi		A 7b	m	2	5,8	2s	137	2	+(?)	—	—	—)
2#	Algutsrum	Alg.ch.		X 20	m	3	10	—		6	—	—	+	—
(4–6 are inscribed on same sarcophagus)														
4[180]	Resmo	Resmo ch.	rec.	B 1	m	3	10	—	128	öl	—	+	—	—
5#	Resmo	Resmo ch.	rec.	AB 01/20	m	3a	10	—		öl	—	—	—	—
6[181]	Resmo	Resmo ch.	rec.	C 5 or A 7b?	s	3a	10	—		öl	—	—	—	—
9[182]	Resmo	Resmo ch.		X			10	fr.	(64)		—	—	+	—
10#	Mörbylånga	Bårby		A 1	m			—		6	—	—	—	—
11[183]	Mörbylånga	Mör.ch.yd.		B 5	s	3a	10	fr.	(38)	öl	—	—	—	—
12#	Mörbylånga	Mör.ch.yd.		X 60	s	2	10	—		6	—	—	+	—
15[184]	Mörbylånga	Mör.ch.		X	m	3a	10	fr.	(40)		—	—	—	—
18[185]	Mörbylånga	Mör.ch.		A 1	m	3a	10	—	221		+(?)	—	—	—
19#	Kastlösa	Kast.ch.		A 1	s	2	10	—		6?	—	—	+	—
20#	Smedby	Alvlösa		X	m			—		6?	—	—	—	—
21[186]	Smedby	Alvlösa		X 30				fr.	(61)		—	—	—	—
22#	Smedby	Smed.ch.yd.		A 2	s	3a	10	—		6?	+	—	+	—
23#	S.Möckleby	S.Möck.		X 10	s			—		3	—	—	—	—
24#	S.Möckleby	S.Möck.ch.yd.		X 40?			10	fr.			—	—	—	—
25#	S.Möckleby	S.Möck.ch.yd.		A 1/2	s	2	10	—		6?	—	—	—	—
26[187]	S.Möckleby	Gårdstorp		X 10				fr.	(56)		—	—	—	—
27#	Gräsgård	Gräsg.ch.yd.		A 6	m	2	10	—		6?	—	—	+	—
29#	Segerstad	Säby		A 2	s	2		—		5	—	—	—	—
30[188]	Segerstad	Säby		A 1	m	2		—	307	6?	—	—	—	—
31#	Hulterstad	Hult.ch.		C 5	s	3a	10	—		öl	—	+	+	—
32#	Hulterstad	Hult.ch.yd.		C 5 or A 7b?			10	fr.			—	—	—	—
33[189]	Hulterstad	Hult.ch.yd; ch.		A 1	s	3a	10	—	96	öl	—	—	—	—
36[190]	Hulterstad	Hult.ch.		X 30			10	fr.	(33)		—	—	—	—
37[191]	Hulterstad	Hult.ch.yd.		C 5 or A 7?		3a	10	—	(47)		—	—	—	Korp?
40[192]	Hulterstad	Hult.ch.yd.; ch.		X	s		10	fr.	(52)		—	—	—	—
44[193]	Hulterstad	Hult.ch.		X 4?			10	fr.	(90)		—	—	—	—
45[194]	Hulterstad	Hult.vic.; ch.		B 5	s		10	fr.	(67)		—	—	—	—
50#	Stenåsa	Sten.ch.yd.		A 1	m	2	10	—		6	—	—	+	—
51#	Stenåsa	Sten.ch.yd.		X 20+C 3	m	3a	10	—		6?	—	—	+?	—
54[195]	Sandby	Dröstorp		A 2	s	3a		—	105	2	—	—	—	—
55m[196]	Sandby	Sand.ch.yd.		E 05.10	m	3a	10	—	190	öl	—	—	—	—
56m[197]	Sandby	Sand.ch.yd.		AB 02/10	m	3a	10	—	179	öl	—	+	—	—
57	Sandby	Sand.ch.yd.		X 10			10	fr.			—	—	—	—
58[198]	Gårdby	Gårdby ch.yd.		C 3	s	2	10	—	146	6	C?	—	—	Brand
59#	Gårdby	Gårdby ch.		X 30			10	fr.			—	—	—	—
62[199]	Runsten	Run.ch.		A 6	s		10	—	148	6	—	—	—	—
66[200]	Runsten	Åkerby		A 1	m	2		fr.	(120)		—	—	+	—
68[201]	Runsten	Bjärby		E 10.05	m	2		—	180	6	A?	—	church	—
69[202]	Runsten	Lerkaka		E 10.05	m	3a		—	218		—	—	—	—
70[203]	Runsten	Lerkaka		X 10		2		fr.	(87)		—	—	—	—
72[204]	Gärdslösa	Bägby		A 1	s			—	209	6	—	—	—	—
73[205]	Gärdslösa	Bägby		A 2	m	2		—	188		—	—	—	—
74#	Gärdslösa	Bägby		A 1	m	2		—			—	—	—	—
75#	Gärdslösa	Gärd.ch.; br.		X 10			6,10	fr.			—	—	—	—
76[206]	Gärdslösa	Gärd.ch.		A 1	m	3a		3fr.	(124)		—	—	—	Oddvar?
77[207]	Gärdslösa	Gärd.ch.		X	m		10	fr.	(54)		—	—	—	—
79[208]	Bredsätra	Bo		X 10?			2	—			—	—	+	—

Continued

[178] For Öl 90–1, 93–103, 111–13, 122–48, 159–61, and 164, see ATA 3430/57. [179] Öl 1 is the same stone as DR 411; see also ATA 78/81. [180] Öl 4: ATA 4707/43; *Kalmar länsmuseum. [181] Öl 6: ATA 6852/68; *SHM, 14533:2. [182] Öl 9: *Kalmar länsmuseum. [183] Öl 11: ATA 3960/71. [184] Öl 15: ATA 4064/60. [185] Öl 18: ATA 4065/60. [186] Öl 21: ATA 4704/43. [187] Öl 26: ATA 4063/60; *Kalmar länsmuseum 28352. [188] Öl 30: ATA 4689/43. [189] Öl 33: ATA 4684/43; cf. Öl 37 and 40. [190] Öl 36: ATA 4376/56; cf. Öl 44. [191] Öl 37: ATA 4684/43; cf. Öl 33 and 40. [192] Öl 40: ATA 4684/43; cf. Öl 33 and 37. [193] Öl 44: ATA 4376/56; cf. Öl 36. [194] Öl 45: ATA 4375/56; *Hulterstad church. [195] Öl 54: ATA 4698/43. [196] Öl 55: ATA 4694/43; cf. Öl 56. [197] Öl 56: ATA 4694/43; cf. Öl 55. [198] Öl 58: ATA 4695/43. [199] Öl 62: ATA 4693/43. [200] Öl 66: ATA 4686/43; *Himmelsberga. [201] Öl 68: ATA 4690/43. [202] Öl 69: ATA 4692/43. [203] Öl 70: ATA 4691/43. [204] Öl 72: ATA 4697/43. [205] Öl 73: ATA 4696/43. [206] Öl 76: ATA 4699/43. [207] Öl 77: ATA 4700/43. [208] Öl 79: *Skedemosse, Köping parish.

id.	parish	place	type	rel.sh.	s/m	dat.	fsp.	state	height	design	cross	orn.	rel.	sign.
86[209]	Köping	Tingsflisan		A 1	m	2		—	298	6	—	—	+	—
88[210]	Köping	Köp.ch.		X 30		4	10	fr.			—	—	—	—
89#	Köping	Köp.ch.yd.		B 2 ?	m	2	10	—			—	—	—	—
90	Köping	Köp.ch.yd.		X 60			10	fr.	(102)		—	—	+	—
91	Köping	Köp.ch.yd.		X	m		10	fr.	(70)		—	—	—	—
92[211]	Köping	Tingsdal		A 6	m			—	150		—	—	—	—
93	Köping	Köp.ch.		X 60	m	3	10	fr.	(27)		—	—	—	—
96	Köping	Köp.ch.		X 10			10	fr.	(19)		—	—	—	—
99	Köping	Köp.ch.		X	s		10	fr.	(23)		—	—	—	—
103	Köping	Köp.ch.		X	m	3a	10	fr.	(43)		—	—	—	—
109[212]	Köping	Köp.ch.		X	s		10	fr.	(75)		—	—	—	—
111	Köping	Köp.ch.		X	m	3a	10	fr.	(36)		—	—	—	—
113	Köping	Köp.ch.		C 5 or A 7b?		3a	10	fr.	(33)		—	—	—	—
118[213]	Köping	Hässelby		A 1	m	2		—	215		—	—	—	—
122	Köping	Köp.ch.		X 03		2	10	fr.	(29)		—	—		—
126	Köping	Köp.ch.		X 01?		3	10	fr.	(26)		—	—	—	—
130	Köping	Köp.ch.		X		3a	10	fr.	(32)		—	—	—	—
133	Köping	Köp.ch.		X 10	m	3a	10	fr.	(34)		—	—	—	—
135	Köping	Köp.ch.		X	s	3a	10	fr.	(44)		—	—	—	—
136	Köping	Köp.ch.		X 30		3a	10	fr.	(43)		—	—	—	—
140	Köping	Köp.ch.		B 5 or 3?	s?		10	fr.	(55)		—	—	?	—
141	Köping	Köp.ch.		X		3a	10	fr.	(38)		—	—	+	—
142	Köping	Köp.ch.		X	s	3a	10	fr.	(33)		—	—	—	—
143	Köping	Köp.ch.		A 1	s	3a	10	fr.	(45)		—	—	—	—
144	Köping	Köp.ch.		C 5 or A 7?	s	3a	10	fr.	(49)		—	—	?	—
145	Köping	Köp.ch.		X 10		3a	10	fr.	(51)		+	—	?	—
146	Köping	Köp.ch.		X 10		3a	10	fr.	(46)		—	—	—	—
147	Köping	Köp.ch.		X 10+?		3a	10	fr.	(73)		—	—	—	—
148	Köping	Köp.ch.		X 60		3a	10	fr.	(36)		—	—	—	—
149[214]	Köping	Köp.ch.		A 1	m	3a	10	fr.	(75)		—	—	—	—
151[215]	Köping	Köp.ch.		X	s	3a	10	fr.	(33)		—	—	—	—
159	Köping	Köp.ch.		A 3	s	3a	10	fr.	(50)		—	—	—	—
160	Köping	Köp.ch.		X (?.20)	m		10	fr.	(96)		—	—	—	—
161	Köping	Köp.ch.		X	s		10	fr.	(93)		—	—	—	—
162[216]	Köping	Köp.ch.		X			10	fr.	(26)		—	—	—	—
163[217]	Köping	Köp.ch.		X 06		3a	10	—	(74)		—	—	+	—
164[218]	Köping	Köp.ch.yd; ch.		A 1 or 2?	m	3–4	10	—	107	go	B?	—	—	—
169#	Högby	Hög.ch.		X	m		10	—	150		—	—	—	—
170[219]	Källa	Källa des.ch.		E10/20. 05/03	m	3a	10	3fr.			—	—	—	—

Östergötland (Ög): 212 inscriptions

Aska härad

id.	parish	place	type	rel.sh.	s/m	dat.	fsp.	state	height	design	cross	orn.	rel.	sign.
2	Orlunda	Orl.ch.	rec.	A 4?	m		10	dam.	182	7/9?	—	—	—	—
3#	Orlunda	Orl.ch.yd.	rec.	A 3	s		10	dam.	160	7/9?	—	—	+	—
4#	Orlunda	Orl.ch.yd.	rec.	B 1	m?		10	fr.	—	7/9?	—	—	—	—
5	Orlunda	Orl.ch.yd.	rec.	B 5	s		10	dam.	79	7/9?	—	—	—	—
6	Orlunda	Orl.ch.yd.	rec.	A? 2	s		10	fr.	38	7/9?	—	—	—	—
8[220]	V.Stenby	V.Sten.ch.		A 3	s	2a	10	—	190	2(2)	—	—	—	Viking, Grimulv
9	Vinnerstad	Vinn.ch.		X 01			10	dam.	140	3a	—	—	—	—

Bankekind

id.	parish	place	type	rel.sh.	s/m	dat.	fsp.	state	height	design	cross	orn.	rel.	sign.
10[221]	Askeby	L.Greby		E 40.05?	m		5,10	dam.	137	3a+mbd	+(?)	—	—	—
11	Vårdsberg	Vård.ch.		A 1	s		10	—	234	5	—	—	—	—

Björkekind

id.	parish	place	type	rel.sh.	s/m	dat.	fsp.	state	height	design	cross	orn.	rel.	sign.
13	Konungsund	Kon.ch.		A 1	s		10	—	170	6	A+C	—	—	—
14	Konungsund	Kon.ch.		A 3	s		10	—	177	3a	D?	—	—	—

[209] Öl 86: ATA 4702/43. [210] Öl 88: *FV* 1974, 214. [211] Öl 92: ATA 4703/43. [212] Öl 109: ATA 2056/75.
[213] Öl 118: *Forngården, Borgholm. [214] Öl 149: ATA 3430/57; *SHM, 25339:31. [215] Öl 151: ATA 3430/57; *SHM, 25339:33.
[216] Öl 162: ATA 3937/75. [217] Öl 163: ATA 3937/75. [218] Öl 164: together with 165.
[219] Öl 170: ATA 4706/43; one fragment in the disused church; two fragments in Kalmar länsmuseum.
[220] Ög 8: ATA 2831/62. [221] Ög 10: ATA 6635/71.

id.	parish	place	type	rel.sh.	s/m	dat.	fsp.	state	height	design	cross	orn.	rel.	sign.
15#	Konungsund	Svensksund		C 5?	s		2	dam.	77	3a	—	—	—	—
16#	Kuddby	Kudd.ch.		A 2	s		10	dam.	138	3a	C	—	—	—
17#	Kuddby	Kudd.ch.		A 1	m		10	—	?	7?	—	—	—	—
18[222]	Kuddby	Kudd.ch.		A 2	s		10	dam.	130	3a+mbd	?	—	—	—
20	Kuddby	Hjärtrum		A 1	m		5,7	—	180	3a+mbd	C	—	—	—
21	Kuddby	Ingelstad		A 3	s		7	—	155	3a	—	—	—	—
22	Kuddby	Odenstomta		A 1	m		7	—	120	3a+mbd	C?	—	—	—
23#	Kuddby	Örminge		A 1/6	s			—	194	6	A	—	—	—
24	Kuddby	Örminge		X 60			3	—	128	6	?	—	—	—
25#	Ö.Ny	S.Mem		A 2	s		7	—	222	4a	—	—	—	—
26	Ö.Ny	Ö.Skam		A 3	s		7	—	166	3a	A	—	—	—
27#c?	Ö.Ny	Ö.Skam		A 1	s		6,7	—	154	4a	—	—	—	—
28#c?	Ö.Ny	Ö.Skam		X 30			6,7	—	154?	6	—	—	—	—
29	Tåby	Skjorstad		C 5.1	m		5	—	177	6	—	—	—	—
30	Tåby	Skjorstad		A 3	s		5	—	250	6	B	—	—	—
31	Å	Å ch.		A 6	s		10	—	100	3/4?	A	—	—	—
32	Å	Å ch.yd.		A 2.4?	m		10	—	104	5/6?	—	—	—	—
33	Å	Å ch.yd.		X 10			3	fr.		3a	—	—	—	—
34	Å	Lundby		A 2	s		5,7	—	117	4a	C	—	—	—
Boberg														
40#	Vallerstad	Vall.ch.		A 4/2	s		10	—	223	5	C	—	—	—
41#	Älvestad	Älv.ch.		A 6	m		10	dam.	135	6/7?	—	—	+	—
42	Älvlestad	Örevad		A 3	s		5	—	157	3a+	C	—	—	—
Bråbo														
44#	Kvillinge	Björnsnäs		A 1	s			—		3a	—	—	—	—
45	Kvillinge	Björnsnäs	rock	A 2	m		3	—	(495)	6	—	—	—	—
46	Kvillinge	Ströbo äng		A 2	s		5	—	170	6	B	—	—	—
(47+48 = paired stones)														
47m	Kvillinge	Ströbo äng		C 1/2	s		5	—	150	3a+	—	—	—	—
48	Kvillinge	Ströbo äng		—				—	123	—	A	—	—	—
Dal														
N1[223]	Rogslösa	Rogslösa ch.	rec.	X 02			10	3pts.	(110)		—	—	—	—
51#	Väversunda	Väv.ch.	rec.	C 1?	s		10	—	214	7	—	—	+	—
52	Väversunda	Väv.ch.	rec.	A 1?	m		10	dam.	96	7/9?	—	—	—	—
53#	Väversunda	Väv.ch.	rec.	E 2?	m		10	—	110	7/9?	—	—	+	Sven
56	Väversunda	Väv.ch.	rec.	X	s		10	fr.	—	9?	—	—	—	—
59#	Örberga	Örb.ch.	rec.	X 30			10	dam.	(49)	7/9?	—	—	—	—
60#	Herrestad	?		A 2	s			—	?	3b	—	—	—	—
Gullberg														
61	Flistad	Fli.ch.yd.		C 1?	s		10	dam.	153	4a	C	—	—	—
N2[224]	Vreta	Vreta mon.	rec.	X (A 7b or C 5?)			10	—	?	?	—	—	—	—
Göstring														
62#	Allhelgona	Biskopsberga		X	s		7	—	195	?	B/C?	—	—	—
63	Allhelgona	Vistena	?	A 1?	s?		7	dam.	100	3a	C?	—	—	—
N3[225]	Allhelgona	Appuna ch.		A 3	s		5?	—	140	3a	A	—	—	—
64	Bjälbo	Bjälbo ch.		A 5	m		10	—	400	3a	—	—	—	Love
65#	Bjälbo	Bjälbo ch.yd.		B 5?	s		10	—	200	?	—	—	+	—
66	Bjälbo	Bjälbo ch.yd.		A 2	s		3	—	490	6	A	—	—	—
N4[226]	Bjälbo	Norrg.		A 6?					?	?	—	—	—	—
67	Ekeby	Ek.ch.yd.		A 6	s		10	—	157	3a	—	—	—	—
68c[227]	Ekeby	Ek.ch.		C 2	s		10	—	157	3a+mbd	A	—	—	—
70[228]	Ekeby	Ek.ch.		A 1	m		10	—	150	4a+mbd	?	—	—	—
71#	Ekeby	Dala		A 2	s		7	—	178	3a+mbd	—	—	—	—
73[229]	Hov	Hov ch.	rec.	X 60			10	dam.	76	9	—	—	—	—
74[230]	Hov	Hov ch.	rec.	B 6	s		10	dam.	85	7/9?	—	—	+	—
N5[231]	Hov	Hov ch.	rec.	B 6?	s		10		?	?	—	—	—	—
75[232]	Hov	Hov ch.yd.	rec.	X 03	s		10	dam.	92	7/9?	—	—	+	—
76#	Hov	Hov, school	rec.	X	m			fr.	?	?	—	—	—	—
77	Hov	Hovgården		C 5	s		3	dam.	188	5	D	—	—	—

Continued

[222] Ög 18: ATA 3604/47. [223] Ög N1: ATA 6266/59. [224] Ög N2: SKL, 174.
[225] Ög N3: *FV* 1983, 240. [226] Ög N4: ATA 5060/54; *Bjälbo churchyard. [227] Ög 68: ATA 6489/60.
[228] Ög 70: ATA 6489/60. [229] Ög 73: Hov, 20. [230] Ög 74: Hov, 19.
[231] Ög N5: Hov, 14. N5 may be the same stone as Ög 240–1. [232] Ög 75: Hov, 16.

id.	parish	place	type	rel.sh.	s/m	dat.	fsp.	state	height	design	cross	orn.	rel.	sign.
240–1[233]	Hov	Hov ch.	rec.	X 60	s		10	fr.	(145)	7/9?	—	—	+	—
81c	Högby	Hög.old ch.		C 4	s		10	2s	345	5	D	—	—	Torkel
82c[234]	Högby	Högby ch.		A 6	s		10	—	116	3b	D?	—	—	—
83c[235]	Högby	Hög.ch.		C 3	s		10	—	137	6	C	—	—	—
(84c#[236]	Högby	Hög.old ch.yd.		EF 8?	m		10	—	187	3a	C?	—	—	—)
85#	Högby	Hög.old ch.yd.		A 6	s		10	—	175	3a	D	—	—	—
86#	Högby	Hög.old ch.yd.	rec.	X 10			10	fr.	—	9	—	—	—	—
88	Högby	Axstad		A 4	s		7	—	154	3a	—	—	—	—
89	Högby	Skrukeby		A 2	s			—	123	3a+	A	—	—	—
90	Högby	Skrukeby		A 4	s		3	fr.	—	?	—	—	—	—
91[237]	Järstad	Jär.ch.yd.		B 2	s		10	—	185	3a	A	—	—	—
92#	Väderstad	Väd.old ch.yd.		A 1	m		10	—	177	4a	—	—	—	—
93	Väderstad	Haddestad		C 5	s		2	—	150	6	?	—	—	—
94[238]	Väderstad	Harstad ch.yd.		E 6	m		10	—	200	5	C	—	—	—
N6[239]	Väderstad-Harstad	Har.ch.yd.		A 6	m		10	—	205	7	A	—	—	—
96	Väderstad-H.	Karleby		A 4	s		2	—	228	3a	Hr	—	—	—
97	Åsbo	Grönlund		A 1	s		7	—	179	3a+	—	—	+	—
98	Åsbo	Strålsnäs		AB 1?	s		5	3pts.	162	3a	—	—	—	—
Hammarkind														
99	Mogata	Hov		A 1	m		8	—	260	6	—	—	+	—
100	Ringarum	Ring.ch.		A 1	m		10	—	100	6	—	—	—	—
101#	Skönberga	Skön.vic.	?	X	m			fr.	?	?	—	—	—	—
Hanekind														
102[240]	Kaga	Kaga vic.	rec.	B 5	s		10	—	171	7/9?	—	—	+	—
103	Kaga	Kaga ch.		A 1	s		10	—	227	6	—	—	—	—
104	Kaga	Gillberga		A 2	s		5,7	—	?	6	—	—	—	—
105	Kärna	Kärna ch.yd.		A 1	s		10	—	220	3a	C	—	—	—
107	Kärna	Kärna ch.yd.		A 6?	s		10	fr.	—	3a	—	—	—	—
108	Kärna	Kärna ch.yd.		X	s		10	fr.	—	?	D	—	—	—
109[241]	Kärna	Frössle		A 3	s		4	—	165	5	C	—	—	—
110	Kärna	Lagerlunda		X 30	?		2	fr.	—	?	D?	—	—	—
111c	Landeryd	Land.ch.		A 2	s		10	—	260	6	B	—	—	—
112#	Landeryd	Hjulsbro		C 5	s		?	—	?	5	A	—	—	—
113	S:t Lars	Nykvarn		AB 3	s		5	—	257	7	—	—	+	—
N7[242]	S:t Lars	Kallerstad		A 1	m		2	—	298	5	C	—	—	—
117[243]	Slaka	Slaka ch.		X	s	1	10	fr.	88	1/2?	—	—	—	—
118	Slaka	Slaka ch.yd.		A 1/2	m		3	—	132	4a	A	—	—	—
119#	Slaka	Slaka ch.yd.		A 1	s		10	—	153	3a	—	—	—	—
120#	Slaka	Slaka ch.yd.		A 1	s		3	—	217	3a	—	—	—	—
121	Slaka	Slaka ch.yd.		A 1	m		10	—	222	4a	D?	—	—	—
122#[244]	Slaka	Lambohov		A 2	s		3	dam.	241	?	A?	+	—	—
123#	Slaka	Lambohov		A 3	s		3	—	214	3a	A	—	—	—
124#	Slaka	Lambohov		A 1	s		8	—	220	4a	A	—	—	—
N8[245]	Vist	Vist ch.		A 1?	m		10	—	190	?	—	—	—	—
Kind														
127#	Hycklinge	Vallingedal		X	s		3	fr.	(174)	2/3?	—	—	—	—
128[246]	Linköping town	S:t Lars ch.host.		C 5/2	s		10	—	211	3a+mbd	A	—	—	—
N9[247]	Linköping	S:t Lars ch.	rec.	A 3	s		10	—	177	?	—	—	—	—
N10[248]	Linköping	S:t Lars ch.	rec.	C 5.1	m		10	—	203	?	—	—	+	—
129#	Linköping	Modis gård		A 2	m		3	—	140	3+mbd	—	—	—	—
130#	Linköping	Skolemäst.g.		A 2	s		3	—	183	6	A	—	—	—
Lysing														
131	Heda	Heda ch.		A 1	s		10	—	210	4a	C	—	—	—
132	Heda	Heda ch.		A 1	s		10	—	184	5	—	—	—	—

[233] Ög 240–41: Hov, 14. Ög 240–1 may be the same stone as Ög N5. [234] Ög 82: *Högby vicarage. [235] Ög 83: *Högby vicarage.
[236] Ög 84: no commemoration formula: 'Torkel and Helga, they raised the stone'. [237] Ög 91: ATA 7309/71.
[238] Ög 94: ATA 7833/71; *FV* 1975, 175 f. [239] Ög N6: *FV* 1975, 174. [240] Ög 102: *Stifts- och landsbiblioteket, Linköping.
[241] Ög 109: *Lagerlunda. [242] Ög N7: *FV* 1950, 341; *Östergötland Museum. [243] Ög 117: *FV* 1972, 276.
[244] Ög 122: *Östergötland Museum. [245] Ög N8: ATA 6225/65. [246] Ög 128: *Valla.
[247] Ög N9: *FV* 1958, 255. [248] Ög N10: *FV* 1958, 252.

id.	parish	place	type	rel.sh.	s/m	dat.	fsp.	state	height	design	cross	orn.	rel.	sign.
133	Heda	Häggestad		A 1/2	s		7,8	—	153	4a	D	—	+	—
134	Kumla	Gärdslösa		X	s		2	dam.	120	3a	—	—	—	—
135	Kumla	Gärdslösa		A 1	m		2	—	109	5	C	—	—	—
136[249]	Rök	Rök ch.yd.		A 3	s	1	10	4s	382	1+2	—	—	—	Varin
139#	V.Tollstad	V.Toll.ch.	rec.	A 1	s		10	—	248	7?	—	—	+	—
140#	V.Tollstad	V.Toll.ch.	rec.	C 5 or A 7?	s		10?	—	226	7/9?	—	—	—	—
142#	St.Åby	St.Åby ch.		A 1	s		10	—	160	4a	A	—	—	—
143#	St.Åby	St.Åby ch.		A 2	s		10	—	162	4a	—	—	—	—
144	Ödeshög	Öd.ch.		X 10	s		10	—	200	5?	C	—	—	—
Lösing														
145	Dagsberg	Dags.ch.yd.		A 1?			10	fr.		3a	B	—	—	—
146[250]	Dagsberg	Dags.ch.		A 1/?	s		10	—	189	6	—	—	—	—
147	Furingstad	Fur.ch.		A 4	m		10	—	200	3a+mbd	—	—	—	—
148	Furingstad	Fur.ch.		C 3	s		10	—	142	3a	—	—	—	—
149	Furingstad	Fur.vic.		A 1	m		10	—	212	3a+mbd	—	—	—	—
150	Furingstad	Fur.ch.		C 1.5	m		10	dam.	123	5?	A	—	—	—
151	Furingstad	Fur.ch.		A 6	s		10	—	135	4a	A	—	—	—
152	Furingstad	Agetomta		A 4	s		3	fr.	385	6?	B	—	+	—
153	Styrstad	Styr.ch.yd.		A 3	s		10	—	150	5	—	—	—	—
154	Styrstad	Styr.ch.yd.		C 1	s		10	—	?	6	A	—	+	—
155	Styrstad	Bjällbrunna, Sylten		C 3 or A 3?	s		2	—	200	3a+	C	—	—	—
156	Tingstad	Ting.ch.		C 3	s		10	—	188	6	—	—	—	—
N11[251]	Tingstad	Ting.ch.		A 1	s		10	—	212	5	—	—	—	—
157	Tingstad	Ting.ch.yd.		C 3	s		10	—	119	3a+mbd	—	—	—	—
Memming														
160	Kimstad	Kim.ch.		C 5	s		10	—	160	7/9?	—	—	+	—
161	Kimstad	Kim.ch.yd.		A 1	m		10	—	170	4b	C	—	+	—
N12m[252]	Kullerstad	Kull.ch.		A 3	s		10	—	155	3a+2	A	—	—	—
162	Kullerstad	Kullerstad br.		A 3	s		6	—	164	3a+	B	—	—	—
163	Kullerstad	Skattna		C 3	s		7	—	320	5	B	—	+	—
Skänninge town														
165c	Skänninge	Skänninge ch.		E 1	m		10	3s	230	3a+2	—	—	—	Torkel
N13[253]	Skänninge	S:t Ingrid mon.		X 20			10	dam.	150	?	—	—	—	—
N14[254]	Skänninge	S:t Ingrid mon.	rec.	A 1	s		10	—	203	?	+(?)	—	+	—
N15[255]	Skänninge	S:t Ingrid mon.	rec.	A 1	s		10	3pts.	204	?	—	—	+	—
166	Skänninge	hospital chapel		A 2	m		3,10	—	192	4a	—	—	—	—
239[256]	Skänninge	Skänninge	rec.	B 5/3	s		3	—	125	5	—	—	+	—
Skärkind härad														
169#	Gistad	Gistad old ch.		X	s		10	—	266	?	—	—	—	—
170	Gårdeby	Ösby		A 1	s		2	—	174	6	A	—	—	—
172	Skärkind	Skär.old ch.		A 1	m		10	—	285	6	A	—	—	—
176	Skärkind	Karlslund		A 1	s		5	—	107	3a	—	—	—	—
Söderköping town														
177#	Söderköping	Söderköping		E 6	m		3	—	155	3a+	D	—	—	—
N16[257]	S'köping	S:t Lars ch.		A 3	s		10	—	240	5	C	—	—	—
N17[258]	S'köping	?		E 3	m			fr.?	(57)	?	—	—	—	—
Vadstena town														
179[259]	Vadstena			X 10			5	—	193	2(sd)	—	—	—	—
Valkebo härad														
180	Gammalkil	Gamm.ch.		A 1	s		10	—	174	?	C	—	—	—
181[260]	Ledberg	Led.ch.yd.		E 10.05?	m		10	3s	242	2	A	+	—	—

Continued

[249] Ög 136: Wessén (1958). [250] Ög 146: ATA 6576/62. [251] Ög N11: *FV* 1959, 95.
[252] Ög N12: *FV* 1970, 310. [253] Ög N13: ATA 4401/63. [254] Ög N14: *FV* 1943, 317.
[255] Ög N15: *FV* 1943, 317. [256] Ög 239: Wessén (1966), 5; *S:t Ingrid monastery.
[257] Ög N16: *FV* 1966, 102. [258] Ög N17: *FV* 1959, 249; *S:t Ragnhild Guild Museum.
[259] Ög 179: *Klosterkyrkan (Vadstena monastery church). [260] Ög 181: Jansson (1976), 76.

id.	parish	place	type	rel.sh.	s/m	dat.	fsp.	state	height	design	cross	orn.	rel.	sign.
183	Ledberg	Kärrsjö		A 2	s		3	—	162	3b	C	—	—	Åke?
184	Sjögestad	Sjög.ch.yd.		A 2	s		10	—	257	6	C	—	—	—
186[261]	Sjögestad	Frackstad		A 3	s		2	—	156	5	C	—	+?	Anund
187[262]	Sjögestad	Hackstad		A 1	s		7	fr.	220	4a	C	—	—	—
238	Vikingstad	Bankeberg		B 6?	s		2	—	189	3a	A?	—	—	—
189	Vikingstad	Bo		A 2	s		7	—	144	6	—	—	—	—
190	Vikingstad	Nybble		A 6	s		7	—	?	3a	C	—	—	—
191#	Vikingstad	Nybble		A 1	s		?	—	152	3a	—	—	—	—
192#	Vikingstad	Rakered		C 5	s		3	—	157	3a	C?	—	—	—
Vifolka														
193	Herrberga	Herr.ch.		A 4	s		10	2s	164	3a+2	—	—	—	—
194#	Herrberga	Herr.ch.		A 1	m		10	—	293	6	A	—	—	—
195#	Mjölby	Hadelö		X 30			6	—	140	3a	D	—	—	—
196#	Mjölby	Hulterstad		C 2	s		2	—	180	4a	—	+?	—	—
197	Mjölby	Söderby ch.		A 2	s		10	—	264	4a	—	—	—	—
198[263]	Normlösa	Norm. klockareg.		C 1?	m		3,10	dam.	(76)	3a	—	—	—	—
199[264]	Sya	Sya ch.		A 1	s		10	—	263	4a?	—	—	—	—
200	Sya	Uddarp		C 5?	s		2	—	130	2	—	—	—	—
201	Veta	V.ch.yd.		A 2	m		10	2s	130	3a+	—	—	+	—
202	Veta	Gottlösa		A 2?	s		3	—	176	3a	A/B?	—	—	—
203	Veta	Gottlösa		X 30	s		7	—	195	4a	C?	—	—	—
204[265]	Viby	Viby ch.		A 4	s		10	dam.	132	3a	—	—	—	—
N18[266]	Viby	Viby ch.		A 3	s		10	—	283	?	A–C?	—	—	—
205+206	Viby	Viby ch.yd.		C 5	s		10	2pts.	228	3a	A?	—	—	—
207	Viby	Enebacken		A 4	m		7	—	170	5	—	—	—	—
208	Viby	Enebacken		A 1	s		7	—	157	3a	—	—	—	—
209	Viby	Enebacken		A 4	s		2	—	148	5	C	—	—	—
210	Viby	Kårarp		A 1	s		2	—	179	4b	A–C?	—	—	—
211	Viby	Mörby		A 1	s		7	—	160	5	A	—	—	—
212#	Viby	Ålbäcken		C 5	s		5	—	200	2	A–C?	—	—	—
213	Västerlösa	Väst.ch.	rec.	C 3	s		10	—	173	7/9?	—	—	+	—
214	Västerlösa	Egeby		A 1	s		2	—	143	6	—	—	—	—
Ydre														
215#	V.Ryd	Lägernäs		A 3	s		3	—	195	3a	A	—	—	—
217	Sund	Oppeby		AB 10/02	s		7	—	330	4a	A	—	—	—
Åkerbo														
219	Lillkyrka	Övre Lundby		A 4	s		2	—	208	3a	A–C?	—	—	—
220	Ö.Skrukeby	Ö.Skruk.ch.	rec.	A 1	m		10	—	190	7/9?	—	—	+	—
221[267]	Törnevalla	Törn.ch.		A 1	s		10	—	246	6	—	—	—	—
N19[268]	Törnevalla	Törn.ch.		A 5	m		10	—	342	3a	Hr(2)	+	—	—
222[269]	Törnevalla	Törn.ch.yd.		A 6	s		10	fr.	(52)	3a	Hr	—	—	—
223	Törnevalla	Törn.ch.		A 4	s		10	—	178	3a	—	—	—	—
224	Törnevalla	Stratomta		E 10.05	m		2	3s.	185	5?	D	+	—	—
N20[270]	Rystad	Rystad ch.		A 1	s		10	dam.	260	?	—	—	—	—
Östkind														
225	Ö.Husby	Högtomta		A 1	s		5,7	—	133	6	D	—	—	—
226#	Ö.Husby	Lönnbro		X (E 1 or A 1?)	m		6	—	247	5	B	—	—	—
227#	Ö.Husby	Lönnbro		A 1?	m		6	—	?	?	—	—	—	—
228	Ö.Husby	Tuna br.		C 5.1?	m		7	—	153	?	—	—	+	—
229	Ö.Husby	Varby		A 1	m		2	—	237	6	D	—	+	—
230	Häradshammar	Åkerby		A 3	s		7	—	170	6	D?	—	—	—
231	Ö.Stenby	Ö.Stenby ch.		A 1	m		10	2s,dam.	—	6?+2	A	—	+	—
232[271]	Ö.Stenby	Ö.Stenby ch.		A 1	m		10	—	110	6/10 (circle)	—	—	—	—
233[272]	Ö.Stenby	Ö.Stenby ch.		A 2	s		10	—	132	3a	—	—	—	—
234mc	Ö.Stenby	Ö.Stenby ch.		A 2	s		10	—	160	3a	C	—	—	—
235mc[273]	Ö.Stenby	Ö.Stenby ch.		A 4	s		10	—	132	3a	C	—	—	—
236[274]	Ö.Stenby	Ö.Stenby ch.		A 3	s		10	—	180	3a	C	—	—	—
N21[275]	Ö.Stenby	Ö.Stenby ch.		X 30?	s		10	fr.	(173)	3a	A	—	—	—
237c	Ö.Stenby	Ållonö		A 2	m		3	—	253	5	—	—	—	—

[261] Ög 186: *Lunnevad folkhögskola. [262] Ög 187: *Lunnevad folkhögskola. [263] Ög 198: *Normlösa church.
[264] Ög 199: *Tingshuset (*Thing* house). [265] Ög 204: ATA 6573/62. [266] Ög N18: *FV* 1965, 54. [267] Ög 221: *Reva.
[268] Ög N19: *MÖLM* 1960, 230. [269] Ög 222: *MÖLM* 1960, 224. [270] Ög N20: ATA 5503/75. [271] Ög 232: ATA 503/75.
[272] Ög 233: ATA 8114/74. [273] Ög 235: ATA 2035/75. [274] Ög 236: ATA 8101/74. [275] Ög N21: ATA 580/75.

id.	parish	place	type	rel.sh.	s/m	dat.	fsp.	state	height	design	cross	orn.	rel.	sign.

238 follows Ög 187, above
239 follows 166
240–1 follow 77

NEW FINDS

	härad	*follows Ög*		*härad*	*follows Ög*		*härad*	*follows Ög*
N1	Dal	48	N8	Hanekind	124	N15	Skänninge	N14
N2	Gullberg	61	N9	Kind	128	N16	Söderköping	177
N3	Göstring	63	N10	Kind	N9	N17	Söderköping	N16
N4	Göstring	66	N11	Lösing	156	N18	Vifolka	204
N5	Göstring	74	N12	Memming	161	N19	Åkerbo	221
N6	Göstring	94	N13	Skänninge	165	N20	Åkerbo	224
N7	Hanekind	113	N14	Skänninge	N13	N21	Östkind	236

Sweden (excluding Uppland): Further Particulars

Ornaments (indicated by + in column headed 'orn.')

GOTLAND

59 rider and woman with drinking horn; sailing ship with six men
77 horse, wagon, man and woman with drinking horn
92 rider and woman (?) with drinking horn
109 sailing ship
110 sailing ship with nine men; horse with eight legs, rider and woman with drinking horn, dog (?) and building
141 beast
N2 'spiral wheel'
N4 riders, sails

GÄSTRIKLAND

2 tree and four men
7 woman with arms stretched forwards
9 leaves, man, sword
19 tree, bird, people, wagon, he-goat, beast, hooked staff

NÄRKE

34 beast, mask

SMÅLAND

83 house with ornaments
103 mask?
124 animals
133 dog/wolf?

SÖDERMANLAND

39 beast
40 couple, two animals
367 human face
66 beast?
80 beast?
86 Thor's hammer with a face
101 Sigurd's saga
111 Thor's hammer
155 beast?
158 sailing ship
164 sailing ship
167 human face
175 human face
190 man with axe; beast?
192 beast
205 beast
213 beast
377 two beasts
226 beast?
235 beast?
237 beast
239 beast?
270 cock
272 horse and rider
284 animal?
286 front: Christ, angel, dead people rising from their graves; back: animals, leaves
301 two beasts
303 beast?
304 beast
324 man
327 Sigurd's saga
367 follows Sö 40 above
377 follows Sö 213 above

VÄSTERGÖTLAND

4 beast
106 mask
14 two beasts
32 man
51 ship
56 crowned animal ('cenocephalos'?)
80 man with a processional cross
103 bird's head
106 follows Vg 4 above
113 Thor's hammer
119a see Vg 119 (*SRI*)
129 Adam, Eve, serpent?
147 figure
150 bird's head
181 beast
186 figure
196 beast

VÄSTMANLAND

10 beast
12 beast
13 tree ('of life')
15 beast
17 ship
24 beast
29 beast
32 beast

ÖLAND

4 two beasts
31 two beasts, person (woman?)
56 animal

ÖSTERGÖTLAND

122 beast
181 front and back: two warriors and a dog (?)
196 beast
224 ship
N19 ship

Multiple Commemorations

GOTLAND

3. By the same sponsor(s) (in memory of different individual(s))

113+114, by Liknat's sons: 113 in memory of their father; 114 in memory of their mother Ailikn.
134–136, by Rodvisl and Rodälv in memory of their three sons: 134 in memory of Rodfos; 135 in memory of Ai——; 136 in memory of Hailfos.

HÄLSINGLAND

1. Identical

14+15, by Frömund in memory of his father Rike-Gylfe.

SMÅLAND

3. By the same sponsor(s) (in memory of different individual(s))

143+N1, by Germund: 143 in memory of his father ——ger; N1 in memory of **auþelfi** and **uarin** . . .

SÖDERMANLAND

1. Identical

2+141, by Slode and Ragnfrid in memory of their son Igulbjörn.
112+113, by Vigdärv and Djärv: 112 in memory of their father; 113 in memory of both parents.
122+123, by Asgot in memory of his son Hasten.
134+N10, by Gudmund and Gisla in memory of their son Ofeg.
197+203, by Björn and Gärdar in memory of their brothers Viking and Sigfast.
206+208, in memory of ——bärn and Torsten by their mother Gudlög and their sister Hjälmlög.
N10: see this group above, at 134.

2. In memory of the same individual(s) (by different sponsor(s))

34+35, in memory of Torkel and Styrbjörn: 34 by their brothers Styrlög and Holm; 35 by their mother Ingeger(d).
57+58, in memory of Svarthövde: 57 by his brothers Balle and Ofeg; 58 by his sons Livsten, Fröbjörn, and X.

137+N13, in memory of Öpir (Rönö parish): 137 by his widow Tora/Torun; N13 by his son(s?) Öger (?) and X.
N13: see immediately above, at 137.

3. By the same sponsor(s) (in memory of different individual(s))

13+173, by Muskia ('Mus-Gea'): 13 together with Viking in memory of their son (?) Sigbjörn; 173 together with Manne in memory of their brother Rodger and their father Holmsten.
14+15, by Säva and Ragnborg: 14 together with their mother in memory of her husband, their father; 15 in memory of their mother?
280+328, by Underlög: 280 together with her son ——björn in memory of Ulvrik, her husband, ——björn's father and in memory of NN, Underlög's son; 328 together with her brother Torulv in memory of their father Gudvar.
292+N15, by Vigmar: 292 in memory of his in-law and partner Jörunde; N15 in memory of his father Kåre.
173: see this group above, at 13.
328: see this group above, at 280.
N15: see this group above, at 292.

VÄSTERGÖTLAND

1. Identical

11+13, by Tore Skorpa: 11 in memory of his son Kättil; 13 in memory of his son Kättil and his foster-daughter/mother (?).

VÄSTMANLAND

3. By the same sponsor(s) (in memory of different individual(s))

18+19, by Gunnald: 18 in memory of his son Gerfast; 19 in memory of his stepson Orm.

Double monuments ('paired stones') (one with inscription, the other with ornament)

1+2, by Gudlev in memory of his son Slagve.
9+10, by Gisl in memory of his son Ösel.

ÖLAND

2–3. By the same sponsors (almost), in memory of both the same and another individual

55+56, by Gudfast and Nenne: 55 together with their mother Helgun in memory of her husband, their father Sven; 56 in memory of their sister Åfrid and their father Sven.

ÖSTERGÖTLAND

1. Identical

162+N12, in memory of Gunnar by his father Hakon.

3. By the same sponsor(s) (in memory of different individual(s))

234+235, by Karl: 234 in memory of his brother Asmund; 235 in memory of his kinsman Torfrid.

Double monuments (one with inscription, the other with ornament)

47+48, in memory of Eskil and Asbjörn by Torvida, Eskil's daughter and Asbjörn's sister.

Connected Monuments

SMÅLAND

36+37: 36 Önd and Sven in memory of Assur; 37 Assur in memory of his father Önd.
76+77: 76 Tova in memory of her father Vråe; 77 Vråe in memory of his brother Gunne.

SÖDERMANLAND

13+173+374: 13+173, see 'Multiple Commemorations' above, at Sö group 3: 374 X in memory of Manne, Muskia's brother . . .

45+367: 45 Gerfast and Estfare in memory of their father Frösten and their brother Vagn/Vrang; 367 Håmund and Ulv in memory of their father Rolv, and Öborg in memory of her husband. Frösten and Rolv owned the village.

Sö 101+106+U 11+16+617: Sö 101 Sigrid in memory of her husband Holmger, Sigröd's—and Ginnlög's (?) father; Sö 106 Alrik, Sigrid's son, in memory of his father Spjut; U 11 Tolir and Gylla in memory of themselves, Håkon had the runes carved; U 16 Gunne and Kåre in memory of a man, 'the best of bönder in Håkon's *rod* [ship district]'; U 617 Ginnlög, Holmger's daughter, Sigröd's sister, in memory of her husband Assur, Håkon Jarl's son.

137+138+N13: 137+N13, see 'Multiple Commemorations' above, at Sö group 2: 138 in memory of Öpir's and Torunn's (=Tora's) son; no sponsor.

173: see above, at 13.

280+328: see 'Multiple Commemorations' above, at Sö group 3.

292+298+N15: 292+N15, see 'Multiple Commemorations' above, at Sö group 3: 298 Håur (?), Karl, Sighjälm, Vihjälm, and Kåre in memory of their father Vigmar.

328: see this group above, at 280.

367: see this group above, at 45.

374: see this group above, at 13.

N13: see this group above, at 137.

N15: see this group above, at 292.

VÄSTERGÖTLAND

9+12: 9 Gunnur in memory of (her husband?) Olov *nacke* ('neck'); 12 Olov *nacke* in memory of X.

Vg 112+DR 127: in memory of Karl by his *felaga* ('partner') Tore.

ÖSTERGÖTLAND

27+28: 27 by Torer in memory of his father Tialvar; 28 by NN in memory of his son.

68+111: 68 Svena in memory of her brother Övind, dead in Väring's *lið*(?) ('retinue'?); 111 Väring in memory of his brother Tjälve.

81+82+83+84+165: 81 Torgärd in memory of her (maternal) uncle Assur. Torkel carved; 82 Torkel in memory of Övind (Toste's son, who owned Högby); 83 Tora in memory of her son Sven; 84 Torkel and Helga ('raised the stone'); 165 Torunn and the brothers in memory of their father Toste. Torkel carved.

111: see this group above, at 68.

165: see this group above, at 81.

234+235+237?: 234+235, see 'Multiple Commemorations' above, at Ög group 3; 237 Torsten and Sunvid in memory of their brother Karl (?).

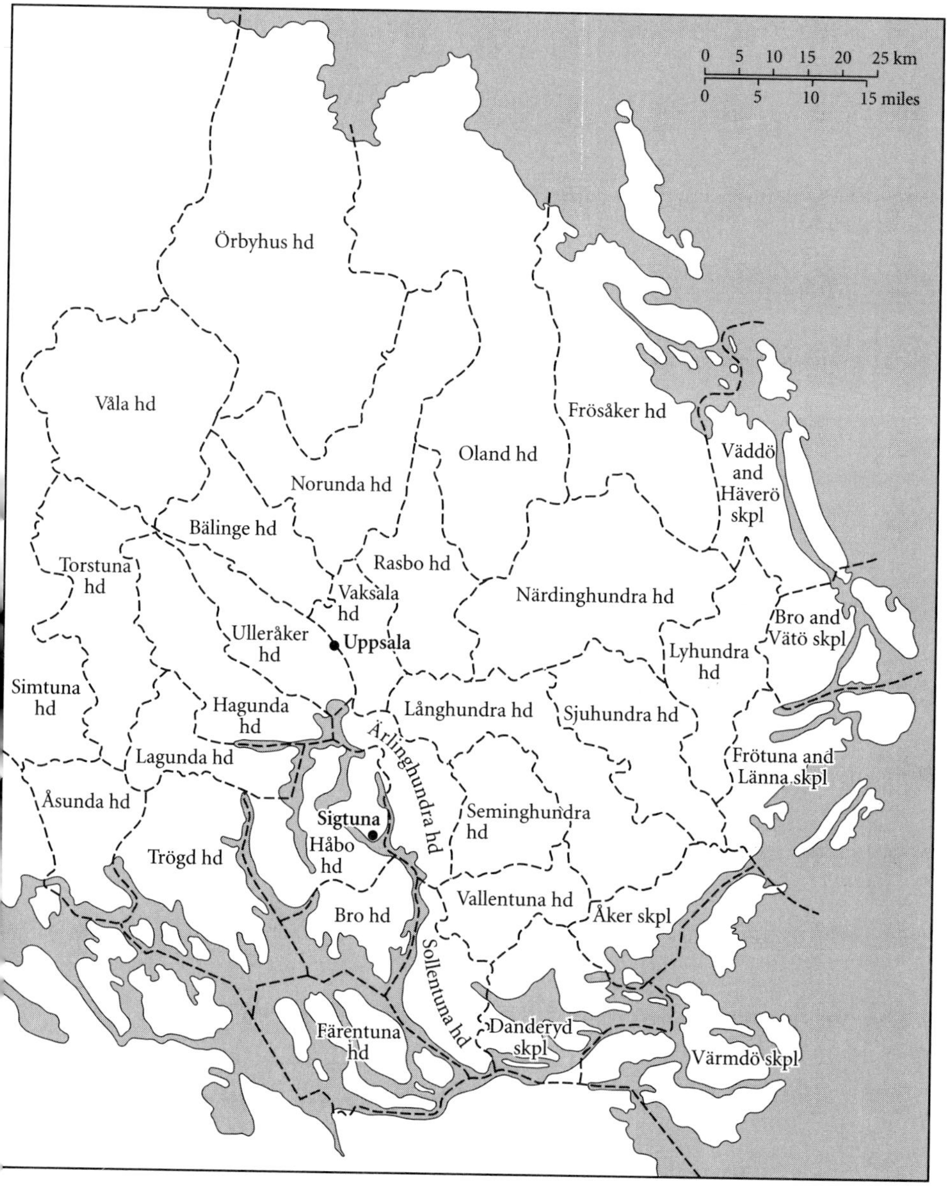

MAP 5. Districts in Uppland

Since the late Middle Ages the administrative districts of Uppland have been *härader* and, along much of the coast, *skeppslag*. There have been many changes in the boundaries of these districts; this map shows those used in *SRI* with the abbreviations 'hd' and 'skpl'.

UPPLAND (U)

(Total no. of inscriptions: 1,016)

Färentuna härad

id.	parish	place	type	rel.sh.	s/m	dat.	fsp.	state	height	design	cross	orn.	rel.	sign.
1	**Adelsö**	Adelsö ch.		A 1	s		10	—	119	6	+(?)	—	—	—
2#		Adelsö ch.		A 1	m		10	—		?	—	—	+	—
4[1]		Björkö		C 6	s	2a	3	fr.	(32)	1(2)	—	—	—	—
9[2]		Björkö		X 10			2	8fr.		?	—	—	—	—
10[3]		Dalby		X 60		3	8	—	93	2(2)	—	—	—	—
11c		Hovgården	rock	EF 8	m	3b	7	—	178	6	—	—	—	—
12#	**Munsö**	Bona		X	s		3	—		7?	—	—	—	—
13		Husby		A 6	m		8	—	65	?	—	—	+	—
14		Österås		E 3	m	2a	5	—	155	6	A	—	—	—
N1[4]	**Ekerö**	Ekerö ch.		A 6	s	2a	10	fr.	(98)	?	—	—	+	—
16c#		Nibbla		A 6	m		7,8	—		6	B	—	—	—
17		Skytteholm		A 2	m	2b	8	—	122	6	C	—	+	—
18		Stavsund		X 40	m?	2b	8	—	265	6(sd.)	A	—	—	—
19		Älby		A 1	s	2a	7	—	126	4a	B	—	—	—
20–21mc[5]	**Färentuna**	Fär.ch.		C 5/1?	s		10	fr.		6?	—	—	+	—
22		Kungsberga		A 1	m	2–3	8	—	205	6	—	—	+	—
23	**Hilleshög**	Hill.ch.		A 1	s	4	10	2pts.	(100)	6	A	—	—	Öpir
24		Hill.ch.		X 10			10	fr.	(65)	?	—	—	+	—
25		Hill.ch.		C 5	s		10	—	182	5	Eg	—	+	—
29		Hillersjö	rock	0		3b	3	—	280	see Pl. 10	—	—	—	Torbjörn
30		Kvarsta		E 10.05	m	2b	2	—	285	6	—	—	+	—
31		Väntholmen		A 2 + X 60	s		5?	2s	170	6+8a	—	+	—	—
32	**Sånga**	Stockby		E 1/2	m	2a	2	—	165	6	B	—	+	—
34		Sundby		E 1/2	m	2a	2	—	210	7	B	—	+	—
35		Svartsjö		A 1	m	2b	7	—	300	6	—	+	—	—
36		Svartsjö		C 5	s	3b	2	—	140	8a	A	—	—	Öpir
37		Säby		E 10.05	m	2b	2	—	340	6	A?	—	+	Torbjörn
38		Säby		A 1?	m	3a	2	—	265	4a	—	—	+	—
39#		Torslunda	rock	A 3	s	2b	1	—		6	B	—	+	—
40	**Skå**	Eneby		E 1	m	3a	7,8	dam.	(85)	6/7?	—	—	—	—
41		Kumla	rock	A 1	m	3a	7	—	161	6	B	—	+	Ärnfast
42		Troxhammar		A 3	s	3b	7	—	240	8a	—	—	—	—
43		Törnby		A 1	m	3a	7	2s	235	6+8a	B	—	—	Ärnfast
44[6]		Törnby		E 10.05	m		7	2s	225	6	—	—	—	Snare
45		Törnby		B 1	s	3–4	2	—	120	6	A	—	—	—
46	**Lovö**	Lovö ch.		B 1?	m		10	—	270	6	A	—	—	—
47		Lovö ch.		A 1	m	3a	10	—	175	6	A–C?	—	—	—
48		Lovö ch.; ch.yd.		A 3.2	m	3b	10	—	178	6	A	—	—	—
49		Lovö ch.; ch.yd.	rec.	X	m	3b	10	—	104	6	A	—	—	—
50		Lovö ch.; ch.yd.		E 10.05	m	3	10	—	113	6	A–C?	—	—	—
51#		Drottningholm		A 1	m	3a	8	—	240	6	—	+	—	—
52		Edeby	rock	C 3/5?	s	3a	8	—	150	6	—	—	—	—

Stockholm town

id.	parish	place	type	rel.sh.	s/m	dat.	fsp.	state	height	design	cross	orn.	rel.	sign.
53	Stockholm	Kåkbrinken		E 3	m	3b	3	—	95	6	—	—	—	—
54#	Stockholm	Riddarholms-kyrkan		A 1 or 2?	m		10	—		6	—	—	+	—

Sollentuna härad

id.	parish	place	type	rel.sh.	s/m	dat.	fsp.	state	height	design	cross	orn.	rel.	sign.
55#	**Bromma**	Ekeby		X 30			2,5	dam.		?	—	—	—	—
56		Glia		A 1	m	2b	8	—	110	6	A+Fg	—	+	—
57c#		Riksby		A 1	m	3a	5	—	155	6	Fr(2)	—	—	—

[1] U 4: *SHM 15825:1126 (the asterisk here and at nn. 2, 3, 7, etc. below indicates the present location of the stone).
[2] U 9: *SHM [3] U 10: Nordén (1943), 220; *Adelsö church.
[4] U N1: *FV* 1954, 1. [5] U 20–21: *FV* 1970, 301. [6] U 44. *FV* 1983, 234.

id.	parish	place	type	rel.sh.	s/m	dat.	fsp.	state	height	design	cross	orn.	rel.	sign.
58c		Riksby	rock	A 1	m	3b	7	—	187	6	B	—	—	—
59		Riksby	rock	A 1	s	3b	7	—	107	6	—		—	—
60		Ängby		A 4	s	3	7	2s	230	6	B	—	—	—
61	Spånga	Spå.ch.; ch.yd.		A 2/1	m	2a	10	2s	230	3a+mbd	A–C +H?	—	—	—
62m		Spå.ch.; ch.yd.		E 10.05	m	3a	10	—	188	6	B	—	—	—
63[7]		Spå.ch.		X 60			10	fr.	(47)	3a?	B	—	—	—
64		Spå.ch.	rec.	E?	m	3–4	10	dam.	122	9	A	—	—	—
67[8]		Spå.ch.		X	m		10	fr.	(50)	?	—	—	—	—
N2[9]		Spå.ch.		A 1	m		10	—	169	6	A	—	—	Snare
69		Eggeby		C 3	s	2a	6,7	2s	155	3(sp)	B	—	+	—
70#		Flysta		X 30			3	—		6?	—	—	—	Torbjörn
N3[10]		Granby	rock	E 03.20	m		5	—	250	7	B	—	—	—
72m[11]		Hansta		A 4	m	3a	7	—	243	6	B	—	—	—
73m		Hansta		0		3a	7,8	—	200	6	B	—	—	—
74		Husby		A 2	s	3a	7,8	—	194	6	B	—	+	Visäte
75		Kista		AB 1/02 or EF 1?		3b	7	—	130	6	B	—	—	—
76		Kista		A 2?	s?		3	2fr.	(193)	6?	—	—	—	—
77m		Råsta		E 10.05	m	3	3	—	165	6	—	—	—	—
78m[12]		Råsta		E 2	m	4	3	2fr.	(99)	6	A	—	—	—
79[13]		Skesta		A 1.4	m	3a	2	2s	240	6	B	+	—	Ärnfast
80		Sundby	rock	E 10.05	m	3b	5,8	—	310	6	B	—	—	—
82#	Järfälla	Järf.ch.		X 4	s		10	dam.		7?	—	—	—	—
84		Egglunda		A 7 or C 5?	s	3	3	—	107	6?	B	—	—	—
85[14]		Lövsta		A 4?	m		5	—	140	?	A	—	—	—
86		Skylsta	rock	A 2	s	3b	2	—	172	7	B	—	—	—
87#		Skylsta		X 60			1	—	?	?	—	—	—	—
88		Skälby		A 1?	m	3b	7,8	—	120	8a	B	—	—	—
89		Skälby		E 1	m	2b	7	—	132	7	—	—	—	—
90		Säby	rock	A 2.4	m	3b	7	—	164	6	B	—	—	—
91[15]		Vible		E: C 6+A 6	m	3a	2	—	177	8b	A+Fg	—	—	—
92[16]		Vible		AB 1/2	s	2a	2	—	175	4a	A–C?	—	—	—
93#		Väddesta		A 6	m		2	—	?	?	—	—	—	—
94	Sollentuna	Soll.ch.; ch.yd.		A 1	m	3a	10	—	175	6	A	—	+	—
95		Soll.ch.; ch.yd.		X 60		2a	10	fr.	(65)	3a?	A	—	+	—
N4[17]		Soll.ch.		A 1	m		10	fr.	(87)	6	—	—	—	—
96		Edsberg		A 1	m	2b	7	—	65	6	B	—	+	—
N5[18]		Kummelby		C 5/3	s		3	—	200	6	A	—	—	Igulfast
97#		Rotebro		E 05.10?	m		6,7	—	?	5+mbd	A	—	—	Kättil
98#		Rotsunda		E 01.40?	m		6,8	—	?	5	—	—	—	—
99		Skillinge	rock	A 1/2	m	3b	1	—	225	6	A	—	—	—
100mc		Skälby		EF: CD 30 + AB 22	m	3b	5,7	—	215	6	B	—	—	—
101mc		S.Sätra	rock	E 10.03	m	3b	7	—	190	6	—	—	+	—
102		Viby	rock	E 3	m	3b	8	—	235	6	B	—	—	—
103[19]		Ytterby		A 1	m	2a	2	—	265	6+mbd	—	—	—	—
104[20]	Ed	Ed ch.		AB 1/20	s	4	10	—	135	6	—	—	—	Öpir
106		Ed, vic.		B 1	m		2	dam.	(102)	6	B	—	—	—
107		Antuna		AB: A 3 + B 5/3?	m	2b	2,8	2s	208	6	A	—	—	—
108		Bisslinge		E 1	m	2	3	dam.	(132)	6	A	—	+	—
109#		Bisslinge		A 1/2	m		?	—		?	—	—	—	—
111#		Ed, Hjältarängen		AB 60/01	s		?	—		6	—	—	—	—
112c(×2)		Ed, Kyrkstigen	rock	B 1	s	3b	7	2s	192, 191	6+8a	—	—	+	—
113#		Ed, Stenbron		X 60			6	dam.			—	—	—	—
114(×2)		Runby	rock	C 5/3	s	3b	5	2s	170, 127	6+7	—	—	+	—
115[21]		Runby		A 6	s		3,6	4fr.		5	—	—	—	—
116		Älvsunda	rock	A 2	m	3a	3,8	—	225	8a	B	—	—	—
117		Älvsunda		E 3	m	3b	3	—	165	6	—	—	—	—
118		Älvsunda		A 1	s	3b	6	—	160	8a	A	—	—	Öpir
119[22]		Älvsunda		A 1	s	3a	6	—	78	6	B	—	—	—

Continued

[7] U 63: one fragment, *Spånga pastorsexpedition (parish office). [8] U 67: *Stockholm town museum. [9] U N2: *FV* 1953, 266.
[10] *RR* 1987, 134. [11] U 72: *Skansen. [12] U 78: *Sundbyberg hembygdsmuseum. [13] U 79: *Hässelby manor.
[14] U 85: *Hässelby museum. [15] U 91: *Jakobsberg. [16] U 92: *Jakobsberg. [17] U N4: *FV* 1968, 279.
[18] U N5: *FV* 1953, 263; 1972, 16. [19] U 103: *Sollentunaholm [20] U 104: *Ashmolean Musuem, Oxford.
[21] U 115: *FV* 1954, 12. [22] U 119: *Antuna park.

id.	parish	place	type	rel.sh.	s/m	dat.	fsp.	state	height	design	cross	orn.	rel.	sign.

Danderyd skeppslag

id.	parish	place	type	rel.sh.	s/m	dat.	fsp.	state	height	design	cross	orn.	rel.	sign.
121	**Solna**	Frösunda		A 6	m	3a	7,8	—	180	6	B	—	—	—
122#		Järva krog		X	m		7	—		6?	—	—	—	Öpir
123#		Karlberg		A 8	m		2	—		6	A–C?	—	—	—
124		Karlberg		A 6	m	3a	7	—	185	6	B	—	—	—
126[23]		Över-Järva		A 3/6	s	2b	2	—	160	6(sp)	—	—	+	—
127mc	**Danderyd**	Dand.ch.; ch.yd.		A 8	s	2b	10	—	214	7	B	—	+	—
128		Dand.ch.		A 1	m	4	10	2pts.	(113)	6	(+?)	+	—	—
129		Dand.ch.		X	s		10	fr.	(60)	?	A	—	+	—
130m		Nora	rock	A 2	s	3b	5	—	190	6	A	—	+	—
131[24]		Rinkeby		E 10.05	m	3a	8	—	213	6	B	—	—	—
132#		Rinkeby		X 40			2	—		?	—	—	—	—
133m	**Täby**	Täby ch.		CD 30/08	s	3a	10	2pts.	(147)	6	—	—	—	—
N8[25]		V.Arninge	rock	C 5/3	s		1	—	180	8a	A	—	—	—
134[26]		Ö.Arninge		X			3	fr.	(49)	6?	—	—	—	—
135mc		Broby		A 1	m	2b	6,7	—	202	6	B	—	—	—
136mc		Broby		C 5	s	2b	6,7	—	173	6	B	—	pil-grim	—
137mc		Broby		E 3	m	2b	6,7	—	138	6	A	—	—	—
138#		Broby		X			2	—		6?	—	—	—	—
139		Broby		X 60	s		3	fr.	(32)	6	—	—	+	—
140c		Broby		A 6	s	3a	3	fr.	(50)	6	—	—	—	—
141m#		Fittja		C 3	s		5	fr.	(45)	6	B	—	—	—
142c		Fällbro		E 10.05	m	3b	7	—	155	8b	Eg	—	—	Öpir
N6[27]		Fällbro, Hagby	rock	A 1	m		1	—	223	6	—	+	—	Visäte
143mc		Hagby	rock	E 05.10 +C 3	m	3b	3	—	294	8b	—	—	—	—
144m		Hagby	rock	E 10/20.05	m		3	—	295	6	A?	—	—	—
145		Hagby, Brohammaren	rock	A 1	m	3b	6,7	—	159	6	A	—	—	Olev
146		Hagby, Brohammaren	rock	C 5/3	s	2a	6,7	—	170	4a+mbd	A	—	—	—
147mc		Hagby, Sparingsberg		C 5/4+3?	m	3b	5,7	—	115	6?	—	—	—	—
148mc		Hagby, Sparingsberg	rock	B 5.1	m		5,7	—	131	6	A–C?	—	—	—
149mc#		Hagby		A 8	s	3a	8	—	165	6	B	—	—	—
N7#[28]		Hagby		E 6	m		?	—		?	—	—	+	—
150c		Karby		E 3	m		7	—	122	6	C	—	—	—
151		Karby		E 1.05	m	3a	7	—	117	6	B	—	—	—
152m		Lissby		C 5/3	s	3b	2	—	135	6	—	—	—	—
153m		Lissby		A 2	m	3a	3	—	260	6	B	—	—	—
154		Lissby		X 20	s	3a	3	—	123	6	—	—	—	—
155–157m[29]		Lissby		A 2	m		3	7fr.		6?	+(?)	—	—	—
158#		Löttinge		E 05.10?	m?		6	—		6	—	—	—	—
159[30]		Löttinge		A 1	m		7	4fr.	102	7	—	—	—	—
160mc		Risbyle		A 1	m	2a	7	—	275	7	A	—	+	—
161mc		Risbyle		A 4	s	2a	5	—	198	7	A+ H?(3)	—	—	Ulv
N9[31]		Roslags Näsby	rock	CD: D 3 +C 3	m		1	—	175	?	—	—	—	—
162#		Skogsberga		A 1	s		?	—		6	—	—	—	Olev
163		Såsta	rock	A 1	m	3b	7	—	240	6	A	—	—	——fast
164mc		Täby tä		A 8	s	2–3	6,7	—	220	7	B	—	+	—
165mc		Täby tä		A 8	s	2–3	6,7	—	186	6	B	—	+	—
166m	**Ö.Ryd**	Ö.Ryd ch.		E 3	m	3a	10	—	130	8a(2)	—	—	—	—
167		Ö.Ryd ch.		A 4	s	3a	10	—	147	7	—	—	—	Fot
168#		Björkeby	rock	A 7a	m	3b	?	—		6	A	—	—	Öpir
169		Björkeby		AB 3	s	2a	3	—	175	3b	—	—	—	—
170m#		Bogesund		E 3	m		8	—		7	A–C?	—	'ch.yd.'	Fastulv
171m		Söderby	rec.	A 3/8	s	3b	5	—	155	6	—	—	—	Faste
172	**Lidingö**	Islinge		A 1	m	3a	5	fr.	(100)	6	—	—	+	—
N10[32]	Bo g.	rock	A 4	s		7,8	—	—	200	6	B	—	—	Åsmund

[23] U 126: *SHM 21389. [24] U 131: *Klockaregården (Danderyd parish). [25] U N8: *FV* 1976, 99.
[26] U 134: THS 10:60; ATA 5938/64; *Rönninge. [27] U N6: *FV* 1946, 258 [28] U N7: ATA 4909/78.
[29] U 155–157: *FV* 1964, 155; U 156: *Täby centre. [30] U 159: *SHM 22757. [31] U N9: THS 10:58.
[32] U N10: *FV* 1986, 84; *RR* 1987, 140

id.	parish	place	type	rel.sh.	s/m	dat.	fsp.	state	height	design	cross	orn.	rel.	sign.

Värmdö skeppslag

id.	parish	place	type	rel.sh.	s/m	dat.	fsp.	state	height	design	cross	orn.	rel.	sign.
173	**Värmdö**	Väsby		E 10.05	m	4	2	—	179	6	A	—	—	—

Åker skeppslag

id.	parish	place	type	rel.sh.	s/m	dat.	fsp.	state	height	design	cross	orn.	rel.	sign.
174#	**Österåker**	Öst.ch.		A 2	m		10	—	?	3b	—	—	—	—
175		Öst.ch.		AB 1 or CD 1	s?		10	2fr.	?	6	B	—	—	—
176#		Berga		A 1	m	3a	2	—	?	6	—	+	—	—
177	**Roslagskulla**	Stav		C 1/5	s	3b	5	—	295	6	A–D?	—	—	Fot
179	**Riala**	Riala ch.		A 1	m	4	10	dam.	(94)	6	—	—	—	Öpir

Vallentuna härad

id.	parish	place	type	rel.sh.	s/m	dat.	fsp.	state	height	design	cross	orn.	rel.	sign.
180	**Össeby Garn**	Öss.G.ch.		A 2	m	3b	10	—	275	7	B	—	—	—
181		Öss.G.ch.		E 1	m	4	10	—	195	6	A	—	—	Öpir
182		Öss.G.ch.		X	m		10	fr.	?	6/7?	—	—	—	—
183[33]		Öss.des.ch.		X 30			10	fr.	(68)	6/7?	A	—	—	—
N11[34]		Öss.des.ch.		X 01?	m		10	fr.	(65)	?	—	—	—	—
N12[35]		Öss.des.ch.		X 4?	m		10	fr.	(60)	?	—	—	—	—
186m		Gillberga		A 1	m	2b	7	—	154	7?	A	—	—	—
188m		Gillberga		A 1?			7,8	—	130	5	A(2)	—	—	—
N13[36]		Hacksta		X10?20?			3	fr.	(60)	?	—	—	—	—
189#		L.Karby		A 1	m		3,8	—	?	5	—	—	—	—
190		Kumla		A 1	s	3b	7	—	226	6	C	—	—	—
191#		Morsta		A 1	m		2,8	fr.	?	6/7?	—	—	—	—
192		Sjöberg		X			2,5	fr.	(39)	?	—	—	—	—
193		Svista		E 05.10?	m	3a	5	—	176	6	B	+	—	—
194m		Väsby		A 8	s	3a	5	—	210	6+mbd	A	—	+	—
195[37]		Åby		X 60/30	s?	4	7	—	144	6	Eg	—	—	—
198[38]	**Vada**	Vada ch.		E 3?	m	4	10	3fr.	?	?	—	—	—	—
N14[39]		Vada ch.		X ? + X 03			10	fr.	(52)	?	—	—	—	—
(199=235)		(Vada vic.)												
200		St.Benhamra		AB 20/01	s	2a	5,7	—	192	5	—	+	+	—
201	**Angarn**	Ang.ch.		A 1	m	2a	10	—	225	6	A	—	+	—
202		Ang.ch.		A 1	m	3a	10	—	120	6	—	—	—	—
203		Ang.ch.; roadside		A 3	s	3a	10	—	194	6	—	—	—	—
204		Ang.ch.; roadside		E 3	m	2b	10	—	214	6	A	—	—	—
205#		Ang.ch.		X			10	fr.	(70)	?	—	—	—	——älv
206#		Ang.ch.		X	m?		10	fr.	(105)	?	—	—	—	—
207m		Råcksta		A 1	m	3a	7?	—	122	6	—	—	—	—
208m		Råcksta		A 1	m	3a	7	—	128	6	B	—	—	Visäte
209m		Veda	rock	A 3	s	3b	7,8	—	90	8a	—	—	—	—
210c		Åsta	rock	E 10.05	m	3b	6	—	153	8b	A	—	—	—
211[40]		Örsta		C 5	s		3	—	140	6	B	—	—	—
212mc	**Vallentuna**	Vall.ch.; ch.yd.		A 8	s	2–3	10	2s	188	7(2)	B	—	+	—
214m		Vall.ch.		C 5	s	2a	10	—	134	3a+	A	—	—	—
215m[41]		Vall.ch.		C 1/2	m		10	fr.	115	6	—	—	—	—
216c[42]		Vall.ch.		A 1	s	4	10	—	105	6	—	—	—	Drosboe
217c?#		Vall.ch.		A 3?	s		10	—	180	9	—	—	—	—
221		Vall.ch.		X 60			10	—	115	6	—	—	—	—
224#		Vall., klockarestugan		A 1	s		10	—	120	6	—	—	—	—
225mc		Bällsta		A 1	m	2a	5,9	—	180	7?	Hg	—	—	—
226mc		Bällsta		C 5	s	2a	5,9	—	170	7	—	—	—	Gunnar
227		Grana		E 20.03	m	3b	8	—	142	6	B	—	—	—
229c		Gällsta		A 1	m	3b	7	—	265	6	A	—	—	Öpir
231c		Gällsta		E 1	m	4	7	—	130	6	A+H?	—	—	—
232c		Gällsta		A 1	m	4	7	—	130	6	—	—	—	—
233		Kusta		E: A 1 + C 3	(m)	3b		—	130	6	—	—	—	—
234#		Kusta		E 1	m			—	?	?	—	—	—	—
235=199[43]		Kusta		E 6	m	2a	8	2pts.	156+	3b	B	—	—	—
236m		Lindö		A 1/2	m	3a	6	—	180	6	D	—	—	Visäte
237m[44]		Lindö		A 1/2	m	3b	6	2fr.	220	8b	B	—	+	—

Continued

[33] U 183: *FV* 1972, 275; *SHM. [34] U N11: *FV* 1972, 272; *SHM.
[35] U N12: *FV* 1971, 213; *SHM 29217. [36] U N13: ATA 4822/64. [37] U 195: *Stångberga school. [38] U 198: *SHM 22799.
[39] U N14: *FV* 1971, 212. [40] U 211: *FV* 1974, 212. [41] U 215: *SHM 29956. [42] U 216: SHM 8355; *Apoteket, Vallentuna.
[43] U 235=199: Westlund (1980), 136; *Vada church. [44] U 237: *Nedernäset.

id.	parish	place	type	rel.sh.	s/m	dat.	fsp.	state	height	design	cross	orn.	rel.	sign.
238m		Lindö		C 3/5	s	3a	6	—	220	8a	—	—	—	—
239		Lindö		C 5	s		6,7	dam.	135	6	—	—	—	—
240m		Lingsberg		E 10.05	m	3a	6	—	260	6	B	+	—	—
241m		Lingsberg		A 4	m	3a	6	—	176	8b	B	—	+	—
242		Lingsberg		X	m		3	fr.	(28)	?	—	—	—	—
243m#		Molnby		E 3	m			—	160	6	B	—	bap-tism	—
244m		Mällösa		A 3	s	3a	8	—	125	6	—	+	—	—
245#		Mällösa		A 4	m		3	—	160	6	B	—	+	—
247		Lilla Mällösa		C 2	s		6,7	—	165	6	—	—	—	Sven
249		Näle, S.gården	rock	A 1	m	3	1	—	137	6	—	—	—	—
251m		Sursta	rock	A 3	s	3a	1	—	?	6	—	+	—	—
252	**Fresta**	Fresta ch.		B 1	m	4	10	—	160	6	A	—	—	—
253=264[45]		Fresta ch.		C 5	s	3a	10	2pts.	102	6	—	—	—	—
255m		Fresta ch.		E 20.03	m	3b	10	—	200	6	B	—	—	—
256		Fresta ch.		A 1	m	3a	10	—	259	6	B	—	—	—
257		Fresta ch.		X	s?	—	10	—	114	1?	—	+	—	—
258		Fresta ch.		A 1	m	2a	10	—	176	3a(2)	A	—	—	—
259		Fresta ch.		A 3	s	3b	10	—	121	6	A?	—	—	—
260		Fresta ch.		A 1	m	3b	10	—	220	6	B	—	—	—
261mc[46]		Fresta ch.		A 8	s	3a	6	—	145	7	B	—	+	—
262#		Fresta ch.		A 2?	s		10	2fr.h.	160	8b	—	—	—	Öpir
263#		Fresta ch.		E 3?	m		10	h.	?	?	—	—	—	—
(264=253)		(Fresta ch.)												
N15[47]		Fresta ch.		X 10	s		10	fr.	(33)	?	—	—	—	—
265m		Ekeby	rock	C 3	s	3b	7	—	145	6	—	—	—	—
266m		Ekeby	rock	A 1	m	3b	7	—	158	6	—	—	—	—
267m		Harby		C 3	s	3b	6	—	140	6	—	—	—	Fot
269m		Harby		A 2	s	3b	3	—	117	6	B	—	—	—
270#		Smedby		C 1+?	s		2	dam.	250	6	—	—	—	—
272	**Hammarby**	Hamm.ch.		C 3	s	3a	10	—	114	6	—	—	+	—
273c		Hamm.ch.		A 1.2	m	3b	10	—	170	6	B	—	—	—
N16[48]		Hamm.ch.	rec.	C 3	s	3–4	10	—	143	?	—	—	+	—
N17[49]		Hamm.ch.		A 3	s			—	145	6	—	—	—	—
274#		Hamm., klockareg.		X 30	s		10	fr.	?	6?	—	—	—	—
275		Brunnby		A 2	m	3b	6	—	160	6	A	—	—	—
276c[50]		Hammarby		A 1	m	2a	7	—	285	7	B	—	+	—
277c		Hammarby		E: C 5 + A 6	m	3b	7	—	180	8b	—	—	—	—
N18m[51]		Hammarby		E 3? (6?)	m?		4	fr.	(125)	6	—	—	—	—
278		Nibble		A 1?	s?			fr.	(75)	8b	A+ Fg(2)	—	—	—
279		Skälby		A 2	m	3b	7	—	164	8b	A+ Fg(2)	—	—	Öpir
280m		Smedby	rock	B 5	s	3b	7	—	93	8a	A	—	—	—
281m		Smedby		A 1	m	3b	8	—	190	6	B	—	—	—
282#		Torsåker		X	s			fr.	?	?	A	—	—	—
283#		Torsåker		A 1?	m		2	—	165	6	B ?	—	—	—
284		Torsåker	rock	A 1	m	3b	7	—	199	7	B	—	—	Sven
285m[52]		Tryninge		C 3/2	s	3b	2	—	158	6	B	—	—	—
286m[53]		Tryninge		C 3.6	m	3b	2	—	129	6	B	—	—	—
287		Vik		A 3.2	m	3b	2,5	—	223	8b	A	—	—	Öpir
288		Vik		E 3.20	m	4	2,5	—	212	6	A+H	—	—	Öpir
289m		Vik		A 1	m	3a	7	—	162	6	B	—	—	—
292		St.Vilunda		A 1	s	4	2,5	—	65	6	A	—	—	—
293c		L.Vilunda		A 1	m	3b	8	—	165	6	B		+	—
294c		L.Vilunda		C 5.1?	m	3a	7,8	—	202	8b	B	—	—	—
N19[54]		L.Vilunda		C 5	s			—	215	?	—	—	—	—

Seminghundra härad

id.	parish	place	type	rel.sh.	s/m	dat.	fsp.	state	height	design	cross	orn.	rel.	sign.
295c	**Skånela**	Skån.ch.; ch.yd.		E: A 3 + C 2	m	3b	10	—	182	7	B	—	—	—
296m		Skån.ch.		E 3	m		10	—	100	6	B	—	—	—
297m[55]		Skån.ch.		A 1	s	3b	10	—	195	6	A–C?	—	—	—
300#		Skån.ch.		C 5?	s		10	—	150	6	A–C?	—	—	—

[45] U 253=264: *FV* 1959, 254; ATA 5316/85.
[46] U 261: *FV* 1959, 252. [47] U N15: *FV* 1959, 255. [48] U N16: *FV* 1959, 196. [49] U N17: *FV* 1993, 233.
[50] U 276: *Löwenströmska lasarettet (hospital). [51] U N18: *FV* 1959, 188; *Löwenströmska lasarettet (hospital).
[52] U 285: *Torsåker. [53] U 286: *Torsåker. [54] U N19: *FV* 1972, 172. [55] U 297: *FV* 1953, 270.

id.	parish	place	type	rel.sh.	s/m	dat.	fsp.	state	height	design	cross	orn.	rel.	sign.
301#		Skån.ch.		X	s		10	—		6	—	—	+	Åsmund
302[56]		Skån.ch.		X	m		10	fr.	(121)	?	—	—	+	—
N20[57]		Skån.ch.		X 20			10	fr.	(65)	?	—	—	—	—
304c[58]		Bensta		A 1	m		2	—	158	6–8	+(?)	—	—	—
305c		Bensta	rock	E 05.11?	m	3a	7	—	103	8a	—	+	—	—
306mc		Dal	rock	E 05.11?	m	3b	1	—	152	6	A	—	—	—
307c		Ekeby	rock	A 2	m	3b	1	—	107	8a	—	—	—	Öpir
308		Ekeby	rock	A 8	s	3b	1	—	130	6	B	—	—	Torgöt
(309–311 = same rock)														
309mc		Harg	rock	A 1/2	m	3b	5	—	156	6	—	—	—	—
310mc		Harg	rock	C 5/4	s	3b	1	—	110	6	—	—	—	—
311mc		Harg	rock	F 03.20	m	3b	1	—	160	6	A	—	—	—
312mc		Harg		B 4	s	3b	6	—	138	6	A	—	+	—
313mc		Harg		F 40.03	m	3a	2	2s	133	8+2	A	+	—	—
314mc#		Harg		D 3	s		8	—	145	6	A	—	—	—
315mc#		Harg		E 3	m	3b	5,8	—	200	8	A	—	—	Öpir
316mc		Harg		0			5	—	150	2	B	—	—	—
317#		Harg		E 10.05	m		6	—	150	6	B	—	—	—
318		Harg	rock	C 5.1	m		1	—	140	6	—	—	—	—
319		Kimsta		E 6	m	2a	7	—	163	4a+3a	A–C?	—	+	—
320#		Kimsta	rock	X	m		1	—	?	6	B	—	—	—
321		Skalmsta		A 3.2 + A 6	m	3a	2	2s	158	6	B–C?	—	—	—
322		Stensta		C 6	s	3a	3	—	173	6	B	—	+	—
323[59]		Sälna		A 1	m	2a	6	—	314	3a(2)	—	—	+	—
324		Tjursta		E 20.03	m	2a	7	—	217	6	—	—	—	—
325	**Markim**	Markim ch.; ch.yd		A 1.4	m		10	4fr.	250	6+8a	A?	—	—	—
326m		Husby		E 3	m	2a	7	—	199	3a	A–C?	—	—	—
327m[60]		Husby		E 3	m		7	—	276	3a(3)	A–C?	—	+	—
328mc		Lundby		C 1 + C 5	m	2a	5	—	176	7	A	—	—	—
329m		Snottsta		C 5	s	3a	7	—	188	6	B	—	—	—
330m		Snottsta		C 5	s	3a	7	—	226	6	C	—	—	—
331m		Snottsta	rock	C 5	s	3a	1	—	145	7	B	—	+	—
332m#		Vreta		C 5	s	3a	?	—	145	6	B	—	—	—
333m	**Orkesta**	Ork.ch.		A 1	m	3a	10	—	154	6	B	—	—	—
334		Ork.ch.		AB 1	s	3b	10	—	142	8b	C?	—	+	Kättil
335		Ork.ch.		A 1	s	2a	10	—	156	6	B	—	—	—
336mc		Ork.ch.; school		A 4	s	2a	10	—	165	3c	—	—	—	—
N21[61]		Borresta		A 2	s		?	—	255	6?	—	—	—	—
337mc		Granby	rock	E 1 ?/4	m	3b	1	—	413	6	B	—	+	Visäte
338c		Granby		E 4	m	2a	7	2s	172	3a	B	—	+	—
339#		Granby		X			6	3fr.	?	?	B	—	+	—
340		Orkesta		X	s		3	fr.	(50)	?	—	—	—	—
341mc		Söderby		AB 1/20	s	2a	5,6	—	232	3b	—	—	+	—
342mc[62]		Söderby		X 20?			6	fr.	?	3/4?	A	—	—	—
343mc#		Yttergärde		A 1	m	3a	?	—	250	7	—	—	+	—
344mc[63]		Yttergärde		0		3a	3	—	170	6	—	—	—	—
345#		Yttergärde		X 30/8	s	2a	7	—	?	4a+	—	—	+	—
346m#	**Frösunda**	Frösunda ch.		C 3	s	3a	10	—	200	6	B?	—	+	Åsmund
N22[64]		Frös.ch.	rec.?	A 1	m	3–4	?	—	143	4a	A	—	—	—
347m		Näs	rock	AB 8/05/30	s		7	—	222	3a	Fr	—	+	—
348m		Näs	rock	0		2a	7	—	135	2	Fr	—	—	—
349#		Odenslunda		A 1	m	2a	3	—	125	3c	A	—	+	—
350		Solsta	rock	E 10.04	m	3b	8	—	176	6	C	+	—	Orökja?
351		Solsta	rock	E 10.05	m	3b	1	—	154	6	B	—	+	—
352		Vreta		C 3	s	3b	7	—	225	6	C	—	—	—
353	**Lunda**	Lunda ch.		A 6	s		6,10	—	155	3a+2	—	+	—	Sune
354		Lunda ch.; ch.yd.		C 2	m	2b	10	—	210	7	H?	—	+	—
355[65]		Lunda ch.		A 2	m		10	fr.	(150)	3b	—	—	—	—
356m		Ängby		C 3	s	3a	8	—	225	7	A	—	+	Åsmund
N23[66]		Ösby		X 60	s	2a	2	fr.	(130)	3a	—	+	+	—
357	**Skepptuna**	Skepptuna ch.		E 10.05	m	3b	10	—	227	6	A	—	—	—
358		Skepp.ch.		A 3	s	2a	10	—	205	3c	B	—	+	—
N24[67]		Fröby		X 60			7,8	fr.	(130)	3a	A–D?	—	—	—
360m		Gådersta	rock	A 3/1	s	3b	7	—	200	8b	—	—	—	—
361#		Gådersta		E 6	m		3	—	275	6	A	—	—	—

Continued

[56] U 302: *FV* 1953, 275.
[57] U N20: *FV* 1953, 270.
[58] U 304: *FV* 1953, 278.
[59] U 323: *Skånelaholm.
[60] U 327: *Torslunda.
[61] U N21: *FV* 1975, 169.
[62] U 342: *FV* 1976, 98.
[63] U 344: *Orkesta church.
[64] U N22: *FV* 1993, 231.
[65] U 355: ATA 5923/69.
[66] U N23: *FV* 1978, 226.
[67] U N24: ATA 3019/65.

id.	parish	place	type	rel.sh.	s/m	dat.	fsp.	state	height	design	cross	orn.	rel.	sign.
362#		Gådersta		A 1	m	3b	3	—	220	6	—	—	—	—
363#		Gådersta	rock	E 03/05. 20/10	m		2	—	160	6	A	—	+	—
364mc[68]		Gådersta		X 40	m		3	fr.	160	7	—	—	bap-tism	—
366#		Gådersta		X 60			?	fr.	?	?	—	—	—	—
368#		Helgåby		X	m		3	fr.	(100)	3b	—	—	—	Åsmund
371		Lövhamra		A 1	m	2a	7	—	230	3b	—	—	+	—
N25[69]		St.Ullentuna		A 6	s		3	fr.	(100)	3a	A	—	+	—
N26[70]		St.Valla; ch.		X 60			3	fr.	(100)	?	—	—	+	—
372		Ånsta		A 1	m	2b	8	—	198	6	A/D?	—	+	—
373		Örby		A 3	s	3a	7	—	160	6	—	—	—	—
374[71]		Örby		X 60	m		3	—	150	6?	A?	—	+	—
375	**Vidbo**	Vidbo ch.		E 3	m	2b	7	3pts.	190	7	—	+	—	—
376m		Vidbo ch.; ch.yd.		C 3.5	m	3–4	10	—	144	6	A	—	—	Sten
377m#		Velamby		F 3	m		2,8	fr.		6	A	—	—	Sven
378		Åsby		AB 1	m	3–4	7	3pts.	100	6	A	—	—	—

Sigtuna town

id.	parish	place	type	rel.sh.	s/m	dat.	fsp.	state	height	design	cross	orn.	rel.	sign.
379	**Sigtuna**	Sig.ch.yd.		A 5	m		10	dam.	184	4b	A	—	+	Torbjörn
380		Sig.ch.yd.		X	m		10	dam.	(87)	?	—	—	—	—
381		Sig.ch.yd.		X			10	fr.	(61)	?	B	—	+	—
382[72]		Sig.ch.		X 60	s	3–4	10	dam.	(75)	4a?	A	—	—	Sven
384[73]		Sig.mon.		X	m?		10	2s,fr.	(67)	?+2	—	—	—	—
N27[74]		S:t Lars' (ruin)		A 8	s		10?	—	192	6	B	—	—	—
385		S:t Olov's (ruin)		A 5?	s		10	fr.	(42)	?	A	—	—	—
386[75]		S:t Olov's (ruin)		X 10			10	3fr.		?	—	—	—	—
387#		S:t Olov's (ruin)		X 03			10	—		?	A	—	—	—
388[76]		S:t Olov's (ruin)		X	m	3b	10	2fr.		6/7?	—	—	—	—
389[77]		S:t Lars' (ruin)		E 03.20?	m	3b	10	—	179	6	B	—	—	—
390[78]		Storgatan		E 10.05?	m	2b	3	dam.	156	7	B	—	+	—
391		Prästgatan		A 5	m		3	—	110	4b	A	—	+	Torbjörn
392		Klockbacken	rock	A 3	s	2a?	3	dam.	80	4a+3a	—	—	—	—
393		Borgmästar-vreten		B 2	s	3a	7	2s	225	6	A	—	—	—
394		S:t Per's (ruin)		A 2	s		10	—	215	4a	B	—	—	—
395[79]		S:t Per's (ruin)		B 5?	s	3b	10	dam.	(88)	6	B	—	—	—
398[80]		S:t Per's (ruin)	rec.	X 10		3–4	10	—	110	?	C	—	—	—
399[81]		S:t Per's (ruin)		X 60?	s		10	2fr.		?	—	—	—	—
403[82]		kv.Professorn		X 10	s	2a?	3	2fr.		?	B–C?	—	—	—
N28[83]		kv.Handels-mannen		X 10			3	fr.	(92)	6/7?	—	—	—	—
405[84]		?		X 10				4fr.		?	—	—	—	Torbjörn

Ärlinghundra härad

id.	parish	place	type	rel.sh.	s/m	dat.	fsp.	state	height	design	cross	orn.	rel.	sign.
407	**S:t Per**	Bärmö		X	m			fr.			—	—	—	—
408		Bärmö; Granby house		X	m?		3,4	2fr.	(53×2)	3c?	—	—	+?	—
N29[85]		Bärmö		A 3	s		2	—	260	6	A–C?	—	—	—
N30[86]		Billby		E 3	m	2b	2	—	130	?	B	—	+	—
409	**S:t Olov**	Lövstaholm		A 1	m	3a	2	—	160	7	A	—	+	—
410		N.Til		A 1	s	3a	8	—	155	7	B	—	—	—
411		N.Til		A 1	s	3b	7	—	174	6	B	—	+	—
412		Viby		E 10.05	m	3b	5	—	170	6	B	—	—	—
413	**Norrsunda**	Norr.ch.	rec.	A 3.2	m	4	10	3s	175	1(sds)	A	—	—	—
414#		Norr.ch.		A 2	m	2a	10	—	?	6(go)	A?	—	—	—
415[87]		Norr.ch.		X 10?20?			10	h.fr.		?	—	—	—	—

[68] U 364: ATA 4374/50. [69] U N25: *FV* 1979, 244; *FV* 1993, 234. [70] U N26: ATA 3500/43. [71] U 374: ATA 2502/72.
[72] U 382: SHM 8455; *Sigtuna Fornhem. [73] U 384: *Sigtuna Fornhem. [74] U N27: *FV* 1958, 250.
[75] U 386: SHM 12272; *Sigtuna Fornhem. [76] U 388: *FV* 1970, 305; SHM 8272:2 and 29114; *Sigtuna Fornhem.
[77] U 389: *Sigtuna Fornhem. [78] U 390: *FV* 1958, 252; *Sigtuna town park. U N28 is part of U 390. [79] U 395: *Sigtuna Fornhem.
[80] U 398: *Sigtuna Fornhem: 1397. [81] U 399: *Sigtuna Fornhem: 1401. [82] U 403: 'Sigtuna Fornhem: 1253.
[83] U N28: this is part of U 390. [84] U 405: SHM 29973; *Sigtuna Fornhem. [85] U N29: *FV* 1983, 228. [86] U N30: *FV* 1955, 216.
[87] U 415: *FV* 1986, 87.

id.	parish	place	type	rel.sh.	s/m	dat.	fsp.	state	height	design	cross	orn.	rel.	sign.
418		Brista		E 1	m	3a	7,8	dam.	190	7+mbd	A	—	+	—
419[88]		Norslunda		E 6	m	2b	7	—	302	7	A	—	+	—
420		Rosersberg		X 30			5	fr.	(122)	6?	B	—	—	—
421		Rosersberg		C 1.5	m		5	—	120	6	B	—	—	—
422		Rosersberg		A 10?20?.4	m?	2a?	3	2s	85	3a+2(2)	A	—	—	—
423[89]		Rosersberg		A 1	s	3a	2	—	200	6	B?	—	+	—
424#		Rosersberg		A 3	s	3a	2	—	200	6	—	—	+	—
425#[90]		Rosersberg		A 1?	m		3	—	120	6	—	—	—	—
N31[91]		Rosersberg	rock	A 1	s		7	—	137	6	B	—	—	Heriar?
426		Vallstanäs		A 3	s	2a	2,7	—	160	6	B	—	—	—
428[92]		Viggeby		E 3	m	3a	7,8	dam.	256	6	—	+	—	—
429c		Åshusby		E 3	m	2b	7	—	120	5/6	—	—	—	—
430c[93]		Åshusby		E 3	m	2a	7	—	80	5/6	H?	—	—	—
431[94]		Åshusby		E 3	m	2b	7	—	195	5/6	A	—	+	—
432#		Åshusby		A 3	s		1,4	—		?	—	—	—	—
433m	Husby-Ärlinghundra	Hus.-Ärl.ch.		A 8	s	3b?	10	—	104	5/6	—	—	—	—
434[95]		Hus.-Ärl.ch.		X 10	s	4?	10	2fr.	(90 +52)	?	—	—	—	—
435		Hus-Ärl.ch.		E 10.05?	m	2b	10	—	195	6	A	—	+	—
436[96]		Arnberga		X	s?	2a?	3	pt.	(80)	2(2)	—	—	—	—
437[97]		Broby		E 6.10	m	2a	6,7	—	325	7?	A	—	—	—
438[98]		Ekilla		E 1? 10.05?	m	3a	2	—	240	6	A	—	+	—
N32[99]		Måby		A 2	m	2b		—		7	D	—	—	—
439#		Steninge		C 1	m	2b?		—		7	D	—	—	—
440	Odensala	Odensala ch.	rec.	E 3	m	4	10	—	140	9	A	—	+	—
441#		Odens.vic.	rec.	X	m?	3–4	10	—	110	1(2)	—	—	—	—
443		Odens.vic.		X 10			10	fr.	(63)	?	A–D?	—	—	—
444c		Bromsta		A 1	m	2b?	8	—	180	6	B	—	—	—
445c		Bromsta		E 10.05	m	3b	8	2s	215	6	B(2)	—	—	—
446#		Droppsta		X 10?20?	s	3a	2	fr.	(110)	6	—	—	—	—
447#		Fransåker		A 2	m	2a	8	—	185	6	H?	—	+	—
448		Harg		A 1	m	2b	7	—	180	6	—	+	—	—
449		Harg		X	m	2a	8	fr.	(80)	?	—	+	—	—
451#		Hova		X 20		2b	3	fr.	(90)	6	B	—	—	—
452#		Hova		X	m		3	fr.		?	A–D?	—	—	—
453m		Kumla		A 1	m	3a	5	dam.	155	5/6	B–C?	—	+	—
454m		Kumla		A 2.6	m	3a	2	—	106	6	B	—	—	Visäte
455		Näsby		AB 1	s	3b	8	—	275	8a	—	—	—	—
456		Tollsta		X 10	m		7	2s,dam.	126	6	A	—	—	—
457c	Haga	Skråmsta		A 3	s	2a	8	—	180	6	B	—	+	—
458c[100]		Skråmsta		A 1	s?		3	2fr.	(55)	?	—	—	—	—
459c		Skråmsta		E 10.03	m	2b	5,7,8	—	270	8b	B	—	—	—
460		Skråmsta		E 10.05	m	3a	5,8	—	338	8	—	—	—	—
461		Torslunda		E 1.05	m	2b	2	—	215	6/7	D	—	+	—
462	Vassunda	Vass.vic.		E 1.05	m	3a	7	2s	215	8a+2	B	—	—	Öpir
463		Ala		E 10.05	m	3a	5,8	—	235	8a	B	—	—	—
464		Edeby		C 3	s		7	—	190	6	C	—	+	Fot
465#		Smedby		C 5	s	2a	7	—	205	6	D	—	+	—
467		Tibble		X 60	s?	2a	7	dam.	230	6	A–D?	—	+	Torbjörn
470	Knivsta	Knivsta ch.		X 10			10	—	85	?	B	—	+	—
471		Segersta		A 1	m	3a	7,8	—	207	6	B	—	+	—
472m		Skottsela		C 4	s	3b	7	—	170	6	B	—	—	—
473m		Skottsela	rock	A 2	s	3b	7	—	128	6	—	—	—	—
474		Vickeby		E 20.03	m	2a	10	—	206	6	A+B	—	+	—
475		Vickeby	rock	B 1	s	3b	5	—	151	6	A	—	—	—
476#		Vickeby		A 6	m	2b	6	dam.	160	6	A	—	—	—
477#		Vickeby		X 30		2a	7	fr.	(150)	?	A–D?	—	—	—
478		Ängby		E 05.10	m	2a	6	—	175	5/6	B	—	+	—
N33[101]	Alsike	Alsike ch.		E 3.20	m		10	—	190	6	A	—	—	Öpir
479c		Alsike vic.		A 1	m	2a	7	—	180	5/6	A+D	—	—	Ulvkel
480c		Tagsta		A 1	m	3a	7	—	220	7	B	—	—	—

Långhundra härad

id.	parish	place	type	rel.sh.	s/m	dat.	fsp.	state	height	design	cross	orn.	rel.	sign.
481	**Lagga**	Lagga ch.; ch.yd.		A 1	m	3b	10	—	174	6	B	—	—	—

Continued

[88] U 419: *Skansen. [89] U 423: *FV* 1988, 240. [90] U 425: *NOR* 1996, 16. [91] U N31: *FV* 1988, 241.
[92] U 428: Källström (1998), 27 f. [93] U 430: *Norrsunda church. [94] U 431: *Norrsunda church. [95] U 434: *FV* 1992, 155.
[96] U 436: *SHM 31326. [97] U 437: ATA 5368/56. [98] U 438: *Steninge. [99] U N32: *FV* 1992, 157; *Arlanda.
[100] U 458: *FV* 1979, 240. [101] U N33: *FV* 1948, 168.

id.	parish	place	type	rel.sh.	s/m	dat.	fsp.	state	height	design	cross	orn.	rel.	sign.
482		Kasby		A 2	m	2a?	3	—	197	6	—	—	—	—
484		Kasby		A 1	s	2b	5	—	150	6	—	+	—	—
485		Marma		E 10.05	m	4	7	—	184	6	A	—	—	Ofeg Öpir
486[102]	(Mora stenar)	Morby		X 10/?			8	—	83	?	—	—	—	—
488[103]		Morby		X			2	fr.	(83)	?	B?	—	+	—
489[104]		Morby		D 3	s	3b	7	—	164	8a	A	—	+	Öpir
490		Olunda		A 2	m	2a	7	—	188	3a(2)	A	—	+	—
491		Årby		X		3a?	3	fr.	(60)	?	—	—	—	—
492		Örby		A 1	m	3b	7,8	—	169	8a	—	—	—	—
N34[105]	Östuna	Risberga		AB 1	m?		8	—	147	?	B	—	—	—
494	Husby-Långhundra	Hus.-Långh.ch.		A 1	s		10	dam.	141	6	—	—	—	—
495		Hus.-Långh.ch.		A 1	m	3a	10	—	200	6	B	—	—	—
496m		Tibble		A 1/6	s	3b	6,8	dam.	162	6	A	—	+	—
497m		Tibble	rock	AB 1	s	3b	5	—	225	8a	A	—	—	—
498#		Åby		A 6/1	m		2	—	175	5?	A?	—	—	—
500	Gottröra	Johannesberg		X 10	m	4	2	—	166	6	—	—	—	—
501	Närtuna	Närtuna ch.		A 1/?	m	4	10	—	240	6	—	—	—	—
502		Ingelsta		A 1/2	s?	2a	5	fr.	(145)	3/4?	—	—	—	—
503c		Malmby		A 1	m	3b?	2?	—	207	6	B	—	—	—
504c		Ubby		A 1	s	2a	8	—	188	3c	A	—	+	—
505	Kårsta	Kårsta ch.		A 3.2	m	3–4	10	—	162	6	A	—	—	Sven
506#		Broby		A 1/2	m		7	—	250	6	—	—	—	—
508		Gillberga		C 1/6	m	2a	2	—	164	3c	—	+	—	—
509		N.Hall	rock	A 1/2	s		8	—	115	6	—	—	—	—
510c		Mälsta		A 1	m		8	—	225	6	B	—	—	—
511c		Mälsta		A 1	m	3b	8	—	164	6	B	—	—	—

Sjuhundra härad

id.	parish	place	type	rel.sh.	s/m	dat.	fsp.	state	height	design	cross	orn.	rel.	sign.
512	Fasterna	Tjäran		A 1/2	m	2a	2	fr.	(80)	3/4?	—	—	+	—
513m	Rimbo	Rimbo ch.		A 2	m	2a	10	—	227	6	A/C?	—	+	—
514m		Rimbo ch.		A 1.6	m	4	10	—	243	6	H?	—	—	—
515		Rimbo ch.		A 1	s	3b	10	—	167	6	—	—	+	—
516#		Rimbo ch.		X	m		10	fr.	?	?	—	—	—	—
517[106] (+558?)	Skederid	Sked.ch.		E 20.05	m		10	fr.	(107)	3a?	A	—	—	X
518		V.Ledinge		E 6	m	2a	8	—	?	3c	B	—	+	—
519		Salmunge		A 1	m	2b	5	—	148	5/6	H?	—	+	Tolir?
520#		Salmunge		X	m		5	fr.	(40)	?	—	—	—	—

Frötuna and Länna skeppslag

id.	parish	place	type	rel.sh.	s/m	dat.	fsp.	state	height	design	cross	orn.	rel.	sign.
521#	Länna	Länna ch.		X	m		10	fr.	(110)	5/6?	—	—	—	—
524		Penningby		A 6	m		5,7,8	—	150	7	—	—	—	Vidbjörn
525		Österlisa		X 10			?	—	146	6	A–C?	—	—	—
526	Frötuna	Frötuna ch.		X 10 + A7 or C5?			10	2fr.	?	?	—	—	—	—
527[107]		Frötuna ch.		A 1	s		10	dam.	(84)	8b?	—	—	—	—
530#	Norrtälje	Norrtälje		A 1	m		5	—	?	6	—	—	—	—
531		Kvisthamra	rock	X 30/10		4?	5	dam.	155	6 ?	A–C?	—	—	—

Bro and Vätö skeppslag

id.	parish	place	type	rel.sh.	s/m	dat.	fsp.	state	height	design	cross	orn.	rel.	sign.
532m	Roslagsbro	Rosl.ch.		C 5	s	2a	10	—	150	6	C?	—	+	Torbjörn
533m		Rosl.ch.		C 3	s		10	—	127	6	—	—	—	—
537		Bredsätra		X	m		8	dam.	(110)	?	—	—	—	—
538[108]		Ösby		X (C 5?)	s?		3	fr.	(70)	6?	—	—	—	—

Lyhundra härad

id.	parish	place	type	rel.sh.	s/m	dat.	fsp.	state	height	design	cross	orn.	rel.	sign.
539	Husby-Lyhundra	Hus.-Lyh.ch.		A 2	m	2a	10	3s	248	3a	A–C?	—	+	—
540		Hus.-Lyh.ch.		E 6	m	3a	10	—	150	8b	—	—	+	—
541		Hus.-Lyh.ch.rec.		0		3–4	10	—	142	6	—	—	—	Öpir
545m[109]		Hus.-Lyh.ch.		C 5/1	s		10	3fr.	(142)	8b	—	—	—	—

[102] U 486: *SHM 25555. [103] U 488: ATA 5369/58. [104] U 489: *Uppsala University park. [105] U N34: *FV* 1980, 237.
[106] U 517: *FV* 1949, 249; *FV* 1984, 255. [107] U 527: ATA 4761/62. [108] U 538: *FV* 1954, 10. [109] U 545: *FV* 1979, 242.

id.	parish	place	type	rel.sh.	s/m	dat.	fsp.	state	height	design	cross	orn.	rel.	sign.
546m[110]		Hus.-Lyh.ch.		A 1	m		10	2pts.	163	7	A?	—	—	—
547		Hus.-Lyh.ch.		X	s	3b	10	fr.	(83)	?	—	—	+	—
550		Hus.-Lyh.ch.		X 10			10	fr.	(48)	?	A–C?	—	—	—
555		Hus.-Lyh.ch.		X 20			10	fr.	(44)	?	A	—	—	—
557#		Hus.-Lyh.vic.		X	m		3	fr.	?	?	—	—	—	—
558 (+517?)[111]		Hus.-Lyh.vic.		X	m		?	fr.	(106)	5+	—	—	+	—
560	Malsta	Malsta ch.		X	m		10	fr.	(102)	6?	—	—	—	—
565m#		Ekeby skog		E 3.20	m	3b	1	—	200	6	A	—	—	Öpir
566m		Vällingsö	rock	A 2	s		5,7	—	176	8b	—	—	—	Öpir
568#	Lohärad	Lohärad vic.		A 7b? C 5?			10	fr.	?	?	—	—	—	—
570		Hållsta		A 1	m	3a	7	dam.	118	7	—	—	—	—
571		Hållsta		X 10			3	fr.	(52)	?	—	—	—	—
572		Kragsta		E 05.20	m	3b	2	—	126	6	—	—	—	—
573		Kragsta		A 1	m	3a	2	—	180	6	B/C?	—	—	—
574	Estuna	Estuna ch.		E–EF?	m		10	fr.	(106)	?	—	—	—	—
575		Estuna ch.		X 20/60?			10	2fr.	?	?	—	—	—	—
576		Estuna ch.		X 60?			10	2fr.	?	?	—	—	—	—
577#		Estuna ch.		X 60?			10	—	?	?	—	—	—	—
578#		Eneby		E 20.03?	m		?	—	?	8a	—	—	+	—
579		Hårdnacka		A 2			5,6	dam.	176	6	—	—	—	—
580		Hårdnacka		X 30	m		3	3fr.	?	?	—	—	—	—
582#	Söderby-Karl	Söd.-Karl ch.		E 3	m		10	—	180	5	—	—	—	—
585#		Igelsta		A 3.6	m		7	—	180	5	A–C?	—	+	—

Närdinghundra härad

id.	parish	place	type	rel.sh.	s/m	dat.	fsp.	state	height	design	cross	orn.	rel.	sign.
586[112]	Edsbro	Bro		E 10.05?	m	2a	2	2s,2pts.	175	3c	—	—	+	—
590	Knutby	Burvik		A 4?	s		5	—	161	6	—	+	—	Östen
592		Gränsta		A 1	m	4	3	2s,fr.	(43)	5+2	—	—	—	—
N35[113]	Ununge	Berga		X 30			3	—	220	3a	A?	—	—	—

Väddö and Häverö skeppslag

id.	parish	place	type	rel.sh.	s/m	dat.	fsp.	state	height	design	cross	orn.	rel.	sign.
593	Väddö	Ortala		A 2	m		5,8	—	102	5	A/H?	—	—	—
594[114]		Ortalalund		X	m		2,8	fr.	(80)	?	—	—	—	—

Frösåker härad

id.	parish	place	type	rel.sh.	s/m	dat.	fsp.	state	height	design	cross	orn.	rel.	sign.
595	Harg	Harg skog		AB 10/04	m		7	2s	242	5/6	H+A	+	—	—
597	Hökhuvud	Hök.vic.		A 1	m	3b	6	fr.	(145)	8b?	—	—	—	—
598		Borggårde	rock	A 2	m		7	—	142	6	A	+	—	Ödmund?
599		Hanunda		A 1	m		7	—	185	7	—	+	—	Torfast
600	Börstil	Sund		C 3	s	3b	8	—	128	6	A	—	—	—

Bro härad

id.	parish	place	type	rel.sh.	s/m	dat.	fsp.	state	height	design	cross	orn.	rel.	sign.
604	Stockholms-Näs	Stäket		A 2	m		7	—	136	6	B	—	—	—
605#		Stäket	rock	D 8	s		6,7	—	120	7	—	—	pil-grim	Fot
606#	V.Ryd	V.Ryd ch.		E 10.05	m	2a	10	—	160	6	B?	—	—	—
608m[115]		V.Ryd vic.; ch.		X	m		3	dam.	135	4a	B		—	—
610#		Granhammar		X 30	s		3	fr.		4?	A–D?	—	—	—
611		Tibble		E 3	m	2a	2	—	155	5/6	B		—	—
613m[116]		Torsätra		C 3	s	3b	7	—	155	6	B	—	bap-tism	—
614m[117]		Torsätra		A 2	m	3a	7	—	145	6	—	—	—	—
615#		Tranbygge		A 1	s		2	—	195	4b	D?	—	+	—
616		Tång		A 1/2	s	2a	7	—	190	5/6	B	—	+	—
617c	Bro	Bro ch.		C 5	s	2a	6,10	—	157	3a+4a	A	—	+	—
618		Bro ch.		C 1.5	m	4	10	—	127	6	—	—	—	—
619[118]		Bro ch.		X	m?	4	10	fr.		6?	—	—	—	—
620[119]		Finnsta		A 2	m	2b	7	dam.	185	6	B	—	+	—
621mc		Härnevi		E 10.05	m	2b	6	—	200	7	B	—	—	—
622mc		Härnevi; vic.		E 03.60?	m?	2–3	7	dam.	150	6	—	—	+	—

Continued

[110] U 546: *FV* 1979, 241. [111] U 558 (+517?) *FV* 1984, 255; *Husby-Lyhundra church. [112] U 586: *FV* 1954, 9; ATA 4144/52.
[113] U N35:: *FV* 1992, 169. [114] U 594: *Väddö folkhögskola. [115] U 608: *Västra Ryd church. [116] U 613: *SHM.
[117] U 614: *SHM. [118] U 619: *FV* 1973, 191. [119] U 620: ATA 6420/86.

id.	parish	place	type	rel.sh.	s/m	dat.	fsp.	state	height	design	cross	orn.	rel.	sign.
623		Jursta		E 1	m	3a	7	—	135	6	C	—	—	—
624		Ullvi, Toresta		A 1	m	3b	8	—	237	6	B	—	—	—
625[120]		Välla tä		X 4?	m	3b	7	—	188	6	A?	—	—	—

Håbo härad

id.	parish	place	type	rel.sh.	s/m	dat.	fsp.	state	height	design	cross	orn.	rel.	sign.
626	Håbo-Tibble	Bälby		A 2/1	m		3	fr.		6+1	A?	—	—	—
627#		Jädra tä		A 1	m		7	—	175	6	B?	—	+	—
628#		Jädra tä		A 1	m		7	—	185	5/6?	A?	—	—	—
629		Grynsta backe		A 1	m	3a	7	—	225	7	A?	+	+	Torfast
630		V.Tibble		A 1	s	2b	8	—	260	8b	B	—	—	—
631m[121]	Kalmar	Kalmar ch.		A 1	s		10	2s	167	6	—	+	—	—
632m		Kalmar ch.		A 2?	m?	3b?	10	2s,7fr.		6?	Eg(2) +C?	+	—	—
633		Broby		C 5	s		6	—	138	5	—	+	—	—
634#		Enby	rock	A 1	s		7	dam.	125	8a	A	—	—	—
635c		Låddersta		A 1	m	3b	7	—	160	6	B	—	—	—
636c		Låddersta		C 3	s	2b	2	—	127	5/6	A	—	—	—
637		Låddersta		E 10.05	m	2b	2	—	160	6	B	—	—	—
638#		Mansängen		0	?		7	dam.	225	3b	—	—	—	—
639#		Skörby		X 10	s		7	fr.		6?	A–D?	—	—	—
640mc		Väppeby		A 1	m	3a	6	—	212	6	B	—	—	—
641m	Yttergran	Brunnsta br.		A 6	m		5,7	—	205	6	C	—	—	—
642m[122]		Ekilla br.		A 1	m	3b	6,8	—	220	6	C	—	—	—
643c[123]		Ekilla br.		A 1	m	3a?	6,8	—	227	6	—	—	—	—
644mc		Ekilla br.		A 1	m	2b	7,8	—	220	7	D(2)	—	+	—
645		Lundby		A 2	s	3a	7	—	118	8a	B	—	+	—
646		Yttergrans by		A 1	s	3a?	7	—	160	8b	B	—	—	—
647m[124]	Övergran	Övergran ch.		C 1	s	2b	10	—	157	4a	—	—	—	Balle
648mc		Övergran ch.		A 2	s	3b	10	—	168	6	A–C?	—	—	—
649		Övergran ch.		A 1	m	2b	10	—	155	8a	B	—	—	—
650[125]		Jädra		A 1	m	3a	2	—	229	4a	B	—	+	—
651[126]		Kumla		A 2	m	2b	2	—	170	8a?	—	—	—	—
652		Kumla		CD 08/30	s	2b	2	—	246	7	B	—	—	Arbjörn
653		Kumla		A 1	m	3a	2	—	215	8b	B	—	—	—
654mc		Varpsund		A 1	m	2b	5	—	294	7+2	D	—	+	Alrik?
655	Håtuna	Håtuna ch.		A 2	m	2a	10	—	189	6	—	—	—	—
656[127]		Bjursta		C 3	s		8	—	190	6	B	—	—	—
657[128]		Kålsta		A 1	m	2b	7	—	152	5/6	A	—	—	—
658[129]		Nibble		A 1	s		3	5fr.		?	B	—	—	—
659		Nibble		A 6	m	3a	1	—	150	6	B	—	—	—
660[130]		Norränge		A 1	m	3b	5	—	238	6	B	—	—	—
661		Råby		C 1	m	2b	8	—	200	7	A–C?	—	+	—
662		Signhildsberg		E 6?	m	2b	5,7	—	151	5/6	H?	—	—	—
663		Signhildsberg		C 3	s	2a	?	—	111	4a	A	—	—	—
665	Häggeby	Finstaholm		A 1	m	2b	7	—	145	5/6	D (circle)	—	—	—
667		Hassla		A 1	m	2b	7	—	185	6	B	—	—	—
668m		Kålsta		A 1	m	3a	3	—	204	7	A–C?	—	+	—
669m#		Kålsta		A 2	m		3	—	210	5–6	B	—	+	Visäte, Ofeg
670		Rölunda		X 30			8	—	145	3a?	—	—	+?	—
671		Rölunda ås		A 1	s	2b	2,7	—	110	5/6	D	—	—	—
672		Rölunda		X 10	m		8	dam.	132	?(circle)	—	—	—	—
673#		Rölunda		X			?	fr.		?	—	—	—	—
674		Skadevi		A 1	m	3a	2,7	—	130	6	B	—	—	—
675#		Skadevi		A 3	s		2,7	fr.	(95)	6	—	—	—	—
676		Viksjö		A 2	m	2b	7	—	235	8b+3	B	—	—	—
677		Viksjö		X	m		7	fr.	(93)	?	—	—	—	—
678	Skokloster	Skokl.ch.		A 1	m		10	2s	220	4a+1	B	+	—	Fot
679		Skokl.ch.		X 10	m	2b	10	—	125	6	A	—	—	—
681		Skokl.ch.		A 4	s		2	—	108	5	A	—	+	—
682#		Kaddala		C 5?/3	s		2	—	150	6	—	—	—	Arbjörn
683		Linda		A 1	m	2b	2,7	2fr.	?	6	—	—	—	—
684		Råberga		A 1	m	3b	2,8	—	195	8a	A	—	—	—
685		Sanda		A 1	m	2b	2	—	126	6	B	—	—	—
686		Sanda		A 1	m	2b	2,8	—	195	6	B	—	—	—

[120] U 625: *Säbyholm, Låssa parish. [121] U 631: *SHM 24732. [122] U 642: *Ekolsund, Husby-Sjutolft parish.
[123] U 643: *Ekolsund, Husby-Sjutolft parish. [124] U 647: Jansson (1964), 10. [125] U 650: *Signhildsberg.
[126] U 651: *Övergran church. [127] U 656: *FV* 1954, 8; *Markeby. [128] U 657: *Nyborg. [129] U 658: *Håtuna church.
[130] U 660: *Håtuna church.

id.	parish	place	type	rel.sh.	s/m	dat.	fsp.	state	height	design	cross	orn.	rel.	sign.
687		Sjusta	rock	C 3 + C 5	m	3b	1	—	(148)	8b	A	—	'church'	Öpir
688[131]		Stavsund		A 1	m		3	3fr.	250	7	B	—	—	Arbjörn
689		Säby		A 2	m	2b	7	—	137	8b	—	—	—	—

Trögd härad

id.	parish	place	type	rel.sh.	s/m	dat.	fsp.	state	height	design	cross	orn.	rel.	sign.
690	Arnö[132]	Hälsingbo		C 3	s	3a	7	—	212	7	—	+	+	—
691[133]		Söderby		A 3	s	3a	7	—	300	7	—	+	+	—
692		Väppeby		A 1	m	3b	3,5	2s	137	4a	—	+	—	Ödbjörn
N36[134]	Torsvi	Torsvi gård		X 20?				fr.	(96)	?	—	—	—	—
695	Veckholm	Veck.ch.		E 3	m	3a	10	—	140	4a?	—	—	—	—
696		Veck.ch.		X 70a	s	3a	10	—	150	4a	A	+	+	—
697#		Veck.ch.		X 10	m		10	fr.	?	?	—	—	—	—
698#		Veck.ch.		A 3	s		10	—	?	5?	—	—	—	—
699[135]		Arnö		C 5	s	3a	2	—	152	4a	A	—	baptism	Balle
700m		Kynge		A 2	s	2b	2	—	142	5/6	—	—	+	—
701m#		Kynge; ch.		A 2	s		10	—	140	5/6	—	—	+	—
(702m cross D: no inscription)														
703		V.Väppeby		C 3	s	3a	5	dam.	230	7	—	+	—	—
(704 beast)														
705m[136]		Ö.-Dalby		X	m	3a	2,7	fr.	?	6/7?	B	—	—	Balle
706m		Ö.-Dalby	rock	A 1	m	3a	7	dam.	110	8b?	—	—	—	—
707[137]	Kungs-Husby	Kungs-Hus.ch.		A 1	s		10	dam.	161	6–8	—	—	—	Balle
708		Kungs-Hus.ch.		A 2	s	3a	10	—	167	4a	—	—	—	—
710[138]		Kungs-Hus.; ch.		X 60			3	fr.	?	?	—	—	—	—
712m[139]		Skeberga		A 2	s		6,7	dam.	109	4	—	—	—	X
713m#		Skeberga		A 2	m		7	dam.	?	3/4?	—	+	—	—
714#		Skeberga		X			7	—	?	?	—	—	—	—
716	Lillkyrka	Viggby		E 10.05?	m	3b	2	—	205	4a	—	+	—	—
718#	Vallby	Vallby ch.		X	m		10	—	?	?	—	—	—	—
719		Folsberga		A 6	s	3b	7	—	226	5/6	—	+	+	—
720		Hånningby		A 1	m	2b	7,8	—	180	6	—	—	—	—
721	Löt	Löt ch.		C 6	s	3a	10	—	119	4a	—	—	—	Balle
722		Löt ch.		A 2	s	3a	10	2s,dam.	133	2(2)sd	—	—	+	—
723m		Hummelsta		A 1	m	3a	7	—	108	5/6	—	—	—	—
724m		Hummelsta		A 1	m	3a	7	—	133	7	B	—	+	—
(725m beast: no inscription)														
726		Ramby		A 1	s	2b	2	2s	194	6	—	+	+	Balle
727		Tängby	rock	A 1	m	3a	7	dam.	150	8a(2)	—	—	+	—
729		Ågersta		A 1	s	3b	7,8	—	207	8b(2)	—	—	—	Balle
731#	Villberga	Grillby		X	s		10	fr.	?	?	—	—	—	—
732		Grillby		A 2	s	2b	10	—	178	5/6	B	—	—	—
733#		Hässleby		A 3	s	3a	3	dam.	?	6/7?	—	—	—	Tidkume
734		Linsunda		A 8	s		7	—	138	5/6	—	+	—	Lidsvald?
735m		Långarnö		E 3	m	3a	2	—	190	7	B	—	—	—
736m#		Långarnö		X			?	fr.	?	?	—	—	—	—
738		Villberga by		X 40		2	3	fr.	?	?	B	—	+	—
739	Boglösa	Gådi		A 8	s	3a	7	—	144	7	B	—	—	—
740		Hemsta		A 2	s	3a	7	dam.	236	7	—	—	—	Balle
741#		Hemsta		A 3	s	2	7	—	?	4b	A/H?	—	—	—
742		Myrby		A 1	s	3b	2	—	150	4a	—	+	—	Tidkume
744[140]	Husby-Sjutolft	Gidsmarken		C 5	s	3a	2	—	185	4a	—	—	—	Balle
745#		Hammaren		E 2?	m	2b	7	—	?	6?	—	—	—	—
746		Hårby		A 3	s	3b	7	—	160	8a	—	+	—	Torgöt
749		Sävsta		A 1/2 + A 1	m	3	7	—	187	7	—	+	—	—
750		Viggby		A 2	m	3a	7	—	173	8a	—	—	—	Balle
751		Viggby		A 1	m	3a	2,7,9	dam.	220	7	—	+	—	—
753	Litslena	Litslena vic.		C 5/6	s	3a	8	—	230	7	—	+	—	Balle
755		Kälsta		A 6	m	2b	7,8	—	195	5/6	B	—	—	—
756		Ullstämma	rock	A 1	m	3a	7	—	326	6	B	—	—	Balle
757		Ullstämma		A 6	m		2	dam.	180	5	—	—	—	—

Continued

131 U 688: *FV* 1971, 210.
132 Arnö parish is now divided between Kungs-Husby parish in Uppland and Aspö parish in Södermanland.
133 U 691: *Veckol, Aspö parish, Södermanland. 134 U N36: *FV* 1993, 235. 135 U 699: *Ekholmen. 136 U 705: *Mobacka.
137 U 707: *FV* 1966, 29. 138 U 710: *Kungs-Husby church. 139 U 712: *FV* 1969, 302.
140 U 744: *Ekolslund, Husby-Sjutolft parish.

Åsunda härad

id.	parish	place	type	rel.sh.	s/m	dat.	fsp.	state	height	design	cross	orn.	rel.	sign.
758[141]	Enköping town	Enköp.ch.		A 1	m	3b	10	—	232	7	—	+	+	Tidkume
759[142]		Enköp.ch.		A 1	m	3b	10	—	186	7	—	+	+	Tidkume
(760 = same stone as 796; one part in Enköping church, the other in Sparrsätra church)														
761#		Enköp.		X 10				fr.		?	—	—	—	—
762m	Vårfrukyrka	Brunna		A 3	s	2b		dam.	115	6	B	—	—	—
N37[143]		Gånsta		X 60			7	—	140	?	—	—	—	—
763m		Klista		A 1	m	3a	7	—	183	7	—	+	—	—
764m		Klista		A 1	m	3a	7	—	180	7	—	+	—	—
766m		Norrby		A 3/8	s	3b	8	—	120	6	—	+	—	—
767m		Norrby		A 6	s	3b	8	—	135	4a	—	+	—	Livsten
768m		Norrby		A 6	m	2b	8	—	162	6	B	—	—	—
769[144]		Testeby		A 3	s	2b	2	—	165	6	B	—	+	—
770mc?		Tjursåker		C 1	m	3a	6,7	2s	242	7	—	+	—	Balle
771		Tjursåker	rock	A 3	s	3a	6	—	225	?	—	+	—	Tidkume
773	Enköpings-Näs	Enk.-Näs ch.		E 6	m	3a	10	—	155	7	—	—	—	—
774		Hjulsta		A 4	m	2b	6	—	180	6	B	—	+	—
775[145]		Väppeby		E 6	m	3b	7,8	—	250	7	—	+	—	Tidkume
776[146]		Väppeby		A 1?	s		3	5fr.	187	4a	—	—	—	—
778	Svinnegarn	Svinn.ch.		E 3	m	2b	10	—	235	7	B	—	+	Eskil
779m		Svinn.ch.		A 3	s	2b	10	—	182	6	B	—	+	—
780		Svinn.ch.		A 2	m	3b	10	—	110	7	—	+	—	—
781[147]		Svinn.ch.	?	X		?	10	2fr.	200+	?	—	—	+	—
785	Tillinge	Tillinge ch.		A 2	s	2a	10	—	169	?	—	—	+	—
786m		Hansta		A 2	s	2b	2	—	155	6	—	—	+	—
(787m)		Hansta		0			2	—	142	?	C?	—	—	—
788		St.Järstena		X 30			3	2fr.		?	—	—	—	—
789		Mälby		C 5	s	3b	2	—	190	6	—	+	—	—
790#		Mälby		A 3	s		8			?	—	—	—	—
N38[148]		Skinna		A 1	m		2,5?	—	220	7	—	—	—	—
791		Tibble	rock	A 3	s	3b	7	—	150	6	—	+	—	—
792		Ulunda		A 1.4	m	2b	6,8	—	165	6	B	—	—	—
793		Ulunda		C 5	s	2b	6,7	—	174	6	B	—	+	—
794		Vindsberga	rock	X 10			1	—	175	5?	—	+	—	—
795	Bred	Bred ch.		A 3	s	3b	10	—	128	8b	—	—	—	—
796=760[149]	Sparrsätra	Sparr.ch.		A 3	s	3b	10	2pts.	194+	7	—	+	—	Livsten
797		Nyby		A 1	m	3b	7	—	204	7	—	—	—	—
798#		Torgesta		A 6	s	2b	7	—		6	B	—	+	—

Lagunda härad

id.	parish	place	type	rel.sh.	s/m	dat.	fsp.	state	height	design	cross	orn.	rel.	sign.
799	Långtora	Långt.ch.	rec.	A 6	s	3–4	10	—	190	9	—	—	—	Johan
800[150]		Långt.ch.		A 3	s		10	fr.	139	4a	—	—	—	—
802		Långt.field; ch.yd.		A 3	s	2b	2	—	114	7	B	—	—	—
803		Långt.by		A 8	s	3b?	6,7	2s	190	3a	A?	+	—	—
805d	Fröslunda	Frös.ch.		A 2.1?	m		10	—	(130)	?	—	—	—	—
807		Enberga; Frös.ch.		X 60			7	fr.		?	—	—	+	—
808		Enberga		AB 1	m	3a	7,8	—	207	7	D	—	+	—
809		Härvesta		A 1	m	2b	7	—	156	5/6	A	—	—	—
810		Nopskäl		X	m	3a	3	—	109	7	B	—	—	—
812	Hjälsta	Hjälsta ch.		X 10		2b	10	—	130	6	D	—	—	—
813		Brunnsta		A 3?	s		2	dam.	(105)	3/4?	—	—	+	—
814		Bälsunda		A 1	m	3a	2,8	—	140	6	B	—	—	—
815		Bälsunda		AB 1	s	3a	2,5	—	188	4a	A(2)	—	+	—
816#		Bälsunda		X	s		7	—		?	—	—	—	—
817#		Bälsunda		A 1	m		7	—		8	—	—	—	—
818	Kulla	Gryta		E 6	m	2b	2,6,7	—	128	5/6	D+A	—	+	—
819m[151]		Mysinge		A 1	s	3a	2,8	—	180	7	B	—	+	Balle
(820m[152]		Mysinge		0	—		2,8		—	—	—	—	—	—)
821c[153]		Mysinge		C 1 + CD 50/03	m	3b	5,7	—	202	6	B	—	—	—
823m# (+822)		Rävsta		X	s		2	—		?	—	(+)	—	—

[141] U 758: *Afzeliusparken, Enköping. [142] U 759: *Skolparken, Enköping. [143] U N37: ATA 6243/65. [144] U 769: *Valla.
[145] U 775: *Hjulsta. [146] U 776: *FV* 1972, 269. [147] U 781: ATA 365/61. [148] U N38: *FV* 1973, 146.
[149] U 796 and 760 are parts of the same stone: one part is in Enköping church, the other in Sparrsätra church; *FV* 1995, 45.
[150] U 800: *FV* 1955, 222. [151] U 819: *Friberg's allé. [152] U 820: ATA 5056/64, without inscription. [153] U 821: *Friberg's allé.

id.	parish	place	type	rel.sh.	s/m	dat.	fsp.	state	height	design	cross	orn.	rel.	sign.
824	**Holm**	Holm ch.		E 6	m	3b?	10	—	222	5/6	—	+	—	Åsmund
825		Gymminge		X 30	s	3b	7	—	130	6	—	—	—	—
826#		Mysinge		A 1	s		7	—	170	6	B	—	—	—
827[154]		Valby		E 60.03	m	3b	8	—	168	6	A	—	—	—
828	**Fittja**	Bodarna		A 1	m	3b	7	dam.	193	6	—	+	+	Tidkume
829	**Giresta**	Furby	rock	A 1	m	3a	8	—	220	7	B	—	—	Balle
831[155]		Giresta by; ch.		X 30	s		2,10	dam.	(117)	3a?	—	—	—	—
836	**Nysätra**	Alsta		A 1	m	3b	2,7	—	208	6	—	—	—	—
837		Alsta		X 60			2	fr.		?	—	—	+	—
838		Ryda kungsg.		E 10.05	m	3a	7	—	260	6	—	+	—	—
839c		Ryda kungsg.		E 3	m	3b	7	—	215	6	—	—	—	—

Hagunda härad

id.	parish	place	type	rel.sh.	s/m	dat.	fsp.	state	height	design	cross	orn.	rel.	sign.
840	**Dalby**	Dalby ch.		E 1	m	3b	10	—	175	6	—	—	—	—
841[156]		Dalby ch.		X 60	s		10	fr.	(95)	?	B	—	—	—
842		Hållberga		E: C 2 + A 6 (m)		4	2,7	—	137	6	A	—	—	—
843#		Hässle		A 1	m		7	—	200	6	—	—	—	—
844m		Viggby br.		A 1	m		6,7	—	127	6	B	—	—	—
845m[157]		Viggby br.		A 2	m	2b	6,7	—	180	8b	—	—	—	—
846	**Västeråker**	Västeråker ch.		E 01.40.05?	m	3a?	10	—	272	7	B(2)	—	—	—
847		Västeråker ch.		E 3	m	3b	10	dam.	270	6	—	—	—	Åsmund
848		Torresta	rock	A 6	m	3b	7	—	137	6	—	—	—	—
849#	**Balingsta**	Bal.ch.		X	m		10	—		4a+2	D	—	—	—
851[158]		Bal.ch.	rec.	X 6	m	3b	10	—	104	6?	—	—	—	—
853[159]		Bal.school		X	s		3	—	(68)	?	—	—	—	—
854		Bal.vic.		E 05/03.60	m	3b	10	—	156	6	—	—	—	—
855[160]		Bal.vic.		E 3.20	m	2b	7	—	257	4a	—	+	—	—
856		Frövi		X		3b	5	—	125	?	—	—	—	—
857		Frövi		E 6	m	2b	5	—	150	6	B	—	+	—
859m		Måsta		E 1? 10.05?	m	3a	6,7	—	144	6	B	—	+	Åsmund
860m		Måsta; Bal.by		E 1? 10.05?	m	3a	6,7	—	170	6	B	+	+	Åsmund
861		Norsta		AB 3 +?	m	3a?	5	several fr.	250	6?	A	—	—	—
862		Säva		A 2	m	3b	7	—	140	6/8b?	—	—	—	Visäte
863#		Tibble		X 60			7	fr.		?	A	—	—	—
864#		Vik		C 1/2	s		3	—		8a	B?	—	—	—
865		Vik		A 1	m	2b	6	—	125	6/7?	B?	—	—	—
866	**Gryta**	Björnome		A 1	s	3a	?	—	230	6	B	—	+	—
867[161]		Gryta		EF: B 3 + E 10.05	m	3a	2	2pts.	180	8b	A+Eg	—	+	—
868		Ransta		X	m	3b	7,8	fr.		6	—	—	—	—
870		Säva	rock	A 2	m	2–3	7	dam.	200	7?	—	—	—	Ödbjörn?
871[162]		Ölsta		E 1	m	3b	2	—	184	6	A	—	—	Åsmund
873		Örsunda		A 1	s	3a	5,8	—	240	7	B	—	+	Balle
874#	**Hagby**	Hagby ch.		X 10	m	—	10	—	200	6/7?	—	—	—	—
875		Focksta		E 1.05	m	3a	7,8	—		6	B	—	+	—
876		Focksta		E 1	m	2b	5,7	—	155	?	D	—	—	—
878		Möjbro; Hagby ch.		C 5.1	m	3a	2	—	265	6	B/C?	—	—	—
879	**Ramsta**	Bragby	rock	A 1	m	3b	7	—	192	6	—	—	—	—
880	**Skogstibble**	Skogs.ch.		X		4	10	2s,dam.	142	8+7?	—	—	—	Öpir
881		Skogs.ch.	?	X 30?	s?	—	10	fr.		?	—	+	—	—
884c		Ingla	rock	E 10.04 +?	m	3a	7	3s	175	6?	B	+	—	Åsmund
885c		Ingla		A 1	m	3a	7	—	150	6	A	—	—	—
887		Skillsta		A 1	m	3b	8	—	291	6	—	—	—	Örik
889	**Åland**	Västerby		X	m	3b	5,6,7	dam.	200	6	—	—	+	—
890		Österby		E 10.05?	m	3b		dam.	248	7	B	—	—	—

Ulleråker härad

id.	parish	place	type	rel.sh.	s/m	dat.	fsp.	state	height	design	cross	orn.	rel.	sign.
891	**Uppsala-Näs**	U.-N. ch.		X 10	m	2b	10	fr.		7	—	—	—	—
893		Högby		E 1	m	3a	5,6,7	—	160	8b	A+Fr(2) +Fg(2)	—	—	Öpir
894		Söderby		A 1	m	3b	6,7	dam.	218	6	A	—	—	—
895[163]	**Bondkyrka**	Flogsta		A 1	m	3b	6	2s	200	8a+2	B	—	—	—

Continued

[154] U 827: *Sjö-allé. [155] U 831: *Giresta church. [156] U 841: *FV* 1959, 257. [157] U 845: ATA 4851/61. [158] U 851: *Vik.
[159] U 853: *FV* 1975, 168; ATA 441/75; *Museet för nordiska fornsaker, Uppsala. [160] U 855: *Böksta backe. [161] U 867: *FV* 1976, 97.
[162] U 871: *Skansen. [163] U 895: *Håga.

id.	parish	place	type	rel.sh.	s/m	dat.	fsp.	state	height	design	cross	orn.	rel.	sign.
896[164]		Håga		X 30	m	2a?	3	—	200	3a+	A+Fg?	—	baptism	Öpir
897		Norby	rock	B 4	s	3b	1	—	165	6	Fr	—	—	—
898		Norby	rock	E 1/20?	m	3b	8	—	148	8b	—	—	—	Öpir
899		Vårdsätra		A 1	m	3b	7	—	195	6	B	—	—	—
901m[165]	Läby	Håmö		A 1	m	3a	3	3fr.	(140)	5/6?	B	+	+	—
903		Västerby		A 2	m		7	—	146	6	B	—	—	—
904m		Västerby		A 1	m	3a	6,7	—	155	6	B	+	—	—
905[166]	Vänge	Vänge ch.; ch.yd		C 6	s	3	10	—	157	4a	Eg	+	—	—
906#		Brunna		E 03.2	m		3	—	180	6	—	—	—	—
907		Bärby		A 1	m	3b	2	—	156	8b	A	—	—	—
908		Fiby		E 10.05	m	3b	2	—	200	8a	—	—	—	—
909[167]		Finnsta		A 6	s	2a	3	—	200	5	A–C?	—	+	—
910[168]		Körlinge		E 10.05?	m?		?	—	190	6	A	—	—	—
911		Åltomta br.		X 20? E 2?	m	3a?	6	—	162	6	—	—	—	—
912	Börje	Börje ch; ch.yd.		A 1	s	2	10	—	213	4b	A	—	—	—
913		Brunnby		A 1	m	3b	8	—	167	6	A	—	—	Sven?
914		Ströja		EF: C 1 + B 4?	m	4	7,8	—	151	6	—	—	—	—
915#		Tiby		E 1	m	3b	2,6	—	170	8a	—	—	—	—
917	Jumkil	Jum.ch.; ch.yd.		A 1? E 10.06?	m	3b	10	—	188	8b	B	—	—	Disälv?
918m		Blacksta		A 3	s	4	7	—	164	6	A	—	—	—
919m		Blacksta		E 10.05	m	3b	7	—	197	8b	A	—	—	—
920[169]		Broholm		A 6(2?)/1	m		7	dam.	197	4b(2)	B+A?	+	+	—
921		Holmsta		A 3	s	—	5,7	—	182	6	A(2) +Eg	—	—	—

Uppsala town

id.	parish	place	type	rel.sh.	s/m	dat.	fsp.	state	height	design	cross	orn.	rel.	sign.
922[170]	Uppsala	domkyrkan		A 1/6	m	3b	10	—	310	8b	B	—	—	Öpir
923[171]		domkyrkan		B 2/3 +?	s	4?	10	—	310	6	A+Eg	—	—	—
924		domkyrkan		X 10/20			10	—		?	A	—	—	—
925		domkyrkan		A 3.1	m	3b	10	—	225	8b	A	—	—	—
926#		domkyrkan		X 30	s		10	dam., ph.	(100)	8	—	—	—	Öpir
929[172]		domkyrkan		A 1	s		10	2pts.	185	6	Eg	—	—	Ingulv
931		domkyrkan		C 1?			10	fr.		6	C	—	—	—
932[173]		domkyrkan		E 20.06?	m	3	10	3s	175	6(2)	C	—	—	Åsmund, Ingjald?
933		domkyrkan		E 03.20?	m	4	10	dam.	198	6	A–C?	—	—	—
934		domkyrkan		X	m	3b?	10	fr.		?	—	—	—	—
935		domkyrkan		E 10.05?	m	3b	10	fr.		6	—	—	—	—
N39[174]		domkyrkan		A 1	m		10	—	165	6	A	—	—	Likbjörn
N40[175]		domkyrkan		X	m		10	—	295		—	—	baptism	—
N41[176]		domkyrkan		A 1.2	m		10	—	200	8a	A	—	—	Öpir
937mc[177]		Svartbäcks-gatan		A 2	m	3a	3	—	160	6	—	+	—	—
938[178]		kv.Torget		A 1/6	s	3b	10	—	191	6	A	—	—	—
939[179]		kv.Torget		A 1	m	3b	10	—	122	8a	—	—	—	—
940[180]		kv.Torget		A 1 (E 10.05?)	m	3a	10	—	278	6	A	—	+	Öpir
N42[181]		kv.Torget		X 4			10	fr.	(115)		—	—	—	—
N43[182]		kv.Torget		X 60	m		10	—	120	8a	B	—	—	—
N44[183]		kv.Torget		X 10			3	fr.	(65)	?	—	—	—	—
N45[184]		academic hospital	E–EF?	m		3	fr.	(110)	?	—	—	—	—	
942[185]		Bredgränden		A 3	s	2a	3	—	200	6	A–C?	—	+	—
943[186]		ärkebiskops-gården		X	m	2b	10	—	203	6	B	—	+	—
944[187]		Uppsala		A 1? E 1?	m			fr.		?	A	—	—	—

[164] U 896: *Uppsala University park. [165] U 901: SHM 22437; *Umeå University. [166] U 905: *FV* 1966, 24. [167] U 909: *FV* 1993, 237; *Upplandsmuseet, Uppsala. [168] U 910: *Brunna. [169] U 920: ATA 6044/90. [170] U 922: *FV* 1973, 196. [171] U 923: *FV* 1973, 195. [172] U 929: *FV* 1976, 103. [173] U 932: *Uppsala University park. [174] U N39: *FV* 1976, 104. [175] U N40: *FV* 1973, 194. [176] U N41: *FV* 1976, 107. [177] U 937: *Uppsala University park. [178] U 938: *Uppsala University park. [179] U 939: *Uppsala University park. [180] U 940: *Uppsala University park. [181] U N42: *FV* 1977, 163. [182] U N43: *FV* 1972, 271. [183] U N44: *FV* 1973, 198. [184] U N45: *FV* 1988, 243; *Upplandsmuseet. [185] U 942: *Upplandsmuseet. [186] U 943: *Uppsala University park. [187] U 944: *Upplandsmuseet.

id.	parish	place	type	rel.sh.	s/m	dat.	fsp.	state	height	design	cross	orn.	rel.	sign.
Vaksala härad														
945	**Danmark**	Danmark ch.		A 1	m	3a	10	—	220	6	B	—	+	Fot
946		Danmark ch.		A 6	s		10	—	164	4b	A/H?	—	—	—
947		Berga, Fålebro		A 4	m	2a	6	—	223	6	B	—	+	Esbjörn
948		Danm.by; Fålebro		A 1.2	m	3b	5,8	—	235	8b	—	—	—	—
949		Lunda		X 10			7	dam.	155	?	—	—	—	—
950		Myrby		A 3.2	m	3b	7	—	166	8b	A/H?	—	—	—
951		Säby		E 6	m	2b	7	2s	131	8a+4b	A/H?	—	—	Grim skald
952#		Sällinge		A 3 + A 1?	s+m	3b	7	—	220	8a	A	—	—	—
953#		Sällinge		A 1	s		8	dam.	190	6	A?	—	—	—
954#		Söderby		A 2	m	2a	7	—	175	6(sp)	—	—	+	—
955#		Tjocksta		E 1	m	3a	2	—	220	6	—	+	—	—
956		Vedyxa	rock	C 5	s	3a	7	—	227	6	A	—	+	Åsmund
957		Vedyxa		E 10.05	m	3b	2	—	237	6	A+ Eg(2)	—	—	—
958		Villinge		A 1	s		2	fr.		4a+1	B	—	—	Torgöt
959	**Vaksala**	Vaks.ch.		E 3	m	4	10	pt.		6	A	—	—	—
960[188]		Vaks.ch.		E 3	m	10	fr.	150	7	—	—	+	—	
961[189]		Vaks.ch.		C 1.5	m	3b	10	—	190	8b	A	—	—	Öpir
962		Vaks.ch.		A 8	s	4	10	dam.	148	6	A	—	—	—
963		Vaks.ch.		E 10.05	m	2a	10	—	200	4a(2)	—	—	+	—
964		Vaks.ch.		C 5	s	2a	10	—	145	7	B	—	+	—
967		Vaks.ch.		X 10			10	fr.		?	—	—	—	—
968		Bolsta		E 20.03	m		8	3fr.		6	B	—	—	—
969		Bolsta		A 1	s	3a	8	—	133	6	B	—	—	Åsmund
970		Bolsta		X	s	4	8	—	105	6	—	—	—	Öpir
971		Eke		A 1	s	2b	6,7	pt.	160	5/6	—	—	+	—
972#		Gnista	A 6?	m			7,8	—	165	6	—	—	—	—
973[190]		Gränby		C 4	s	4?	7	fr.		6	—	—	—	Öpir
974		Jädra		A 2	m	4	2	—	133	6?	A	—	—	—
976		Råby	rock	A 2	s	3b	8	—	232	6	A(2)	—	—	—
977#		Vittulsberg		E 1.05.20	m		7	—	175	6	A	—	—	—
978	**Gamla Uppsala**	G.Upp.ch.		A 1	s	2b	10	—	229	6	B	—	—	—
980		G.Upp.vic.; ch.		A 1	m		10	several fr.		6	—	+	—	—
981#		G.Upp.vic.		C 5/1?	s		10	—		?	—	—	—	Åsmund
982#		Bredåker		X10			7	fr.		?	—	—	—	—
984#		Ekeby		A 1	m		6,7,8	—	210	8b	B?	—	—	Öpir
985		Hämringe		A 1	s	3b	7	—	210	6	—	—	—	—
986#[191]		Kungsgården		E 10.05	m	—	6,8	—	230	6	B	—	—	Åsmund
Rasbo härad														
987	**Funbo**	Funbo ch.		E 3.20	m	3a	10	—	176	7	A	—	+	—
990mc		Broby		A 1	m	2b	6,7	—	150	7	B	—	+	—
991mc		Broby		A 2	m	3a	6,7	—	147	6	—	+	—	—
992		Broby		X 40/ 10/06		2b	6	—	90	5/6	A–C?	—	—	—
993[192]		Brunnby		E 1	m	3b?	7	dam.	150	6	B	—	—	Öpir
995#		Funbo br.		X	m	3b	6	—		8b	B	—	—	—
996		Karberga		C 1	m	3b	7	—	224	8b	A	—	+	—
997		Lövsta		A 1	s	3b?	2	—	155	6/8	—	—	—	—
998		Skällerö		A 2	m	2b	8	pt.	190	7+mbd	A	—	+	Åsmund
999c		Åkerby		A 1	m	2b	5,7	—	238	3b	Fg(2)	—	—	—
N46[193]		Ärenvi		A 1	m		7	—	240	6	C	—	—	—
1005	**Rasbo**	Hov		A 1/2/3	s		6	—	215	6	A	—	—	—
1006		Lejsta		A 1	m	3b	2	—	184	6	C?	—	—	—
1007		Visteby		A 1	s	3b	8	—	184	6	A	—	—	Manne
1008c[194]		Västerberga		B 5	s	3b	1,7	fr.		8b	A	—	+	—
1009		Yrsta		X 10	m	3a	7,8	dam.	120	6?	—	—	—	—
1010		Årsta		X 10	m	3b	8	—	160	8b	—	—	—	—
1011[195]		Örby		A 8(+E)	s	3b	7	2s	185	6+8a	A(2)	—	+	—
1012c	**Rasbokil**	Rasbokil ch.		E 1	m	3a	10	—	203	6	A	—	—	—

Continued

188 U 960: *FV* 1970, 307. 189 U 961: *Vaksalahöjden. 190 U 973: *Upplandsmuseet. 191 U 986: *NOR* 1995, 19.
192 U 993: *Bärby. 193 U N46: *FV* 1990, 32. 194 U 1008: *FV* 1969, 302; *Rasbo church.
195 U 1011: *Uppsala University park.

Norunda härad

id.	parish	place	type rel.sh.	s/m	dat.	fsp.	state	height	design	cross	orn.	rel.	sign.
1013	Ärentuna	Ärentuna ch.	X	s		10	fr.		?	—	—	—	—
1014		Ärentuna ch.	A 3	s	4	10	—	132	6	Fg	—	—	—
1015		Ärentuna ch.	AB 30/05	s		10	—	125	6	—	—	—	—
1016[196]		Fjuckby	A 3	s	2b	7,8	dam.	191	5/6	D	—	—	—
1017		Fjuckby; Är.ch.	E: A 6 +C 1	(m)		2	fr.	180	8b	B(3)	—	—	—
1018		Kolje	A 1	m	3–4	8	—	136	6	A	—	—	—
1019		Kyrsta	A 1	m	3b	7	—	205	6	A	—	—	—
1020		Kyrsta	A 6?	s	3b	7	—	158	8b	A	—	—	—
1021[197]		Nederbacka	X	s		6	dam.	146	6?	Eg	—	—	—
1022		Storvreta	E 1	m	3b	8	—	195	6	B	—	—	Öpir
1023#		Vallby	E 1	m		5	—	170	6	A	—	—	—
1024		Vaxmyra	A 4	s	3b	2	—	155	6	B	—	—	—
1025#		Vaxmyra	A 2	m		2	—		?	—	—	—	—
1026	Lena	Lena ch.	A 2	m	3b	10	—	160	6	A	—	—	—
1027		Lena ch.	X	m		10	dam.	116	6	A	—	—	—
1028		Lena ch.	X 60			10	fr.		?	—	—	+	—
1030#		Björnhammar	X 30	s		2	—	185	6	A	—	—	—
1031		Hånsta	A 1	m		2	—	114	6	B	—	—	—
1032		Ånge	A 1+A 1	(m)		2	2fr.		8b	B	—	—	—
1033		Årby	A 1	m	2a?	7,8	2s	150	3a(2)	B+Fg	—	+	—
1034	Tensta	Tensta ch.	A 1	m	4	10	—	200	6	A	—	—	Öpir
1035		Tensta ch.	E 10.05	m		10	dam.	180	8a	B	—	—	—
1036		Tensta ch.	E 60.03?	m	3b	10	—	169	8b	B	—	bap- tism	—
1037#		Tensta ch.	X 10	s		10	h.	150	?	—	—	—	—
1038#		Altomta	A 2	s		2	—		8b	A	—	—	—
1039		Bräcksta	A 1	m	3b	8	2s	215	6+5	A	—	+	Kjule
1040		Fasma	A 8	s	3b	7	—	186	6	A	—	—	Kjule
1041		Golvasta	EF 1	m	3a	2	—	166	6+	B	+	—	Ingulv
1042		Källbo	AB1	s	3b		fr.	250	6	A?	—	—	Kjule
1043		Onslunda	A 1	m	3a	7	—	163	6	B	+	+	—
1044		Onslunda; ch.	E 10.05	m	4	7	fr.		6	A	—	—	—
1045	Björklinge	Björk.ch.	A 1	s	4	10	—	134	6	—	—	—	—
1046		Björk.ch.	A 2	s	3b	10	—	165	8b	A	—	—	—
1047		Björk.ch.	A 1	m	3b?	10	—	155	6	B+ E(2)	—	—	—
1048		Björk.ch.	C 3	s	3b	10	—	132	6	A	—	—	—
1050 m		Björk.ch.	X 10	m		10	dam.	96	6	A?	—	—	—
1051		Björk.vic.	E 40.01	m	3a	2,5	—	90	6	A	—	—	—
1052		Axlunda	A 4	m	3a	2	—	136	6+	Eg+ Fg	+	—	Ingulv, Tjälve
1053		Hammarby	E 3+?	m	3b?	6,8	pt.	(185)	6	A?	—	—	—
1054		Lund	X 10	s		7	dam.	170	6	B	—	—	—
1056		Ramsjö	A 1	m	3b	2	—	182	8b	B	—	—	—
1057		Sandbro	X 4?		3b	2	dam.	114	6	—	—	—	—
1058#		Sandbro	X	m		?	dam.		6	—	—	—	—
1060 m		Tibble	A 1	m	3a	3	—	215	6	A	—	—	—
N47[198]		Åby	X 30			2,6	—	120	6	A(2) +Eg	—	—	—
1062	Viksta	Dalboda	A 6	m	3b	7	—	160	6	A	—	—	—
1063		Källslätt	C 1	m	3b	7	dam.	212	6	A	—	—	Öpir
1064#		Nyvalla	X			2	fr.		6	A	—	+	+?
1065		Rångsta	A 1+A 1	s+m	3	8	—	183	7	A(2)	+	—	—

Bälinge härad

id.	parish	place	type rel.sh.	s/m	dat.	fsp.	state	height	design	cross	orn.	rel.	sign.
1066	Åkerby	Åkerby ch.	X	m	2a	10	—	175	7	Fg	—	—	—
1067		Åkerby ch.	X 10	s	2a	10	—	243	7	C	—	+	Brand
1068		Åkerby ch.	X 10+?	m		10	fr.	(97)	5	—	—	—	—
1069		Berga	A 3+A 6	(m)	3b	6,8	—	199	6	A	—	—	—
1070		Kroksta	A 1	m	3b	8	—	193	6	A	—	—	—
1072	Bälinge	Bälinge ch.	X	m	3b	10	dam.	180	6	A	—	—	Öpir
1073#		Bälinge ch.	A 1	m		10	—		6?	—	—	—	—
1074#		Bälinge ch.	E 03.20	m		10	—		6	A+ Eg(3)	—	—	Likbjörn
1075#		Bälinge ch.	A 1	m		10	—		6	A(2)	—	—	Ingulv?

[196] U 1016: Wulf (1997), 185 ff.

[197] U 1021: *Rosta kvarn, Bälinge parish.

[198] U N47: *FV* 1947, 203.

id.	parish	place	type	rel.sh.	s/m	dat.	fsp.	state	height	design	cross	orn.	rel.	sign.
1076#		Bälinge ch.		A 2	s		10	—		8b	Eg(3)	—	—	—
1077[199]		Bälinge ch.		X 60			10	fr.	(150)	?	B	—	—	—
1078b		Bälinge ch.		X			10	fr.		6	A	—	—	—
1079[200]		Forkarby		B 5	s		7	fr.	130	6	A	—	—	—
1080[201]		Forkarby		A 1	m		7	fr.		6	A	—	—	—
1081		Forkarby		A 2?	m	4?	5	—	140	6	A	—	—	—
1083#		Gysta		E 10.05. 20?	m		8	—		6	A	—	—	—
1084		Hämringe		A 1	m	4	7	—	152	6	A	—	—	—
1085		Högsta		X 60	m	3b	6	—	142	6	A	—	—	—
1086#		Högsta		A 1	s		7	—		8b	A	—	—	—
1087#		Lövsta		C 3	s	3b	8	—	220	8a(2)	A	—	—	—
1088#		Lövsta		E 1?	m		2	—		6	A	—	—	—
1089		Marsta		A 1	s	3b	7,8	—	172	8b	A	—	—	Jovurfast?
1090#		Marsta		X 20+?	m		3	—		?	A	—	—	—
1091#		Målsta		X 10	m		3	dam.	140	?	A	—	—	—
1092		Nyvla		A 6	m	3b	2,8	—	205	6	A	—	—	—
1093		Nyvla	rock	EF 8	m	3b	2,9	—	173	6	A(2)	—	+	—
1094#		Rosta br.		A 1	m		6	—		6/8?	A	—	+	—
1095		Rörby		E 10.05	m	3b	7,8	—	170	6	A	—	—	Likbjörn
1096		Rörby		C 3	s	4	8	—	150	6	A	—	—	—
1097		Sundbro		E 1.05	m	3b?	2,8	dam.	158	6	—	—	—	—
1098		Sundbro		E 1	m		6	2s, fr.	220	6(2)	A	—	—	—
1099#		Sundbro		X 10	m	3b	6	—	90	6/7?	—	—	—	—
1100		Sundbro		X	s?		6	fr.	(124)	6/8?	—	—	—	Öpir
1101#		Sundbro		X 60			?	fr.		?	—	—	—	—
1102#		Svista		E 1	m	3b	2	—	210	6	A	—	—	Otvagen
1103#		Svista	rock	A 6	s		2	—	135	8a	A	—	—	—
1104		Tuna		X	m	3a	7	—	220	6	A?	—	—	Nase, Kättil
1105#		Åloppe		X 10	s		2	dam.	200	8b	A+Eg	—	—	—
1106		Äskelunda		A 1	m	3b	2,6	—	195	8b	A+Fg	—	—	Öpir
1107		Äskelunda		E 03.6?	m	3b	2,8	—	165	6	A	—	—	—
1108#	Skuttunge	Skuttunge ch.		E 3	m	3a?	10	—	200	6	—	—	—	—
1110		Broddbo		A 4	s	3b	8	dam.	(143)	6	A	—	—	—
1111		Eke		E 10.05	m	3b	7,8	—	203	6	A	—	—	—
1114#		Myrby		A 8+?			8	dam.		?	—	—	—	—
1115#		Norrby		X	m		8	dam.	170	6?	—	—	—	—
1116#		Skuttunge by		E 1.05	m		10	—	210	6	A	—	—	Gudfast
1117		Vigle		A 1?2?	s	3b	2,7	dam.	160	8b	—	—	—	Kol
1118		Örke		X 20	m	3b	7	—	162	6	A	—	—	
1119[202]		Örke		C 1	s	2b	2	fr.	190	6	Eg	—	—	—
1120#		Örke		C 5 or A 7b?	?	—	7	dam.	100	?	—	—	—	—

Oland härad

id.	parish	place	type	rel.sh.	s/m	dat.	fsp.	state	height	design	cross	orn.	rel.	sign.
1122	**Stavby**	Stavby ch.		A 1	m	3b	10	—	270	8a	A	—	+	—
1123	**Tuna**	Tuna ch.		X 10	m	3b	10	dam.	145	6	A	+	—	—
1127	**Alunda**	Alunda ch.		A 2	m	3a	10	—	145	5	—	—	—	—
1129#		Alunda ch.		A 2+?	s		10	—	160	?	—	—	—	—
1130#		Klev		X	m	3a	10	dam.		6	A–D?	—	—	—
1131#		Långörn		A 1	s		6	—	160	6	B	—	—	—
1132	**Skäfthammar**	Gimo		AB 1	m	3b	6	—	234	6	A	—	—	Ödmund
1133m#	**Morkarla**	Norrby		AB 6	s	2a?	2	—	125	3a+	—	—	—	—
1134m		Söderby		AB 05.30	s		7	fr.	(90)	4a	—	—	—	—
1135	**Dannemora**	Ackarby		X			3	fr.	(90)	6	A	—	—	—
1137#	**Österlövsta**	Skärplinge		X 10			3	fr.	(65)	?	—	—	—	—
1138	**Hållnäs**	Hållen		X 30+?		7,8	dam.	275	6	—	—	—	—	
1139		Ängvreta		A 2.3	m	2b?	2	—	180	5/6	—	—	—	Fasttegn

Örbyhus härad

id.	parish	place	type	rel.sh.	s/m	dat.	fsp.	state	height	design	cross	orn.	rel.	sign.
1140	**Vendel**	Burunge		E 3	m	3b	2	—	214	8b	A	—	—	—
1142		Åbyggeby		A 1	s	3a	8	—	149	6	B	—	—	Åsmund, Vigmar
1143	**Tierp**	Tierp ch.		A 1	m		10	dam.	164	7	Fr+Eg	—	+	Tore

Continued

[199] **U 1077: *FV* 1980, 235.** [200] **U 1079: *FV* 1978, 223; *Sundbro, Bälinge parish.**
[201] U 1080: *FV* 1978, 225; *Sundbro, Bälinge parish. [202] U 1119: *Högsta bridge, Bälinge parish.

id.	parish	place	type	rel.sh.	s/m	dat.	fsp.	state	height	design	cross	orn.	rel.	sign.
1144[203]		Tierp ch.		A 1	m	3a	10	—	182	4a+mbd	B	+	+	Åsmund, Heriar?
1145		Yttrö		E 10.05?	m	3a	2	dam.	200	7	A	—	+	—
1146	Tolfta	Gillberga		A 1	m		7,8	dam.	185	6	—	—	—	—
1148#	Älvkarleby	Älvkarleby ch.		X 60	m		10	—	180	6	—	—	—	—
1149		Fleräng		A 1	m	2b	2	—	220	7	A	—	+	Sven, Åsmund

Simtuna härad

id.	parish	place	type	rel.sh.	s/m	dat.	fsp.	state	height	design	cross	orn.	rel.	sign.
1151mc?	Frösthult	Brunnby		C 5/3	s	2b	7	—	150	5/6	B	—	+	—
1152m?		Brunnby		C 5	s	3b	7	—	209	8b	—	+	—	Livsten
1153#	Simtuna	Bärby		A 2	s	2b	7	—	220	5/6	B	—	—	—
1154		Forsby		C 5	s	2b	7	—	123	5/6	B	—	—	—
1155		Hjälteberga		A 6	m	2b	2	—	142	5/6	B	—	+	—
1156		Hjälteberga		A 1	m	2b	2	—	173	5/6	B	—	—	—
1157		Isby		A 6	s	2b	7	—	135	5/6	B	—	+	—
1158		St. Salfors		A 1	m	3a	7	dam.	183	7+8b	—	—	—	Livsten
1159		Skensta	rock	A 1	m	3b	2	dam.	160	8a	A	—	—	Öpir
1160[204]		Ändersta		A 1	s	3b	2	2s	154	8a	—	+	—	—
1161	Altuna	Altuna ch.		A 1/2	m	3a	10	3s	196	7+2(2)+	—	+	—	Balle, Frösten
1162		Buska		E 10.05	m	3b	7	—	231	6	A	—	—	—
1163[205]		Drävle		A 1	m	2b	2	—	185	6	H?	+	—	—
1164m?	Västerlövsta	St.Runhällen		X	s	3b	7	—	167	6	—	+	—	Livsten

Torstuna härad

id.	parish	place	type	rel.sh.	s/m	dat.	fsp.	state	height	design	cross	orn.	rel.	sign.
1165m	Härnevi	Rotbrunna		E 6	m	2b	2	—	165	5/6	B	—	—	Erik
1167	Torstuna	Ekeby		X	s	3b	7,8	—	177	6	—	—	—	—
1168	Österunda	Österunda ch.		E 3?	m	3b	10	dam.	195	?	—	+	—	—
1172	Vittinge	Holm, Sveden		A 6	m	2b	3	—	182	6	B	—	—	—
1173[206]		L.Ramsjö		A 1	s	2b		2s	144	?	B+A	—	+	—
1174		St.Ramsjö		X 30/10	s	3b	8	—	175	7	—	—	—	—

Våla härad

id.	parish	place	type	rel.sh.	s/m	dat.	fsp.	state	height	design	cross	orn.	rel.	sign.
1176	Huddunge	Huddunge by		E 2.40	m	3b	2	—	185	6	A	—	—	—
1177	Harbo	Hässelby		A 6	m	3b	2,8	2s	200	6+2	A(2)	—	—	Öpir
1181	Nora	L.Runhällen		A 8	s	2b	7	fr.		6	—	—	—	—

NEW FINDS

	härad/skeppslag	*follows* U		*härad/skeppslag*	*follows* U		*härad/skeppslag*	*follows* U
N1	Färentuna	14	N17	Vallentuna	N16	N33	Ärlinghundra	478
N2	Sollentuna	67	N18	Vallentuna	277	N34	Långhundra	492
N3	Sollentuna	70	N19	Vallentuna	294	N35	Närdinghundra	592
N4	Sollentuna	95	N20	Seminghundra	302	N36	Trögd	692
N5	Sollentuna	96	N21	Seminghundra	336	N37	Åsunda	762
N6	Danderyd	142	N22	Seminghundra	346	N38	Åsunda	790
N7	Danderyd	149	N23	Seminghundra	356	N39	Uppsala	935
N8	Danderyd	133	N24	Seminghundra	358	N40	Uppsala	N39
N9	Danderyd	161	N25	Seminghundra	371	N41	Uppsala	N40
N10	Danderyd	172	N26	Seminghundra	N25	N42	Uppsala	940
N11	Vallentuna	183	N27	Sigtuna	384	N43	Uppsala	N42
N12	Vallentuna	N11	N28	Sigtuna	403	N44	Uppsala	N43
N13	Vallentuna	188	N29	Ärlinghundra	408	N45	Uppsala	N44
N14	Vallentuna	198	N30	Ärlinghundra	N29	N46	Rasbo	999
N15	Vallentuna	263	N31	Ärlinghundra	425	N47	Norunda	1060
N16	Vallentuna	273	N32	Ärlinghundra	438			

[203] U 1144: *FV* 1988, 243. [204] U 1160: *Ashmolean Museum, Oxford.
[205] U 1163: *Göksbo. [206] U 1173: *Castle Rock, Edinburgh.

Uppland: Further Particulars

Ornaments (indicated by + in column headed 'orn.')

FÄRENTUNA

31 bird
35 two beasts
51 two beasts

SOLLENTUNA

79 beast (side)

DANDERYD

128 man
N6 man

ÅKER

176 beast

VALLENTUNA

193 beast?
200 serpent's head
240 beast
244 beast
251 beast
257 bird

SEMINGHUNDRA

305 winged dragon
313 two men
350 beast
375 rider and horse
N23 beast

ÄRLINGHUNDRA

428 beast
448 horse and rider; bird
449 animal

LÅNGHUNDRA

484 trikvetra
508 man's head

NÄRDINGHUNDRA

590 beast

FRÖSÅKER

595 belfry; woman; two men, and a kettle over a fire
598 two beasts
599 horse and rider; bird

HÅBO

629 two men; bird
631 two men
632 two heads
633 winged animal
678 horse and rider and sword (×2)

TRÖGD

690 beast
691 beast; horse and rider and sword
692 eagle and beast
696 beast
(704 beast)
703 beast
713 bird
716 beast
719 two beasts
(725 beast)
726 beast
734 beast?
740 beast
742 beast
746 bird
749 beast
751 two beasts
753 two beasts

ÅSUNDA

758 beast
759 beast
760 beast (=796 below)
763 beast
764 beast
766 beast
767 beast
770 two beasts
771 beast
775 beast
780 beast
789 beast
791 beast
794 beast
796 =760 above

LAGUNDA

803 beast
(822 beast)
824 face; mask
828 beast
838 beast

HAGUNDA

855 hunting scene: horse and rider and spear; two dogs; deer (elk?); bird (falcon?), man on skis with bow and arrow
860 four animals
881 flower
884 beast

ULLERÅKER

901 three men: one lying down (dead?), one holding a cross (or axe?); a horse
904 two animals (bears?)
905 two beasts
920 bird

UPPSALA

937 trikvetra

VAKSALA

955 beast
980 beast

RASBO

991 beast

NORUNDA

1041 ship
1043 man and woman
1052 ship's keel
1065 face

OLAND

1123 beast

ÖRBYHUS

1144 two beasts

SIMTUNA

1152 beast
1160 beast
1161 beast; man with a hammer in a boat; horned head as a bait on a rope
1163 figures
1164 beast

TORSTUNA

1168 beast

Mutliple Commemorations

1. Identical (or almost identical)

101+143, in memory of Ingefast by his sons Häming and Jarlabanke: 101 together with Ingefast's mother Estrid; 143 together with Estrid and Ingefast's widow Jorun.
133+141, in memory of Holme by his mother Gudlög; 133 also in memory of Gudlög herself.
143+147, in memory of Ingefast by his wife Jorun and mother Estrid (?); 143 also by his sons; 147 uncertain whether the mother is a co-sponsor. See also under 101.
153+155–7, in memory of Halvdan and Gunnar by their brothers Sven and Ulv.
160+225, in memory of Ulv in Skålhamra by his sons: 160 by his sons Ulvkel, Gye, and Une; 225 by his sons Ulvkel, Arnkel, and Gye.
186+188, in memory of Jarger by his sons Trane and Äsbjörn (+187).
207+208, in memory of Sterkar by his sons Ulv, Tormund, and Gammal.
209+360, in memory of Ärnmund by his father Torsten; 360 also in memory of Torsten's father Gerbjörn.
225: see above, at 160.
236+237, in memory of Ulv and Sven by his brothers Gärdar, Fullhuge, Sigrev, Sibbe, and Sigvat, Ulv's sons.
244+251, in memory of Fastulv by his father Faste.
285+286, in memory of Olev: 285 also in memory of Kättilmund by Holmlög, Olev's mother and Kättilmund's sister; 286 by Holmlög and Gillög.
326+327, in memory of Sven by his parents Holmgärd and Sigröd.
329–32, in memory of Ragnfast by his wife Inga.
346+356, in memory of Björn by his mother Ragnfrid.
360: see above, at 209.
641+642, in memory of Gilde (?) by his sons Hedenger and Björn.
644+654, in memory of Gunnelv by his sons Andvätt, Kår **kiti**, Bläse, and Djärv.
700–2, in memory of Ingjald by his brother Gute.
712+713, in memory of Gerbjörn: 712 by his brother Olev; 713 by his brothers X and Olev.
723–5, in memory of Gute by his sons Öger and Fröger (+725).
735+736, in memory of Sigtrygg by his parents Vädralde and Arngärd.

762+779, in memory of Jarl by his father Järund.

763+764, in memory of Gunnbjörn by his sons Brune and Holmsten.

779: see above, at 762.

859+860, in memory of Ingefast by Fastbjörn and Torunn.

901+904, in memory of Jovur by his sons, Jarl/X, Karl, and Igulbjörn.

937+991, in memory of Väder by his brothers Tägn and Gunnar.

1050+1060, in memory of Est by his sons Holmger and Karl (?).

1133+1134, in memory of Karlung and Gudvar by Agvid, father and husband.

1152+1164, in memory of Torsten by his wife Ärnlög.

NB: four cases where the same individuals are commemorated (a) *both by the same and by other sponsors;* (b) *alone or together with other people:*

170+171, in memory of Önd: 170 by his parents Gunne and Åsa; 171 by his father Gunne and in memory of Gunne himself.

255+269, in memory of Björn: 255 by his brother Illuge and his mother Gillög; 267 by his mother Gillög; 269 by his brother Illuge.

312–14, in memory of Jovurfast: 312 by her stepfather Gunnar; 313 by her stepfather Gunnar and mother Holmdis; 314 by her mother Holmdis.

496+497, in memory of Ingefast by his son Ragnfast; 496 also in memory of Gullev; 497 also in memory of his mother Ingefrid.

2. *In memory of the same individual(s) (by different sponsor(s))*

72+73, in memory of Gärdar and Jorund, Inga's sons: 72 by their (maternal) uncles Ärnmund and Ingemund; 73 no sponsor mentioned.

101+143+147, in memory of Ingefast (for 101 and 143, see also under 'Identical' above): 101 by his sons Häming and Jarlabanke, together with Ingefast's mother Estrid; 143 by his sons Häming and Jarlabanke, together with Ingefast's widow Jorun and his mother Estrid; 147 by his widow Jorun (and his mother Estrid?).

135+136, in memory of Östen: 135 by his sons Ingefast, Östen, and Sten; 136 by his widow Estrid.

143+147: see this group above, at 101.

144+152, in memory of Björn and Sigvat: 144 by their sons/brothers Gammal, Torsten, and Torgils; 152 by Holmfrid, Björn's widow and Sigvat's mother.

160+161+225+226, in memory of Ulv in Skålhamra (for 160 and 225, see also under 'Identical' above): 160 by his sons Ulvkel, Gye, and Une; 161 by his kinsman Ulv in Bårresta; 225 by his sons Ulvkel, Arnkel, and Gye; 226 by his widow Gyrid.

214+215, in memory of two men: 215 by their daughters/sisters Ragnhild and Ulvhild; 214 in memory of one of the men by his widow Ingeberg (?).

225+226: see this group above, at 160.

236+237+238, in memory of Ulv and Sven: 236–7 by Gärdar, Fullhuge, Sigrev, Sibbe, and Sigvat, Ulv's sons, Sven's brothers (see under 'Identical' above); 238 by Astrid, Ulv's widow, Sven's mother.

309+310, in memory of Ingvar: 309 by his sons Sigvid, Ingvar, and Jarlabanke . . . ; 310 by his widow Estrid . . .

328+336, in memory of Onäm: 328 by his daughters Gyrid and Gudlög; 336 by his nephew (brother's son) Ulv (in Bårresta).

337+341+342, in memory of Kalv: 337 also in memory of several others, by Häming, Själve, and Johan; 341 also in memory of Igul and Ragnvi by Ingjald, Kalv's and Ragnvi's son, Igul's brother; 342 by his brother(s?).

631+632, in memory of **syhsa**: 631 by his son Nigulas; 632 by his brothers ——i and Stenbjörn (?).

704+705+706, in memory of Vigöt by his sons: 705 by Olev, Holmfast, X, and Ännebrant; 706 by X, Holmfast, and ——ger.

766+767, in memory of Gudfast and his son Est by Gudfast (himself); 767 'Livsten carved'.

768+1165, in memory of Nocke: 768 by Agute, Assur, and Björn; 1165 by Hjälmdis and Torsten.

3. *By the same sponsor(s) in memory of different individuals*

(20+21?, see 329 below)

77+78, by Hosve: 77 together with Holmsten and Gyrid in memory of Jobjörn, Hosve's and Holmsten's father, Gyrid's husband; 78 together with Sigrid and Kättilö in memory of their brother Holmsten.

100+226+328, by Gyrid: 100 in memory of her son Ulvkel, together with Gye in memory of his brother and his sister Holmdis; 226 in memory of her husband Ulv (in Skålhamra); 328 together with her sister Gudlög in memory of their father Onäm . . .

101+143+148, by Häming: 101+143 see group 2 above; 148 together with his father Ingefast in memory of Ragnfrid, his mother, Ingefast's wife.

127+149+164+165+212+261, by Jarlabanke in memory of himself.

130+433, by Björn Finnvid's son: 130 in memory of his brother Olev; 433 in memory of himself.

135+148, by Ingefast: 135 see group 2 above; 148 see this group above, at 101.

136+137+143(+147?), by Estrid: 136 in memory of her husband Östen; 137 together with Östen in memory of their son Gag; 143 together with Jorun, Häming, and Jarlabanke in memory of Ingvar (see this group above, at 101).

143: see this group above, at 136.

148: see this group above, at 101.

149: see this group above, at 127.

160+225, by Ulvkel and Gye in memory of their father Ulv (in Skålhamra): 160 together with their brother Une; 225 together with their brother Arnkel.

161+336, by Ulv in Bårresta: 161 in memory of his kinsman Ulv in Skålhamra; 336 in memory of his (paternal) uncle Onäm.

164+165: see this group above, at 127.

194+203, by Alle: 194 in memory of himself; 203 in memory of his son Ulv.

212: see this group above, at 127, and 'Connected Monuments' below, at 101.

225: see this group above, at 160, and group 2 above, at 160.

226: see this group above, at 100, and group 2 above, at 160.

240+241, by Dan, Huskarl, and Sven: 240 together with their mother Holmfrid in memory of Halvdan, their father; 241 in memory of their (paternal) grandfather Ulvrik.

261: see this group above, at 127.

265+N18?, by Ärenvi: 265 in memory of her son Elev; N18 together with Sigsten in memory of (their son Elev?).

266+N18?, by Sigsten: 266 together with Visten in memory of their father (Ingv)ar; N18 together with Ärenvi (?) in memory of (their son Elev?).

280+281, by Vibjörn: 280 in memory of his wife, 'Gunne's daughter'; 281 together with Huskarl in memory of their father Sibbe.

306+311, by Ingrid: 306 together with her sons Ingemar, Ingevald, Karl in memory of Jobjörn, her husband/their father; 311 together with her sons Ingemar and Karl in memory of Ingegärd, her daughter/their sister.

312+313+314+315+316, by Gunnar and/or Holmdis: 312–14 in memory of Jovurfast: 312 by her stepfather Gunnar; 313 by her stepfather Gunnar and mother Holmdis; 314 by her mother Holmdis; 315–16 in memory of Tord by his parents Gunnar and Holmdis.

328: see this group above, at 100.

329+330+331+332+(20+21?), by Inga: 329–32 in memory of her first husband Ragnfast; (20–1 in memory of her second husband Erik and her father Gudrik?)

336: see this group above, at 161.

343+344(+364?), by Karse: 343–4 together with NN in memory of their father Ulv (in Bårresta); (364 also X in memory of Y).

347+348, by Livsten in memory of himself, his wife Ingerun, and sons Jorund, Niklas, and Luden.

433: see this group above, at 130.

453+454, by Torkel and Gisl: 453 in memory of their father Ganse; 454 in memory of their brother Styrbjörn—and Säfare (?).

496+497, by Ragnfast: 496 in memory of his father Ingefast and in memory of Gullev; 497 in memory of his parents Ingefast and Ingefrid.

513+514, by Anund: 513 together with Erik, Håkon, and Ingvar in memory of their brother Ragnar; 514 together with Farulf in memory of Anund's father Kättilfast.

532+533, by Sigrud: 532 in memory of her husband Kåre; 533 in memory of her son Anund.

565+566, by Manne: 565 together with Åfrid in memory of their son Olev, and Johan in memory of his brother; 566 in memory of his brothers Hulte, Torkel, and Själve.

621+622, by Gunnhild: 621 together with her sons Åbjörn and Sigbjörn in memory of her husband, their father; 622 in memory of her son Horsämne (?) . . .

640+648, by Sighjälm: 640 together with **kus** in memory of their father Andvätt; 648 in memory of his brother **kus**.

668+669, by Stärkar and Hjorvard: 668 in memory of their father Gere; 669 in memory of their brother Gisl.

770+1151, by Hedendis: 770 together with Ärndis in memory of their father Ofeg; 1151 in memory of her husband Holmfast and her son Ängle.

(819+820, by Sven: 819 in memory of his father; 820 an empty serpent.)

(822+823: 823 by X in memory of Y; 822 a beast.)

844+845, by Gisl and Åsger: 844 together with Björn in memory of their father Torsten; 845 in memory of their brother Björn.

918+919, by Gudfast: 918 in memory of his son Kättilmund; 919 together with Trond in memory of their father Hals, and Frögunn in memory of her husband.

937+990+991, by Tägn and Gunnar: 990 together with Väder in memory of their father Hörse; 937+991 in memory of their brother Väder.

1151: see this group above, at 770.

N18: see this group above, at 265 and 266.

Connected Monuments

11+16: see 617 below (+Sö 101+Sö 106).

(20+21)+29+329–32: 'Hillersjö–Snottsta family': 329–32 see 'Multiple Commemorations' above, group 3; 29 no sponsor: the 'story' about Gerlög and her daughter Inga.

57+58: 57 Senar, Torkel, and Vifast in memory of their father Björn; 58 Sigvid and Sigrev in memory of their father Senar.

100+112+160+161+225+226+328+336+343+344+364: 'Skålhamra' and 'Bårresta families': 112 Ragnvald in memory of his mother Fastvi, Onäm's daughter; for the rest, see 'Multiple Commemorations' above.

101+127+135+136+137+140+142+143+147+148+149+150+164+165+212(+216+217?)+261+309+310: 'Jarlabanke family' (see also under 'Multiple Commemorations' above): 101 Häming and Jarlabanke in memory of their father Ingefast, and Estrid in memory of her sons (Ingefast and Ingvar); 127 Jarlabanke in memory of himself; 135 Ingefast; Östen, and Sten in memory of their father Östen; 136 Estrid in memory of her husband Östen; 137 Östen and Estrid in memory of their son Gag; 140 Jarlabanke in memory of X (=Östen?); 142 Ingefast in memory of his father Jarlabanke, and Kättilö in memory of her husband; 143 Jorun in memory of Ingefast, her husband, Häming and Jarlabanke in memory of their father, and Estrid in memory of her son; 147 Jorun (and Estrid?) in memory of Ingefast and Ingvar; 148 Ingefast in memory of his wife Ragnfrid, and Häming in memory of his mother; 149 Jarlabanke in memory of himself; 150 Jarlabanke and Fastvi in memory of their son Sven; 164 Jarlabanke in memory of himself; 165 Jarlabanke in memory of himself; 212 Jarlabanke in memory of himself; 216? Johan in memory of Östen (son of Jarlabanke and Kättilö?); 217? Ingefast in memory of Östen (son of Jarlabanke and Kättilö?); 261 Jarlabanke in memory of himself; 309 Sigvid, Ingvar, and Jarlabanke in memory of their father Ingvar and their brother Ragnvald; 310 Estrid in memory of her husband Ingvar and his son Ragnvald.

112: see this group above, at 100.

127: see this group above, at 101.

135–137: see this group above, at 101.

140, 142, 143: see this group above, at 101.

147–150: see this group above, at 101.

160–161: see this group above, at 100.

164–165: see this group above, at 101.

210+229+231+232: 210 Finnvid and Holmger in memory of their father Holmgöt, and Hedenvi in memory of her husband; 229 Halvdan and Tobbe in memory of their father Udde; 231 Hedinvi, Östen, Ulv, and Olov in memory of their father Halvdan; 232 Toste, Sigus, and Sigmar in memory of their father Tobbe.

212: see this group above, at 101.

216–217: see this group above, at 101.

225–226: see this group above, at 100.

229: see this group above, at 210.

231–232: see this group above, at 210.

261: see this group above, at 101.

273+276+277: 273 Illuge in memory of his father, and Assur and Fulluge in memory of their brother

Djärv; 276 Djärv, Andsvar, and Fulluge in memory of their father Gerbjörn; 277 Kättilgärd in memory of her husband Assur, and Ulv in memory of Björn.

293+294: 293 Forkunn and Tore in memory of their father Kättil; 294 Gudlög in memory of her husband Forkunn, and Kättilälv in memory of her father?

295+304+305: 295 Viger in memory of his son, and Fastlög in memory of her brother Fulluge; 304 Fulluge and Hök (?) in memory of their father Manne; 305 Åskatla in memory of Fulluge her husband (?), and Illuge and Signy in memory of their father (?).

306+307+311: 306+311 see 'Multiple Commemorations' above, group 3; 307 Jorund and Jarl, Ingemar's and Kättilö's sons, in memory of their brother Ingvar.

309–310: see this group above, at 101.

311: see this group above, at 306.

312+313+314+315+316: see 'Multiple Commemorations' above, group 3.

328: see this group above, at 100.

329–332: see this group above, at (20+21)+29 ('Hillersjö–Snottsta family').

336: see this group above, at 100, and 'Multiple Commemorations' above, group 3 (at 161).

337+338+341+342: 337 Häming and Själve in memory of their father Finnvid and of several other individuals; 338 Torsten and Ragnfrid in memory of Björn (in Granby); 341+342 see 'Multiple Commemorations' above, group 2 (at 337).

343+344+364: see this group above, at 100, and for the same inscriptions and 161+336, see also 'Multiple Commemorations' above, group 3.

429+430: 429 Tore and Roda in memory of their father Borgulv; 430 Borgulv and Gudlög in memory of their son Torbjörn.

444+445: 444 Ulv, Härbjörn, Näsbjörn, and Häming in memory of their father Borgulv; 445 Kylving in memory of his father Näsbjörn and Gillög in memory of her husband.

457+458+459: 457 Svarthövde in memory of his son Anund; 458 Est in memory of his father Svarthövde; 459 Saxo in memory of his father Est, and Torgunn in memory of her son.

479+480: 479 Åsmund and X, Gyrid's sons, in memory of their father Sigulv, Sote's brother; 480 Holmger and Gunne in memory of their father Sote.

503+504: 503 Ärnfast and Ärngöt in memory of their father Kättilfast; 504 Kättilfast in memory of his father Åsgöt.

510+511: 510 Frösten, Torbjörn, Faste, Vinjut, Ulv, and Gunndjärv in memory of their father Torsten; 511 Vidjärv, Dan, Fast, and Halvdan in memory of their father Faste.

U 617+11+16+Sö 101+Sö 106: 617 Ginnlög, Holmger's daughter, Sigröd's sister, in memory of her husband Assur, Håkon Jarl's son; 11 Tolir and Gylla in memory of themselves, Håkon had the runes carved; 16 Gunne and Kåre in memory of a man, 'the best of bönder in Håkon's *rod* [ship district]'; Sö 101 Sigrid in memory of her husband Holmger, Sigröd's and Ginnlög's (?) father; Sö 106 Alrik, Sigrid's son, in memory of his father Spjut.

621+622: 621 Åbjörn and Sigbjörn in memory of their father Assur, and Gunnhild in memory of her husband; 622 Gunnhild in memory of her son Horsämne (?) . . .

635+636: 635 Rolv (?), Arnfast (?), Arfast, and Arne in memory of their father; 636 Alve in memory of her son Arnfast.

640+648: see 'Multiple Commemorations' above, group 3.

643+644+654: 643 Gullev and Kår in memory of their father Andvätt *röde* [the red]; 644+654 see 'Multiple Commemorations' above, group 1.

770+1151: 770 Hedendis and Ärndis in memory of their father Ofeg; 1151 Hedendis in memory of her husband Holmfast and their son Ängle.

821+839?: 821 Estrid (?) in memory of her father Hedenfast and Öda in memory of her husband and in memory of her daughter Ödgärd; 839 Anunde and Ödgärd in memory of their son Anund.

884+885: 884 Holmger, Sigrid, and ——fast in memory of Holmger's father Vig; 885 Vig, Sigsten, and Karls in memory of their father Sigvat.

937+990+991+999: 937+990+991 see 'Multiple Commemorations' above, group 3 (Tägn and Gunnar . . .); 999 Hörse and Kättil in memory of their father Tägn.

1008+1012: 1008 Gunne in memory of his wife Ginnlög; 1012 Sprake, Torbjörn, Otvagen, Ginnlög, and Åfrid (?) in memory of their father Björn.

1151: see this group above, at 770.

REFERENCES

ÅHLÉN, MARIT (1986), 'Sex vikingatida släkter i Mälardalen', *Släkthistoriskt Forum*, 1/1986: 1–7.

——(1994), 'Runinskrifter i Hälsingland', *Bebyggelsehistorisk tidskrift*, 27: 33–50.

——(1997), *Runristaren Öpir: en monografi* (Uppsala).

ÅKERBERG NORBERG, MIKAEL (1997), 'Gunnunn och Torgöt—ett vikingatida föräldrapar i Medelpad, *Studia anthroponymica Scandinavica*, 15: 59–72.

AAKJÆR, SVEND (1927–8), 'Old Danish Thegns and Drengs', *Acta Philologica Scandinavica*, 2: 1–30.

ADAM OF BREMEN (1961 edn.), *Gesta Hammaburgensis Ecclesiae Pontificum*, ed. W. Trillmich, in Trillmich and Buchner (1961), 137–499.

AGGESEN, SVEN (1917 edn.), *Svenonis Aggonis filii Brevis Historia Regum Dacie*, ed. M. Cl. Gertz (Scriptores minores historiae danicae medii aevi; Copenhagen).

ALBRECTSEN, ESBERN (1994), 'Harald Blåtand og Danmark', in Karsten Due-Nielsen *et al.* (eds.), *Struktur og Funktion: Festskrift til E. Ladewig Petersen* (Odense), 17–26.

ANDERSON, PERRY (1978), *Passages from Antiquity to Feudalism* (London).

AXELSON, JAN (1993), *Mellansvenska runristare: Förteckning över signerade och attribuerade inskrifter* (Runrön, 5; Uppsala).

BESKOW, PER (1994), 'Runor och liturgi', in Per Beskow and Reinhart Staats (eds.), *Nordens kristnande i europeiskt perspektiv: Tre uppsatser* (Skara), 16–36.

BETHURUM, DOROTHY (1957), *The Homilies of Wulfstan* (Oxford).

BRAKELY, THERESA C. (1950), 'Mourning Songs', in *Funk and Wagnall's Standard Dictionary of Folklore, Mythology and Legend*, ii (New York).

BROWN, PETER (1961), 'Aspects of the Christianisation of the Roman Aristocracy', *Journal of Roman Studies*, 51: 1–11 (repr. in Peter Brown, *Religion and Society in the Age of Saint Augustine* (London, 1972), 161–82).

——(1997), *The Rise of Western Christendom: Triumph and Diversity AD 200–1000* (Oxford).

CARLQVIST, KNUT (1977), 'Vad säger runstenarna?', *Meddelanden från arkivet för folkets historia*, 5.4: 8–21.

CHRISTIANSSON, HANS (1959), *Sydskandinavisk stil: Studier i ornamentiken på de senvikingatida runstenarna* (Uppsala).

CLAESSON, EIVIND (1989), 'Cuius ecclesiam fecit: Romanska stenkyrkor i Västergötland' (diss. Lund).

CLOVER, CAROL (1986), 'Hildigunnr's Lament', in John Lindow *et al.* (eds.), *Structure and Meaning in Old Norse Literature: New Approaches to Textual Analysis and Literary Criticism* (Odense), 141–83.

DAVIES, WENDY, and FOURACRE, PAUL (1986) (eds.), *The Settlement of Disputes in Early Medieval Europe* (Cambridge).

DÜWEL, KLAUS (1975), 'Runische Zeugnisse zu "Bauer"', in R. Wenskus *et al.* (eds.), *Wort und Begriff 'Bauer': Zusammenfassender Bericht über die Kolloquien der Kommission für die Altertumskunde Mittel- und Nordeuropa* (Göttingen), 180–206.

Düwel, Klaus (1983), *Runenkunde* (Stuttgart).

Elmevik, Lennart, and Peterson, Lena (1989), *Projektet De vikingatida runinskrifternas kronologi: En presentation och några forskningsresultat* (Runrön, 1; Uppsala).

Eriksson, Manne (1935), 'Jordbruk och jordbruksredskap', in J. Sahlgren *et al.* (eds.), *Vår hembygd: Dess historia och hur den utforskas* (Stockholm), 194–205.

Erixon, Sigurd (1919), 'Svenska gårdstyper', *Rig. Tidskrift utg. av Föreningen för svensk kulturhistoria*, 2: 1–39.

von Friesen, Otto (1933), 'De svenska runinskrifterna', in his *Runorna* (Nordisk kultur, 6; Stockholm, Oslo, and Köpenhamn), 145–248.

Fuglesang, Signe Horn (1998), 'Swedish Runestones of the Eleventh Century: Ornament and Dating', in *Runeninschriften als Quellen interdisziplinärer Forschung: Abhandlungen des Vierten Internationalen Symposiums über Runen und Runeninschriften in Göttingen vom 4.–9. August 1995*, ed. Klaus Düwel (Berlin and New York), 197–218.

Gillingham, John (1995), 'Thegns and Knights in Eleventh-century England: Who was then the Gentleman?', *Transactions of the Royal Historical Society*, 6th ser. 5: 129–53.

Gräslund, Anne-Sofie (1987*a*), 'Pagan and Christian in the Age of Conversion', in *Proceedings of the Tenth Viking Congress, Larkollen, Norway, 1985*, ed. James E. Knirk (Oslo), 81–94.

——(1987*b*), 'Runstenar, bygd och gravar', *Tor. Tidskrift för nordisk fornkunskap*, 21: 241–62.

——(1989), '"Gud hjälpe nu väl hennes själ": Om runstenskvinnorna, deras roll vid kristnandet och deras plats i familj och samhälle', *Tor. Tidskrift för nordisk fornkunskap*, 22: 223–44.

——(1992), 'Runstenar—om ornamentik och datering, II', *Tor. Tidskrift för nordisk fornkunskap*, 24: 177–201.

——(1996), 'Kristnandet ur ett kvinnoperspektiv', in Bertil Nilsson (ed.), *Kristnandet i Sverige: Gamla källor och nya perspektiv* (Uppsala), 313–34.

——(1998), 'Ornamentiken som dateringsgrund för Upplands runstenar', in Audun Dybdahl and Jan Ragnar Hagland (eds.), *Innskrifter og datering* (Senter for middelalderstudier, Skrifter 8; Trondheim), 73–91.

Gustavson, Helmer, and Klas-Göran, Selinge (1988), 'Jarlabanke och hundaret: Ett arkeologiskt/runologiskt bidrag till lösningen av ett historiskt tolkningsproblem', *Namn och Bygd*, 76: 19–85.

Hagenfeldt, Stefan E., and Palm, Rune (1996), *Sandstone Runestones: The Use of Sandstone for Erected Runestones* (Sällskapet Runica et Mediævalia; Stockholm).

Hagland, Jan Ragnar (1998), 'Innskrifta på Kulisteinen: Ei nylesing ved hjelp av Jan O. H. Swantessons mikrokarteringsteknologi', in Audun Dybdahl and Jan Ragnar Hagland (eds.), *Innskrifter og datering* (Senter for middelalderstudier, Skrifter 8; Trondheim), 129–39.

Hansen, Lars Ivar (1994), 'Slektskap, eiendom og sosiale strategier i nordisk middelalder', *Collegium Medievale*, 7: 103–54.

von Harnack, A. (1908), *The Mission and Expansion of Christianity in the First Three Centuries*, ii (New York).

Helgason, Jón (1944), 'Bällsta-inskriftens "i grati"', *Arkiv för nordisk filologi*, 59: 159–62.

Hellbom, Algot (1979), *Medelpads runstenar* (Sundsvall).

Hult, Bengt (1992), 'Ej strid—utan frid: En omtolkning', *Kyrkohistorisk årsskrift*, 1992: 107–16.

Hultgård, Anders (1992), 'Religiös förändring, kontinuitet och ackulturation/synkretism i vikingatidens och medeltidens religion', in Bertil Nilsson (ed.), *Kontinuitet i kult och tro från vikingatid till medeltid* (Uppsala), 49–103.

Hyenstrand, Åke (1973), '... bättre än han förtjänade: En parentes om runstenar', *Tor. Tidskrift för nordisk fornkunskap*, 15: 180–90.

Iversen, Mette (1985), 'På vej til kirke?', *Museerne i Viborg amt*, 13: 56–65.

Jämtlands kristnande (1996), ed. Stefan Brink (Sveriges kristnande, 4; Uppsala).

Jansson, Sven B. F. (1951), 'Ett par hälsingska runstenar', *Hälsingerunor—en hembygdsbok* (Norrala), 15–23.

——(1960 = abbr. MÖLM 1960), 'Törnevalla kyrkas runstenar', *Meddelanden från Östergötlands och Linköpings stads museum*, 1960–1: 219–37.

——(1963), *Runinskrifter i Sverige* (Stockholm).

——(1964), 'Runstenen i Övergrans kyrka', in *Uppland 25* (årsbok för medlemmarna i Upplands fornminnesförening och hembygdsförbund, 1940–), Uppsala: 7–12.

——(1976), 'Linköpingsbygdens runstenar', in Salomon Kraft (ed.), *Linköpings historia*, i: *Från äldsta tid till 1567* (Linköping), 45–84.

——(1985), *Två runstenar i Hälsingland: Malsta och Sunnå* (Filologiskt arkiv, 33; Stockholm).

——(1987), *Runes in Sweden*, trans. P. Foote (Stockholm).

Jesch, Judith (1993), 'Skaldic Verse and Viking Semantics', in Anthony Faulkes and Richard Perkins (eds.), *Viking Revaluations: Viking Society Centenary Symposium, 14–15 May 1992* (Viking Society for Northern Research; London), 160–71.

Jochens, Jenny (1985), 'En Islande médiévale: A la recherche de la familie nucléaire', *Annales, Économies, Sociétés, Civilisations*, 40: 95–112.

Johansen, Erling, and Liestøl, Aslak (1982–3), 'Kong Haralds "mishandlede" Jellingstein', *Kuml. Årbog for Jysk Arkaeologisk Selskab*, 1982–3: 205–11.

Johansson, Hilding (1986), 'Skara som stiftsstad', in Arne Sträng *et al.* (eds.), *Skara*, i: *Före 1700: Staden i stiftet* (Skara), 387–542.

Johnsen, Ingrid Sanness (1968), *Stuttruner i vikingtidens innskrifter* (Oslo).

Jómsvíkinga saga (1962 edn.) = *The Saga of the Jomsvikings: Text and Translation*, ed. N. F. Blake (Edinburgh).

Källström, Magnus (1998), 'Ett otolkat mansnamn på Viggebystenen (U 428)', *Studia anthroponymica Scandinavica*, 16: 27–34.

Knirk, James (1987), 'Recently Found Runestones from Toten and Ringerike', in *Proceedings of the Tenth Viking Congress, Larkollen, Norway, 1985*, ed. James E. Knirk (Oslo), 191–202.

——(1994), letter dated 21 August 1994, addressed to Birgit Sawyer.

Krogh, K. J. (1982), 'The Royal Viking-Age Monuments at Jelling in the Light of Recent Archaeologiccal Excavations', *Acta Archaeologica*, 53: 183–216.

LAGMAN, SVANTE (1990), *De stungna runorna: Användning och ljudvärden i runsvenska stseninskrifter* (Runrön, 4; Uppsala).

LANGE, JOHAN (1982–3), 'Danmarks bod (Tanmarkar bøt): Et nyt tolkningsforsøg', *Kuml. Årbog for Jysk Arkaeologisk Selskab*, 1982–3: 213–18.

LARSSON, MATS G. (1990), *Runstenar och utlandsfärder: Aspekter på det senvikingatida samhället med utgångspunkt i de fasta fornlämningarna* (Acta Archaeologica Lundensia, 18; Lund).

LIESTØL, ASLAK (1964), 'Tre nyfunne runesteinar frå Rogaland', *Stavanger Museums Årbok*, 74: 29–39.

——(1972), 'Innsksrifter på Eiksteinen', *Stavanger Museums Årbok*: 82, 67–76.

LINDKVIST, THOMAS (1997), 'Saga, arv och guld i 1000-talets Södermanland', in Janne Backlund *et al.* (eds.), *Historiska Etyder: En vänbok till Stellan Dahlgren* (Uppsala), 139–47.

LINDOW, JOHN (1975), *Comitatus, Individual and Honor: Studies in North Germanic Institutional Vocabulary* (University of California Publications in Linguistics, 83; Berkeley and Los Angeles).

LINDQVIST, SUNE (1915), *Den helige Eskils biskopsdöme: Några arkeologiska vittnesbörd om den kristna kyrkans första organisation inom mellersta Sverige* (Antikvarisk tidskrift för Sverige, 22; Stockholm).

——(1923), 'Jarlabankes-släktens minnesmärken', in Gustaf Hallström (ed.), *Nordiska Arkeologmötet i Stockholm* (Stockholm), 123–41.

——(1942), *Gotlands Bildsteine*, ii (Stockholm).

LJUNGBERG, HELGE (1938), *Den nordiska religionen och kristendomen: Studier över det nordiska religionsskiftet under vikingatiden* (Uppsala).

LÖFVING, CARL (1986), 'Var Knut den store kung även över Västergötland? Ett diskussionsinlägg', *Västergötlands Fornminnesförenings Tidskrift*, 1986: 168–75.

LUNDBERG, STIG (1997), 'Gravmonument i sten från sen vikingatid och äldre medeltid i Västergötland' (diss. Göteborg).

MACLEOD, MINDY, 'Samnordisk runtext- databas' http://www.nordiska.uu.se/samnord.html

MOLTKE, ERIK (1958), *Jon Skonvig og de andre runetegnere: Et bidrag til runologiens historie i Danmark og Norge*, ii: *Skildring og kommentar* (Bibliotheca Arnamagnæana, Suppl. 2; Copenhagen).

——(1976), *Runerne i Danmark og deres oprindelse* (Copenhagen).

——(1985), *Runes and their Origin, Denmark and Elsewhere* (Copenhagen).

MUNDAL, ELSE (1983), 'Kvinner og dikting: Overgangen frå munnleg til skriftleg kultur—ei ulukke for kvinnene?', in Silja Aðalsteinsdottir and Helgi Þorlaksson (eds.), *Förändringar i kvinnors villkor under medeltiden* (Reykjavik), 11–25.

——(1992), 'Gjennom diktinga til røyndomen bakanfor', in Berit Jansen Sellevold *et al.* (eds.), *Fokus på kvinner i middelalderkilder* (Skara), 69–84.

MURRAY, ALEXANDER C. (1983), *Germanic Kinship Structure: Studies in Law and Society in Antiquity and the Early Middle Ages* (Toronto).

MUSSET, LUCIEN (1965), *Introduction à la runologie* (Paris).

NÄSSTRÖM, BRITT-MARIE (1996), 'Från Fröja till Maria: Det förkristna arvet speglat i en folklig föreställningsvärld', in Bertil Nilsson (ed.), *Kristnandet i Sverige: gamla källor och nya perspektiv* (Uppsala), 335–48.

NEILL, THOMAS, and LUNDBERG, STIG (1994), 'Förnyad diskussion om Eskilstunakistorna', *Fornvännen*, 89: 145–60.

Nielsen, Karl Martin (1974), 'Jelling Problems: A Discussion', *Mediaeval Scandinavia*, 7: 156–234.

Nielsen, Michael Lerche (1997*a*), 'To utolkede danske runefølger og navneelementet-gisl', *Studia anthroponymica Scandinavica*, 15: 49–57.

——(1997*b*), 'Omkring Harby-stenens personnavne: Tolkning og datering', in *Blandade runstudier*, ii (Runrön, 11; Uppsala), 59–82.

Niermeyer, J. F. (1954–76), *Mediae Latinitatis lexicon minus* (Leiden).

Nilsson, Bruce Eugene (1973), *The Runic Inscriptions of Öland* (Ann Arbor (University Microfilms International)).

Nordén, Arthur (1943), 'Bidrag till svensk runforskning', in *Antikvariska studier*, 1 (Vitterhetsakademiens handlingar, 55; Stockholm).

Norseng, Per (1987), 'Lovmaterialet som kilde til tidlig nordisk middelalder', in *Kilderne til den tidlige middelalders historie: Rapporter til den XX nordiske historikerkongress*, ed. Gunnar Karlsson (Reykjavik), 48–77.

Ölands runinskrifter, ed. Sven Söderberg and Erik Brate (Stockholm, 1900–6 (=*SRI* i)).

Owe, Jan (1995), *Svensk runbibliografi, 1880–1993* (Stockholm).

——(1996), *Svenskt runnamnsregister* (Stockholm).

Page, Raymond, I. (1987), *Runes* (London).

Palm, Rune (1992), *Runor och regionalitet: Studier av variation i de nordiska minnesinskrifterna* (Uppsala).

Palme, Sven Ulrik (1959), *Kristendomens genombrott i Sverige* (Stockholm).

Peterson, Lena (1991), 'Gæra bro fyriʀ sial: En semantisk studie över en runstensfras', in Gullbrand Alhaug *et al.* (eds.), *Heidersskrift til Nils Hallan på 65-årsdagen, 13 desember 1991* (Oslo), 341–51.

——(1994), *Svenskt Runordsregister* (Runrön, 2; Uppsala).

Pollock, F., and Maitland, F. W. (1898), *The History of English Law*, ii (Cambridge).

Randsborg, Knud (1978), *The Viking Age in Denmark: The Formation of a State* (London).

Runor och runinskrifter: Föredrag vid Riksantikvarieämbetets och Vitterhetsakademiens symposium, 8–11 september 1985 (Konferenser 15; Stockholm, 1987) (abbr. *RR*).

Ruprecht, Arndt (1958), *Die ausgehende Wikingerzeit im Lichte der Runeninschriften* (Palaestra, 224; Göttingen).

Sandnes, Jørn (1996), 'Jämtene kristnet sig selv. Jämtlands kristning sett fra vest', in Stefan Brink (ed.), *Jämtlands kristnande* (Projektet Sveriges kristnande, publikationer 4; Uppsala), 107–16.

Sawyer, Birgit (1988), *Property and Inheritance in Viking Scandinavia: The Runic Evidence* (Alingsås).

——(1989), 'Det vikingatida runstensresandet i Skandinavien', *Scandia*, 55: 185–202, 327–8.

——(1990), Women and the Conversion of Scandinavia', in W. Affeldt (ed.), *Frauen in Spätantike und Frühmittelalter* (Sigmaringen), 263–81.

——(1991*a*), 'Women as Bridge-builders: The Role of Women in Viking-Age Scandinavia', in Ian Wood and Niels Lund (eds.), *People and Places in Northern Europe 500–1600* (Woodbridge), 211–24.

SAWYER, BIRGIT (1991*b*), 'Viking-Age Rune-Stones as a Crisis Symptom', *Norwegian Archaeological Review*, 24: 97–112.

——and SAWYER, PETER (1993), *Medieval Scandinavia: From Conversion to Reformation* ca. *800–1500* (Minneapolis and London).

SAWYER, PETER (1987), 'The Process of Scandinavian Christianization in the Tenth and Eleventh centuries', in B. and P. Sawyer and Ian Wood (eds.), *The Christianization of Scandinavia* (Alingsås), 68–87.

——(1988), *Da Danmark blev Danmark* (=*Danmarks Historie*, pt. 3, ed. Olaf Olsen; Copenhagen).

SAXO GRAMMATICUS (1931 edn.), *Saxonis Gesta Danorum*, 1, ed. J. Olrik and H. Raeder (Copenhagen).

——(1979 edn.), *Saxo Grammaticus: History of the Danes*, I: Text, trans. Peter Fisher, ed. Hilda Ellis Davidson (Cambridge).

SCHMID, TONI (1934), *Sveriges kristnande: Från verklighet till dikt* (Stockholm).

SJÖHOLM, ELSA (1988), *Sveriges medeltidslagar: Europeisk rättstradition i politisk omvandling* (Stockholm).

SNÆDAL, THORGUNN (1984), *Runstenar i Södermanland: Vägvisare till runristningar i Södermanlands län* (Södermanlands Museum, Nyköping).

SRIGLEY, MICHAEL (1988–9), 'The Dream of Troy: An Interpretation of the Gotland Picture-stones of the Late Vendel and Viking Periods', *Tor. Tidskrift för arkeologi*, 22: 161–87.

STÅHLE, CARL IVAR (1950), 'Sockenbildningen i Törens prosteri', *Namn och Bygd*, 38: 100–12.

STILLE, PER (1996), 'Myskia—ett sörmländskt runstensnamn', in Eva Brylla *et al.* (eds.), *Från göterna till Noreens kor: Hyllningsskrift till Lennart Elmevik på 60-årsdagen, 2 februari 1996* (Skrifter utgivna genom Ortnamnsarkivet i Uppsala, serie 8, Meddelanden, 11; Uppsala), 158–60.

STOKLUND, MARIE (1991), 'Runesten, kronologi og samfundsrekonstruktion: Nogle kritiske overvejelser med udgangspunkt i runestenene i Mammenområdet', in Mette Iversen *et al.* (eds.), *Mammen: Grav, kunst og samfund i vikingetid* (Aarhus), 285–97.

STRID, JAN PAUL (1987), 'Runic Swedish Thegns and Drengs', in *Runor och runinskrifter: Föredrag vid Riksantikvariämbetets och Vitterhetsakademiens symposium, 8–11 september 1985* (Konferenser 15; Stockholm), 301–16.

——(1988), 'Jädra runsten', *Västmanlands Fornminnesförening och Västmanlands läns museum, Årsskrift* 66: 7–20.

SVÄRDSTRÖM, ELISABETH (1936), *Johannes Bureus arbeten om svenska runinskrifter* (Kungl. Vitterhets Historie och Antikvitetsakademiens handlingar, 42.3; Stockholm).

——(1971), *Runorna och Runverket* (RAÄ, Småskrifter och särtryck, 18; Stockholm).

TESCH, STEN (1989), 'Sigtuna—anlagd stad', *Kulturmiljövård*, 5: 6–17.

THOMPSON, CLAIBORNE W. (1975), *Studies in Upplandic Runography* (Austin, Texas and London).

THORPE, B. (1840) *Ancient Laws and Institutes of England*, ii (London).

TRILLMICH, W., and BUCHNER, R. (1961), *Quellen des 9. und 11. Jahrhunderts zur Geschichte der hamburgischen Kirche und des Reiches* (Berlin).

Vikstrand, Per (1996), 'Jämtland mellan Frö och Kristus', in Stefan Brink (ed.), *Jämtlands kristnande* (Projektet Sveriges kristnande, publikationer 4; Uppsala), 87–106.

Wamers, Egon (1997), 'Hammer und Kreuz: Typologische Aspekte einer nordeuropäischen Amulettsitte aus der Zeit des Glaubenswechsels', in Michael Müller-Wille (ed.), *Rom und Byzanz im Norden: Mission und Glaubenswechsel im Ostseeraum während des 8.–14. Jahrhunderts* (Stuttgart), 82–107.

Weibull, Lauritz (1948), 'Tyre Danmarkar bot', in his *Nordisk historia: Forskningar och undersökningar*, i (Stockholm), 225–43.

Wessén, Elias (1927), *Nordiska namnstudier* (Uppsala).

——(1958), *Runstenen vid Röks kyrka* (Stockholm).

——(1966), *Skänningebygdens runinskrifter* (Filologiskt arkiv, 10; Stockholm).

Westlund, Börje (1964), 'Om runstensfragmenten vid Hagby i Täby socken', *Fornvännen*, 59: 152–6.

——(1980), 'Namntolkning i runinskrifter', *Namn och Bygd*, 68: 128–40.

Williams, Henrik (1990), *Åsrunan: Användning och ljudvärde i runsvenska steninskrifter* (Runrön, 3; Uppsala).

——(1996*a*), 'Vad säger runstenarna om Sveriges kristnande', in Bertil Nilsson (ed.), *Kristnandet i Sverige: Gamla källor och nya perspektiv* (Uppsala), 45–83.

——(1996*b*), 'Runtexternas teologi', in Bertil Nilsson (ed.), *Kristnandet i Sverige: Gamla källor och nya perspektiv* (Uppsala), 291–312.

Wilson, Lars (1994), *Runstenar och kyrkor: En studie med utgångspunkt från runstenar som påträffats i kyrkomiljö i Uppland och Södermanland* (Uppsala).

Winberg, Christer (1985), *Grenverket: Studier rörande jord, släktskapssystem och ståndsprivilegier* (Rättshistoriskt bibliotek, 1.38; Stockholm).

Wulf, Fred (1989), '*Goðr* in Runeninschriften Götalands', in E. Walter and H. Mittelstädt (eds.), *Altnordistik: Vielfalt und Einheit. Erinnerungsband für Walter Baetke (1884–1978)* (Weimar), 109–18.

——(1997), 'Der Name des zweiten Sohnes in der Fjuckby-Inschrift', in *Blandade runstudier* (Runrön 11), Uppsala: 185–99.

Zachrisson, Torun (1998), *Gård, gräns, gravfält: Sammanhang kring ädelmetalldepåer och runstenar från vikingatid och tidigmedeltid i Uppland och Gästrikland* (Stockholm).

INDEX

This index, generously prepared by Jan Meijer, includes all references to rune-stones in the text and footnotes, but not to those in the Appendices and Catalogue. Illustrations are not indicated; they are listed on pp. xii–xiii. The identification numbers explained on p. xvii are used. Further details, including locations, are given in the Catalogue. References in footnotes are indicated by 'n' after the page number, and inscriptions mentioned in the text and a footnote on the same page by page number + 'n'. For new Swedish finds the publications in FV, MÖLM, SKL, and THS are noted.

Uppland, U

Västergötland, Vg

Västmanland, Vs

Öland, Öl

Östergötland, Ög